Cases in International Relations

PORTRAITS OF THE FUTURE
Second Edition

Donald M. Snow
University of Alabama

PEARSON
Longman

New York San Francisco Boston
London Toronto Sydney Tokyo Singapore Madrid
Mexico City Munich Paris Cape Town Hong Kong Montreal

Executive Editor: Eric Stano
Acquisitions Editor: Edward Costello
Senior Marketing Manager: Elizabeth Fogarty
Production Manager: Eric Jorgensen
Project Coordination, Text Design, and Electronic Page Makeup: Electronic
    Publishing Services Inc., NYC
Cover Design Manager: John Callahan
Cover Designer: Maria Illardi
Cover Photos: Getty Images
Senior Manufacturing Buyer: Alfred C. Dorsey
Printer and Binder: Courier Corporation
Cover Printer: Courier Corporation

Library of Congress Cataloging-in-Publication Data

Snow, Donald M.,
Cases in international relations : portraits of the future / Donald M. Snow.—2nd ed.
   p.   cm.
Includes bibliographical references and index.
ISBN 0-321-33797-2 (paperbound)
1. International relations. I. Title.
JZ1242.S658 2006
327—dc22
2005006303

Please visit us at http://www.ablongman.com

ISBN 0-321-33797-2

 2 3 4 5 6 7 8 9 10—CRS—08 07 06

Contents

Preface
Portraits of the Future

The twenty-first century is now several years old. While the century is still in its early stages, it is natural to want to know how it compares with the last century and how it will likely look in the future. How will the relations between states and other entities change or remain the same? What forces are likely to emerge to promote and resist change? Where will the world's most serious troubles occur? Where will there be positive signs of hope and improvement in the human condition? For that matter, how has the future changed since the first edition of this book was released in fall 2002?

In early September 2000, more than 150 heads of state, the largest assemblage of its kind in history, met at the United Nations headquarters for a two-day meeting to discuss these kinds of problems. Conferees at this event, known as the Millennium Summit, met and passed a truly remarkable series of pronouncements and approaches to solving the problems they identified. After acknowledging the process of globalization and the challenges that process poses to the membership of the international system, the Millennium Declaration (the name given to its statements) emphasizes the need for international cooperation to help ensure that responsive "needs of developing countries and economies in transition are formulated and implemented." As summarized by the *New York Times* on September 9, 2000, the declaration produced a stunning list of what it calls values essential for international relations in the twenty-first century. These values are: freedom, equality, solidarity, tolerance, respect for nature, and shared responsibility for worldwide economic and social development.

In many ways, these themes reflected the concerns of the post–Cold War 1990s, when international security concerns were relaxed by the collapse of the global competition between communism and anticommunism. The values the Millennium Declaration portrays—human rights, development, cultural diversity, the role of state in international problem solving, and the role of the United Nations—are certainly emphases more associated with the 1990s than with the more troublesome 2000s.

Although it set forth a comprehensive, ambitious international agenda that could form the basis for international activity for this decade and beyond, the Millennium Summit is no more than a largely forgotten event. The leaders of the world's powers arrived in New York, gave rousing speeches, signed the declaration, had their pictures taken, and left. Whether the summit was indeed no more than a "photo-op" or whether events like the terrorist attacks of September 11, 2001, simply overwhelmed its implementation is a matter of speculation. The Millennium Summit offered one vision of the international agenda for the future, and it is interesting to compare its view with the more geopolitical agenda that now dominates our view of the world. Which vision will hold true is one of the questions of the future.

We operate, of course, in the opacity of the future. Because political science is not a precise science like physics or chemistry, we lack the quality of theory possessed by the hard sciences that could aid our predictive ability. With imprecise theoretical lenses, we can only guess—draw portraits of the present and extrapolate them into a future about which we cannot be sure.

A word about what this book is and is not is appropriate at this point. It is a case book, presenting a series of individual instances of problems and trends within the international arena in the early 2000s. Some of the cases reflect concerns raised at the Millennium Summit, but others, notably those dealing with security issues, do not; however, all cases provide the reader with the opportunity to apply IR concepts to real-world situations, with the hope that in doing so they will come to better understand current and enduring problems facing the international system.

This book is not a systematic overview of the system or its history, which is the province of core textbooks in the field. Many of the most interesting historical cases have been written, and their rewriting would not be terribly helpful. At the same time, the book is not a systematic exposition of various political science theories explaining international phenomena, which I view as less than optimally helpful for the undergraduate students whom I assume will be the primary readers of this book.

A word about pedagogy may help at this point. Each of the cases begins by identifying a particular problem or dynamic in the international system. The case study on Kashmir, for instance, begins with the observation that there are some international disputes that are so intractable as to be essentially irresolvable. The situation in Kashmir is then examined as an instance of this irreconcilability. The case concludes by looking at some options and why they have failed; it then ends with study/discussion questions and references for future reading and research, including a sample of relevant Web Sites.

What distinguishes this effort from other supplementary texts is that all the essays included are original papers written by the author for this volume. This was done to allow more timely coverage of situations that are ongoing than is possible with the lag time involved in publication in scholarly journals and the like, and also to allow the cases to be cast within a more standard format than is possible with preexisting materials written for other purposes. In addition, writing original articles means that it is possible to update and modify materials as events and dynamics change and, it is hoped, to facilitate both the freshness and accuracy of the material that appears in these pages. Certainly, doing these things has been a major intent and concentration of this second edition.

The rationale for choosing the cases flows from the book's subtitle, "Portraits of the Future." Clearly, it is not possible to include as much breadth in a casebook as in a core text without either making the casebook encyclopedic and massively long or making the cases so brief as not to be particularly helpful. Rather, a casebook is by its nature a set of examples presented in sufficient depth to highlight and explain principles, events, and the like in more detail than in a conventional text. The trick is in picking the right cases to meet the reader's needs.

Why did I pick the cases I did? Beyond their amenability to case treatment, I used five criteria in choosing the subjects included in this volume. The first was that the subject was important and represented an enduring issue or problem. Cases such as continuing terrorism, the fate of Israel and the Palestinians, the direction of China, and AIDS in Africa meet this criterion. Second, I wanted to look at problems that are fresh and timely, but not covered extensively in other places. The study of asymmetrical warfare as the military problem of the future fits this criterion, as does the problem of resource scarcity and the future of nongovernmental organizations in peacekeeping.

Third, I wanted subjects that represent real-world problems with which the international system will have to come to grips and about which students need to know in order to be informed citizens. Missile defense as an international problem clearly fits this criterion, as does the problem of the future of war crimes. Fourth, I wanted subjects that are future oriented and that likely will endure for a period of time. The precedential value of how the world deals with the AIDS pandemic in Africa meets this criterion, as does the question of how countries and groups deal with globalization and how the process of democratization evolves. Fifth, I wanted subjects that were inherently interesting, so that the reader would approach and consume them with some enthusiasm that, I hope, will translate into a broader interest in international relations. At a practical level, the intractability of the Kashmir and Israeli-Palestinian questions and how the rules of globalization are applied fall into this category. At a more abstract level, the question of the future of sovereignty and the future of war meet this criterion.

Individual cases were chosen with these criteria in mind, and the book was then divided into five parts. Within each part, my intention was to select substantive topics that both illustrate important principles operating within the international system and exemplify important concerns in the contemporary environment. In doing so, I decided there were visible themes that needed to be included. I selected four general topics—new forces and evolutionary change in the post–Cold War world (which comprise the first two parts of the text), globalization, national and international security, and transnational issues—and then proceeded to try to find cases that would provide illustrations of these dynamics. In picking the cases I did, I tried to invoke the five criteria cited above—importance, freshness and timeliness, real-world importance, endurance, and interest.

Each case meets these criteria. For the problem of new forces (Part 1), I chose three cases that are not unique to the post–Cold War world but that have attracted increasing attention since the fall of the Soviet empire. The case on China reflects both the growing economic and political importance of China and provides some criteria by which people look at how China may evolve in the future—as either a looming threat or a strategic partner. Nongovernmental organizations (NGOs) are not a new phenomenon, but they have become more prominent and even intrusive actors in diverse situations such as peacekeeping. *Medecins sans Frontieres* (Doctors without Borders) are a prime example. Similarly, the dynamics of democratization began to emerge as an important force in the 1990s, but the certainty and process for achieving the "democratic peace" has been questioned, especially in light of the experience of trying to impose a democratic system in Iraq.

The dynamics of change are addressed in Part 2. The roots of the problem of war crimes and how to deal with them emerged originally after World War II but have been reenergized by atrocities in diverse parts of the developing world, including the Balkans and Iraq. It is an evolving problem that has yet to be resolved and to which the United

States has been a major barrier because of its refusal to ratify the International Criminal Court statute. The assault on national sovereignty is an important theme that will continue to reverberate through the 2000s and beyond, prominently within the context of the debate over American foreign policy. Finally, the issue of Israeli-Palestinian conflict, which seemed near resolution in 2000 but which continues to cloud the international relations of the Middle East, remains a testimony to the difficulty of resolving extraordinarily complex situations.

The other concerns in the book are more discrete, although I have attempted to choose my "portraits" from parts of the subject matter that are outside normal textbook treatment. Part 3 deals with globalization and how it affects those to whom globalization is being sold as the vehicle to their success. The "New Trinity of Globalization" looks at how the "movers and shakers" of globalism operate by examining the dynamics of the triangular relationship between the International Monetary Fund, the United States and target countries seeking to globalize, and ways private providers of foreign direct investment fit into the scheme. Much of the controversy surrounds questions of free trade, the history and issues surrounding which form the subject of the second case in Part 3. The third case deals with adverse reactions to globalism, beginning with he debate over its impact in Indonesia and moving to the so-called rejectionists and the impact of outsourcing.

Part 4 deals with security in the international environment. While there is general agreement that environment has changed fundamentally since September 11, 2001, there is much less agreement on exactly how it has changed, which is the focus of the cases in this part. The section begins with an assessment of what future war will be like, with particular emphasis on the rise of increasingly asymmetrical challenges to American (and other Western) conventional warfare prowess, drawing examples from places like Afghanistan and Iraq. The problem of how the proposed actions of one power to increase its security can decrease the security of its neighbors—the classic security dilemma—is investigated through the vehicle of the national missile defense proposal of the Bush administration. To demonstrate the endurance and intractability of some problems, I have chosen the case of Kashmir, which, along with the Israeli-Palestinian confrontation, has been one of the most difficult world problems to solve.

Part 5 deals with transnational issues, and it attempts to follow the criteria of the rest of the volume by bringing fresh looks at how some transnational issues can be viewed in a new light and how some other problems can usefully be examined through the lens of transnational issues. I begin with the familiar problem of global warming and the Kyoto Protocol, because this is clearly a problem that is not going to go away. If the Kyoto Protocol itself may be seriously or mortally wounded, what will we do about the underlying problem, which remains? Conflicts over scarce resources other than petroleum represent a second global problem that can be viewed as a transnational issue. Similarly, there has been a great deal of rhetorical concern and promises of action given to the problem of AIDS in Africa, but there has been little attention to thinking of it as a transnational issue and the precedent that will be set for dealing with outbreaks of AIDS elsewhere or other diseases like Ebola. Finally, international terrorism is the overriding concern of our day and one that can only be surmounted by concerted international efforts as terrorism has evolved in the post–September 11, 2001, environment.

What I have provided is a stack of portraits of the future that I hope the reader will find both broad and enriching. I have dedicated this edition of the book, like the original, to my longtime friend, the late D. Eugene Brown. Gene and I met in 1989 and shared an office at the U.S. Army War College for two years before he returned to Lebanon Valley College and I to the University of Alabama. Our time together led to a collaboration that produced several book projects brought to fruition. In most cases, Gene was the ideational force who suggested new projects that were completed by collaborative effort.

Cases in International Relations was to be a continuation, even culmination, to our joint efforts. The idea of a casebook of original essays was Gene's; unfortunately, he was unable to complete the task we had set for ourselves, and I had the burden of completing the work after Gene left us over the Thanksgiving holiday, 2000. I hope Gene would have been pleased with how our final collaboration has evolved.

I would like to thank the reviewers who made useful comments on the manuscript and first edition. Their feedback helped give shape to this second edition. They are:

Douglas Blum, Providence College; J. Barron Boyd, LeMoyne College; John Calhoun, Palm Beach Atlantic University; Dan Cox, University of Nebraska–Kearney; Ruth Ediger, Lee University; Larry Elowiz, Georgia College and State University; Gregory Hall, St. Mary's College of Maryland; Linda Petrou, High Point University; Brian Potter, Tulane University; Michael A. Preda, Midwestern State University; Abdoulaye Saine, Miami University of Ohio; Michael E. Smith, Georgia State University.

DONALD M. SNOW

PART 1

New Forces in International Relations

A common theme in the post–Cold War international environment is change, the extent to which that environment is somehow different than it was before, and the implications of those changes for the operation of international relations.

Part I identifies three ways in which the system appears to have changed. There is nothing systematic or inclusive about the changes that are included in the three cases; rather, they seek to be illustrative of the ways in which change has occurred. The three themes that are developed are the changing nature of power by states in the system, the emergence of significant new actors in the process, and a new dynamic in the politics within and between states.

Chapter 1, "China Rising," looks at the emergence of the People's Republic as a major player in the system, a so-called rising power. In the past decade, China has become a major economic force in the world as its economy grows more capitalist and it has become a major world manufacturing center. At the same time, China has engaged in a program of military expansion and diplomatic initiative. The question the case study raises is how much difference that makes: will a more powerful China be a disruptive or a supportive part of the evolving international system?

Chapter 2, "The Growing Significance of NGOs," looks at a form of actor, the non-governmental organization (NGO), that has become an increasingly prominent part of international interactions. The focus of the case is how these international organizations make a difference. To study this phenomenon, the case looks at one particularly active NGO, *Medecins sans Frontieres* (MSF, which translates as "Doctors without Borders"), and its role in an important post–Cold War phenomenon, participation in peacekeeping operations (PKOs) in the bloody internal wars that are the main source of violence in the international system.

Chapter 3, "The Democratic Peace," looks at a prominent new emphasis in the post–Cold War international environment: the spread of democratization worldwide. The case begins by describing this phenomenon and its relationship to the process of globalization in the economic realm. The case then focuses on challenges to democratization by examining instances (e.g. "mini-cases") where the process has been resisted.

CHAPTER ONE

China Rising
LOOMING THREAT OR GLOBAL PARTNER?

PRÉCIS

One of the ways in which the international system appears different than it did before the end of the Cold War is the increasingly prominent role played by the People's Republic of China. China was a consequential country during the Cold War, but its significance was overshadowed by its relative position within the communist world. With the demise of the Soviet Union and the adoption of different policies, especially in the economic realm but increasingly in military matters, China has become a much more important factor in the international politics of the new century.

The question is how this "rising power" will fit into the international politics of the twenty-first century. With its growing economy and increased military might, will China be a force for stability and peace or a disruptive force? Will China challenge American world leadership or become a productive part of the globalizing international scene? As issues as diverse as China's role in the World Trade Organization and military confrontation with Taiwan continue to draw headlines, an assessment of what kind of power China is rising to be is an important concern for the international system.

It has become commonplace in the early 2000s (and even before) to refer to China as a "rising" power. What does that mean? In the most general sense, a rising power refers to a country that, by virtue of increased military, economic, or other power, is or has the potential to play a more prominent role in the international system than it has heretofore played. The United States was such a rising power in the late nineteenth and early twentieth centuries, as was the Soviet Union during the middle of the twentieth century. Now, it would appear to be China's turn.

The impact of rising powers is important. At the level of the international system, rising powers change the relative power balance between the major powers, creating ripple effects throughout the system, often in ways that are controversial and difficult to predict. Will, for instance, a rising China eventually challenge American international predominance and lead to a transformation from an essentially unipolar to a bipolar or multipolar balance? Would such a transformation be stabilizing or destabilizing?

The impact of rising states also creates foreign policy questions for countries affected by the rising power. The basic question is whether the impact will help or make more difficult the realization of interests of the affected power. Will the rising power be, to borrow from the subtitle, a looming threat to those interests or a global partner assisting in their accomplishment? Like the systemic impacts, these impacts are never entirely clear in advance, leading to speculation and disagreement. Europe worried about the impact of an industrially gigantic United States, and the United States worried about the impact of a militarily powerful Soviet Union. The United States ended up a strategic partner of Europe, and the Soviet emerged primarily as a threat. Where does China fit?

The world's oldest continuous civilization with a history rich in both creativity and tragedy, China has stood largely outside the quantum leaps in wealth and power made possible by Western-centered advances in modern science, technology, and industrialization since the eighteenth century. From the mid-nineteenth to the mid-twentieth centuries, China endured its "century of humiliation," as the once grand but then defenseless country fell under the domination and exploitation of the West and of newly industrialized Japan.

Today, however, China is again on the rise economically, politically, and militarily. Though still much less economically advanced than nearby Japan or South Korea, for example, China's sheer mass—it accounts for fully one-fifth of the earth's population—means that already no Asian state can contemplate its own strategic requirements without taking China into account. Should its ascent continue, China will become a leading power of global, not merely regional, status.

China already possesses some of the trappings of superpower status: it has nuclear weapons and is one of the five permanent members of the United Nations Security Council. If its economy continues the robust growth of the past two decades, then China may truly arrive as a state capable of wielding power on a large scale. China's growth raises two questions about its future: will China continue to grow to the point that it *can* upset the power balance? And will a newly robust China (if it emerges) accommodate itself to the existing international system or instead act in ways that defy international norms and threaten international stability and security? In other words, will China pose a threat to the emerging international order, or will it become another major, but orthodox, member of the international system?

The purposes and structure of the case study follow from this introduction. The first purpose is to describe how China has risen from the status of a semicolonized state in the early twentieth century to its current position as a rising power. To this end, we will look briefly at that evolution, culminating in the 1979 promulgation of the Four Modernizations and their applications to raising Chinese economic, military, and political power. There is, of course, disagreement on each of these dimensions. The second purpose is to apply these descriptions of China's rise to the questions of whether China will be a looming threat or global partner, a question prominently imbedded in the American foreign policy debate about China. The overall purpose, of course, is to show how uncertainties affect the assessment of the impact of rising powers more generally.

THE SETTING: FROM HUMILIATION, CHAOS, AND POVERTY TO MODERNIZATION

China's "century of humiliation" reduced it to a semicolony. The situation resulted from the loss of creativity, corruption, and resistance to reform within the imperial court; the obsolescence of its emperor-based political system that relied upon a corps of bureaucrats chosen for their mastery of Confucian classics rather than their command of modern ideas; and the numerous unequal treaties imposed upon it by foreign powers since its defeat in the Opium War with Great Britain in the 1840s. Westerners roamed throughout China. Merchants, adventurers, diplomats, and missionaries all enjoyed special privileges that placed them beyond Chinese authority, a situation that was simply humiliating to all Chinese. Those privileges included foreign spheres of influence and foreign concessions, foreign troops and police, foreign post offices and telegraph agencies, and consular jurisdiction that kept foreigners beyond the reach of Chinese justice.

Layered atop all of China's other discontents was a split between two centers of political and military power, each of which was determined to unify, govern, and strengthen China against the domestic and foreign ills that had befallen it. The Guomindang—or Nationalist—forces led by Chiang Kai-shek were generally supported by the United States. But beginning in the 1920s, an initially small upstart group of communists led by Mao Zedong made clear its own vision of mobilizing mass support to overthrow China's antiquated social order and to restore unity to the nation.

As the two forces began their titanic struggle in earnest, China endured yet another devastating blow, this time from Japan's exceptionally brutal aggression, first in its invasion of Manchuria in 1931 and then throughout its bloody drive through China proper from 1937 to1945.

The defeat of Japanese forces by the United States in 1945 gave the people of China not a new era of peace but rather a renewal of the violent and conclusive phase of the titanic struggle between Chiang Kai-shek's Nationalist forces and Mao Zedong's communist followers. By the autumn of 1949, China's communists emerged victorious and drove Chiang's forces to the island refuge of Taiwan.

In October 1949, Mao could boast to the assembled mass in Beijing's Tiananmen Square that "China has stood up." He meant, of course, that China was at long last unified under a strong central authority and that foreign intervention in its internal affairs would no longer be tolerated. Beyond unification and the reclamation of China's sovereignty, it was Mao's abiding passion to create within China a radical, egalitarian society. In so doing, he ensured that China remained largely outside the international community, terribly repressive within, and its people mired in poverty throughout his rule from 1949 to 1976.

Upon Mao's death, a scramble for power ensued among China's ruling elites. Within a year, Deng Xiaoping had effectively consolidated governing authority within his own hands. Purged three times during Mao's reign and standing less than five feet tall, Deng seemed at first glance to be an unlikely ruler of the world's most populous state. But more remarkable than his personal tenacity or physical diminutiveness was the boldness of his vision for China. Deng soon implemented his famous "Four Modernizations" campaign. Undaunted by the giant shadow cast by Mao, Deng announced an audacious series of reforms designed to advance China beyond the revolutionary dogma of Maoism and to create instead a stronger, more modern country by loosening the reins of state authority; more fully embracing economic globalization in search of foreign markets, technology, and investment; and frankly accepting income differentials in a society that had so recently been singularly animated by radical egalitarianism.

The Four Modernizations—agriculture, science and technology, industry, and military—began in the countryside, home to three-fourths of all Chinese. Gradually, socialist-style communal farming was phased out. Under the new "household responsibility system," peasants were now allowed individually to lease land from the state. Without quite admitting it, Deng's regime injected market—that is, *capitalist*—incentives by allowing peasants whose production surpassed their obligatory quotas turned over to the state at fixed prices to sell any surplus they could produce for as much money as they could get for it. A system of rural markets and distribution systems sprang up to buy farm produce and sell it to independent urban vendors. As longer land leases gave peasants new incentives to undertake capital improvements, food production soared. With it, rural incomes rose sharply, and the most successful peasant families reaped the greatest awards.

The older norm of imposed egalitarianism was quietly shelved. What the regime today calls "Socialism with Chinese Characteristics" took its place. With the passage of time this slogan has simply become a euphemism for capitalism with state supervision, but with much less direct central control. Gradually the limited market system begun in the countryside spread to the cities. Individuals were allowed to open restaurants, shops, and factories. Workers could be hired and fired, something utterly unthinkable under Mao's "people's" regime. The wheels of a more market-driven economy were thus set into motion.

The second and third modernizations—industry plus science and technology—inherently required China's leaders to turn outward to the most advanced industrial countries for investment capital, markets for Chinese goods, scientific know-how, and the most modern production technology and management skills. Four Special Economic Zones (SEZs) were established in southeastern China in which foreign corporations were allowed to form joint ventures with Chinese partners and thus transfer their leading-edge technological, manufacturing process, and managerial expertise to initially quite limited enclaves of capitalist experimentation.

As local laboratories of industrial modernity, the SEZs were intended to, among other things, create a new leadership cohort of technologically sophisticated managers whose expertise, it was hoped, would in time fan out from the SEZs themselves and help jump-start China's obsolescent and inefficient state-owned enterprises (SOEs). During Mao's era, "redness"—that is, communist ideological purity—was more highly prized than substantive expertise in filling leadership ranks. But Deng was much more of a pragmatist. In his famous aphorism, he said, "it doesn't matter if a cat is white or black, as long as it catches mice." Results, then, would be the new measure of the country's rising managers and leaders, not their ritual incantation of Marxist-Maoist dogma. The Deng program provided the launching pad for China's ascent into the realm of world powers. How far will it ascend? How will China use its new status? To answer these questions, we will assess China on three dimensions: economic growth, military strength, and diplomacy.

ECONOMIC GROWTH, BUT QUESTIONS

The economic results have been the most dramatic. Riding a boom powered by foreign capital inflows and an aggressive export strategy, China's economy grew at an average annual rate of around 10 percent throughout the 1980s and 1990s and into the 2000s. Not all Western China specialists accept these astounding government-promulgated growth statistics at face value. But regardless of the figures one accepts, there is no denying the fact—easily observable to any return visitor to the country—that China's economy has grown dramatically during the past quarter century. It is today the third-largest economy in the world, ranking only behind the United States and Japan. In critical consumer sectors such as clothing, shoes, toys, and other low-technology products, China dominates U.S. and world markets.

China's recent leaders—Deng Xiaoping and Jiang Zemin—have realized that, for their country to develop and modernize economically, they would have to thoroughly repudiate Mao's policies of economic self-sufficiency and instead fully embrace economic globalization. The international trend toward reducing barriers to the free movement of goods and capital has very much worked to China's advantage. In recognition of this fact, the current leadership's commitment to globalization has been most clearly demonstrated by its single-minded drive to gain membership in the World Trade Organization (WTO), a goal it achieved late in 2000. As a precursor to its accession to the WTO, China negotiated a complex commercial agreement with the United States. The agreement contains a number of key concessions on China's part. Especially notable among them are market-opening measures that place many of its state-owned industries at a competitive disadvantage, thus risking a substantial loss of jobs for Chinese workers. This process has produced both WTO membership and permanent trade relations for China with the United States, but at the cost of forcing China to accept international norms that tie the country more fully to the international community and limit its ability to act outside systemic rules.

Even as we sketch China's dramatic economic ascent, however, we must also note that it is a country beset by a litany of domestic woes that, taken together, raise the alarming possibility of widespread social unrest. Its internal preoccupations include a mounting political crisis of regime legitimacy as faith in communism has atrophied, severe environmental degradation, immense population pressures, almost-daily revelations of official corruption, a growing gap in urban versus rural incomes, high unemployment, a steady loss of arable land, a diminished social safety net for the poor and displaced, and secessionist movements in Tibet and in the westernmost province of Zinjiang.

China's rise as an economic power is thus paradoxical. China has made great strides as an industrial power, but it has done so within the confines of a political and social system that places serious constraints on the ability of China to expand, especially into a world power, if that is its desire. Thus, individually and collectively, what do these trends and problems mean, and how do they affect our assessment of China as a rising power?

ASSESSING CHINA'S ECONOMIC RISE

Does China's economic and technological rise pose a threat to the world power balance? The sheer potential size of an economy energized by one-fifth of mankind raises concern: if China were to become competitive structurally with the world's most advanced economies, would that size not pose a danger of simply overwhelming the global economy and establishing itself as an "800-pound gorilla," which everyone else would have to treat with care and deference? As an illustration of this possibility, China's announced intent to increase automobile production and to expand, possibly greatly, its domestic market has created palpitations in the petroleum market worldwide; such a move would greatly increase China's presence in the petroleum-buying market, hence increasing demand worldwide and driving up prices.

Opinions vary on this subject, based on differing assessments of the nature of the Chinese economy and the impact on the Chinese political system. Analysts critical of the notion that China poses a threat tend to point to factors in Chinese development that limit the potential threats. In a recent *Foreign Affairs* article, for instance, Hale and Hale point to three of what they call the "dragon's ailments." The first is demographic and relates to the extremely uneven character of Chinese development. There are, they point out, "great disparities between the integrated, largely urban coastal areas in the eastern part of the country and the fragmented, rural economies in the western part." In addition, there is a considerable unemployment problem, especially in western China, that results in considerable migration to the industrialized areas. China also faces the need "to find a way to support its rapidly aging population," a dilemma shared by many industrialized countries.

That is not all. As already noted, much of the prosperity associated with the SEZs is the result of foreign collaboration and investment that limit future independence for the Chinese economy and thus potentially threatens further development. In the July/August 2004 *Foreign Affairs*, Gilboy accentuates how this situation attenuates the threat posed by Chinese growth. "First, China's high-tech and industrial exports are dominated by foreign, not Chinese, firms. Second, Chinese industrial firms are deeply dependent on designs, critical components, and manufacturing equipment they import from the United States. . . .Third, Chinese firms are taking few effective steps to absorb the technology they are importing." Huang and Khanna, writing in *Foreign Policy*, agree, pointing out that, "Few of these products are made by indigenous Chinese companies. In fact, you would be hard-pressed to find a single homegrown Chinese firm that operates on a global scale and markets its own products abroad. The Chinese economy has taken off, but few local firms have followed." In fact, most of the collaboration is between foreigners and the notoriously inefficient SOEs.

Most observers also agree that the emergence of a technologically competitive China requires political reform. As Schell argues in the July/August 2004 *Foreign Affairs*,

"Whether the PRC will be able to continue straddling the widening divide between the economic system and its anachronistic political system is the most critical question China faces." The situation is ironic because of the likely effect political reform would have on China's role as a world power. As Gilboy puts it, "The paradox of China's technological and economic power is that China must implement structural political reforms before it can unlock its potential as a global competitor. But if it were to undertake such reforms, it would likely discover even greater common interests with the United States and other industrialized democracies." In this view, China can be either antagonistic and not very threatening or competitive, vibrant, and friendly.

THE "FOURTH MODERNIZATION:" MILITARY ENHANCEMENT

In recent years China's leaders have introduced major equipment modernization, battle-field doctrine, and a slimming down of the old, low-tech People's Liberation Army (PLA). Originally configured to wage defensive "people's war" on the ground, the PLA tradi-tionally stressed massive numbers of light infantry and sought to compensate for China's low industrial and technological base by presenting to any would-be intruder the specter of a numerically overwhelming mass of ground forces.

More recently, the focal concept guiding China's battlefield doctrine, force struc-ture, and weapons procurement policy is "local war under high-tech conditions." Three principal factors account for this altered strategy. The first was China's 1979 armed incursion into neighboring Vietnam (then a Soviet client state), an attempted reprisal for Vietnam's overthrow of Cambodia's Khmer Rouge regime (a Chinese client). But the attempt to "teach Vietnam a lesson" went very badly. Chinese forces were outma-neuvered and outfought by the battle-tested Vietnamese. So it was China, not Viet-nam, which was dealt the harsh lesson that its warfighting capabilities were in serious need of modernization.

Secondly, China's commanders and strategists were deeply affected by Operation Desert Storm, the 1991 U.S.-led rollback of Iraq's invasion and annexation of neighbor-ing Kuwait. Chinese military leaders could watch on CNN real-time demonstrations of America's advances in C3I (command, control, communication, and intelligence), which allowed battlefield commanders to coordinate their technologically advanced, excep-tionally mobile, and lethal air, land, and sea forces. The Gulf War created in China a heightened awareness of its own backwardness in weapons technology, unit coordina-tion, and force mobility.

Third, China's strategic priority has shifted somewhat away from defending against receding threats of ground invasion of its core home territory. Today, its political-mili-tary strategy is more focused upon (1) defending its new industrial centers concentrated along its Pacific coast, (2) preventing the Chinese-claimed Taiwan from making a formal bid for independence, and (3) securing China's claim of sovereignty over all of the Spratly Islands in the South China Sea, a potentially oil-rich assortment of islets also claimed in whole or in part by Taiwan, Brunei, Malaysia, and the Philippines. With the end of the Cold War, China's potential for military confrontation with traditional rivals like Russia,

Map 1.1 Map of China and surrounding areas, including Spratly Islands.

Japan, India, and even the United States has unquestionably receded, but the new environment is more fluid and unpredictable.

Elements of Modernization

China clearly has invested heavily in updating its military forces. Two measures of this commitment are changes in the size of the military and in the amount of military spending.

In terms of *size*, China's forces have recently shrunk from a three million to a two-and-one-quarter million–man force in 2003. Additional uniformed slots are currently being phased out. Prevailing doctrine has it that a leaner, better trained, and more technologically equipped force is better suited to meet the country's security requirements in light of the extraordinary advances made by other states, particularly the United States. As measured by *spending*, China has made military modernization a leading priority. In 2000, for example, official on-the-books defense spending rose by 12.7 percent in an economy that grew by only 7 percent. In 2002–03, Chinese defense spending was $46 billion, compared to $322 billion by the United States. While these figures are not directly comparable (the Chinese pay their soldiers far less than do their American counterparts, for instance), the gap is in orders of magnitude.

What has this increased spending bought? China's recent *weapons acquisition* program has proceeded along two tracks: (1) indigenous development and (2) foreign purchases. As noted earlier, Beijing's strategic focus has shifted toward potential clashes over disputed islands in the South China Sea, with Taiwan should it make a formal attempt at independence, and against any threat to its new industrial centers near the Pacific Ocean. Each emphasis requires modernization efforts in China's air and naval forces.

China's fleet of fighter aircraft is outmoded by today's standards. Its domestically produced F-8II (one of which crashed after colliding with an American "spy" plane off the Chinese coast in April 2001) is broadly comparable to a United States F-4, a 1960s aircraft. The J-10, a more advanced fighter, is now under development. Based in part on Israeli technology, the J-10 will enhance China's jet fighter capabilities, but a substantial amount of time is required to develop, test, manufacture, and deploy complex modern aircraft.

As to warships, China's "blue water" fleet—that is, its oceangoing ships as opposed to its "gray water" coastal vessels—is relatively small and not terribly advanced by contemporary standards. Its navy has equipped some of its fleet with radar-guided surface-to-surface missiles. In some ways, this represents a substantial enhancement of its naval might, but it must be noted that the missiles deployed—the old fashioned HY-2—are liquid-fueled, are inherently volatile, and could thus be quite dangerous to China's navy itself. Also, they can be reloaded only while the ships are in port. So what at first glance appears as a major addition to naval capability turns out to be a rather problematical development. Four relatively modern submarines and several destroyers have been purchased from Russia.

To date, however, China has been unable to acquire the one naval asset that represents true long-distance power-projection capability—a fleet of aircraft carriers. Attempts to negotiate foreign purchases have thus far been unsuccessful. And indigenous development seems quite unlikely for the near future due to the extraordinary cost involved, the specialized and highly advanced engineering skills required for carrier construction, and the logistical capacity necessary to manage the substantial flotilla of supply ships necessary to support a carrier's operations. Moreover, there is growing agreement that carriers are increasingly vulnerable to missile attacks that will make them obsolescent in the future, making development questionable.

Assessing China's Military Strength

Defense analysts agree that China possesses the military manpower and equipment needed to fend off any foreseeable land-based assault upon its core homeland. The sheer size of both the country and of the PLA make a "defense in depth" strategy both feasible for China and daunting to any would-be invader. Any currently imaginable scenario in which an aggressor sought to quash the Beijing regime through invasion would require it to penetrate deep into the country's heartland. It is thus essentially a given that China is able to defend its home continental territory and population against ground invasion.

Similarly, Chinese defense planners believe that the probability that the country will be attacked by nuclear weapons is rather low. Absent an extraordinary escalation of a regional conflict, the states that currently possess both proven warhead and missile delivery capability—the United States, Russia, Britain, France, India, and Pakistan—lack a rational incentive to launch a doomsday nuclear assault on China. So despite the considerable technological gap between Western and Chinese defense capabilities, its home territory is currently rather secure against either major ground-based penetration or wholesale destruction from nuclear assault.

What, then, of China's power projection capabilities; that is, what is its ability to impose its will outside of its borders? Here we are principally interested in the broader question of China's ability to challenge the current balance of power and stability within the crucial East Asian region. For greater clarity, this issue is best divided into two distinct questions: its strategic position vis-à-vis nearby states within continental Asia, and its ability to project its power beyond its territory into the more distant continental and maritime states of East Asia. It is the possibility that China will assert itself regionally that concerns those who see China as a future threat.

As to its potential to coerce its continental neighbors, it is necessary to stress that China's *latent* strategic dominance of both the Korean peninsula in Northeast Asia and of Indochina (Laos, Cambodia, and Vietnam) in Southeast Asia is a widely accepted reality. The likelihood of China actually employing its coercive capabilities in either location will be discussed later. But its capacity to wield power in both theaters is simply a reality.

In order to be able to alter significantly the existing balance of power in the broader East Asian region, however, China would have to achieve the ability to project power beyond the mainland. Doing so would require attaining sufficient aerial and naval power projection capability both to operate in distant locales and to do so with capabilities that surpass those of other states in the region.

As Robert Ross has shown in his insightful "Beijing as a Conservative Power" (*Foreign Affairs*, March/April 1997), China must contemplate the requirements of acting in three distinct maritime theaters in East Asia: (1) the East China Sea, (2) the northern portion of the South China Sea, and (3) the southern reaches of the South China Sea.

China would have to establish its clear dominance over the first—the East China Sea—in order to seize Taiwan or to reassert its historical primacy over Japan and South Korea. Acquiring and sustaining that primacy would require superior air power in support of naval operations against an adversary. In this theater, China could take advantage of its geographic proximity to utilize its land-based aircraft. But, as noted earlier, China's air force is technologically primitive and severely limited in range. Its outdated inventory of 1960s and 1970s aircraft would fare poorly against Japan's much more sophisticated F2 fighter jet. Also, Japan's aerial defenses are greatly enhanced by its possession of modern AWACS (airborne warning and control system) aircraft, and its fighters are being equipped with much more advanced air-to-air missiles than are China's. In addition, Japan possesses a science, technology, and industrial base that far exceeds China's.

Much the same could be said of Taiwan. More economically advanced than mainland China, Taiwan possesses the wealth, the technology base, and the manufacturing capability to maintain a sophisticated defense against a potential armed takeover by Beijing. Equipped with both an advanced navy and a highly sophisticated air force that includes U.S.-built F-16s, Taiwan can most likely repulse a military assault from the mainland. The important caveat for Taiwan, however, is China's current drive to acquire a growing arsenal of quite accurate cruise and ballistic missiles, virtually all of which are deployed in coastal southeast China and targeted at Taiwan. The warning time for launch of these modern missiles is brief, and in any case Taiwan is unable fully to defend itself against a missile barrage. This is the instrument of choice for Beijing to prevent Taiwan from carrying out a policy of formal independence from the mainland during the next decade or two while China lacks a credible air, sea, and land capability to hold the island against formal secession. Such a barrage could virtually destroy Taiwan, but the results would be a Pyrrhic victory, wiping out one of the largest sources of foreign investment in China. In other words, China can destroy Taiwan if it so chooses, but what would be the point?

China is similarly currently incapable of effectively projecting a great deal of armed might into the southern portion of the South China Sea, a region which includes Indonesia, the Philippines, Singapore, and Malaysia. Absent either aircraft carriers or difficult-to-master aerial refueling, the sheer distances involved buffer this region against any potential threat from China's land-based aircraft. Singapore, Malaysia, and Indonesia all have fleets of sophisticated American and British fighters capable of repulsing hostile intrusion by China's navy. Thus in two of the three East Asian theaters where a Chinese challenge to the current balance of power would carry both regional and even global consequence, China currently is incapable of presenting a credible threat, even if it had the desire to do so.

It is in the third regional theater—the northern portion of the South China Sea—where China's land-based aircraft could provide aerial support for both ground operations in Indochina and for operations in the waters near the Paracel Islands east of Vietnam and in the northernmost disputed Spratly Islands. Rightful ownership of the Paracels—which China seized from Vietnam in 1974—is a matter of dispute among Taiwan, Vietnam, and China. China's unyielding stance on the islands was captured in an interview with a Chinese official in Beijing in the summer of 1999. "We can discuss the Spratlys," he said, "but the Paracels are simply off the table. Period."

On current evidence, then, fears of a militarily predatory China both bent upon and capable of imposing its will across East Asia would appear to be minimal. It is true, of course, that China's "Fourth Modernization" is an evolving phenomenon, and that with the passage of time the country's power-projection capabilities will become more potent than they are today. Whether those forces evolve in a menacing way that poses a threat to its neighbors and to American interests in Asia is the main foreign policy question discussed in the next major section.

NONCOERCIVE INFLUENCE: CHINA'S NEW DIPLOMACY

Well aware of its military backwardness and of its economy's growing dependence upon trade, China has in recent years adopted what for it is a new style of diplomacy. Until quite recently, the characteristic style of Beijing's envoys abroad was one of secrecy, aloofness, inaccessibility to host media and public organizations, and a pronounced rigidity in repeating abroad the "line" laid down by the Chinese government. Today, however, there is a growing awareness that the old-style diplomacy was an ineffective instrument of advancing China's interests abroad.

Increasingly, Chinese diplomacy reflects a growing sophistication about how best to get the country's message out, an appearance—at least—of sensitivity to the other state's apprehensions, and the appearance in prominent posts of a new generation of diplomats skilled at the arts of gentle persuasion rather than the dogmatic assertion of unilateral pronouncements. This change represents what Deng and Moore call "a new foreign policy choice [that] highlights the potential role of globalization in transforming great-power politics from an unmitigated struggle for supremacy...to a more cooperative form of interstate competition that increases prospects for China's peaceful rise."

Beyond mere style, Chinese diplomacy has recently focused upon (1) joining literally hundreds of international organizations from which it was previously aloof and (2) mending fences with its Asian neighbors. In Southeast Asia, for example, China has adroitly cultivated bilateral ties (its preferred method in international dealings) in order to dilute the political will of the region's states to adopt a common stance in opposing China's claims in the South China Sea. In initiatives as diverse as resolving its long-standing border dispute with Vietnam in 1999 or agreeing to import more of Thailand's goods in exchange for Thai diplomatic efforts on China's behalf in 1997, China's concerted drive to improve its bilateral ties throughout Asia are beginning to pay off.

Diplomacy has become an important foreign policy instrument for a developing China whose coercive and economic instruments of influence remain quite constrained. Unable to emulate Japan's generous foreign aid and—for now, at least—unable to present a credible military threat to most of Asia, it is learning how to employ age-old diplomatic arts in order to advance its strategic intentions. Deng and Moore suggest a strategic motivation for this change: "To the extent that globalization can create constraints for American power—power that might otherwise be used to pursue unmitigated unilateralism—China believes it can pluralize and democratize the hegemonic order and strengthen incentives for Washington to engage Beijing rather than constrain it." The meaning of China's rise thus becomes an American foreign policy concern.

POLICY ALTERNATIVES: CONTAINMENT OR ENGAGEMENT?

In June 2004, the Organization of Economic Cooperation and Development announced that, for the first time, foreign direct investment to China exceeded that to the United States, knocking the United States from its perpetual position as the number one recipient of global investment. This reversal was partly the result both of declines in investment in the United States (foreign direct investment to this country went from $167 billion in 2002 to $40 billion in 2003) and steady levels of investment in China ($55 billion in 2002 and $53 billion in 2003). Generally, such fluctuations reflect the judgment of investors about the strength of recipient economies. By this measure, at least, China's rise is concrete and undeniable.

But what does China's rise mean for America and the world? Should we worry about it, or should we embrace it?

Answers to these questions vary considerably and sharply along lines developed throughout this case study. The basis of difference is largely the interpretation of the implications of China's rise. One line of argumentation, largely associated with the neo-conservatives prominent in the George W. Bush administration, sees China's rise in largely negative, geopolitical terms and concludes the American policy should be to curb or contain China's rise and to use American influence to force China to change into a less threatening place. The opposite position is that the way China is evolving is evidence of the policy of engagement and enlargement of the Clinton years and that, as a result, the United States should continue to emphasize cooperation with an increasingly close global partner. Doing so, they argue, will encourage continued evolution of China to a position as a peaceful member of the international system.

These contrasts are at the heart of the purpose of the study. There are two aspects of the analysis on which the sides agree. First, they agree on the basic data describing China's rise on both the economic and military levels: China rising is not a point of disagreement. Second, they agree on the desired outcome of China's rise: both the containers and the engagers desire a liberalized, democratic, and capitalist China that is a responsible, "normal" member of the international system. They disagree on which way China is headed. Each position will be briefly described.

Containing the Looming Threat

Those concerned with the trajectory of China's rise begin from the premise that China presents a serious geopolitical threat to the United States. As a close advisor to Vice President Richard Cheney argues, "Virtually every serious strategic thinker in the United States agrees that China, if current trends continue, represents a greater potential threat in the long run than any other nation in the world." Kagan and Kristol, writing in *Present Dangers* (a kind of neo-conservative bible), put it this way: "The past decade also saw the rise of an increasingly hostile and belligerent China." The bases of these assessments include greater Chinese spending on defense coupled with the conviction that the Chinese will divert their growing economic resources to geopolitical ends, including establishing China as the major power in Asia. As Friedberg argues, "The bottom line is simple: one way or another, China's economic growth will provide it with an increasing array of instruments with which to try to exert influence on other countries and, if it chooses, to carry forward a strategic competition with the United States."

In order to respond to this situation, the answer is a policy of containment of China. In Kagan's words, "A successful containment strategy will require increasing, not decreasing, overall defense capabilities. . . .Containment would seek to compel Beijing to choose political liberalization as the best way to safeguard their economic gains and win acceptance in the international community." Kagan dismisses the idea that China will move toward political liberalization on its own as "Marxian foolishness" and concludes that, "as long as China maintains its present form of government, it cannot be peacefully integrated into the international community." This notion that China can be pressured into reform is, one might add, roughly the policy the Bush administration followed in Iraq before 2003. According to Friedberg, the alternative to accepting this analysis of China's intention is strategic competition: "the first order of business is to see the situation plain— namely, that in several important respects a U.S.-PRC strategic competition is already underway, and there is a good chance that it is only going to become more intense and open. In recognizing these realities, the Chinese are well ahead of the United States."

Engaging the Global Partner

Not everyone accepts the neo-conservative facts as true or their realities as real. Looking at the same set of conditions and trends, Gilboy, for instance, finds those conclusions overblown but potentially dangerous: "overestimates of China's achievements and potential are fueling fears that the country will inevitably tilt global trade and technology in its favor, ultimately becoming a military threat to the United States." In addition, these fears are based, according to Segal, "on the fear that the United States provides China both with money and particularly advanced technologies."

This latter point clearly demonstrates conflicting interpretations of trends. As noted earlier, the Chinese indeed import American technology, mostly from American firms operating in China. But does this create a problem, and for whom? One interpretation can be that such importation increases China's technological base, which can be applied to military prowess. Another interpretation is that importing technology simply makes China more dependent on the United States (a position cited earlier).

Those who interpret China's rise positively contradict the assertion of increased Chinese hostility. Medeiros and Fravel, for instance, suggest that "in recent years, China has begun to take a less confrontational, more sophisticated, more confident, and, at times, more constructive approach toward regional and global affairs." Moreover, Deng and Moore maintain the Chinese have basically accepted their role in the evolving order: "In the minds of most Chinese observers, the persistence (and even strengthening) of U.S. primacy after the Cold War has rendered balancing a relatively impractical alternative." Medeiros and Fravel concur: "Chinese analysts now acknowledge that their country cannot (and will not) challenge U.S. global dominance anytime soon." China, in other words, will become a responsible global citizen because it has little choice.

CONCLUSION

China is, as pointed out at the beginning, unquestionably a rising power, and like rising powers in the past, the consequences of its rise are uncertain and subject to varying, even diametrically opposed, interpretation. Because no one can reliably look into the future and know for certain how it will be, whether China will be an increasingly looming threat or a global partner cannot be known with certainty. While the facts are not terribly at odds with one another, what they mean are very different, depending on one's perspective.

Of course, there is a third alternative: China could evolve as *both* a rival and as a partner. Or, it may be that the kinds of policies that evolve for dealing with China will influence the trajectory of that development. In his latter regard, Mead makes a case for using American economic power—what he calls sticky power (institutions and policies that attract others toward U.S. policies and then trap them in it)—to influence China's rise. "As China develops economically, it should gain wealth that could support a military rivaling that of the United States; China is also gaining political influence in the world. Sticky power offers a way out. China benefits from participating in the U.S. economy and integrating itself into the global economy."

The consequences of China's rise for regional and global stability and security will be closely monitored in the coming decades. As other states seek a better understanding of China's intentions, Chinese leaders would do well to keep in mind that their unique place in Asia means they must be especially sensitive to how others view both their ascent and what they plan to do with it.

In the end, what kind of a rising power will China be? Clearly, historical experience suggests to the Chinese their clear mission to become a central actor on the international scene and the dominant actor in East Asia. While China has some of the wherewithal (a huge population, a growing economy) to realize these goals, it has restraints as well. The Chinese military, despite efforts at modernization, is technologically behind; the economy is large but comparatively primitive; and the web of global interdependence constrains Chinese assertiveness. Being a rising power in the new global system may prove to be quite different from being a rising power in an earlier time.

 STUDY/DISCUSSION QUESTIONS

1. What is a rising power? Why is the concept important in understanding the nature of international politics and changes in the balance of power? As suggested in the introduction, rising powers arise periodically. To get some flavor of the process and why it is confusing and controversial, put yourself in the position of being a European in the late nineteenth century trying to assess the impact the United States would eventually have. Would you view the United States as a looming threat or a global partner? Why?

2. A primary source of China's rise is economic. While China's economy has indeed expanded greatly, there is disagreement on the nature of that growth and what it means. Try to construct two arguments, one of which points to the emergence of China as a major competitor and rival and one suggesting that Chinese economic development is less ominous. Compare the two arguments. Where do they agree and disagree?

3. China has also been engaged in military development. Describe the nature and outcomes of that development and the military problems to which they are aimed. Based on your reading, do these development provide basic threats to the United States and its interests? Why or why not?

4. What are the commonly accepted facts about China's rise on which analysts on both sides of the question agree? How do they reach diametrically opposed conclusions based on these facts?

5. Describe and assess the arguments that a rising China is primarily a looming threat and that it is moving toward being a global partner. Based on your understanding of the facts and arguments, which do you find more compelling? Why?

READING/RESEARCH MATERIAL

Deng, Yong, and Thomas G. Moore. "China Views Globalization: Toward a New Great-Power Politics?" *Washington Quarterly* 27, 3 (Summer 2004), 117–136.
Friedberg, Aaron L. "The Struggle for Mastery in Asia." *Commentary*, November 2000.

Gilboy, George J. "The Myth Behind China's Miracle." *Foreign Affairs* 83, 4 (July/August 2004), 33–48.

Gurtov, Mel, and Byong-Moo Hwang. *China's Security: The New Roles of Military.* Boulder, CO: Lynne Rienner Publishers, 1998.

Hale, David, and Lyric Hughes Hale. "China Takes Off." *Foreign Affairs* 82, 6 (November/December 2003), 36–53.

Huang, Yasheng, and Tarun Khanna. "Can India Overtake China?" *Foreign Policy,* July/August 2003, 74–81.

Kagan, Robert. "What China Knows That We Don't: The Case for a New Strategy of Containment." *The Weekly Standard,* January 20, 1997.

Kagan, Robert, and William Kristol, eds. *Present Dangers: Crisis and Opportunity in American Foreign and Defense Policy.* San Francisco, CA: Encounter Books, 2000.

Khalilzad, Zalmay M., et al. *The United States and a Rising China: Strategic and Military Implications.* Santa Monica, CA: RAND, 1999.

Mead, Walter Russell. "America's Sticky Power." *Foreign Policy,* March/April 2004, 46–53.

Medeiros, Evan S., and M. Taylor Fravel. "China's New Diplomacy." *Foreign Affairs* 82, 6 (November/December 2003), 22–35.

Nathan, Andrew J., and Robert S. Ross. *The Great Wall and the Empty Fortress: China's Search for Security.* New York: W. W. Norton, 1997.

Ross, Robert S. "Beijing as a Conservative Power." *Foreign Affairs,* March/April 1997, 33–44.

Schell, Orville. "China's Hidden Democratic Legacy." *Foreign Affairs* 83, 4 (July/August 2004), 116–124.

Segal, Adam. "Practical Engagement: Drawing a Fine Line for U.S.-China Trade." *Washington Quarterly* 27, 3 (Summer 2004), 157–173.

Segal, Gerald. "Does China Matter?" *Foreign Affairs,* September/October 1999, 24–36.

Starr, John Bryan. *Understanding China: A Guide to China's Economy, History, and Political Structure.* New York: Hill and Wang, 1997.

Swaine, Michael D., and Ashley J. Tellis. *Interpreting China's Grand Strategy: Past, Present, and Future.* Santa Monica, CA: RAND, 2000.

WEB SITES

A general overview of China at www.insidechina.com

Comprehensive overview of the Taiwan question at http://taiwansecurity.org

A compendium of online sources about Chinese military policy and capabilities

Chinese Military Power at http://www.comw.org/cmp

Index of web-based information relating to Chinese foreign relations

Chinese Foreign Policy Net at http://www.Stanford.edu/-fravel/chinafp.htm

A compendium of Chinese foreign affairs position papers

State Council Information Office at www.china.org.cn

Ministry of Foreign Affairs at www.fmprc.gov.cn

Systematic overview prepared by Federal Research Division of Library of Congress

China, a Country Study at http://memory.loc.gov/frd/cs/cntoc.html

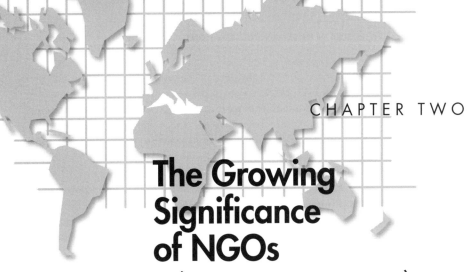

CHAPTER TWO

The Growing Significance of NGOs

MÉDECINS SANS FRONTIÈRES, PEACEKEEPING, AND BEYOND

PRÉCIS

The phenomenon of international activity being conduced by international organizations whose members are not governments of state—referred to as nongovernmental organizations or NGOs—is not a unique attribute of the contemporary period. NGOs, in a number of guises, have been in operation for more than a century, and some, such as the International Red Cross, have been prominent actors on the international scene.

In the contemporary world, NGOs have become more obvious actors in at least two distinct ways. First, they have become increasingly activist in the pursuit of their interests, and this is especially true in the area of peacekeeping and other military operations. Second, at least some of the more activist NGOs pose an open challenge to the principle of state sovereignty, snubbing the idea when it interferes with their work. The *Médecins sans Frontières*, the NGO that is the subject of this case, is especially open in its disdain for trappings of sovereignty like national frontiers, particularly when great physical suffering is occurring. The two factors combine to help form the thrust of this aspect of NGO activity in the contemporary environment, including places like Iraq and Afghanistan.

Nongovernmental organizations (NGOs) are playing an increasingly important and in some cases controversial role in the international relations of the post–Cold War world. Much of this controversy arises from their independence from the controls of national governments, which frees them to engage in activities unconstrained from governmental concerns. One area where they have become particularly active and are playing a significant but controversial role is in their participation alongside governments in a variety of humanitarian efforts falling under the category of peacekeeping operations (PKOs). French-based *Medecins sans Frontieres* (MSF), whose title in English is Doctors without Borders, is one of the most prominent examples of this phenomenon and one of the best examples of NGOs not only ignoring but virtually flaunting their independence from national control.

International organizations (IOs) are generally divided into two groups for analytical purposes. The most prominent kind is *intergovernmental organizations (IGOs)*. The defining characteristic of an IGO is that its members are the governments of states. The most obvious examples of IGOs are the United Nations and its specialized agencies such as the International Monetary Fund or the World Bank (discussed in Chapter 7, "The New Trinity of Globalization").

The other kind of international organization is the nongovernmental organization (NGO). The NGOs are also international in their membership, but unlike IGOs, their members are private individuals or groups from different countries rather than governments. NGOs are far more numerous than IGOs, and their numbers have swelled markedly in an Internet age where communications across borders is both easy and cheap. For instance, there were around 200 NGOs in 1909, according to Stephen Krasner. Today, there are more than 17,000. Most NGOs are narrow in their focus and operate well outside the public eye. Some, however, have very ambitious agendas and play a role in the most public areas of international relations. MSF is one of those prominent organizations.

One of the venues in which MSF and other high-profile, activist NGOs have been prominent is peacekeeping operations (PKOs). The origin of these operations, normally conducted with at least a mandate from the United Nations and often under UN authority, goes back to the Cold War. In that environment, PKOs generally were mounted to separate physically two formerly warring states and to oversee either implementation of some form of peace agreement or, more minimally, to prevent formerly warring parties from resuming hostilities by providing a physical barricade of blue-helmeted soldiers to a potential attacker that he would have to penetrate before reaching the foe. The prototype of this kind of operation was the United Nations Emergency Force (UNEF), which separated Israel and Egypt from the end of the Suez War in 1956 until the outbreak of the Six Days War in 1967 (the UNEF was asked to leave Egypt, where it was stationed, prior to the war). Other examples include the United Nations Force in Cyprus (UNFICYP), which has been in operation since 1964, and the United Nations Interim Force in Lebanon (UNIFIL), which operated between 1976 and 2000.

The nature and thrust of peacekeeping changed radically with the end of the Cold War. During the Cold War, most civil conflicts were fought between a recognizable government and an armed and organized insurgent movement. The clear purpose of the two sides was to gain (or maintain) control of the political system of the country in question. Although civilians were sometimes the victims of terrorist or other forms of suppression by one side or the other, the major form of combat was between armed units of the government and the insurgency. In most cases, the Soviets supported one side (usually the insurgents until the Reagan Doctrine championed U.S. support of anticommunist insurgents in places like Nicaragua and Afghanistan) and the United States supported the beleaguered government. Among the effects of sponsorship was the ability to place some restraints on how the client group conducted hostilities.

All internal wars during the Cold War did not conform to this "model" of conduct. The most prominent exception was the genocide in Cambodia, where the infamous Khmer Rouge gained power after an internal struggle and engaged in the massive extermination of all Cambodians who opposed them between 1976 and 1979, when the country was invaded and conquered by Vietnam in an extension of the Sino-Soviet competition in Asia (the Khmer Rouge were aligned with the People's Republic of China, the Vietnamese with the Soviet Union). The massive slaughter by the Khmer Rouge of innocent civilians proved to be a chilling premonition of the kind of violence that has shaken the post–Cold War world.

The post–Cold War pattern, which I have called *new internal war* (NIW) in *UnCivil Wars* and *When America Fights,* has become the distinctive, if not the exclusive, form of violence in the post–Cold War world. The list of places where this pattern of violence has occurred is familiar—Somalia, Bosnia, East Timor, Sierra Leone, Kosovo—and so is the aura of tragedy and savagery that has been a major characteristic of these conflicts. The countries where they have occurred generally have had governments in tatters where they existed at all, and the armed insurgents have been little more than armed thugs who roam the countryside, terrorizing, uprooting, or murdering innocent, unarmed civilians, usually for criminal or other non-exemplary purposes. With the retreat of the former Cold War competitors from much of the developing world, there is little to restrain the participants in their reigns of terror.

The results of these "wars" were familiar during the 1990s: the starving children of Somalia with their distended bellies and pencil-thin extremities, the emaciated prisoners of war in Bosnian detention camps, the homeless natives of East Timor sitting outside their burned-down homes, the Sierra Leoneans with their multiple amputations, and the displaced Kosovars in refugee camps or attempting to return home after the ethnic cleansing ceased. The common thread in all these cases has been the extreme human suffering endured by the victim populations and the obviously compelling need for someone to take actions somehow to alleviate the human tragedies being endured.

These tragedies raise multiple questions for the international system and its members. Some of these questions, such as the right to intervene (see Chapter 5) and the prosecution of war criminals (see Chapter 6), are dealt with elsewhere in this volume, and the question of whether involvement should be part of U.S. policy was one of the few foreign policy issues that dented the electoral agenda during the 2000 presidential campaign.

During the 2000s a permutation and extension of these dynamics has occurred. Wars in places like Afghanistan and Iraq have resulted in human conditions of suffering not unlike those associated with the new internal wars. The situations are somewhat different: ameliorating chaos to facilitate the alleviation of suffering in the NIWs, dealing with formal occupiers and ineffective government to help the needy in Iraq and Afghanistan. How does an organization like MSF adapt?

Part of the short-term question is how to stem the worst of the immediate effects of war or an imperfect peace; in the longer run, there is also the question of making the target societies whole and stable once again (if they ever were). MSF is a major part of the answer to the short-term question; increasingly it is also part of the long-term solution.

The current case study thus has two related focuses. The major focus is on MSF as an example of a highly activist, dedicated, and visible NGO. Because it is a medical organization, there is a natural bridge to the second focus on civil and post–September 11, 2001, conflicts, because the kinds of human medical suffering that MSF is dedicated to relieving is nowhere more obvious than in these conflicts.

MÉDECINS SANS FRONTIÈRES

Although it has been active for nearly 28 years, MSF did not attract the broad public eye until 1999. Between its formation in December 1971 and its emergence in the public spotlight with the receipt of the Nobel Peace Prize in 1999, its relative anonymity was, to a large degree, a matter of choice; its mission is to provide relief to those suffering through natural and man-made disasters, and its methods are often highly unorthodox (some would argue occasionally controversial and even illegal). The doctors who work for MSF prefer to operate in the shadows of the international stage. These shadows were illuminated when the organization was awarded the Nobel Prize for Peace, thereby making its low profile less possible to maintain.

Background and Evolution of MSF

MSF is largely the result of the experiences of a handful of young doctors attempting to relieve the hardships of the civilian population during the Nigerian-Biafran Civil War of 1967–70. The "French doctors," as they are known, worked under the auspices of the International Red Cross, a highly respected but very conservative NGO, during that conflict. The Red Cross has a tradition of strict neutrality and deference to political and legal authorities that makes it respected and trusted by governments in matters such as the conformance of prisoner-of-war camps to international conventions on the treatment of military prisoners. In the eyes of the young, idealistic doctors who formed MSF, this conservatism came at the expense of providing maximum relief and succor to those civilians suffering the kinds of indignities associated with modern new internal wars. The French doctors were frustrated by the impact of the International Red Cross's conservative approach and practices; MSF was their answer.

The Biafran experience convinced a small group of participating doctors who had attempted to alleviate the worst civilian suffering by Nigerian soldiers against Ibo tribesmen in Biafra that the approach practiced by the Red Cross had worsened the suffering there (for instance, the Red Cross would not go into certain areas the government forbade it to enter). They thus set out to form a more aggressive, interventionist, and independent organization. The result was MSF, whose first activity was to provide medical care for victims of flooding in Pakistan and which gradually enlarged its activities to encompass both man-made and natural disasters that have carried them around the world to locations as diverse as Ethiopia, Honduras, El Salvador, Peru, Yemen, Mozambique, Liberia, and Sudan. Their goal is to find those suffering medical problems and to alleviate those problems; overt political and other concerns are excluded from their motivations.

The organization has grown dramatically. There were originally six founding members of MSF, the most prominent of whom was Dr. Bernard Kouchner, who later became the French Health Minister and who served as the Special Representative of the Secretary-General (SRSG) of the United Nations effort in Kosovo. Kouchner was the operational leader of peacekeeping and state-building efforts in that bitterly torn land, the first time someone with a primary background in an NGO has ever occupied that kind of position.

The organization has gradually grown in size. In 1999, for instance, MSF had 23 offices in various countries (the American chapter of MSF uses the English translation Doctors without Borders to designate itself). MSF has more than 2,000 medical volunteers at work in 80 countries. Underlying its operation is a budget of more than $167 million, almost four-fifths of which comes from private donations worldwide. Such an extensive operation with such a modest budget is possible because most of the medical personnel, including physicians and nurses, act voluntarily and do not receive remuneration beyond living and travel expenses.

Most of MSF's medical activities are carried out far from the public eye. In 1980, for instance, MSF sent medical teams into Afghanistan to care for the wounded that resulted from the Soviet invasion and occupation of that country. In the process, they gained some reputation as a human rights monitor because MSF doctors witnessed and reported violations. In 1984, it instituted a nutrition program in Ethiopia and ended up denouncing the misuse of humanitarian assistance to that country. In 1988, MSF had the only medical team to reach the Kurdish town of Halabja in Iraq after Saddam Hussein's forces had attacked the Kurdish stronghold with chemical weapons. When the Persian Gulf War broke out, it set up camps in the no-man's land between Iraq and Jordan to provide aid to refugees. When the Kurds fled Iraq at the end of the war to avoid the vengeance of Saddam Hussein, MSF was the first to arrive on the Turkish mountainsides to provide relief to the 70,000 refugees clinging to the most tenuous existence until global publicity, much of it created by MSF itself, resulted in the United States government intervening under the banner of Operation Provide Comfort (later renamed Northern Watch).

MSF has grown to be the world's largest nonprofit medical relief agency. In addition to its willingness to involve itself in man-made emergencies, it has been active in other, less controversial activities such as programs of inoculation against deadly diseases and its Access to Essential Medicines Campaign, which seeks to raise awareness about and to bring relief to poor peoples who are routinely denied access to medical treatment.

But it is MSF's willingness to insert itself in highly political situations—notably war zones where civilians are subjected to grossly inhumane treatment—that has become its international claim to fame. No one argues that its basic mission, the alleviation of human suffering from whatever source, is not noble or praiseworthy. But MSF is also the subject of criticism, much of which follows from its origin. MSF was, after all, born out of a fairly scornful rejection of the means of international medical care giving by the most establishment of caregiving organizations, the International Red Cross. MSF was born as something of a "maverick," and it is a reputation in which it takes satisfaction, even pride. That fact does not always sit well with the organizations with which it must interact in providing its services.

Controversies Surrounding MSF

In some ways, MSF resembles another highly activist organization: Greenpeace. Although Greenpeace has a different substantive mission, they share the characteristic of being reasonably scornful "of governments and journalists," according to *The Economist*. MSF and Greenpeace share a level of devotion to their mission that borders, to some observers, on near zealotry. It also leads to a set of controversies about what MSF does and how it carries out its mission that has an impact on its ability to work effectively within the framework of PKOs. Five interrelated sources of controversy are worth mentioning.

The first controversy surrounds the very core of the reason for MSF's existence, the notion of being "without borders." The idea that political boundaries cannot and should not be a barrier to the provision of medical attention is the basic reason MSF was created in the first place. As one of the cofounders, Rony Brauman, explained in an interview in *Time International* in 1999, "International relief agencies were too respectful of notions of non-interference and sovereignty. When we saw people dying on the other side of the frontiers, we asked ourselves, 'What is this border? It doesn't mean anything to us.'"

This statement summarizes a major source of irritation between MSF and other helping agencies and also governments in the countries where MSF operates. The organization Brauman accuses of being "too respectful" was, of course, the International Red Cross, suggesting a less-than-cordial relationship with that NGO. MSF regularly ignores the sovereignty of states where it operates; when officially denied permission to enter countries to provide medical relief, the response by MSF has been simply to sneak across borders, in effect illegally infiltrating the sovereign territory of states in an act of overt defiance of international norms. Aside from a firm belief in the righteousness of what it is doing, MSF understands that the nature of their mission and their willingness to publicize unfortunate conditions means governments are reluctant to arrest and deport MSF personnel (although this occasionally does happen), making them less than welcome guests some of the time.

This leads to the second controversy surrounding MSF, which is its explicitly political character and nature. Generally speaking, it is a hallmark of international organizations that they must remain fundamentally politically neutral in order to be effective. Certainly this is true of most IGOs, and in most cases, it is true of NGOs as well. The constraints on NGOs in this regard are less than IGOs, since they are not accountable to the national governments of their origin or where they do business.

MSF has never denied that it is political, at least in the impact it has on situations where it acts. As cofounder Kouchner (who split with MSF in 1980 to form a competitior, *Medecins du Monde*) puts it, "The movement was political from the start. The tradition was medical, the action was medical, but we had to convince people that borders should not protect disgraceful conduct and suffering." This frank admission, of course, puts MSF at direct odds with governments that are the source of suffering in their countries; MSF's virtually monomaniacal devotion to the mission also puts the group at odds with peacekeepers and occupying powers on occasion.

The role MSF has taken upon itself leads to a third controversial characteristic: its tendency to view itself and be viewed as a loner. The doctors who work for the organization have a mission, "a 'duty to interfere' in troubled areas and to speak out about what they saw," in the words of the *Time International* article. This notion of special mission sets MSF aside as something different from others around it. MSF volunteers are proud of the fact that they are often the first caregivers on the scene (e.g., ministering to the Kurds in the wake of the Persian Gulf War) and that, when all the others have left, they will still be there. Being aloof is, indeed, part of MSF's effectiveness, as its Nobel citation observes: "By maintaining a high degree of independence, the organization has succeeded in living up to its ideals." It does so, of course, at the expense of being thought of as something less than a team player.

The tendency to be viewed as a loner reinforces the fourth characteristic, MSF's penchant for honesty and integrity, some would argue to a fault. The agency's single-minded concern (even obsession) not only with treating but also with publicizing the human causes of suffering clearly does not endear it with those organizations (which are often national governments) against whom it levels charges. The leaders of MSF are medical personnel, not diplomats, and while this may endow them with a refreshing degree of candor not usually present in complex international situations, it may also compromise their effectiveness in dealing with others.

Finally, MSF has particular disdain for peacekeeping operations. The basic reason for this feeling arises from the MSF perception that peacekeeping missions simply get in the way of their performance of their duties and that the peacekeepers rapidly adopt self-protection as their basic mission rather than the promotion of the well-being of the target population that MSF seeks to protect.

The attitude of MSF toward peacekeepers was expressed explicitly in a 1993 report dealing with the UN effort in Somalia, titled "Life, Death, and Aid." The report begins by criticizing governments for their selectivity in terms of which humanitarian disasters they deal with and which they ignore—mounting a major effort in Somalia but turning a blind eye toward the equally horrendous slaughter in nearby Sudan. Turning to the actual operation in Somalia, MSF argues additional points. On one hand, MSF maintains that UN PKOs often have imprecise mandates that tie their hands in providing needed assistance to those suffering the effects of war. Instead, the peacekeepers come to define their mission as self-protection rather than the promotion of agendas such as MSF's. Moreover, in their efforts to be fair and impartial, the peacekeepers may actually make it more difficult to conduct operations than was the case before their arrival. In Somalia, for instance, the report alleges that UN efforts to provide protection to food supplies being convoyed to remote locations disrupted an informal arrangement MSF had with various warlords whereby the warlords would be allowed to plunder a share of humanitarian relief supplies in return for allowing the rest to get through. When the peacekeepers arrived and restored an open transportation system, this informal arrangement was interrupted and the clans then began attacking the supply caravans, with the effect that delivery became more, rather than less, difficult than it had been under the clan-MSF arrangement.

PEACEKEEPING OPERATIONS

As noted earlier, international involvement in the internal violence in the third world has become an increasingly prominent component of contemporary international affairs. The frequently gory nature of these conflicts makes them difficult to ignore, especially if television's roving eye happens to capture the gross human suffering that accompanies them. A few places, such as Sudan, avoided scrutiny for years by terrorizing journalists to keep them out of the country until refugees flowed into Chad and told their horrific stories. In any case, there will be a great temptation to intercede to right the situation.

The problem is controversial and revolves around three questions. The first is what outcomes one expects from intervention: a mere cessation of the hostilities? Is a return to the status quo from which the violence emerged in the first place enough? Or is a stable environment that will nurture a post-involvement peace the desired end we seek? The second question has to do with what must be done to accomplish whatever end one has in mind: the alternatives are interceding into the violence and forcefully making sure it does not resume (what I call conflict suppression) and building viable institutions and structures that will create an atmosphere in which peace will be built (what I call state building). The third question is who should engage in this process and how, which gets to the heart of the involvement of NGOs such as MSF.

Nature of the Problem

When a PKO is first considered, the potential target situation is either an active war zone or a former war zone where some form of ceasefire (probably not very durable) is in place. In all likelihood, the violence has largely been perpetrated against civilian groups within the country by other indigenous groups, leaving a strong residue of bitterness, hatred, and suspicion among the warring parties. Peacekeepers will normally enter with an initial mandate to restore the order and to stop the killing. As the report by MSF cited in the last section indicates, they may have little mandate beyond that.

The initial conditions frame the sequential tasks that the peacekeepers may undertake. Their first duty, unless a peace of sorts is in place, is to stop the fighting, what I call *peace imposition* (PI). This is a combat job and requires well-equipped combat soldiers. Once peace has been imposed, the task moves to making sure the situation does not revert to fighting once again, or what I call *peace enforcement* (PE). This task requires combat soldiers to convince or intimidate the former fighters into remaining peaceful, but it also involves providing conditions conducive to a return to normalcy, such as reinstating some form of physical order and civil justice (police and courts) or instituting such structures if they did not preexist the violence. Providing health care and basic services such as power and water also falls into this category. Military forces may provide the necessary safety— or shield—to undertake these tasks, but the actual tasks are more clearly civil in nature. If peace enforcement produces an atmosphere where animosities are overcome to the point that the former warring parties prefer continuing peace to the resumption of war, then the task can move to simply maintaining the peace, or *peacekeeping* (PK). Once peacekeeping has reached the point that peace will likely be maintained in the absence of the peacekeepers, then the mission is accomplished and the PKO can be terminated.

Three comments should be made about this continuum at this point. The first is that experience over the past decade has demonstrated that the international system has become reasonably proficient at imposing and even enforcing peace. The second is that no mission in the post–Cold War world has reached the point of successful peacekeeping, the point where there is confidence the peace will hold after the mission has been withdrawn. Missions have been terminated, as they were in Somalia, but not with the assurance the peace would remain intact (and in that case, the peace did not hold). Third, the sequence appears to hold equally well in places like Afghanistan and Iraq.

If leaving behind a stable peace is the goal (which it almost always is), then any PKO must successfully complete all three stages of the PI-PE-PK sequence. If the situation in a country has deteriorated to the point that a new internal war has raged, there must have been underlying reasons that need to be addressed if there is to be a reasonable chance for a stable post-mission peace. The same is true when a government has been overthrown with no obvious successor. In all likelihood, political institutions and processes are dysfunctional or nonexistent; economic conditions are either so wretched or so skewed toward a minority that most people have little stake in the ongoing system; and social, cultural, ethnic, or religious differences are so deep as to leave a thoroughly noncohesive social structure. When one adds the animosities generated by the war itself, it is clear that a simple cooling-off period provided by peace imposers and enforcers is not going to be sufficient to heal the wounds and scars that war has produced. Something more must be done.

In order to reach stable peace, the system must be built (or rebuilt) so that the population prefers the peaceful situation to war, the task of *state building* (the term "nation building" is sometimes used as a synonym, but that is technically incorrect, as the actions are aimed at changing the nature of the political unit, the state). Only by creating political, economic, social, and psychological conditions that the population prefers to war can a PKO move along the continuum from a war zone (PI) to a stable post-mission peace where war is unlikely to recur.

The task of state building is complex, and one of the complexities is the large and varied number of tasks that must be performed and the variety of actors that must be involved in the enterprise. Moreover, there is no agreement on how these tasks can be completed or who should undertake them. International experience in this realm is simply too limited for definitive answers to state-building questions. Among the actors who have a part in any operation are NGOs; for the medical needs that are always one of the major byproducts of these wars, that means MSF.

The Structure of State Building

Outsiders entering a former internal war zone face one of two major political problems. They may enter a country that at one time was reasonably well ordered, although in all likelihood any form of political organization was authoritarian in one way or another (Iraq or Afghanistan, for instance). In these circumstances, the war has likely disrupted whatever organization there was (indeed, the political structure may well have been the major target of fighting), leaving behind a dysfunctional, disrupted set of institutions that can only be rebuilt with some effort and care to avoid replicating whatever it was about the old order that was a precipitant of violence in the first place. In addition, it is very likely that the economic and social systems, whatever their prior condition, have suffered similar disruptions.

The other possibility is virtual chaos, where either there never was a viable political and economic system or whatever system preexisted has been so thoroughly destroyed that no semblance of order and authority can be identified. Most of the countries where this condition holds are deeply divided along ethnic, religious, or some other (e.g., clan) lines and can agree on no form of organization that is acceptable to all groups. These states are generally grouped together under a category name such as failed states; Sierra Leone is a current example.

In either case, the situation is bleak, and its alleviation is going to be difficult, if not impossible. Once the fighting is stopped, which is often the easier of the tasks, outsiders are faced with a solid wall of problems, many of them life-threatening. The scourges of war have left many victims as refugees, living in squalid conditions without adequate shelter, sanitary conditions, medical help, or food. Others have had their homes destroyed and huddle in the ruins. Electrical power has long since gone out, as has water, garbage pickup, and other services. Employment has ceased for many as factories have been destroyed and crops torched. Many are suspicious of neighbors as the sources of their suffering, which may include the violent loss of loved ones that leaves physical and psychological wounds that need to be tended. And either there is no political authority to turn to or available officials are viewed as part of the problem.

The human needs fall into several categories. One is the simple restoration of order and safety, a task that intervening troops can perform for a time but that must eventually be provided indigenously. A second is basic survival needs, including an adequate supply of food, potable water, shelter against the physical elements, cooking facilities, medical care for those who need it, inoculations against diseases (the occurrence of which may increase because of the wretchedness of conditions), and more. A third need is the rebuilding of whatever structures have been destroyed, beginning with basic services and infrastructure. Finally, there is the need to begin to expand the preexisting structures to improve conditions so that there will be no incentives for a recurrence of the violence in the future.

Enter the NGOs

The list of tasks is obviously extensive, and it all cannot be performed simultaneously. For better or worse, disasters attract those organizations and individuals who want to provide assistance in the specific areas of their expertise. The soldiers arrive to restore the order, the Red Cross is there to coordinate aid and to provide things like warm clothing and blankets. CARE and other food providers are not likely to be far behind. And, of course, MSF will be among the first to arrive.

The problem is coordination of the overall effort. A welter of governmental and nongovernmental agencies will almost certainly descend on the scene, each with a specific agenda of assistance that it wants to provide but with no coordinated plan for the comprehensive provision of services in an ordered program. In fact, each aid giver is likely to view its own mission as supreme and to treat other priorities and providers whose missions conflict with theirs as detrimental or less important. Those who would help thus can become part of the problem as well as part of the solution.

Here is where the case of MSF, specifically in terms of its relations with military forces on the scene, becomes illustrative. MSF is likely to be one of the first international agencies on the scene when disaster befalls a particular location. In fact, they will probably be present before the problem reaches the level of suffering and atrocity that creates international awareness and the impetus necessary to authorize some form of international action. When the peacekeepers "hit the beaches," MSF will be there to see them ashore, if not necessarily to greet them.

Part of the problem is perspective. For MSF, the central problem is medical, and alleviating the immediate medical suffering of the target population is by far the most important task it believes needs to be undertaken. Anything that other agencies do to make the provision of medical assistance easier is valued; anything that does not contribute to that end, and especially if it makes medical caregiving more difficult, is to be opposed.

Military forces entering a new internal war are likely to have a different perspective on the problem. Certainly they are aware of medical problems and want them dealt with; in Haiti, for instance, military doctors became an integral part of the health-care system during the 1994–98 operation there. But the military also realizes that medical attention is only one of a number of priorities within the general mandate of peace imposition and enforcement. Securing areas from military violence and restoring physical order are likely to be their highest priorities, followed closely by providing reasonable security for the peacekeepers themselves. Once these objectives are achieved, then more strictly humanitarian concerns can be undertaken. While the basic mission is being implemented, however, the caregivers like MSF who want to get out into the field—usually in unsecured areas—simply get in the way and make the accomplishment of their mission more difficult. At this point, the caregivers (MSF) and the soldiers may come into direct conflict. In Afghanistan in 2004, for instance, an MSF team of caregivers traveling in an unsecured part of the countryside (an area not controlled by the Afghan army or NATO forces) was attacked by Afghan tribesmen, and all five members of the team were killed.

This type of instability was apparently the situation in Somalia in the early 1990s. MSF doctors were in the country dispensing medical aid and assisting in the distribution of food in those areas where it was most needed before the United Nations arrived to help alleviate the starvation. In order to carry out their function, MSF was forced to compromise with the clan warlords who controlled various parts of Somali territory. To insure that enough food got to its needed destinations, MSF worked out an arrangement where the clans were allowed to commandeer enough grain to feed their followers in return for allowing the rest of the supplies to go forward, a practice the UN peacekeepers ended. At the same time, MSF doctors working in war zones sometimes allowed themselves to be put into service to run military hospitals to treat the wounds of soldiers wounded in battle.

Such compromises became unacceptable when the UN mission entered the country. The first and major mission of the UNISOM (United Nation in Somalia) was to reestablish the integrity of the food distribution system, which required securing the country's road network and convoying food supplies. As noted, these actions deprived the warlords of the ability to skim their previous shares, thereby interrupting their bargain with the MSF. To the United Nations forces, this was simply a matter of restoring order and integrity to the country; to MSF, it amounted to the disruption of a functional—if extralegal—means to insure that people got the medical services they required.

MSF also believes that peacekeepers are likely to get in the way of solving problems the longer they stay. Partly, this is the case because, as the "Life, Death, and Aid" report maintains, "humanitarian aid permits intervention by armed forces yet gives them no precise political programme." In some sense, this charge is true, but it may be misleading as well. The purely military aspect of PKOs is peace imposition and peace enforcement. During peace enforcement it has an ongoing role in maintaining the absence of a return to violence, but it has little other intrinsic role to play. It may be asked to perform other roles, such as constructing temporary housing facilities (tent cities and the like), but peace enforcers basically do exactly that: enforce the peace.

The problems go beyond conflicts of mission definition, reflecting very different institutional and organizational cultures. MSF is, quite openly and proudly, antiestablishment and iconoclastic. It was, after all, born because the traditional, establishment providers of medical assistance, were, in its view, dysfunctionally hamstrung by conventions (in this case, honoring sovereign borders) from performing necessary medical tasks. In some ways, Doctors without Borders is Doctors *against* Borders, a way of thinking hardly likely to endear them to political authorities and their agents, notably the military. One result is that each group and its members tends to treat the other with suspicion, even disdain. From a military viewpoint, MSF personnel are likely to be viewed as impractical dreamers who obstruct orderly operations and who make demands that can put military forces in unnecessary danger. From an MSF viewpoint, the military is likely to be seen as a reactionary barrier to mission accomplishment, a force to be avoided and circumvented rather than a partner in a broader enterprise to build states and leave behind conditions of stable peace.

Yet, both military forces and organizations like MSF have roles throughout the various purposes for which PKOs may be mounted. When the mission is conflict suppression, the military has the job of bringing the fighting to an end, and MSF has the imperative of treating the wounded and suffering. When the mission turns to state building, their roles continue: the peacekeepers as shields behind which state building occurs, organizations like MSF helping to build or rebuild a medical infrastructure to leave behind when peace is ensured.

MSF in Afghanistan and Iraq

The experience that MSF has built in its 30-year existence has been applied in the different but linked experiences in Afghanistan and Iraq. The two situations are different in that there was a civil war in Afghanistan where the outcome was decisively affected by outside (principally American) military intervention, whereas the Iraqi government was overthrown by a cross-border invasion by U.S.-led forces. At the same time, the two situations are similar in that the restoration (or creation) of a stable peace in each case required a massive state-building operation for which prior planning or resource commitment were either entirely lacking or woefully inadequate, and there was no obvious government or governmental structure to hand power or with whom to negotiate. In both cases, long-term success required (and continues to require) running the entire PI-PE-PK gamut in a chaotic situation. Because part of the chaos was medical, MSF was, and is, there.

MSF involvement in the region goes back to 1980, when MSF teams entered Afghanistan—illegally crossing the border to get there, of course—to aid medical victims of the Soviet invasion of 1979. They remained active within the country throughout that war and into the early 1990s, when their emphasis shifted toward favorite MSF projects such as inoculation of children and the provision of basic medical care in a country whose primitive health-care system had been essentially destroyed by years of war (a not unusual circumstance in war-torn third world countries). After the Afghan Taliban government was overthrown by the indigenous Northern Alliance with the help of the United States, MSF returned in force to lend its expertise and experience to state building in the medical arena. In 2003, the group launched a parallel effort in Iraq after the United States overthrew the Saddam Hussein regime and occupied the country.

MSF efforts in both countries have been low profile in the tradition of the organization, except in instances such as the murder of the MSF team in Afghanistan. As has been the case elsewhere, MSF has found itself at odds with the occupying powers in both countries, for familiar reasons noted earlier. MSF continues to ignore national boundaries, including informal clan boundaries in Afghanistan. These efforts must be carried out by putting its members in harm's way with little protection from allied (or governmental, in the case of Afghanistan) forces reluctant to patrol unsecured areas where MSF insists the medical needs are. At the same time, MSF's insensitivity to political realities when they interfere with the conduct of its mission and its legendary penchant for honesty often puts it at odds with what it views as unjustifiably optimistic assessments of conditions by the occupiers.

An additional problem for MSF in both countries has been in maintaining the appearance of neutrality in the ongoing hostilities aimed at the occupiers. MSF personnel are overwhelmingly (although by no means exclusively) European and North American, and some Afghan and Iraqi opponents of the occupation thus automatically associate them with the occupying powers, thereby making them targets for resistance violence. MSF has no political position in either situation and intends to serve the medical needs of both countries and their citizens regardless of the politics involved (although it is likely most MSF personnel privately oppose the occupation). The result is ironic: MSF has the contradictory problems of disassociating itself from the occupying state builders while simultaneously carrying out a critical state-building function. It is the kind of dilemma that a self-consciously apolitical NGO operating in a highly politically charged atmosphere is bound to endure. MSF has been in this kind of situation before, and it doubtless will be again.

CONCLUSION

This case study is only a microcosm of the growing roles of NGOs in important international situations, in this case the provision of services in circumstances where PKOs are involved. Real situations, of course, are often far more complicated than has been portrayed. In any real PKO, for instance, there will be a wide variety of actors coming together; in addition to military forces and caregivers like MSF, there will be numerous IGOs (the UN and its representatives), the media, representatives of governments providing assistance, and a whole host of other NGOs with other specialized roles, responsibilities, and perspectives.

What this very narrow case (narrow in the sense of the mandate and goal of MSF) seeks to illustrate is how difficult it is to coordinate the relations among emerging international actors in a new and largely uncharted environment. The MSF-peacekeeper relationship is no more than the tip of the iceberg in suggesting the multiple difficulties and opportunities that interaction may produce.

What lessons can we draw from this experience? The question is worth exploring, both because peacekeeping opportunities and situations bearing a resemble to Iraq and Afghanistan are likely to continue, possibly even proliferate, in the international relations of the upcoming years, and because nongovernmental organizations like MSF will probably play an increasing part in the system generally and in PKOs in particular. The problem, in other words, is both prominent and difficult.

There is little agreement on what evolving relationship NGOs like MSF and governmentally based international state-building missions will have in the future. Part of the reason has to do with the lack of consensus on exactly what state building is and how to organize and accomplish its goals. The evolving situations in Afghanistan and Iraq, where the efforts have arguably been half-hearted efforts begun as a virtual second thought, have done little to create the "guidebook" for future operations. Part of the reason is also institutional and perspectival. MSF is not only a *non*governmental organization, it is also, in many cases, an *anti*governmental organization. Its disdain for politics means it shies away from entering the kinds of authority relations on which governments are based. A quick reference to the MSF Web page quickly reveals the scorn MSF has for government; in some ways, the relationship is reciprocal. At the same time, both sides in fact need one another for maximum effectiveness: state building will always have a medical component, and MSF is there. It is not clear who would take their place if MSF were to withdraw or cease to exist.

What makes these situations controversial? Partly, it is the intractability of the circumstances where PKOs with state-building intentions are contemplated. Generally, these are very difficult, bitter situations, where it is unclear how much assistance outsiders can bring beyond stopping (or interrupting) the violence and tending to the immediate suffering of populations. Long-term solutions have remained elusive, at least in part because we have no reliable methods for moving situations toward positive outcomes. A good bit of our uncertainty in this regard is the absence of anything like a plan to integrate and coordinate the activities of a large number of individual organizations with the differing and sometimes contradictory missions they seek to accomplish. Some of these actors will be NGOs like MSF, and some of them will be contentious and even contemptuous of other authorities, as MSF often proudly is. Dealing with programmatic elements that provide vital services but are likely to resist or refuse coordination is part of the PKO problem that needs to be addressed.

The blossoming of organizations like MSF also points to a more general international phenomenon, the privatization of international interactions. This trend has been most apparent in the area of economic globalization where, for many purposes, the interaction of states has become nearly irrelevant as a factor in economic and financial transactions. The 1980s trend toward privatization and deregulation of economic activity has included an assault on underlying dynamics of the international order, including the principle of state sovereignty that has underlaid the system for more than 300 years.

The rise of NGOs may represent a similar assault from another direction. Certainly, MSF fits the bill: it was born explicitly as a reaction to the strictures placed on the provision of medical assistance that honoring sovereignty created for the medical caregivers. Its very name in English, Doctors *without Borders*, is indicative of exactly what it thinks about the underlying truisms of the international order. How much of a threat organizations like MSF represent to the conventional order is a question worth pondering.

STUDY/DISCUSSION QUESTIONS

1. What is a nongovernmental organization (NGO)? Contrast NGOs with intergovernmental organizations (IGOs).

2. Compare and contrast the pattern of internal wars in the third world during the Cold War and post–Cold War periods.

3. How and why did *Medecins sans Frontieres* (MSF) come into being? What are its major self-proclaimed missions and purposes?

4. Why is MSF a controversial organization?

5. Discuss the nature of contemporary peacekeeping operations (PKOs), including the sequential military problems they have and the goals for which they may be commissioned.

6. What is state building? Why is it a controversial goal for a PKO? Where do organizations like MSF fit into state-building operations?

7. MSF has been active in both Afghanistan and Iraq, but its activities have hardly been reported in the press. Why is this so? Why does MSF have a stormy relationship in this area of the world, especially with the U.S. government, as the leader of the occupation force in both countries? Are there lessons to be learned from this experience?

8. How is the relationship of an NGO like MSF with PKO military forces a microcosm of the kinds of difficulties that a complex PKO faces in the field? Explain.

9. Why are both PKOs and NGOs like MSF important to the future evolution of the international system?

READING/RESEARCH MATERIAL

Dorozynski, Alexander. "*Medecins sans Frontieres:* 20 Years Old." *British Medical Journal* 303, 6817 (December 21, 1991), 591.

Krasner, Stephen D. "Sovereignty." *Foreign Policy* (January/February 2001), 20–30.

Nolan, Hanna. "Learning to Express Dissent: *Medecins sans Frontieres.*" *British Medical Journal* 319, 7207 (August 14, 1999), 446.

"No Thanks: Armed Protection for Aid." *The Economist (U.S.)* 329, 7839 (November 27, 1993), 43.

Sancton, Thomas. "Distinguished Service: *Medecins sans Frontieres* Receives the Nobel Prize." *Time International,* October 25, 1999, 68.

Snow, Donald M. *UnCivil Wars: International Security and the New Internal Conflicts.* Boulder, CO: Lynne Rienner Publishers, 1996.

———. *When America Fights: The Uses of U.S. Military Force.* Washington, DC: CQ Press, 2000.

Spencer, Miranda. "The World is Their Emergency Room: *Doctors* Without *Borders.*" *Biography* 4, 6 (June 2000), 55–58.

WEB SITES

Database on intergovernmental and nongovernmental international organizations

Geneva International at http://geneva-international.org/GVA/Directory/Welcome.E.html

Home page for Doctors without Borders

Doctors without Borders at http://www.doctorswithoutborders.org

Worldwide organizations promoting human rights

Amnesty International at http://www.amnesty.org

Human Rights Watch at http://www.hrw.org

Alphabetical listing of NGOs affiliated with the United Nations

NGO Global Network at ttp://www.ngo.org

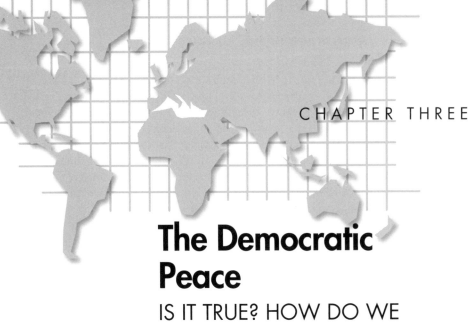

CHAPTER THREE

The Democratic Peace

IS IT TRUE? HOW DO WE GET THERE?

PRÉCIS

Almost no one would argue that the 1990s was not an expansive period for the growth of political democratization in the international system. With the collapse of the ideological opposition to political democracy as Marxism-Leninism imploded operationally and philosophically, the "third wave of democracy" washed across the globe, resulting in a net increase in the number of democratic states in the world.

While hardly anyone would deny this trend, many wonder whether it will endure through the 2000s, and it is a major burden of this case study to examine two questions posed in the subtitle. The first is whether the spread of democracy is inevitable and whether there is greater peace and stability as the process unfolds. The second is what is the better way to promote democracy. The question of democratic success is raised and examined and ways in which it might fail are grouped around five possible sources of failure. The discussion then contrasts approaches of the 1990s and 2000s to promote democracy.

In 1991, Harvard political scientist Samuel P. Huntington published a book titled *The Third Wave of Democracy*. His basic thesis was that the end of the Cold War was ushering in a worldwide movement toward political democratization around the globe. His concern was over the nature and durability of this phenomenon. In addition, he sought to place it in historical perspective within the twentieth century. He chose to call this trend the "third wave" purposefully: a similar phenomenon had occurred twice before in the twentieth century, after the triumphs of the Western democracies in the two world wars.

His choice of the analogy to a wave was both symbolic and controversial, because it suggested an underlying thesis that many others either denied or at least hoped was untrue. The symbolism arises from the actions of waves: they rise in the sea and crash onto the shore. And then they recede. In the cases of the first two twentieth century waves, there was the emergence of democratization, as formerly authoritarian countries overthrew (or had overthrown for them by the victorious allies) their governments and replaced them with democratic forms. As time passed, however, a number of those states reverted to nondemocratic forms in much the same way that a receding wave acts. The controversial aspect was that Huntington predicted the same thing would likely happen again this time: the euphoria of post–Cold War decommunization would produce a series of political democracies (especially in the formerly communist world), but some would revert to nondemocratic form.

We are now a decade and one-half removed from the beginning of the physical end of the Cold War. The wave of democratization has continued to roll in; standard monitors of the process like the Freedom House and its Map of Freedom show a steady increase in the number of countries where individual freedom is exercised and where political democracy is in place. The two lists are not, of course, identical. Citizens of China exercise a large number of individual freedoms in the day-to-day conduct of their private lives. These freedoms do not, however, extend to political participation, as noted in Chapter 1. More to the point, there have been virtually no reversions, and where democracy has been suspended, that act itself has been reversible (Peru, which had its constitution suspended in the 1990s but democracy reinstated, is a good example).

It is possible that the analogy does not hold this time. At the end of each of the world wars, the world situation was different than it was after the end of the Cold War. Most obviously, 1918 and 1945 were the ends of very hot wars, where countries were defeated and devastated, in some cases torn apart (the Ottoman and Austro-Hungarian Empires in 1918, for instance); not a shot was fired to end the Cold War. In 1918 and 1945, there were viable ideological alternatives to political democracy, most notably communism. With the collapse of communism, there were still a number of authoritarian governments, but there was no intellectual defense (as opposed to practice) of antidemocratic principles. One important question to ponder is whether circumstances are sufficiently different this time to invalidate Huntington's thesis.

Optimistic analysts argue there is little evidence that the trend toward greater democratization of the globe has crested. Certainly, the forces of democracy are having more success in some parts of the word than in others. Almost no Latin American expert, for instance, would have predicted fifteen years ago that there would only be one country in the Western Hemisphere that would greet the new millennium with a nonelected government (Cuba). At the same time, there is much less progress toward democracy in much of war-torn Africa, where grinding poverty and deprivation join violence as impediments to democratic growth. The process of democratization is also uneven in Asia. Democratization remains a force in the world, but it is not clear that its continued momentum is somehow inevitable or inexorable.

Whether democracy will prevail and lead to greater peace in the future and how to promote that phenomenon are the subjects of this case study. From the Western perspective shared by most who will read this study, this is an assessment about which it is somewhat difficult to be entirely objective—a condition particularly pointed for Americans. The democratic peace, along with the spread of capitalist economics, is the symbol of the *pax Americana* that began with the end of the Cold War and continues into the new century. Moreover, most of us believe in the virtue of an international system dominated by political democracies—the reason people speak of a democratic *peace* is that they believe political democracies are more peaceful than other forms of government. As Westerners we are not only observers of the process; because it is our system, we are also its proponents, and we must be mindful to separate advocacy from observation.

The subtitle suggests the thin line between our observations of trends and our preference for particular outcomes. Liberal political democracy is a distinctively Western value, and the uneven spread of democracy worldwide is, according to critics, due to the fact that it represents values and outcomes incompatible with the cultural norms and values of others. While people robustly disagree about the extent and effects of such incompatibility, we must remember that everyone does not necessarily want democracy to prevail.

The remainder of this study will be concerned with the post–Cold War experiences with two aspects of democratization, using case examples to illustrate points along the way. First, we will examine the dynamics of the third wave, including the relationship of democracy to the development of the globalizing economy and the advocacy of democracy as a means to induce change more generally, especially in the developing world. The analysis will then turn to potential threats, looking at a number of possible sources of contrary trends to the general movement toward more democracy. This will lead to a discussion of ways to view promotion of democracy in currently nondemocratic stats and regions. We will conclude with some assessment of the future prospects, in particular the impact of more or less democracy on the stability of the international system.

Our perspectives on these questions have altered with changes in the international environment. The 1990s were, generally speaking, highly optimistic about the desirability and inevitability of democracy's spread. Tied closely to the phenomenon of globalization, most observers were convinced that, with narrow exception in places where fundamentalist Islam prevailed, democracy would triumph. The main question was how best to nurture and accelerate the trend. In the wake of the worldwide economic recession of 2000 and the rise of international terrorism associated with September 11, 2001, that optimism has become more muted.

THE DEMOCRATIZATION MOVEMENT

Few observers would dispute that the 1990s were good years for advocates of political democracy. As the decade began, the single greatest intellectual and physical challenge to democracy, Soviet-led communism, disappeared with hardly a murmur, and the successor states to the old second world spent the decade scrambling, with varying success, to adopt democratic forms. Combined with the spread of the globalizing economy, the advocates of democracy were on a roll. But would it last?

The road to democracy has not been easy, and different countries have had to travel it in their own distinctive ways. For some of the formerly communist countries like Poland and Hungary, the route has been fairly smooth; for others, especially parts of the former Soviet Union and notably Russia itself, the process has been tense and uncertain. Especially for the Russians, there has been no shortage of doomsayers predicting the collapse of their democratic experiment and a Faustian descent back into the long history of Russian authoritarianism.

But the Russians continue to defy the doomsayers. No one would make the pretension that Russian democracy is a model for anyone to emulate, but despite the collapse of the Russian economy and most other institutions, the system endures. In 1991, the then Soviet Union endured a coup attempt by erstwhile communists that ended by propelling Russian president Boris Yeltsin into the world public limelight. Yeltsin was elected and reelected president of the Russian Republic, and in 2000, Valdimir Putin succeeded Yeltsin in an orderly exercise of the ballot box. Some political scientists contend that a country that has successfully passed power along through the ballot box twice (the two turnover test) provides an indication that democracy has taken root. Actions by the Putin government in 2004 and 2005 to restrict political liberties have rekindled old fears, at least for the time being.

What explains this phenomenon in Russia and elsewhere? Why has the third wave of democracy appeared to be more successful and even resilient in places that do not seem particularly promising candidates for democratic systems in terms of their histories and national experiences? Is there something about this wave that is more powerful and thus enduring than the other waves of the last century? Its advocates tie continued success to the inherent attractiveness of the democratic system and to its relationship to, and association with, globalization.

Transparency and Soft Power

There is no real basic agreement on the answers to any of the questions posed above. The contending arguments are emotional and, in many cases, implicitly mask a prejudice about the place of the United States in the world. Analysts who see the twenty-first century as a continuation of American intellectual dominance tend to be optimistic about the future spread of Western-style democracy. What Joseph S. Nye Jr. has called American soft power (the appeal of American ideals) has arguably pointed the way for the present and will continue to witness the gradual increase of democracy and a spreading global peace among democratic states. It is an optimistic view of the world that finds the United States at the center of the picture, existing as something like Ronald Reagan's depiction of the "shining house on the hill."

Not everyone agrees with his vision by any means. Some, for instance, argue that the trend toward democratization is exaggerated by using very generous definitions of democracy. In a number of the former republics of the Soviet Union, elections have been held for top leaders, but these have resulted in putting the same people in power as under communism. Belarus, the Ukraine, and a number of the central Asian republics are cited as examples. Although thirty-four of the thirty-five states of the Western Hemisphere have elected governments, calling them democratic stretches credulity. Pakistan continues to elect governments, but unless the military approves the outcome, elected governments are overthrown and replaced by military juntas. As Thomas Carothers puts it, there exists "a profusion of hazy situations—countries with consistently stated democratic intentions but hazy political realities."

Skeptics also warn that the connection between the trend toward democracy and its chief advocate, the United States, may have a darker side. The general argument is that, although the promotion of democracy is not a bad thing, the United States also ends up pushing its culture down the throats of others who may not be interested and often acts as an arrogant upstart. If there is, as some predict, an anti-American reaction in the international system, the trend toward democracy could conceivably be both a cause and a victim of negative developments. The current wave of anti-Americanism in parts of the Middle East in reaction to American military action in Iraq and Afghanistan offers some support for this idea of a "clash of civilizations" (another Huntington construct).

A number of critics also contest the idea that a democratically dominated system will be more peaceful than a less democratic one. While acknowledging that stable, developed democracies do not go to war against one another, these critics contend that during the democratization process "countries attempting to become democratic are more rather than less prone to go to war." Moreover, statistical tests demonstrate that democracies are no less likely to go to war (admittedly against nondemocratic opponents) than are authoritarian regimes. The United States did invade Iraq, not the other way around.

The critics notwithstanding, the trend toward democratization has survived the 1990s and appears to be continuing as the 2000s unfold. This fact suggests a tenacity to the trend, which skeptics downplay or deny. To what can we attribute the longevity of the trend?

Clearly, there are numerous possible explanations. One centers on the idea of *the transparency of democratic practices.* The term transparency has gained considerable prominence in economic circles to describe the necessary conditions for financial institutions in countries seeking to join the globalizing economy (see Chapter 7, "The New Trinity of Globalism," for a discussion). In a political context, democracies are exceedingly open to inspection by those who do not possess political freedom. Overwhelmingly, people exposed to political democracy like what they see and aspire to a similar situation for themselves. Once again, Carothers captures the phenomenon: "what is notable about the recent democratic trend is the similarity of the political aspirations of such different societies." Why might this be the case?

There are several driving factors at work in spreading the democratic gospel, two of which stand out as examples of global political transparency. One is the role of the electronic media, including the Internet. Historically, one of the primary tools of repressive regimes was their ability to withhold and manage information, including comparisons of the political and economic living conditions of their citizens compared to others. The electronic revolution has completely destroyed what was left of that control (global television has also played a part). George Orwell was wrong: rather than aiding authoritarian ends, progress in telecommunications destroyed the ability to control information. There is no place poor or isolated enough in the world that it does not have access to global television (thanks in no small measure to the satellite dish). While some governments still attempt to restrict access to the World Wide Web with varying degrees of success, their attempts are increasingly forlorn and futile.

There is also a prodemocratic elite in virtually every country of the world. Usually, the "democracy movement" (to borrow the phrase used by the Chinese students urging democracy in Tiananmen Square in Beijing in 1989) is composed mainly of young people in their twenties and thirties who are highly westernized, often educated in the United States and other Western countries, and frustrated by conditions in their own countries, and they demand the introduction of freedom and democracy into their countries. They often succeed, as in the case of the mass demonstrations in Indonesia in 1999 that led to the forced retirement of longtime dictator Suharto.

Transparency has a kind of contagion effect that transcends political borders and which, according to Carothers, "[has] been a major factor in the proliferation of democratic transitions around the world." This contagion, in turn, has resulted in a parallel phenomenon, which comes in the form of an increasingly global expectation about democratization. Not only does this manifest itself as an expectation that democracy should spread, but also that the reversal of democracy is increasingly unacceptable behavior for states. The overthrow of an elected government by a military coup d'état was a fairly common event in the 1960s and 1970s that was generally decried but tolerated; now it brings massive amounts of international condemnation, even in places like Pakistan where the precedent is firmly entrenched.

Democracy and Globalization

To many of its proponents, political democratization is part and parcel of the general trend toward the creation of the globalized economy, or what Friedman and others call the international system of globalization.

The assertion that democracy and capitalist economics go hand in hand has both philosophical and practical elements. Philosophically, the argument is made that the two phenomena are simply expressions of the same basic dynamic, which is freedom. Capitalism is the economic expression of freedom, because it is the system in which individuals have the ability (at least in theory) to make all their own economic choices. Similarly, democracy represents the ability for individuals to make political decisions for themselves.

The practical side of the combination is made by Singer and Wildawsky in their description of what constitutes "quality economies." In their description, the most advanced states in the world are market democracies, and this combination is not coincidental. They argue that political freedom of choice and the ability to make your own economic choices results in a highly motivated and productive workforce, where the members can decide how hard they want to work and what their rewards will be. Because the possibility of very hard work and very large rewards is part of that mix, the result is the encouragement of innovative entrepreneurs who, in turn, produce goods, services, and ideas that become the cutting edge of the most advanced countries and keep them ahead of the rest. They emphasize that both forms of freedom are necessary to produce an adequately motivated and satisfied population to be a world-class economy. Thus, countries (like China, for instance) that provide economic incentives but withhold political freedoms will ultimately either have to democratize or fail to become fully competitive at the cutting edge.

Friedman adds the element of transparency to this calculation. Part of the inherent strength of the most advanced economies is that most of the practices of the private firms, and especially financial institutions, are subject to effective oversight that both makes certain they are not engaged in corrupt practices and gives potential investors confidence in those institutions. Creating and enforcing the kinds of legal regimes that allow this oversight is difficult to attain in political systems that are not directly accountable to the general population through devices like elections. Thus, democratic institutions become part of the necessary base for entry into the globalization system.

Walter Russell Mead, as noted in Chapter 1, argues that the attraction of the combination of democracy and globalization provides the United States with leverage to lead the prodemocracy movement through what he calls sticky power: "a set of economic institutions and policies that attracts others toward U.S. policy and then traps them in it."

WHAT COULD GO WRONG?

A casual examination of the global trend toward democracy as it has been presented in the previous pages will almost certainly lead to an optimistic outlook. But anyone reaching that conclusion must face a nagging possible reality: that the trend is transitory and will somehow not last. History, of course, supports a measured conclusion; periods of peace have been followed by war, and periods of prosperity have been followed by periods of economic privation. Why should we believe that the current period of democratic ascendancy will not be followed by a period of democratic decline? The question of whether democracy will prevail remains lively.

The hopeful answer is that things are different now, but are they really? If we can conjure good reasons why the democratic peace will prevail, can we also not conceive reasons why it might not?

The following pages will examine a series of arguments about how democracy might be reversed. Although making no claim of exhaustiveness, I will examine five scenarios, each of which represents how political democracy might fail to take hold in different places or how it might not take root, but instead revert to some authoritarian form in the manner suggested by Huntington's wave analogy. Each is based in post–Cold War experience. When we talk about threats to the spread of democracy, it is important to understand where we are and are not examining. The threats are not to the well-established democracies of the most economically advanced countries, where democratic traditions are firmly in place. Rather, we are talking about countries in the developing world, most of which are straining to join the globalizing economy that requires them to increase individual liberties and democratic participation in the process. Where this process is most problematical is in those parts of the world, principally in Africa, parts of Asia, and to a lesser degree parts of Latin America.

Each of the five examples presents a somewhat different challenge. The "Revenge of the Losers" explores the resistance of traditional elites and their reactions as democratic forces erode their power in places like Indonesia. The "Coming Anarchy" looks at the barriers to democratic emergence in the most chaotic, violent places in the world, such as central Africa. The "Clash of Cultures" examines the contention, heard most often in Asia, that some regions' values are incompatible with democracy. The "Rocky Road to Freedom" examines the difficult path to democracy for countries nearly totally unprepared for the process; Russia is the prime example. Finally, "Economic Collapse" explores the more general question of what an economic implosion worldwide of the scale of the Great Depression of 1930s could mean to democratization.

Revenge of the Losers

One of the clearest sources of resistance to democratization within traditionally organized societies comes from those classes and groups who enjoy privilege under whatever form of autocratic rule prevails and who will lose some of their power in a democratic society. This is a familiar problem, well documented in the developmental literature, that accompanied decolonization during the 1950s and 1960s, and it gains a new twist during the third wave, especially in light of the mixed success and resistance to the transplantation of democracy to Iraq.

Although it varies in detail from society to society, the traditional pattern has similarities. Normally, governance is the province of a narrow segment of society, usually hereditary, landowning, and wealthy by the standards of the society. The privileged group is often in league with the country's military; this mutually supportive bond provides the military with prestige and material support in return for buttressing the government's control.

Among the major characteristics of this form of political system is that it is *closed.* What this means is that governmental tasks are performed in secret, outside public purview, and not subject to criticism by a free press or other critics. While the closed nature is often rationalized on cultural or historical grounds (especially in Asia), one of its main outgrowths is governmental corruption, and particularly the misallocation of revenues for the benefit of the privileged class at the expense of the rest of society.

The globalization system does not tolerate these kinds of arrangements for reasons already discussed, and the onslaught of demands for democracy and entrance into the global economy leave the elite and its supporters in a bind. They face the devil's choices of relenting to democratic pressures (and thereby having to relinquish their power and privilege) or of resisting and thus coming under ever-increasing pressure to reform from both outside the country and internally.

The clearest contemporary case of the revenge of the losers has been in Iraq since the beginning of the American occupation in 2003 and the transition to democracy in 2004. Iraq is something of a special case, in that the impetus toward democracy was American imposition rather than the result of a grassroots movement. At the same time, deep divisions within Iraqi society have created a political zero-sum game where there are clear winners and losers in almost all political outcomes and where the losers distrust the motives of the winners and are prone to withdraw from or attempt to destroy any arrangements they fear will leave them losers.

In contemporary Iraq, all three of the major political groups—the Shia, Sunnis, and Kurds—distrust one another, generally with cause. The minority Sunnis have traditionally ruled and suppressed both other groups and fear they will be suppressed in a democratic Iraq unless they have an effective veto over political outcomes. Fearing they will not have such a veto, most of the Iraqi resistance is Sunni. The Shia represent the majority of the population and prefer a one-man, one-vote majoritarian democracy, whereas the Kurds prefer a system in which the Kurdish north is substantially autonomous. With these divisions, it should not be surprising that the transition to democracy is tentative. The relatively free elections of early 2005 offer the hope but not the certainty of success.

The Coming Anarchy

Atlantic Monthly correspondent Robert D. Kaplan has suggested another threat to democratization, a phenomenon which he has termed, in a magazine article and book of the same name, the coming anarchy. It is a horror scenario based on his travels in some of the poorest and most violent places on the globe. While his analysis is centered in the heart of central Africa, the condition he describes could occur in other places as well.

The dynamic that bothers Kaplan is the essential collapse of governance and even society in a number of countries undergoing particularly chaotic, vicious wars within their boundaries. These wars, which the author has elsewhere termed "uncivil wars" or "new internal wars," occur in some of the poorest parts of the world—where governance has always been problematical, where the fighting has appeared to be motivated by no more noble motive than creating chaos as a condition for organized criminality, where the participants are highly irregular fighters, rather than trained and disciplined soldiers, and where it is not always clear that "leaders" in fact control their "followers."

The locus of these conflicts is often the so-called *failed states*, countries so desperately poor that they cannot sustain themselves and demonstrate over time an inability at self-governance. Somalia was the prototype for the failed state phenomenon, but it is a designation that is often applied to places like Liberia, Sierra Leone, and Haiti, to name a few of the more obvious candidates.

If there is a *leitmotif* (recurring theme) for these kinds of conflicts, it is criminally inspired anarchy. In the Andean region, organizations that argue they are revolutionary are in fact little more than agents of the narcotics producers and traffickers whose job is to destabilize the government enough that it cannot interrupt criminal activities (these are sometimes referred to as narco-insurgencies). In other places, roving bands with revolutionary titles do little more than terrorize the population and void the policing activities of the government in order to facilitate stealing natural resources.

Possibly the most vicious example of this phenomenon is in Sierra Leone. An organization known as the Revolutionary United Front (RUF) has been waging a "war" against the government for some years. Occasionally, there are lulls in the fighting, but the general purpose of the RUF has been to weaken the government to the point that it cannot counteract the RUF's other agenda, which is exploiting the diamond-rich region of the country (see discussion in Chapter 14).

Clearly, it is impossible to talk about the emergence of political democracy in the short term in places such as Sierra Leone. The United States attempted to buttress the movement of Haiti toward political democracy in 1994 when it sent troops to the island country to reinstall its elected president, Jean-Bertrand Aristide, who had been overthrown by a military coup. The Americans stayed for almost five years before withdrawing; no one would argue they left much of a democracy behind, and Aristide is out of power.

Kaplan paints a more ominous picture for the future. His fear is that conditions in many of these countries will become so wretched that large numbers of refugees will flee their countries, with the developed states as their destination. He fears that they will also bring with them the criminal habits and animosities that destabilized their countries. The worst-case scenario for the coming anarchy is the stable democracies being flooded and them swamped by the problems of the least-stable parts of the world.

The Clash of Cultures

An allegation is put forward in some parts of the world, notably in Asia, that political democratization is simply culturally incompatible with long-held values. In such cases, the attempt to transpose democratic values and practices is said to be culturally disruptive, even destructive, and thus should be resisted. It is a variant on the argument of the cultural destructiveness of the American model of economic and political organization.

What should we make of this argument? One point is that it does have an historical basis. In most Asian countries, there is a long-standing practice of nondemocratic rule that dates back at least to the imposition of the Mandarin system in China several thousand years ago. The tradition includes a greater degree of communalism than is present in many Western cultures (e.g., the idea that the common good transcends the interests of individuals) and a belief in the veneration of elders, the most conservative element in society but also the element thought to have accumulated the most wisdom. This leads to a deferential element of the culture that facilitates political control by a small group within society. Many Asian societies, but especially those that were influenced by China, contain these cultural elements and also defenders of the sanctity of these values.

There is, of course, a flip side to the culture argument that is increasingly heard in the societies where it is defended. Most of the defenders of the culture argument, whether it is Singapore's Lee Kwan Yew, Malaysia's Datuk Mahathir bin Mohammad, or the current Chinese leadership, are parts of authoritarian regimes where defense of cultural uniqueness is part of the basis for avoiding widening the political base. All of the societies defending cultural uniqueness are under some level of siege from elements of their societies—normally the young, westernized, and highly educated rising elite—who demand democratization.

Which force will prevail? Will it be the defenders of traditional cultural differences? Or will it be the westernizers who seek to bring their countries into the emerging globalization system? It is too early to say in any comprehensive manner, but there are lightning rods that can be watched to see what will occur.

Rocky Roads to Freedom

The Russian experience provides another possibility. While it has already been noted that Russian democracy, at least at the federal level, has become more stable than its detractors have warned, the road has indeed been a rocky one, and the outcome is by no means assured. The ultimate success or failure of democracy in Russia will play a major part in whether the third wave of democracy is ultimately deemed to have succeeded. Will Russia be part of the wave or the wake?

Russian democracy got off to a chaotic start in the late 1980s under former Soviet leader Mikhail S. Gorbachev. When Gorbachev and his followers realized that the Soviet Union was becoming increasingly uncompetitive with the West, he faced unpleasant choices. A devout Marxist, he could not bring himself to believe the underlying flaw was Marxist economics; instead he blamed flaws in the Stalinist system that administered the economy.

When the Soviet Union became Russia on January 1, 1992, it was officially a democratic state—in name if not in operation. The problem was that Russia was not prepared for such a radical departure from its authoritarian past. There was essentially no democratic tradition anywhere in the country, for instance, and the communist system of the Soviet Union did nothing to prepare politicians to work in a democratic atmosphere. The process of democratization also occurred in a politically tempestuous period where political boundaries between the republics of the former union were being redrawn and where separatist movements were emerging in places like Chechnya. Moreover, democracy was instituted with none of the necessary underlying institutions in place to support and nurture it. Two examples demonstrate the consequences.

One hallmark of a democratic system is a free, fair, and impartial criminal justice system—honest police and courts that apply the law in a manner that is accepted by the population as equitable. No such system existed in the Soviet Union, and it could not be created overnight. Much of the lawlessness that undermines the Russian system and threatens its democracy is directly attributable to a deficient criminal justice system that citizens do not trust and criminals do not fear.

A second hallmark of a democratic system is the ability to levy and collect taxes and to distribute the revenues resulting from taxation. The willingness to be taxed is a basic indicator of the amount of legitimacy the people place in the system. In Russia today, tax collection is at best spotty. At the local and provincial levels, there are places where the taxation system works fairly efficiently; at the federal level, however, the central government has had a very difficult time detecting and suppressing tax evasion, which is often aided and abetted by lower levels of government.

Will democracy ultimately succeed in Russia? It is an important question both because Russia, while diminished as a global power from its Soviet past, is still a major power, and because there are other states in the system not unlike Russia. Certainly the Russian situation can have a positive or negative influence on a number of the other successor states of the former Soviet Union. At the same time, whether Russia can hold together in the face of centrifugal influences and remain democratic will have implications for other large countries with similar problems—like India.

Economic Collapse

The fifth prospect is slightly more abstract and general, but it has an historic precedent the possibility of which causes a major concern. That is the possibility of a worldwide economic collapse on the scale of the Great Depression of the 1930s that could conceivably send states scurrying their separate ways, including succumbing to the Faustian bargains that helped grease the path to World War II.

No two historic situations are exactly the same, so it is difficult to make any analogy between a possible future and the situation in 1929, when the stock market crash in the United States helped trigger the onset of the economic maelstrom that became the Great Depression. The depression of the 1930s was, in some ways, an outgrowth of the settlement of World War I's punitive peace against Germany, which contributed to hyperinflation in Germany, the rise of Hitler, extreme economic nationalism in the form of prohibitively high trade barriers, and ultimately the slide toward World War II. This level of political turbulence is not found anywhere today except possibly in those areas included in Kaplan's coming anarchy, and those areas probably lack the economic power or political clout to destabilize the entire system. Moreover, the collapse of the 1930s occurred in an absolutely unregulated international economic environment. Safeguards and rules described in the case study on globalism (Chapter 7) suggest that there are now mechanisms that can soften the impact of economic downturns if not eliminate them altogether.

The fact that we think we have learned from our economic past does not mean we will necessarily avoid that past in the future. In terms of democracy and the democratic peace, the great fear is of economically based panic that turns populations toward authoritarian demagogues, as happened in the 1930s. Such a fear has been associated with Russia and the possible rise of an ultranationalist like Vladimir Zhirinovsky when the Russian economy collapsed in 1998. Even more traumatic would be a systemwide failure of the globalization system that recreated the panic and economic nationalism of the 1930s. We do not think such a downturn could happen now, but we also do not know that it could not. The same optimism that suggests we have had a very good decade for democracy in the 1990s contains the nagging realization that history has rarely been linear and that bad times have generally followed good times. Will it be that way again?

PROMOTING DEMOCRACY: SOFT OR HARD POWER?

The case that democracy either is inevitable or is unlikely to continue is not unassailable, and there are arguments on both sides of each position we have examined. Because it is apparent that the spread of democracy is possible at least some of the time, the remaining question is how it may best be nurtured. Although they by no means exhaust the possibilities, two approaches have come to dominate at least the American debate on the subject: the "soft" power approach of the 1990s and the "hard" power approach of the early 2000s.

Each approach can be described succinctly. The soft power approach is the basic position of the globalizers of the 1990s. It combines an emphasis on promoting basic American values and institutions (the core of Nye's soft power) with the promise of economic prosperity through participation in the globalization system. It contains the premise that economic success and democratization are compatible, reinforcing ideas: economic prosperity and exposure to the global economy will create demands for political freedoms, and a politically free people will demand the economic freedom associated with capitalist economics in the globalization system of quality economies. Thus, participation in globalism becomes the flypaper by which countries are lured into and entrapped by the "sticky power" of the Western system. During the second half of the 1990s, this reasoning underpinned the Clintonian foreign policy of engagement and enlargement.

The advocates of hard power suggest an alternative based on their perception of the inadequacy of the soft power approach. The soft power approach requires economic prosperity as the lure to start the process, and the 2000 recession showed that prosperity is not perpetual or inevitable. Moreover, the seduction of societies along the pathway from globalization to democracy requires the acquiescence of nondemocratic political elites in the transition. If those elites resist that change—which they may do if they perceive themselves to be the losers in the process—then the transition may be neither automatic nor assured of success. China, after all, has globalized but is not democratic (even if people have considerable individual freedoms), and some Middle Eastern countries' leaders would rather eschew economic modernization than potentially suffer the consequences of democratization.

For those places where soft power will not produce democracy, a group of advocates—most prominently the American neo-conservatives—offer an alternative: hard or military power. Hard power can be applied to nurturing democracy in different ways. With regard to China, it is indirect—effectively encircling China militarily, treating it as a potential threat, and tying the provision of American friendly overtures to Chinese actions reducing threats to democratic Taiwan or improving their human rights record. The ultimate use of hard power, of course, is its direct application against nondemocratic regimes, overthrowing them and replacing them with democratic alternatives. This, of course, has been the approach of the early 2000s, most dramatically applied in Iraq. The champions of imposing democracy in Iraq hope that the democratic transformation there will lead to a contagion effect in which neighboring nondemocratic states also adopt political democracy as their political form.

These are clearly not the only ways to improve the quality of living conditions and the political plights of peoples. Economic modernization through the multilateral provision of international developmental assistance is a public alternative to the essentially privatized process of globalization, just as widely publicizing violations of individual human and political rights through international conferences is an alternative way to promote democracy. In a world where the concerns of sovereign states remain dominant and traditional ways of doing business based in national power remain the norm, however, the alternatives of hard and soft power remain central to the debate.

CONCLUSION

Will democracy and peace prevail? How can democracy best be nurtured? An analysis of the prospects of democratization and a subsequent democratic peace reveals a mixed bag. For the most part, during the 1990s a positive third wave began that has not clearly crested and has left recidivists to authoritarian rule in its wake. At the same time, the wave has not washed ashore uniformly; there are clearly parts of the world that have not enjoyed the phenomenon of democratization. It is probably not coincidental that these areas have also enjoyed the least of the benefits of anything like a democratic peace.

What is the environment like in which the progress of democratization will compete? On one hand, there are clearly positive aspects. The most notable of these are the continuing progress of economic globalization and the absence of ideological divide among competing governmental forms. Political democracy and economic prosperity are the norm in large parts of the world and are the aspiration of many not currently enjoying the benefits of the system. In most of the areas that are part of the globalization system, there is also peace.

But the world that Kaplan describes is present as well. Most of Africa remains outside the prosperity, and it remains politically chaotic as well. Add the disaster of AIDS and other infectious diseases (see Chapter 15), and the situation is bleak indeed. Is Africa just a part of the world that the international system will simply write off out of despair for the future? Will the poorest and politically most divided places in Asia suffer the same fate?

What, then, are the possibilities for the third wave of democracy? There are three broad categories of possible outcome that can be sketched in no particular order of probability.

The first is that the wave will continue to rise, with no crest in the foreseeable future. That is, of course, the most optimistic outcome, and its prospect is clearly tied closely to the continuing vitality of economic globalization. If the global economy spreads and brings democratization in its wake, then one would expect the peace to extend as well. Admitting there may be political instability and even violence in some of the places attempting to make the political transformation from authoritarian to democratic rule, the overall prospect should be for growing tranquility.

There is an objection one can make to this rosy projection. It may well be that the positive economic and political process of the 1990s has largely exhausted itself, because democratization and globalization have succeeded in all the manageable places to implement them, leaving only the hard or impossible places left for the wave to wash over. If that is true and, say, the Great Lakes area of Africa is simply impossible to bring into the democratic peace, then the second possibility is that the wave may indeed spend itself and that there will indeed be a wake where some converts to democracy may fall by the wayside.

How damaging to the overall democratically induced tranquility this second scenario is depends on where reversion occurs. Clearly, the outcome of the democratizing process in two countries is most critical. Russia remains the system's work in progress; a Russia that becomes a stable democracy (and that finds a way to join the global economy) could provide great stability to the global system. But a Russia that reverts to its authoritarian, xenophobic past could do more than just about any other country to upset any notion of a democratic peace. The other crucial country is China. While the PRC is an active member of the global economy, its regime resists democratization that would undermine its power, instead granting its citizens personal but not political freedoms.

The third possibility is a continuation of the present, which includes essentially two parallel subsystems. In such an outcome, one could expect what President Clinton liked to call the "ring of market democracies" to continue slowly to expand, but never meaningfully to penetrate some parts of the world. It is this scenario, alluded to above, where some places in the developing world are quietly written off because of the inability to do anything within the resources we are willing to commit to bring them into Clinton's ring. For these areas, the alternatives may be to attempt democratization through hard power or to abandon the quest.

We finish where we began, with a question: will democracy and the democratic peace prevail? The 1990s provided mostly positive evidence, as globalization and democratization washed progressively distant shores. Whether that trend can be sustained in the third millennium will play a major role in determining how tranquil or stormy the next century will be. Beyond the "natural" spread of democracy is the further question of whether it is possible for the system somehow to serve as midwife to the process, inducing movements toward a transition toward democracy through the application of either soft or hard power.

 STUDY/DISCUSSION QUESTIONS

1. Obtain the latest Map of Freedom or online copy of *Freedom in the World* from the Freedom House (http://freedomhouse.org/). What changes does it report from previous years? Which of the various interpretations about trends in democratization are supported by its findings?

2. Much of the optimism that surrounds evolving notions about the spread of democracy derives from the supposed relationship between economic globalization and democratization. Assess that relationship.

3. As noted in the text, there is disagreement about whether there *is* a democratic peace, and if so, exactly what that means. Do you think democracies are more peaceful than other systems? Would a world of democracies be a more peaceful place?

4. The text describes several scenarios that could arrest or reverse the trend toward democratization. Can you add to the list? If so, what other "horror scenarios" can you think of?

5. What are the alternative ways to induce democracy in nondemocratic countries? Which do you feel are more or less likely to succeed or fail? Why?

6. The text describes three broad outcomes of the democratization process. Which do you think are most and least likely to occur? Why?

READING/RESEARCH MATERIAL

Attali, Jacques. "The Crash of Western Civilization: The Limits of the Market and Democracy." *Foreign Policy* 107 (Summer 1997), 54–64.

Carothers, Thomas. "Think Again: Democracy." *Foreign Policy* 107 (Summer 1997), 11–18.

Freedom House. *Freedom in the World, 1999–2000.* New York: Freedom House, 2000. Available online at http://freedomhouse.org/.

Friedman, Thomas L. *The Lexus and the Olive Tree: Understanding Globalization.* New York: Farrar, Straus, Giroux, 1999.

Huntington, Samuel P. *The Third Wave: Democratization in the Late Twentieth Century.* Norman, OK: University of Oklahoma Press, 1991.

Kaplan, Robert D. *The Coming Anarchy: Shattering the Dreams of the Post Cold War World.* New York: Random House, 2000.

Mead, Walter Russell. "America's Sticky Power." *Foreign Policy,* March/April 2004, 46–53.

Nye, Joseph S., Jr. *Bound to Lead: The Changing Nature of American Power.* New York: Basic Books, 1990.

Singer, Max, and the Estate of Aaron Wildavsky. *The Real World Order: Zones of Peace. Zones of Turmoil.* Chatham, NJ: Chatham House, 1996.

Snow, Donald M. *UnCivil Wars: International Security and the New Internal Conflicts.* Boulder, CO: Lynne Rienner Publishers, 1996.

WEB SITES

Global coalition devoted to combating corruption

Transparency International at http://transparency.org

Organization working to advance the worldwide expansion of political and economic freedom

Freedom House at http://www.freedomhouse,ord

Information on a wide range of groups and organizations working to strengthen global democracy

Democracy Resource Center at http://www.ned.org/research/research/html

Project analyzing efforts to promote democracy worldwide

Democracy and Rule of Law Project at http://ceip.org/files/projects/drl/drl home.ASP

Center aimed at better understanding of democratic process

Center for the Study of Democracy at http://www.demo.uci.edu/democ

PART 2

Evolving Dynamics of International Relations

The cases in this part of the book deal, directly or indirectly, with the question of sovereignty within the international system, a major area of concern to both practitioners and students of international relations. Two of the studies deal with areas that represent direct challenges to the total supremacy of the territorial state in specific areas of state practice; the third deals with adjustments of sovereign boundaries within one of the traditionally most volatile parts of the world, the Middle East.

Challenges to sovereignty certainly are not a unique characteristic of the post–Cold War world. The concept has evolved over time from a justification for the ruling monarchs of Europe to hold total sway over their kingdoms (and to treat their citizens however they wanted) to a more restrained version of what constitutes sovereignty authority and how it can be exercised consistent with international norms. Many of the challenges have their genesis in the Cold War period and have continued with the breakdown of the Cold War competition. The two direct challenges in this part are of that general nature.

Chapter 4, "War Crimes," examines the evolution of international consideration of criminal actions taken during wartime. The case traces the emergence of the idea of "crimes against humanity," which is used more or less synonymously with war crimes in contemporary usage, from the war crimes trials against the Axis powers at the end of World War II through the ad hoc tribunals set up in the 1990s in places like Bosnia and Rwanda to the present. The case culminates with the controversy over the creation of a permanent war crimes tribunal, the International Criminal Court, emphasizing the challenge to sovereignty the court represents.

Chapter 5, "International Permission Slips," is connected to the war crimes chapter in two ways. First, many of the war crimes occur in contemporary internal wars, and it is the atrocities that are committed that cause members of the international system to consider intrusion. Second, the assertion of an international right to intervene is a direct assault on the territorial sovereignty of states where it is invoked. The consequences for sovereignty and international norms come in direct conflict in these cases. Iraq serves as an example of these difficult problems.

The third chapter in this section, "Camp David I and II and Beyond," examines the attempts of the parties and outsiders like the United States to negotiate a peace settlement between Israel and its Muslim neighbors. It argues that the enormously successful Camp David meeting of 1978 was a success in part because it did not deal with the most fundamental issues, which have to do with sovereign control of territories that were once Palestinian and are now Israeli, notably Jerusalem and the former home sites of Palestinians that are now Israeli (the question of Palestinian repatriation). Sovereign control of disputed territories ties the case to the others.

CHAPTER FOUR

War Crimes
THE PAST IN THE PRESENT
IN THE FUTURE

PRÉCIS

Although events in the 1990s in places like Bosnia and Rwanda made the idea of war crimes and their prosecution a widely recognized part of international relations, the notion is relatively recent in its derivation. There have always been more or less well-accepted and enforced rules for conducting war, the violation of which was deemed criminal, but the ideas of crimes against peace and, especially, crimes against humanity are largely the result of the prosecution of German and Japanese officials after World War II. The 1990s revived this interest, which had receded during the Cold War.

Two major aspects of the war crimes issue are highlighted in this case. Following an introduction that lays out basic history and concepts, the case concentrates on two related aspects, both of which have placed the United States government in a controversial situation in the international community. One aspect is the International Criminal Court (ICC), a permanent tribunal with jurisdiction over alleged war crimes. The other aspect is the assault on sovereignty implicit in the ICC statute; when the court gains jurisdiction over war crimes, the sovereign control of a country over its citizens who may be accused of war crimes is compromised. This possibility has led the United States and a handful of other states to reject the ICC's jurisdiction.

In the middle of the 1986 Vietnam war movie *Platoon*, the group of American soldiers who are the subject of the story are on patrol and discover one of their fellows killed, presumably by the Viet Cong, searching for whom is the purpose of the patrol. The incident occurs near a small Vietnamese village. This raises the suspicion that it was Viet Cong from the village that perpetrated the killing, although members of the patrol have no direct evidence linking the village to the death of their comrade.

The patrol enters the village, which is apparently populated by innocent civilians, mostly older men, women, children, and one obviously severely retarded young man. The patrol discovers food supplies clearly excessive to the needs of the villagers and concludes this is a VC food stash, providing "evidence" of VC presence. Members of the patrol attempt to coerce admissions from village residents that they are VC. When the villagers refuse to confess, the soldiers become physically abusive: an old woman is executed with a pistol, the young retarded man is beaten to death with a rifle butt, a young girl is raped, and ultimately the village is set on fire as the remaining villagers flee in a panic.

Did the platoon engage in war crimes for which they might—or should—have been punished? At the time the film was released, the major purpose of the scene was to demonstrate the brutality of the Vietnam War, including the outrageous acts committed by both sides, in this case by American soldiers and the psychological effects committing these acts had on them and the war.

Although the scene draws up on the factual My Lai incident, almost no one at the time raised the question of whether the scene depicted war crimes; had the movie been released in 2005, that would have been one of the first questions asked. More recently, revelations of criminal behavior against prisoners in Abu Ghraib prison in Baghdad have reenergized our concern. What had changed in the interim?

The answer is that one of the important phenomena to reenter the international dialogue during the 1990s was the subject of war crimes. The immediate precipitant had been a rash of so-called humanitarian disasters, where intolerable acts against groups within states, often grouped under the name "ethnic cleansing," occurred during the decade. The worst of these occurred in Bosnia during the early 1990s and in Rwanda in 1994. A somewhat more limited case occurred in Kosovo in 1998–99. The result, according to Richard Goldstone, is a paradox: "Humanitarian law and international human rights has never been more developed, yet never before have human rights been violated more frequently. This state of affairs will not improve absent a mechanism to enforce those laws and the norms they embody."

This quote suggests that the contemporary concern with war crimes stems from two parallel developments. One is the assertion that there are universal human rights to which people and groups are entitled and which, when they are violated, are subject to penalty. The second is an interest in some form of *international* mechanism for dealing with violators of these norms.

While the ideas of defining criminal behavior and enforcement of laws in international, universal terms may not seem extraordinary, both are in fact of recent origin in international affairs. The idea of universal human rights transcending state boundaries, which is a recurrent theme in several of the studies in this volume, is really a phenomenon of the post–World War II period; the primary crime that has been identified in war crimes, genocide, was not identified until the word was coined by Richard Lemkin in 1944, and the United Nations Convention on Genocide, which bans the commission of genocide, was not passed until 1948. Similarly, the term war crimes, which now refers to a broad range of activities associated with war, was basically associated with violations of the so-called laws of war (actions permissible and impermissible during wartime) until war crimes trials were convened in Nuremburg and Tokyo to prosecute accused Nazi and Japanese violators after World War II. Following those trials, the subject remained fallow until it was revived in the 1990s.

The subject of war crimes is unlikely to disappear from international discourse any time soon, for at least four reasons. First, acts now defined as war crimes continue to be committed in many of the savage internal wars that plague the developing world. Exclusionary nationalism (where national groups persecute nonmembers) in some developing world states may increase the number of savage acts that are now considered war crimes. Second, the war crimes trials over Bosnia and Rwanda that were empanelled in the early 1990s have only begun their work, and the international legal community fully recognizes that the outcomes of those trials will influence the subject in the future. Third, definitions are rapidly evolving. Rape, for instance, has only recently been added to the list of punishable crimes against humanity. Terrorist mass murders almost certainly qualify as well. The trial of Saddam Hussein will give wide publicity to this phenomenon. Fourth, one outcome of the concern for war crimes has been the negotiation of a permanent International Criminal Court with mandatory jurisdiction over war crimes. This proposal is controversial, primarily because the United States is one of a handful of states that opposes granting universal jurisdiction to the tribunal, specifically over American service members.

This statement of the problem suggests the direction this case study will take. We will begin with a brief historical overview of war crimes, making the major point that, while the idea of crimes of war has long been part of international concerns, war crimes as we now think of them are of recent vintage. We will then look at the various categories of war crimes that arose from the experience of the war crimes trials at the end of World War II. Because concern for war crimes was dormant during the Cold War, the discussion will move forward to the contemporary period, when the existence of well documented atrocities in places like Bosnia and Rwanda rekindled interest in the subject. The Bosnian and Rwandan cases have, in turn, sparked renewed interest in a permanent war crimes tribunal, the International Criminal Court (ICC). The major opponent of the ICC as proposed at the Rome Conference of 1998 has been the United States, for a variety of reasons. The case concludes with an assessment of the problem of war crimes and the barriers to creating a permanent tribunal, the key elements of which revolve around the concept of sovereignty. The problems in Iraq provide examples of points raised.

BACKGROUND OF THE PROBLEM

The idea of war crimes is both very old and very new. Throughout most of history, the term has been associated with conformity to the so-called laws of war. This usage can be traced back as far as 200 B.C., when a code of the permissible behavior in war was formulated in the Hindu Code of Manu. Enumeration of codes of warfare was part of Roman law and practice throughout Europe. These rules began to be codified into international law following the Thirty Years War between 1618 and 1648, when most of Europe was swept in very brutal religiously based warfare. The first definitive international law text, Hugo Grotius's *Concerning the Law of War and Peace*, was published in

1625 and included the admonition that "war ought not to be undertaken except for the enforcement of rights; when once undertaken, it should be carried on only within the bounds of law and good faith." Definitions of the laws of war, and hence violations of those laws, developed gradually during the eighteenth and nineteenth centuries, culminating in the Geneva and Hague Conventions of 1899 and 1907.

While the concerns expressed in the laws of war continue to be an important part of international concern, the idea of war crimes has been expanded to cover other areas of conduct in war in the twentieth century. The precipitant for this expansion was World War II and wartime atrocities committed by the Axis powers (notably Germany and Japan). Some of the crimes fit traditional definitions of war crimes—the mistreatment of American and other prisoners of war (POWs) by the Japanese in instances such as the infamous Bataan death march, for instance. Many actions, however, went well beyond the conduct of war per se, however, as in the systematic extermination of Jews, Gypsies, and other in the Holocaust by Germany and the so-called Rape of Nanking, where Japanese soldiers went on a rampage and reportedly slaughtered nearly 300,000 citizens of that Chinese city (some Japanese sources dispute the numbers) on the pretext that some of them were soldiers hiding among the civilians.

The laws of war as they had evolved to that point were inadequate to deal with this expansion in the use of military force to the systematic use of military force to brutalize civilian populations. There had been discussion about limitations on fighting and the treatment of noncombatants prior to World War I, but there were no real enforcement mechanisms to deal with transgressions, a recurring problem in enforcing war crimes violations that the ICC seeks to rectify.

The Impact of World War II

As noted, World War II provided the impetus for change. It was a truly global and brutal war, and one of its major "innovations" was to extend what the American General William Tecumseh Sherman called the "hard hand of war" during the Civil War to civilian populations. The Allies discussed the problem throughout the war. The first formal statement on the subject was the Moscow declaration of 1943, which stated that Nazi officials guilty of "atrocities, massacres, and executions" would be sent to the countries in which they committed their crimes for trial and appropriate punishment.

The document that defined modern war crimes precedent was the London Agreement of August 8, 1945. That document did two major things. First, it established the International Military Tribunal as the court that would try alleged war crimes and thereby set the precedent for a formal, permanent body later on. At the time, it specifically set the groundwork for the Nuremberg and Tokyo tribunals. Second, the agreement established the boundaries of its jurisdiction, which have become the standard means for defining war crimes.

The London Agreement defines three kinds of war crimes. The first is *crimes against peace*, "namely, planning, preparation, initiation, or waging of a war of aggression, or a war in violation of international treaties, agreements or assurances, or participation in a common plan or conspiracy for the accomplishment of any of the foregoing." This admonition was reinforced by the United Nations Charter that same year, in which the signatories relinquished the "right" to initiate war. Under this definition, the North Korean invasion of South Korea in 1950 and the invasion and conquest of Kuwait by Saddam Hussein's Iraq in 1990 both qualify as crimes against peace. What should be clearly noted is that this definition applies most obviously and directly to wars between independent states due to the emphasis on territorial aggression. Although it is rarely discussed in this manner, it is possible to contend the U.S. invasion of Iraq qualifies as a crime against peace.

The second category is a reiteration of the traditional usage of the concept. *War crimes* are defined as "violations of the laws or customs of war. Such violations shall include, but not be limited to, murder, ill-treatment or deportation to slave labor or for any other purpose of civilian population of or in occupied territory, murder or ill-treatment of prisoners of war or persons on the seas, killing of hostages, plunder of public or private property, wanton destruction of cities, towns or villages, or devastation not justified by military necessity." This enumeration, of course, was a virtual "laundry list" of accusations against the Germans and the Japanese (although the Allies arguably committed some of the same acts). While acts against civilians are mentioned in the listing, the crimes enumerated are limited to mistreatment of general civilian populations rather than their systematic extension to segments of the population.

As modern warfare moves from conventional combat as regulated by these rules toward so-called asymmetrical warfare (the subject of Chapter 10), instances of war crimes are likely to proliferate, because it is part of the definition of asymmetrical warfare to reject conventional norms of conduct. The taking and execution by beheading of hostages in Iraq in 2004 is exemplary.

The third category of war crimes was the most innovative and controversial. It is also the type of war crimes with which the concept is most closely associated in the current debate over war crimes. *Crimes against humanity* are defined as "murder, extermination, enslavement, deportation, and other inhumane acts committed against any civilian population, before or during the war; or persecutions on political, racial or religious grounds in execution of or in connection with any crime…whether or not in violation of the domestic law where perpetuated." The statute goes further, establishing the basis of responsibility and thus vulnerability to prosecution. "Leaders, organizers, instigators, or accomplices participating in the formulation or execution of a common plan or conspiracy to commit any of the foregoing crimes are responsible for all acts performed by any persons in execution of such plan." This latter enumeration of responsibility justified the indictment of former Yugoslav President Slobadan Milosevic, who has never been accused of carrying out acts qualifying as war crimes.

To someone whose experience is limited to the latter part of the twentieth century, this notion of crimes against humanity may not seem radical or possibly even unusual in content. At the time, however, they clearly were, for several reasons. First, they criminalized actions by states (or groups within states) that, while not exactly common in human history, were certainly not unknown but previously not thought of as criminal. Imagine, for instance, Genghis Khan and the leaders of the Golden Horde being placed in the docket. Or the Ottoman Turk executors of the genocidal campaign against the Armenians early in the twentieth century. Or, for that matter, the post–Civil War campaigns by the United States government against the western Indian tribes (e.g., Wounded Knee).

The second radical idea contained in the definition is that of jurisdiction. By stating that crimes against humanity are enforceable "whether or not in violation of the domestic law" of the places they occur, the definition creates a certain universality to its delineation that, among other things, seems to transcend the sovereign rights of states to order events as they choose within their territory. That assertion remains at the base of controversy about the institutionalization of war crimes, because it entwines war criminal behavior (the reprehensibility of which is agreed upon) with the controversy over sovereignty (about which there is considerable disagreement). Third, the statute seeks to remove the defense that crimes against humanity can be justified on the basis they were committed on orders from a superior (a matter of some interest in the Abu Ghraib case). Thus, anyone with any part in crimes against humanity is equally vulnerable under the law, and this provision creates the flexibility of the tribunal to delve as deeply as it wishes into the offending hierarchy.

The statute does not address one element about war crimes prosecution that is almost always raised. It is the problem of so-called "victor's law"; the charge that war crimes are always defined by the winning side in a war, and those tried are always those from the losing side. While the Nuremberg and Tokyo tribunals labored hard and long to make the proceedings as judicially fair as they could, it is nonetheless true that it was Germans and Japanese in the dock, not Americans or Britons. It is possible, but not very likely, that no one on the Allied side ever committed a war crime or a crime against humanity during the events surrounding World War II. It is arguable, for instance, that the officials who ordered and carried out the fire bombing of Tokyo or the leveling of Dresden, in which many innocent civilians were killed, were guilty of crimes against humanity, but none of these officials came before the war crimes tribunal. The recognition of the potential charge that any trial applies victor's law has been an ongoing concern in the further development of the concept of war crimes and is reflected in the jurisdiction of the International Criminal Court.

Post–World War II Efforts

This concern carried over into the postwar world. In 1948, the General Assembly of the United Nations passed the International Convention on the Prevention and Punishment of the Crime of Genocide, known more compactly as the Convention on Genocide. Building upon the assertion of crimes against humanity, the Convention on Genocide provided clarification and codification of what constituted acts of genocide. According to the convention, any of the following actions, when committed with the intent of eliminating a particular national, ethnic, racial, or religious group, constitute genocide: (1) killing members of the group, (2) causing serious bodily or mental harm to members of the group, (3) deliberately inflicting on the group conditions of life calculated to kill, (4) imposing measures intended to prevent births within a group, and (5) forcibly transferring children out of a group.

In important ways, enunciating the Convention on Genocide (and the parallel UN Declaration on Human Rights) was a form of international atonement for Axis excesses, especially for the Holocaust. Most countries signed and ratified the convention, which took force—without, one might quickly add, any real form of enforcement. A few countries, notably the United States, refused to ratify the document for reasons based on infringement of sovereignty discussed later.

EVOLUTION OF THE PROBLEM

With the completion of the war crimes tribunals after World War II and the flurry of activity that produced the Convention on Genocide, the subject of war crimes dropped from the public eye, not to reemerge until the 1990s. Well beneath the surface of public concern, attempts were indeed made to create some sort of enforcement mechanism for dealing with these issues, but they never received much public attention, nor did they generate enough political support to gain serious consideration in the international political debate.

Why was this the case? It was not because crimes against humanity became less unacceptable, although those acts and traditional war crimes certainly continued to occur, at least on a smaller scale than had happened during World War II. Rather, the more likely explanation is that the subject matter became a victim of the Cold War, as did other phenomena such as the aggressive promotion of human rights.

It is almost certainly not a coincidence that the emergence of a broad international interest in war crimes emerged at a time of U.S.–Soviet cooperation right after World War II, that concern and progress ground to an effective halt during the ideological and geopolitical confrontation between them, and that the subject has resurfaced and been revitalized since the cessation of that competition.

Why would the Cold War competition hamstring progress on a subject that would, on the face of it, seem noncontroversial? No one, after all, officially condones acts that we have described as war crimes, and yet, in the Cold War context, neither was the clarification and codification aggressively pursued internationally.

The problem was similar to, and had the same roots as, the advocacy of human rights, which also lay fallow on the international agenda through most of the Cold War period. In a sense, war crimes are one of the flip sides of human rights: the crimes against humanity clearly violate the most basic of human rights, and traditional war crimes violate those rights in times of combat.

In the Cold War context, issues like human rights tended to get caught up in the propaganda war between the superpowers. The Soviets would assume that American advocacy of certain principles (for instance free speech) was championed to embarrass the Soviet Union, where such rights were certainly not inviolate—an assumption with at least some validity. Had the Soviets decided to push for greater progress on war crimes during the American participation in the Vietnam War between 1965 and 1973, the United States would, with some justification, have assumed the purpose was to embarrass American servicemen and discredit the American military effort. The incident depicted in *Platoon* and the reality at My Lai illustrate the extension of this dynamic to war crimes. Innocent civilians were slaughtered at My Lai in what was a clear crime against humanity, but dispassionate consideration was drowned by wartime propaganda duels over Cold War issues. In such circumstances, little if any progress could be expected on issues with a Cold War veneer; by and large, there was little attempt to pursue agreements in areas where one side of the other might impose a formal veto (in the United

Nations Security Council) or informal veto (by convincing its friends and allies not to take part).

There was a second problem with extending the idea of war crimes, and especially the codification of the idea into some enforcement regime, that has been a particular sticking point for the United States government: the issue of sovereignty. Among the major states in the international system, the United States (as well as nondemocratic states like China) has been among the staunchest supporters of the doctrine of state sovereignty, the idea that supreme authority to act (in other words, sovereignty) resides exclusively with states and that any dilution of that status is unacceptable and thus actively to be opposed.

Because the Convention on Genocide is universally applicable to all states that have signed and ratified the convention and thus have acceded to its provisions, it can be viewed, and was viewed by powerful political elements in the United States, as an infringement of the authority of the United States government to regulate its own affairs. This argument may seem strained in the area of genocide: one way of looking at the objection is that it preserves the right of the United States to commit genocide without breaking agreements of which it is part. Nonetheless, the argument against diluting American national sovereignty was sufficient politically to prevent the United States Senate from ratifying the Convention on Genocide until 1993, when it was submitted to the Senate by President Clinton and approved by the necessary two-thirds majority. As we shall see, this same basic objection has caused the United States to be one of a handful of countries, and the only prominent political democracy, to refuse to sign or ratify the statute of the International Criminal Court.

BOSNIA AND RWANDA: THE PROBLEM REVIVED

The problem of war crimes remained a moot point until the 1990s. As suggested, there undoubtedly were instances where questions of war crimes, and especially crimes against humanity, could have been raised previously but, due to entanglement in the Cold War, were not. The extermination of more than one million citizens by the Khmer Rouge in Cambodia between 1976 and 1979 is a good example. Because the struggle in Cambodia was between rival communist forces, one side supported by the Soviets and the Khmer Rouge supported by the People's Republic of China, it was viewed as an intramural struggle in which the West had little direct interest. China's Great Cultural Revolution between 1966 and 1976 probably qualifies as well.

Two other things had changed between the 1970s and the outbreak of concern about crimes against humanity in the 1990s that help explain international indifference to war crimes in the 1970s and international activism in the 1990s. The first change was the emergence of much more aggressive global electronic media with the physical capability to probe much more widely around the globe and thus to expose and publicize apparent violations. In 1976, one must remember, there was no such thing as global television; Cable News Network (CNN), with which we tend to associate the globalization of world news, was not launched until 1980 and did not become a prominent force for some time thereafter. Moreover, media tools such as handheld camcorders and satellite uplinks were theoretical ideas, not the everyday equipment of the reporter. As a result, there was much less coverage of the slaughter in Cambodia than there typically is today of similar events. There were lots of rumors and verbal accounts by escaping refugees and reporters (the gist of the 1980s movie *The Killing Fields*) but little graphic visual accounting of the tragedy. The stacks of skulls of the victims that are our lasting memory of what happened are products of the latter 1980s and early 1990s, well after the fighting and killing were over. Moreover, the death of Pol Pot, the leader of the Khmer Rouge, in 1999 has removed much of the focus on the event.

The other change has been the growing *de facto* (in practice) if not *de jure* (in law) acceptance of the permissibility of international intervention in the internal affairs of states when states (or factions within states) grossly abuse other people or groups—in other words, commit crimes against humanity and especially genocide. Without an elaborate statement of the principle of *humanitarian intervention*, this is what the United Nations authorized when it sent UN forces into Somalia in1992. This action was widely touted by then UN Secretary-General Boutros Boutros-Ghali as a precedent-setting exercise for the future— the establishment of international enforcement of universal codes of behavior.

Thus, by the early 1990s, three dynamics affecting international politics had changed sufficiently to raise to the international agenda the prospect of dealing with war crimes. The end of the Cold War meant atrocities would not be hidden or accusations about them suppressed on ideological grounds or based on the charge that such expressions were mere propaganda. A more aggressive and technologically empowered electronic media with global reach was available to report and publicize atrocities wherever they could reach (which was not universal; government intimidation has kept the media from reporting effectively the slaughter over the last decade in the Sudan). At the same time, the UN operation in Somalia had established something like a precedent about the notion of humanitarian intervention. The only issue that was not resolved was the question of the implications of all this for state sovereignty, a problem that remained latent until the formal call for a permanent war crimes tribunal was issued by the Rome Conference of 1998.

The Bosnian "Ethnic Cleansing"

The first test of this new environment came in Bosnia and Herzegovina (hereafter Bosnia). As part of the general dismemberment of Yugoslavia in 1991 and 1992 (an event itself made possible by the end of the Cold War, since the Yugoslav state had been communist), the multiethnic state of Bosnia joined several other former Yugoslav states like Croatia and Slovenia and declared its independence from Yugoslavia in 1991. Because of its ethnic composition (with sizable Serb, Croat, and Muslim minorities) and its geographical location (bordering both Serbia and Croatia), the result was the bloodiest civil fighting anywhere within the old Yugoslav boundaries. Part of this fighting involved the displacement of ethnic minorities by groups with claims to different parts of Bosnian territory, a process that became known as ethnic cleansing. One of the outgrowths of ethnic cleansing was the allegation of atrocities against different ethnic groups—crimes against humanity, or war crimes.

Map 4.1 Map of Yugoslavia after breakup (featuring Bosnia).

While this is not the place for a detailed description of the Bosnian war, it was (and could easily become again) a triangular affair. The three principal antagonists were: Bosnian Serbs, who wished either for a Bosnian state they controlled or reunion with Serb-controlled Yugoslavia (effectively reduced to Serbia—including Kosovo—and Montenegro); Bosnian Croats, who wanted either an independent state or, in most cases, union with Croatia (one of the other states that had seceded); and Bosnian Muslims, who desired full independence and who had declared the Bosnian state.

The war, such as it was, was primarily a land grab, where one of the three sides would seek to occupy territory in which the other ethnic groups resided, thereby creating a claim to territorial possession when partition inevitably occurred. Although there was some traditional combat in places like the Krajina region between Croatia and Serbia, a great deal of the "action" consisted of "militia" units attacking basically defenseless members of the other groups to force them from territory the attackers desired. In some cases, large numbers of civilians were killed and interred in mass graves, forming one of the strongest bases for later war crimes indictments. All three groups participated in this action at one time and to one extent or another. The Bosnian Serbs, backed physically and politically by the Yugoslav government in Belgrade, were the best armed and most brutal and successful, and their efforts thus attracted the most—negative—attention.

The nature of this decidedly unmilitary conflict inevitably raised the likelihood that its conduct could be described in terms of war crimes defined nearly a half-century earlier. Although the chaotic beginning of the conflict made it difficult to apportion crimes against peace, the fact that much of the "fighting" involved attacks on civilians meant traditional war crimes probably occurred and that it was likely crimes against humanity were committed.

This constellation of dynamics had occurred before, and no one had cried "war crimes." Why was this case different?

Two factors stood out. The first was the role of the media, which, accurately or not, portrayed the slaughter largely in terms of Serb responsibility but, more importantly, in ways that raised the worst memories of World War II and its war crimes. The first and most vivid depiction of the Bosnian war was the publication of still photographs and television footage of Bosnian Muslim prisoners of war in Serb detention camps. The images were explosive: gaunt, sunken-eyed prisoners staring through the wire fences, looking eerily like pictures of Jewish prisoners in the Nazi death camps a half-century earlier. The analogy was impossible to ignore, whether it was accurate or not (a matter of some controversy); the implications that something had to be done to rectify the situation was equally difficulty to resist.

The second factor was the physical presence of the United Nations on the scene. During a lull in the fighting between Croatia and Serbia over contested territory in 1992, a UN peacekeeping mission, the UN Protection Force (UNPROFOR) was put in place to monitor the cease-fire. While the cease-fire quickly (and predictably) broke down and UNPROFOR was incapable of reinstating it, the UN presence had two impacts that helped frame the situation in war crimes terms. First, UN inspectors associated with UNPROFOR investigated allegations of atrocities against civilians and unearthed evidence of atrocity that could not be dismissed by the contestants as mere propaganda. UN presence thus unearthed (in some cases literally) evidence of crimes against humanity in forms like the mass graves in which the bodies of executed civilians had been unceremoniously dumped.

Second, these revelations meant that the parent organization, the UN itself, was involved; in 1993, the UN Security Council passed a resolution setting up a temporary ad hoc war crimes tribunal. The location would be at the International Court of Justice

(ICJ), which is itself affiliated with the UN. On November 29, 1996, the tribunal handed down its first sentence against Serb leader Drazen Erdemovic. It was the first conviction of an individual on war crimes since Nuremberg and Tokyo. The Bosnian tribunal remains in session; the prosecution of its most famous defendant, Slobodan Milosevic, has begun. Its greatest problem has been the ability to capture indicted violators who remain in Yugoslavia, where the government refuses to allow them to be extradited.

The Rwandan Rampage

War crimes in Bosnia were soon followed by even more spectacular, gruesome events in Rwanda, a small East African country. On May 8, 1994, members of the Hutu majority encouraged by Hutu politicians of that country began a systematic, countrywide campaign of genocide against their fellow countrymen, the Tutsi. By the time the slaughter was finally halted, more than one-half million people had been brutally slaughtered.

Although it received less initial publicity than events in Bosnia, the rampage in Rwanda was a crime against humanity on a scale that dwarfed what had happened in the Balkans. Ethnic cleansing in Bosnia had largely had the purpose of displacing, not systematically eliminating, rival groups. Crimes against humanity undoubtedly occurred; systematic genocide with the intent of extinguishing part of the population probably did not.

The campaign in Rwanda was a clear case of genocide. The purpose of the "fighting" was to kill all Tutsi who could be identified and murdered, often hacking them with machetes. Given the scale of the slaughter and the number of people who took part in the atrocities (and one must recall that the standards indicate that there are no limits about how low in the decision process one can go to prosecute offenders), the potential task of sorting out and prosecuting the war criminals was daunting.

Rwanda raised a quandary for the international community. Who should investigate and administer war crimes trials? The UN system offered the best hope for legitimacy and fairness, but it clearly lacked the resources to conduct a comprehensive investigation and trial, given the number of Rwandan Hutu undoubtedly vulnerable to prosecution (the UN initially assigned twelve investigators to the task). The Rwandans themselves (notably the surviving Tutsi who took control of the government) promised swift and comprehensive justice, but that alternative was fraught with the chance that justice would turn into retribution—victor's law at its worst. Ultimately, an ad hoc war crimes tribunal was created at The Hague on the model of the Bosnian panel. Like that panel, it remains in session, with little prospect of an early disbanding.

The impaneling of the Bosnian and Rwandan war crimes tribunals inevitably created momentum for the idea of a permanent court. There was very little objection in principle to the idea of a war crimes court to deal with these two instances. Moreover, it was increasingly clear from atrocities being committed in other countries that there would be no shortage of situations where allegations of crimes against humanity would be commonplace. Internal conflicts in places as widely separated as Sierra Leone in Africa, Kosovo nearly on the Bosnian border, and East Timor on the Indonesian archipelago provided evidence of both geographic diversity and numerous opportunities to enforce sanctions against a new breed of war criminals whose war crimes consisted of gross crimes against humanity perpetrated against their fellow citizens. Beyond the anticipated amount of demand there would be for a permanent structure was the hope that the existence of a court and the knowledge it could bring criminals to justice might deter some future crimes against humanity. But how should the international community react?

PROPOSALS FOR A PERMANENT WAR CRIMES TRIBUNAL

Advocacy of a permanent court to adjudicate war crimes accompanied the flurry of activity surrounding Nuremberg and Tokyo and the adoption of the Convention on Genocide. In 1948, the UN General Assembly commissioned the International Law Commission (a private body) to study the possibility of establishing an International Criminal Court (ICC). The commission worked on this problem until 1954 and produced a draft statute for the ICC. Unfortunately, this document appeared during the darkest days of the Cold War; there were objections from both sides of the iron curtain, and the UN dropped the proposal.

The idea of an ICC lay dormant until 1989, when the tiny island country of Trinidad and Tobago revived the proposal within the UN. Their motive, oddly enough, was to provide an instrument in their struggle against drug traffickers from South America. Nonetheless, the events in Bosnia and Rwanda revived broader interest. As well, the early experience of trying to mount an ad hoc effort suggested the wisdom of assigning a permanent body to provide a more effective, timely approach to war crimes.

The proposal has been controversial. The heart of contention has surrounded the matter of jurisdiction. Champions of the ICC contend that the court must have mandatory jurisdiction over all accused instances of war crimes and that its jurisdiction must supercede national sovereignty to be effective. Opponents object that this infringement on national sovereignty is unwarranted and could form the basis for future abuses of sovereignty. The ICC statute contains provisions for mandatory jurisdiction.

The Case for the ICC

The idea of an ICC has several advantages over impaneling tribunals as the need arises. First, it would avoid having to start essentially from scratch each time suspected war crimes are uncovered. A permanent ICC would have, among other things, a permanent staff of investigators and prosecutors, and it would have vested in its staff the authority and jurisdiction to ascertain when crimes against humanity have indeed occurred.

Second, and related to the first point, a permanent ICC could be much more responsive to the occurrence—or even possibly the likelihood—that war crimes had occurred or were about to occur. Not only would a permanent staff have or develop the expertise for efficient intervention in war crimes situations, they could be rapidly mobilized and applied to the problem.

Third, it was hoped that a permanent ICC would act as a deterrent to future potential war criminals. Would, for instance, the Bosnian Serb leaders who have been indicted (mostly in absentia) for authorizing ethnic cleansing in Bosnia have been dissuaded from doing so if they knew there was an international criminal authority that could bring them to justice for their deeds? What influence would a permanent ICC have had on the planners and implementers of the slaughter in Rwanda? While no one can know the answers to these questions, the chorus that the existence of the ICC might have made a difference continued to grow, particularly as evidence mounted of potential and actual war crimes being contemplated or committed in Kosovo.

Pressure to negotiate a treaty to create an ICC grew during the 1990s. As early as 1995, the Clinton administration became active in support of the tribunal. The movement culminated with the Rome Conference of 1998 (technically the United Nations Diplomatic Conference on the Establishment of a Permanent International Criminal Court). The conference produced a draft treaty that would establish the ICC as a permanent court for trying individuals accused of committing genocide, war crimes, or crimes against humanity and gave the court the jurisdiction over individuals accused of these crimes. When the draft came to a vote, it passed by a vote of 120 states in favor, 7 opposed, and 21 abstentions. In order for the treaty to come into force, at least 60 states had to ratify the treaty. As of April 2004, it had been signed by over 120 states and ratified by 94, meaning the court is officially in force.

The United States government was one of the seven states to vote against the treaty in Rome and has neither signed nor ratified the document—despite the Clinton administration's involvement in promoting and drafting the ICC statute. In one of his final acts in office, President Clinton signed the statute in December 2000. In February 2001, Secretary of State Colin S. Powell announced that President George W. Bush had no intention of submitting it to the Senate for ratification; the Bush administration subsequently announced it was "unsigning" the treaty, an ambiguous international legal act punctuating its high level of opposition.

Objections to the ICC

While the United States advocating and then opposing the ICC statute may seem anomalous, it is not entirely unusual. The apparent schizophrenia represents different views of America's place in the world, the American attitude toward the world, and especially the question of sovereignty. The Clinton administration, broadly internationalist and seeing the ICC statute as a way both to demonstrate responsible U.S. leadership and to improve the quality of the international environment, became a champion of the idea of dealing with war crimes and a war crimes court with "teeth." Other powerful political forces, however, summoned the specter of the loss of sovereignty that joining the treaty possibly entailed. The problem came to focus on the potential loss of control of the United States government over its own forces in the field. Whether converted to this position or accepting the inevitability that it would prevail, the Clinton administration came to accept the critics of the treaty.

David Sheffer, head of the American delegation, delivered the heart of the United States' objection at the end of the Rome Conference. He began by pointing out that the ICC would only have jurisdiction in countries that were parties to the treaty, and he noted that a number of the countries that were producing accusations of war crimes could and would evade prosecution by simply not joining the treaty. Iraq was an example. The qualifying point of this objection was that a UN Security Council Resolution (UNSCR) can extend that jurisdiction in a given case, and that these are common in these circumstances.

The heart of the objection was that the treaty forces countries to relinquish their sovereign jurisdiction over their forces and leave those forces vulnerable to international prosecution with no U.S. ability to come to their aid when the U.S. participates in UN-sponsored peacekeeping operations, such as those in Bosnia and Kosovo. As Sheffer put it, "Thus, the treaty purports to establish an arrangement whereby U.S. armed forces operating overseas could be conceivably prosecuted by the international court even if the U.S. has not agreed to be bound by the treaty. Not only is this contrary to the most fundamental principles of treaty law, it could inhibit the ability of the U.S. to use its military to meet alliance obligations and participate in multinational operations, including humanitarian interventions to save civilian lives."

The sovereign control of American forces potentially accused of war crimes thus stands at the base of the United States' refusal to sign off on the ICC statute. The same fear of diluting the ability of the United States to maintain total control over its citizens and territory has left the United States in anomalous situations before: the failure to ratify either the Convention on Genocide or the Universal Declaration of Human Rights for more than forty years, for instance. More recently, the same logic has put the United States in the virtually singular situation of opposing an international treaty on land mines that was largely the creation of a private American citizen.

In order to get around the problem of sovereignty forfeiture, the United States has dredged up a tactic it used after World War II to ensure Senate ratification of the statute of the International Court of Justice (ICJ or World Court), with which the ICC would be affiliated. In the case of the ICJ, the United States insisted that the statute state the court would only have jurisdiction in individual cases if *both* (or all) parties granted jurisdiction for that action. In other words, countries, including the United States, can only be sued and have judgments made against them in situations where they have given their permission: sovereign control is only abrogated by explicit consent. This so-called Connally Amendment (named after the Texas senator who proposed it) has been used on numerous occasions by the U.S. government. For instance, in 1986, when Nicaragua tried to sue the United States for mining the harbor at Managua, the United States simply refused the jurisdiction.

The same argument is incorporated in the American approach to the question of the jurisdiction of the ICC. The proposed "supplement" to the Rome Treaty reads, "The United Nations and the International Criminal Court agree that the Court may seek the surrender or accept custody of a national who acts within the overall direction of a U.N. Member State, and such directing State has so acknowledged *only in the event (a) the directing State is a State Party to the Statute or the Court obtains the consent of the directing State, or (b) measures have been authorized pursuant to Chapter VII of the U.N. Charter against the directing State in relation to the situation or actions giving rise to alleged crime or crimes.*" [emphasis added] Parties to the statute have consistently rejected this American position.

Is the American position realistic? The U.S. government, and especially the military, argue the United States, as the remaining superpower, is uniquely vulnerable to international harassment in the absence of this kind of protection. More specifically, there are usually American forces involved in major peacekeeping missions globally, where accusations of war crimes are commonplace. The military fears that unfounded accusations against Americans can become a means of harassment of the United States against which they should guard and which the American amendment seeks to protect.

The concern is neither abstract nor academic. During the early stages of American participation in the Kosovo Force (KFOR) peacekeeping mission, American Army Staff Sergeant Frank J. Ronghi was arrested for sodomizing and murdering an 11-year-old Albanian Kosovar girl, whose body was found on January 13, 2000. Under terms of the ICC, Ronghi should have been arrested and tried by the international body for crimes against humanity. Instead, he was tried by an American military tribunal in Germany, before which he pleaded guilty and received a life sentence without parole on August 2, 2000. He will serve his sentence in a U.S. military prison. The swift prosecution of Ronghi and a sentence as severe as the ICC would likely have handed down muted international criticism of this U.S. evasion of the ICC's jurisdiction.

What must the international community, which, by and large, rejects the American objection, do to gain acceptance—including American—of the ICC? Clearly, it must acknowledge that the absence of the world's most powerful state from the regime greatly undercuts its legitimacy and physical clout. As the Clinton administration's Secretary of State Madeleine Albright put it, the ICC without the United States is "dead upon arrival." Thus, some way must be found to overcome the objections of the Americans and others who find fault with the statute as written. But how?

The ICC and Iraq

Neither Iraq nor the United States is a member of the ICC, and as a result, invoking the ICC as a mechanism to deal with issues surrounding the Iraq war with war crimes overtones has not arisen as an option. There are two specific situations in which the ICC could have come into play—the disposition of Saddam Hussein and the Abu Ghraib atrocities. The question is whether eliminating the ICC option aids or hinders solutions to these problems. In other words, would we be better off having an ICC "card" than not?

The answer is probably mixed. Saddam Hussein will be tried in Iraq, accused of crimes also covered as crimes against humanity under the ICC statute. The advantages of trying him under Iraqi law include the satisfaction it will provide aggrieved Iraqis and the demonstration of Iraqi sovereignty as the trying power. But there are disadvantages as well. An Iraqi-controlled trial is vulnerable to depiction as the application of retributive victor's law (the problem in Rwanda), and almost any outcome—lenient or harsh—could inflame Iraqi politics. An ICC option would allow Hussein to be removed from the scene (a la Milosevic) and tried by a neutral and fair tribunal whose verdict would be less likely to be inflammatory. It is a useful, but unavailable, option.

The Abu Ghraib situation is also mixed. U.S. control over those accused salves American concerns that American personnel will turn into scapegoats subject to unfair harassment simply because they are American, and although the United States can cite the much less complicated Ronghi case as precedent, there will undoubtedly be international concern about a cover-up. Turning the case over to the ICC would largely mute those kinds of criticisms through a thorough and fair trial but would run the risk of reversing the direction of the statute's concerns about levels of responsibility. Any U.S.

effort to shield those higher up in the decision chain would be more difficult in an atmosphere where anyone with knowledge or a role in the authorization process is fair game for prosecution.

CONCLUSION

Now that it has been raised and publicly entered the international agenda, the question of war crimes is not likely to go away. In a gradually democratizing world in which authoritarianism is still practiced but rarely extolled, there is no longer any organized, principled objection to the notion that there are limits on the conduct of war and limits on how individuals and groups can be treated. Although the development of something like a consensus on this matter is really quite recent in historical terms (particularly the idea of crimes against peace and humanity), it nonetheless seems well on its way to being established as an international norm.

The major remaining question is institutionalization of war crimes enforcement. As noted in a quote at the beginning of this study, the emergence of a consensus has coincided with a spate of war crimes, principally in the bloody, brutal internal wars in a number of developing world states. The practical implication of this situation is that there are almost certainly going to be places where war crimes tribunals will need to be formed if there is not a permanent court. In the present environment, Kosovo and East Timor would seem to be candidates, and Iraq is a prime candidate.

Is some form of the ICC the answer? Clearly, it would solve some problems and have some advantages, as already noted. It would certainly be more responsive when problems arise, it would maximize whatever deterrent value a potential violator would experience knowing the court was waiting for him or her, and it would insulate the system from accusations of victor's law in future cases. Moreover, it would contribute to the general promotion of lawfulness in the international system. To its proponents, these are powerful and compelling justifications for the ICC.

Then there is the American position. The U.S. objection to the ICC is not a defense of war crimes nor an explicit defense of international disorder. Rather, it stems from a long-standing American fixation with state sovereignty and the need for the American government to have sole jurisdiction over its citizens. In practice, this policy puts the United States at cross-purposes with most of the international community, including most of its closest allies, and on the same side as some rogue states on this and similar issues. Within the United States, there is division on the position we should take: the Clinton administration did, after all, both champion and subsequently back down into opposition about the ICC, and the Bush administration has redoubled that opposition. Given the American status as the remaining superpower, the American decision on ratifying the ICC statute or an amended version is probably critical. If the United States remains opposed, Secretary Albright could well be correct in her assessment about the ICC.

In the end, the international debate pitting the United States against most of the rest of the world (and especially its principal allies) is not about war crimes or the establishment of a court. No one is *for* war crimes or *against* a tribunal to prosecute offenders. The debate is over the nature of the court's jurisdiction. Should that jurisdiction be mandatory, automatic, and supreme? Or should that jurisdiction be tempered by a filter by which states can maintain primary control over their own citizens accused of war crimes? Ultimately, the issue all boils down to the question of sovereignty.

STUDY/DISCUSSION QUESTIONS

1. Assuming that the definitions of war crimes arising from the post–World War II experience are acceptable, should their application be retroactive, either before the standards were adopted or in cases where violations may have occurred since 1947 but where prosecution did not occur at the time? If so, what criteria can you think of to choose among instances?

2. Why do you suppose that war crimes tribunals were authorized for Bosnia and Rwanda but not for Chechnya? Does this suggest a double standard where the weak are vulnerable but the powerful are not? Because the United States is clearly a powerful country, should we also be exempt?

3. Are the arguments in favor of the International Criminal Court compelling? How much of the American objection to the question of automatic, overriding jurisdiction should be accommodated?

4. Is the participation of the United States necessary for the success of the permanent war crimes tribunal? Assess the American objection. Is it reasonable, arrogant, or possibly both? If you were the representative of another government, how would you feel about the American position?

5. The trial of Staff Sergeant Ronghi by an American military court avoids the precedent of American acquiescence to the ICC statute, and his sentence is as severe as it could have been under ICC jurisdiction. Is such an outcome an adequate and justifiable alternative to full U.S. participation in the ICC?

6. Should the option of sending cases to the ICC be an available tool in situations such as Iraq, or is the principle of protecting sovereignty more important?

7. Most of the situations where allegations of war crimes are likely to occur are internal wars in the developing world; how does this fact affect the value of having a permanent court rather than ad hoc tribunals, as we have done up to now? Would a permanent ICC be more effective in deterring or investigating and bringing to justice violators?

8. Should some measure of national sovereignty be surrendered to make the ICC effective? Which value is more important: national control over a country's citizens, or justice for the victims and perpetrators of war crimes when those two values come into conflict?

READING/RESEARCH MATERIAL

Dempsey, Gary. *Reasonable Doubt: The Case Against the Proposed International Criminal Court.* Cato Policy Analysis No. 311. Washington, DC: Cato Institute, 1998.

Gutman, Roy, and David Rieff, eds. *Crimes of War.* New York: W. W. Norton, 1999.

Kahn, Leo. *Nuremberg Trials.* New York: Ballantine Books, 1972.

Neier, Aryeh. *War Crimes: Brutality, Genocide, Terror, and the Struggle for Justice.* New York: Random House, 1998.

Tusa, Ann, and John Tusa. *The Nuremberg Trial.* New York: Atheneum Publishing, 1983.

WEB SITES

Collaboration of journalists, lawyers, and scholars on laws of war and war crimes

Crimes of War Project at http://www.crimesofwar.org

Overview of documents and events leading to Rome Statute

Rome Statute at http://www.un.org/law/icc/index.html

Arguments about ICC and United States security interests

The United States and the ICC at http://ww/amacad.org/projects/icc.htm

"A Summary of United Nations Agreements on Human Rights."
     http://www.hrweb.org/legal/undocs.html

"Sheffer on Why U.S. Opposed International Criminal Court."
     http://www.usembassy.org/uk/

Update on Status of ICC Ratification. http://www.iccnow.org/html/us2000.html

CHAPTER FIVE

International Permission Slips

SOVEREIGNTY AND THE RIGHT OF INTERVENTION

PRÉCIS

The principle of sovereignty, or supreme authority, has been the bedrock principle of operation of the international system since the end of the Thirty Years War in 1648, a process known as the Peace of Westphalia. Over time, sovereignty has come to reside in the governments of states, where it is generally conceded to exist today. Because war is a primary result of the international system that has evolved around the principle of sovereignty, it has never been without critics who would prefer a more peaceful order. The effort to internationalize war crimes, the topic of the previous chapter, is one aspect of that criticism.

This case study looks at the assault on sovereignty through a prominent and very important problem of contemporary international relations—the bloody internal wars raging in the poorest countries of the world and instances of outside invasion. The frustration associated with these situations has called for intervention in a number of cases by outside groups to end the fighting or to restore some international order. Such missions, usually undertaken under the auspices of the United Nations, represent direct violations of the sovereignty on the countries in which they occur. The American invasion of Iraq is a blatant example. Examining the effects on eroding the overall quality of sovereignty in the system is a major purpose of the case.

In his 2004 State of the Union Address, President George W. Bush offered a one-sentence justification for the American invasion of Iraq and a possible harbinger for the future. He declared that the United States would not ask for an international "permission slip" before it intervened in foreign countries in pursuit of American interests. The line was a virtual throwaway, hardly noticed or commented upon. The statement, however, represented a fundamental challenge to the most basic principle of the international system: state sovereignty.

For the past 350 years, the bedrock principle of international relations has been the evolving concept of sovereignty, and more specifically, the idea of state sovereignty. This concept was first formulated formally in a book written in the sixteenth century as the philosophical underpinning for the consolidation of power by Europe's monarchs, and in particular, the authority of the king of France. With the settlement of the extraordinarily brutal, religiously based Thirty Years War in 1648, the triumphant secular monarchs of northern Europe adopted the concept as part of asserting their independence of papal authority.

State sovereignty, the idea that state governments have supreme authority in the international system and that there can be no superior authority to the state, has been around since that time as a first principle by which international relations is organized. The primacy of sovereignty has never lacked its critics, either in terms of the validity of the concept or its philosophical and practical implications. Nevertheless, the principle has endured, and governments cling tenaciously to their possession of sovereignty.

Sovereignty has always done more than provide the philosophical underpinning of international relations. The idea—even the necessity—of possessing and protecting sovereignty has formed the basis of much state action, and particularly the geopolitical task of protecting the state from its enemies. The idea of a "national security state" that was a popular depiction during the Cold War was based in the need to protect the state's supreme authority over its territory from predators that threatened that authority. Among the defenders of this notion, the United States has stood out for its staunch defense of the sanctity of state sovereignty.

The sacrosanct status of unfettered sovereignty is being increasingly questioned. Part of the assault has come from the traditional critics of sovereignty, for instance opponents of war who argue that armed conflict is an integral and inevitable consequence of a world in which sovereignty reigns. From this view, dismantling sovereignty is the necessary prerequisite for world peace. At the same time, the rise of other concerns such as human rights creates collision points with state sovereignty. Why? Because a major historical justification for mistreatment of individuals and groups within states is that sovereign states possess absolute authority over their citizens, and how states act within their sovereign jurisdiction is their own business, not the concern of the international order. This is roughly the position that the Russian government has taken with regard to its treatment of Chechnya during the attempted Chechen secession during the 1990s and into the 2000s. More indirectly, but no less fundamentally, the Bush doctrine's assertion of an American "right" to attack foes preemptively, as in Iraq, represents a de facto denial of the sovereignty it seeks to preserve.

One area where state sovereignty collides most directly with the realities of the post–Cold War world is internal war in the developing world, and that violence is often chaotic, brutal, and bloody. Often, gross violations of human rights occur and instances of war crimes (see Chapter 4) abound. When these kinds of tragedies occurred in the past, the vast majority of the world simply averted its gaze from, for instance, the slaughter of Cambodians by their countrymen, the extermination of Armenians by the Ottoman Turks, or even the Holocaust against European Jews, Gypsies, and others. The reason for ignoring these events was that they were acts of sovereign governments regarding their own citizens, over whom they had total authority. No matter how badly a government treated its citizens within its own boundaries, that was its own problem and prerogative, not the business of outsiders.

This indifference may seem incredible in contemporary terms, but it is an idea that was virtually unchallenged as little as a half-century ago. Take a real example. When the war crimes trials at Nuremberg were being organized, there were questions about what crimes the Nazi defendants could be charged for committing. The leading U.S. jurist at the trials, a member of the U.S. Supreme Court, offered the official view that the Nazis could be charged with killing non-German citizens on German soil, but not with exterminating German Jews, because, as German citizens, they could treat them any way they saw fit. The position was not particularly controversial at the time (partly, of course, because as a practical matter, there were plenty of war crimes with which to charge them).

The bloody internal conflicts in places like the Balkans and parts of Africa have challenged the idea that state sovereignty provides an unfettered license for governments to do as they please to their citizens or, where governments are incapable or nonexistent, not to protect portions of their populations from ravage. Using the United Nations as a vehicle to justify actions, the international system has, upon numerous occasions that will almost certainly continue into the future, intruded itself into these situations in order to prevent further abuse and to protect citizens. The Bush doctrine assertion that the United States does not need an "international permission slip" to intervene in other states in violation of their sovereignty carries the effect a step forward.

The collision of traditional conceptualizations of sovereignty with the evolution of the post–Cold War world generally is thus a major question in international relations, a question of whether the world and its values are changing so much that the principle of sovereignty must be modified or abandoned to adjust to a new reality. One aspect of that reality is the collision between sovereignty and the assertion of an international right or need to intervene in civil wars within states, or more recently to pursue international terrorists. The outcome of that collision will help answer the broader question of the role of sovereignty in the twenty-first century and is thus the focus of this case study.

Does the international system have a right to violate the sovereignty of states when the state is at war with itself—with hideous consequences for its population? In order to examine the problem, we will begin with a brief overview of the content and evolution of the concept of sovereignty, along with some of the major criticisms of the concept and its implications for international relations. We will then look at the problem of internal wars and the justifications that are used when interventions are contemplated and implemented, as well as the assertions of the Bush doctrine. We will conclude by examining the consequences of multiple interventions on the underpinning of sovereignty in the system.

THE CONCEPT OF SOVEREIGNTY

The basic concept of sovereignty has three distinct elements, which collectively define what it means to possess sovereignty. The first element is legitimate authority. Authority is simply the ability to enforce an order; the qualifier "legitimate" means that authority is invested with some legal, consensual basis. Put another way, sovereignty is more than the exercise of pure force.

The second element of sovereignty is that it is supreme. What this means is that there is no superior authority to the possessor of sovereignty; the sovereign is the highest possible authority wherever the sovereign holds sway. The third and related element is that of territory; sovereignty is supreme authority within a defined physical territory. Since the Peace of Westphalia, the political state came to be the territorial definition of sovereignty. Thus states (or countries) have supreme authority over what occurs within their territorial boundaries, and no other source of authority can claim superior jurisdiction to the sovereign.

Before looking at why sovereignty has developed the way it has as a concept, it is worthwhile briefly to look at the consequences of these characteristics politically. In the *internal* workings of states, sovereignty is the basis of the political authority of state governments; the idea of supreme authority provides the state with the power to order its own affairs and the government to create and enforce that order. When the concept of sovereignty was first developed, this internal application was the emphasis. *Externally*, in the relations between states, this same sovereignty creates disorder, because there can be no superior authority to the sovereign within the defined territory of states. The result is *anarchy*, or the absence of government (political authority) in the relations among states. Thus, sovereignty has the schizophrenic effects of creating both order and disorder, depending on the venue in which it is applied.

Early Origins and Evolution

This consequence was not so clear when Jean Bodin formally enunciated the concept of sovereignty in his 1576 book *De Republica*. Bodin, who was French, decried the inability of the French monarchy to establish its authority throughout the country because lower feudal lords instead claimed what amounted to sovereignty over their realms—especially through charging taxes (tolls) to cross their realms. Bodin countered with the idea of sovereignty, which he defined as "supreme authority over citizens and subjects, *unrestrained by law*." [emphasis added] The added and italicized element, Bodin felt, was necessary to avoid the unifying monarch being hamstrung by parochial laws in his quest for establishing the power of the French monarchy. This part of the definition has fallen from common conceptions of sovereignty, but its implications remain and are part of the ongoing controversy central to this case: if the sovereign is above the law, then nothing he or she does can possibly be illegal, at least when committed within the sovereign jurisdiction over which the sovereign reigns.

When Bodin enunciated his principle of sovereignty, he was unconcerned about it as a maxim for international relations. This is not surprising in that the period of its gestation was a period when the monarchs of Europe were consolidating their holds on what became the modern states of Europe and the modern state system. Given that all these states were absolute monarchies, it is further not terribly surprising the presumption quickly evolved (aided by philosophical publicists like Thomas Hobbes) that sovereignty resided with the monarch (which, among other things, helps explain why monarchs are often referred to as sovereigns).

The concept of sovereignty was extended to international relations as the state system evolved and the structure of the modern state emerged and solidifed. Hugo Grotius, the Dutch scholar generally agreed to have been the father of international law, first proclaimed state sovereignty as a fundamental principle of international relations in his 1625 book *On the Law of War and Peace*. By the eighteenth century, the principle was well on its way to being in place, and by the nineteenth century it was an accepted part of international relations.

By the nineteenth century, the content of sovereignty had evolved from its context. Because virtually all countries were still ruled by more or less absolute monarchies (the fledgling, and not very important, United States, revolutionary France, and slightly democratizing Great Britain being the exceptions), the idea of absolute state sovereignty was the rule, and this principle governed both domestic and international relations. From the view of the international system, a prevailing way to describe international politics was in terms of something called the *billiard ball* theory. The idea, never to be taken entirely literally, was that state authority resembled an impermeable billiard ball, and that international relations consisted of these impermeable objects bouncing against one another, causing them to change course in their international behavior from time to time. Important to the theory, however, was that the balls were also impermeable, which meant that nothing in international interactions could affect what went on within the balls, as, for instance, how states treated their citizens. Under this principle, it was simply impermissible for states to interfere in the internal affairs of other states, no matter how distasteful or disgusting domestic practices might be.

Even during its heyday, this conceptualization was not universally accepted. In fact, conceptual challenges tended to be grouped around two related questions that continue to be important in the contemporary debate. How much authority does the sovereign have in the territorial realm over which it is exercised? Within whom, or what body, does sovereignty reside? Different answers have decidedly different implications for what sovereignty means in the relations among states.

As sovereignty was originally formulated and implemented, the answer to the first question was that sovereignty is absolute, that the possessor has total authority over his or her realm. This interpretation flows from, among other places, the idea that the sovereign is "unrestrained by law," to repeat Bodin's term. The contrary view emerged during the eighteenth and nineteenth centuries and reflected the growing notion of political rights asserted in the American and French Revolutions, each of which declared that the sovereign's powers were limited and could be abridged. Among the primary publicists of this view were the English political philosopher John Locke and his French counterpart, Jean-Jacques Rousseau.

The assertion that there are limits on sovereignty reflects the second question: where does sovereignty reside. It was a question about the basis on which that authority is legitimately claimed by those who seek to wield power within their political jurisdictions. The traditional view was that sovereignty resides in the state. In the sixteenth and seventeenth centuries, when sovereignty was taking hold as an organizational principle, this meant the king or queen had sovereignty because the monarch was the unchallenged head of government. It was what we would now call a "top down" concept; the government exercised sovereignty over the population, whose duty it was to submit to that authority.

Beyond the philosophical positions taken by Locke and Rousseau, the contrary argument had its base in, among other places, the American Revolution. A major theme of the American complaint against the British monarch was his denial that the colonists had *rights* in addition to obligations. From that assertion, it was a reasonably short intellectual odyssey to the assertion that the *people*, not the state (or monarch), were the possessors of sovereignty. Under the notion of what became known as *popular sovereignty*, the idea was that the people, as possessors of sovereignty, ceded some of that authority to the state in order to provide the basic legitimacy for the social and political order. Ultimately, however, sovereignty resides with individual citizens, who can grant, withhold, or even, in some interpretations, rescind the bestowing of authority to the state.

These distinctions are more than abstract, academic constructs. Their practical meanings and implications become particularly clear if one combines the two ideas in matrix form.

Sources and Extent of Sovereignty

		Extent of Sovereignty	
		Absolute	*Limited*
Source	State	(Cell 1)	(Cell 3)
	Individuals	(Cell 2)	(Cell 4)

The idea that sovereignty is absolute can be associated with authoritarian governance of one sort or the other. Traditional authoritarian regimes derive their claim to authority on the combination of absolute sovereignty and the state locus of authority (Cell 1). The populist/fascist regimes in Italy and Germany that arose between the world wars combine absolutism with some popular, individual base, Cell 2 (both regimes originally came to power popularly). On the other side of the ledger, the idea that sovereignty is limited is associated with democratic regimes. The idea of state sovereignty derived from the people is the backbone of traditional Western democracy (Cell 3). Where the conferral of sovereignty to the state is denied and maintained by subnational individuals or groups, the result can be the kinds of instability one associates with many of the unstable regimes in the developing world (Cell 4). Much of the debate about intervention in the internal affairs of states derives from the situation depicted in Cell 4. If one accepts the notion that sovereignty resides with individuals, then the possibility of legitimate interference on behalf of those sovereign individuals can be argued to override the sovereignty of the state.

Objections to Sovereignty

The idea and consequences of sovereignty have come under increasing assault as the twentieth century evolved toward the twenty-first century. Two broad categories of criticism, however, relate directly to the question of international intervention in the internal affairs of states and thus have direct relevance to our task of examining the impact of intervention on sovereignty. Both are attacks on the operationalization of the concept.

The first critique is aimed at absolutist conceptions of sovereignty. Critics of this argument maintain that sovereignty in application has never been as absolute as sovereignty in theory. The myth of the impenetrability of states by outside forces, including other states, is no more than a fiction to buttress the principle. States have always interfered in the internal affairs of other states in one way or another. The billiard ball theory is not, in the scientific sense, a theory at all, but instead a false hypothesis.

According to this argument, sovereignty not only has never been as absolute as its champions would assert but also it is becoming increasingly less so. A major reason for this dilution derives from the scientific revolution in telecommunications, which is making national borders entirely more penetrable from the outside, a trend anticipated more than a half-century ago by Sir Anthony Eden in a speech before the British House of Commons on November 22, 1945: "Every succeeding scientific discovery makes greater nonsense of old-time conceptions of sovereignty."

Those "old-time" conceptualizations refer, of course, to state-centered, absolutist interpretations of sovereignty. Forces such as the spread of the Internet, economic globalization, the emergence of a homogenized commercial and popular culture around the world, and the more or less global desire to embrace the globalized world system all make the factual content of total sovereign control by governments over territory increasingly suspect. From our vantage point, however, we must ask whether this factual dilution of sovereign control extends to the "right" of the international system to infringe on the sovereign ability of the state to treat its citizens in ways that the international community disapproves. Is the spread of popular global culture, for instance, any kind of precedent to assert the rightfulness of forceful interposition by foreign troops into civil strife or to affect domestic change?

The other objection to absolute sovereignty has to do directly with the consequences of a system based in state sovereignty. Once again, a number of assertions are made about the pernicious effects of this form of organization on the operation of the international system. Two assertions will be explored here.

The first, and most commonly asserted, objection to state sovereignty is its legitimization and, in some constructs, even glorification of war as a means to settle disputes between states. In a system of sovereign states, after all, there is no authority to enforce international norms on states nor to adjudicate or enforce judgments resolving the disputes that arise between states, except to the extent states voluntarily agree to be bound by international norms or, ironically, can be forced to accept international judgments. If states cannot agree amicably on how to settle their differences, then they can only rely on their own ability to solve favorably those disagreements they have.

The principle involved is known as *self-help*, the ability to bring about favorable outcomes to differences, often at the expense of the other state. This resolution becomes an exercise in *power* (the ability to get people to do what they would not otherwise do), and one of the forms of power available to states is military force. In situations that states deem to be of sufficient importance to settle with armed force, then war may be the conflict-resolution means of choice. In a system of self-help, there is thus no alternative to possessing, and in some instances using, armed force to get your way.

Despite the fact that all member states of the United Nations have renounced the waging of war as a means to resolve conflict (we simply do not call it "war" anymore), the resort to force is understood and accepted in international practice (with some reservations). A fairly large number of analysts, including many scholars and practitioners of international relations, however, decry this situation because they abhor war and would like to see it end. Because sovereignty and the legitimate recourse to war are closely related, therefore, they welcome its dilution and replacement as an international principle.

The other, more contemporary, objection to the consequences of sovereignty is the power it gives governments over their people. In an international sense, governments still are, after all, legally "unrestrained" by international norms in dealing with their own populations, except, once again, to the extent that states have voluntarily limited their rights by signing international agreements. Historically, the notion that governments could do horrible things to their citizens was abhorred by many in the international community, but the right to such behavior was unchallenged on the basis of sovereignty. The phrase "Patriotism is the last refuge of a scoundrel," first uttered by the English author Samuel Johnson in 1775, could easily be paraphrased as, in international terms, "sovereignty is the last refuge of a scoundrel."

Whether this is good or bad is debatable. Governments strongly support sovereignty because it preserves the ability to conducts affairs without undue interference from outside. Unfortunately, the greater the protection of internal actions, the greater is the potential for abuse. In those cases where abuse results in atrocity and human suffering, the calls for outside intervention arise as a challenge to that sovereign authority.

The sanctity of this concept of sovereignty began to erode with the global reaction to the reality of the Holocaust that surfaced after World War II. The active revival of this objection came at the end of the Cold War. Scoundrel-like behavior did not, of course, go into hibernation during the Cold War (Pol Pot and the Khmer Rouge guaranteed that), but condemnation—and especially proposing action to combat it—tended to get entangled in Cold War politics. Could, for instance, the United Nations have proposed a peacekeeping mission to Cambodia in 1975 (when the Khmer Rouge seized power and began their slaughter), when the fighting and killing involved two communist factions, each aligned with a different communist superpower (China and the Soviet Union), each of which had a veto in the Security Council? Of course not!

The Assault on Sovereignty Through the UN

To borrow a term from military tactics, the attack on sovereignty emanating from actions from the United Nations during the 1990s was not a "frontal assault." None of the actions authorized by the UN Security Council has directly challenged the concept of state sovereignty or aligned itself explicitly with a particular interpretation of the concept, such as limited sovereignty residing in individuals. Rather, they have been justified under Chapter VII of the UN Charter, which gives the Security Council the authority to determine threats to or breaches of the peace and to authorize responses, including the use of military force.

The assault on sovereignty has thus been conducted indirectly and inductively. It began when the Security Council authorized a peacekeeping force (UNOSOM I) to go to Somalia on December 3, 1992. The official reason for the mission was to alleviate human suffering (the threat of massive starvation) due to a five-year-long drought and a civil war, one of the consequences of which was that international relief efforts to get food to the afflicted were being interrupted by the combating factions. The motivation for the mission was hence a humanitarian one: to alleviate suffering in what would subsequently be referred to as a major humanitarian disaster.

The UN action was a major precedent in at least two ways, and one influenced by the unique circumstances in Somalia at the time. First and possibly most importantly, it was a mission authorized and implemented without any consultation with the government of the country to which it was dispatched. The idea that the UN would in effect invade a member state presumably for its own good was a major change of policy for the international community working through the world body.

Circumstances on the ground in Somalia made this an easy course to take. The government of Somalia was not consulted before the intervention because *there was no legal government to consult.* Since the overthrow of Siad Barre the previous year, Somalia had been in a state of anarchy, and the overall objective of the civil war was to install one clan leader or another to form a new government capable of rule. The United Nations could not negotiate with any leader because intervention in a civil war at the invitation of any party is illegal under international law. The UN in effect skirted the issue by invoking Chapter VII and using its provisions to determine a breach of the peace and to take appropriate action to restore the peace. One could argue, but no one did publicly at the time, that the absence of a government meant there was no sovereign territory involved; the issue was officially ignored.

The second precedent was that this was the first occasion where the Security Council interpreted its jurisdiction to include purely humanitarian crises. Without going into the legislative history of the UN Charter, it is clear that the framers meant for Chapter VII to be invoked primarily in the case of cross-border invasions by states (interstate wars). The Persian Gulf War effort was the prototype the framers had in mind. While the UN had (rather unhappily) intervened in a civil war in the former Belgian Congo (later Zaire, now the Democratic Republic of Congo), the decision to engage in humanitarian intervention in a civil war in a country for which the term "failed state" was later coined represented a major change of direction. The involvement raised the question of what it meant to the overall nature of the international system if the world body could simply be used to ignore the sovereignty of its members. It did so by deed, not by explicit acknowledgment that this was its intent or its effect. It was the beginning of an inductive process; during the 1990s there arose more situations with similar sources and arguably similar precedents.

The Assault on Sovereignty Outside the UN: The Iraq Precedent

The American invasion of Iraq had by 2004 become controversial on a number of grounds largely concerned with whether it was necessary or whether it did, or eventually will, accomplish its purposes. Lurking behind these questions is a more fundamental systemic concern: did the invasion represent an illegal, precedent-setting assault on the very principle of sovereignty of which the United States has been the most ardent defender?

The Bush administration has argued it was not illegal and thus indirectly against any negative precedent on two debatable grounds. One is the principle of preemption, which says that a state can legally attack another whenever it faces an imminent threat that can be thwarted by preemptive action. The other is the authorization to use force under Article VII of the UN Charter. Alleged Iraqi possession and intention to use weapons of mass destruction in support of terrorism has formed the justification for preemption. UN Security Council Resolution 1441, which demanded Iraqi compliance with weapons inspections and warned of unspecified consequences (that did not specifically include force) were used to justify Chapter VII. A large portion of the international community denies both claims. Why?

One reason is factual: a rejection of the claim of an imminent threat and a denial the use of force was authorized. More fundamental, however, is the principle of sovereignty as elaborated in the UN Charter and UN Resolutions. Members of the UN renounce the right to commit aggression (defined by UN General Assembly Resolution 3314 in 1974 as "the use of armed force by a state"). The underlying rationale, according to Boniface in a 2003 *Washington Quarterly* article, is the sovereignty-based principle of noninterference in the internal affairs of states, a main purpose of which is "to protect weak states against intervention from strong states."

The Bush doctrine argues that the protection of U.S. national interests overrides these rejoinders and that, as a result, the United States does not have to seek "international permission slips" in order to protect those interests. As the world's most powerful country, there is, as a practical matter, little the international community can do to prevent actions based on these assertions. If, however, the United States does not have to get a permission slip, why should anyone else? Or is noninterference only null and void for the most powerful country in the world? Is sovereignty universally undermined, or only for the relatively weak and defenseless? Or is the United States undermining the principle of sovereignty to which it has been slavishly devoted by inadvertence?

INTERNATIONAL INTERVENTION

The Somali case was not the last instance in the 1990s where a chaotic, bloody civil war would break out in a developing world country, which the citizens of that country would prove incapable of resolving and where there would be gross instances of individual and collective human rights abuses. The list of places where these situations have occurred has become familiar and a litany of the world's trouble spots: Bosnia, Haiti, Rwanda, Liberia, Kosovo, Sierra Leone, and East Timor, to name the most obvious. All are fragile states, where full sovereign control by governments is tenuous and where breakdowns of control nearly invite interference from outside on humanitarian bases. Not all situations have evoked the same kind of international responses, but each raised the same kinds of questions about international rights and obligations in situations where humanitarian issues arise and the degree to which traditional views of sovereignty are applicable or require amending. In addition to involvement in these new internal wars, the invasion of Afghanistan and Iraq pose other questions about the impact on sovereignty.

New Internal Wars

The existence of organized armed violence within countries for the purpose of displacing a government and replacing it with some alternative is certainly not a unique characteristic of the period since the end of the Cold War. Largely connected to the unraveling of the European colonial empires that began shortly after the end of World War II, internal—or civil—war has been the dominant form of political violence for a half century.

This pattern has continued since the end of the Cold War, although with some changes. During the Cold War, civil conflicts generally took on a Cold War ideological flavor, with one side (usually the insurgents) "sponsored" by the major communist states and the other (usually the government under siege) aligned with the West. This provided a surrogate battleground for the superpowers, and it also meant that the sponsoring states could (and usually did) impose some constraints on how their proxies conducted themselves. Moreover, these wars were clearly for the political purpose of gaining or maintaining political control in order to govern the state.

The new internal wars of the post–Cold War international environment are often not like this traditional pattern. The end of the Cold War was accompanied by the retreat first of the dying Soviet Union and then the United States from active participation in much of the developing world. The restraint they imposed on their clients left with the superpowers, and the result was a new breed of war.

These wars have tended to be especially brutal and chaotic, accompanied by large-scale accusations and evidences of atrocities that have, among other things, resuscitated interest in war crimes. Part of the bestial, bloody conduct of these conflicts (for instance, the systematic amputation of hands and feet by Sierra Leone's Revolutionary United Front and the genocide in Rwanda) reflects the absence of outsider influence on the "rebels." At the same time, many of the participants, rather than being trained and disciplined soldiers, are instead untrained "fighters" who are only nominally under anyone's control. Especially in African variants of new internal war, the forces are often little more than children (the 10- to 12-year-old "child soldiers" of the Liberian civil war, for instance). Moreover, beyond pure criminality (much of the war in Sierra Leone is about who will control the diamond-rich area of the country), it is often difficult to discern the purposes of the wars.

These wars are generally occurring in the poorest, most destitute parts of the world. Somalia was, as mentioned, the prototype of the so-called "failed state" (countries that have historically shown an inability to govern themselves in a stable manner), and a number of other conflicts have been in similar countries (Haiti and East Timor, for instance). The failed states also tend to be very poor, meaning there is little materially to fight over but also meaning that ending them and restoring a stable order is difficult, because there is little material base on which to build. Moreover, most of the countries and regions where these wars occur are clearly outside the areas of important interests of the major powers (the Balkans are an arguable exception); as a result, it is difficult to argue that any outcome would much discomfort major countries like the United States and thus to generate great enthusiasm for involvement. In a growing number of instances, the internal parties seem totally incapable of resolving their differences, either by one side prevailing militarily or through negotiations.

Ignoring the problem is made difficult by the very public nature of the conflicts. Modern electronic media were able to penetrate, cover, and report on the tragedy in Rwanda in a manner that would have been quite impossible two decades earlier in

Cambodia. The world knew of the rampage by the Khmer Rouge as they decimated their own population, but the accounts were in the print media, not on television, as the slaughter of the Tutsi by the Hutu was in Rwanda. The steady flow of wretched refugees in Kosovo was a daily CNN story that could only be avoided if one did not watch the news. The result is to activate a desire to alleviate the problem (what I call the "do something syndrome"). The question is, what?

Afghanistan and Iraq

These two neighboring countries offered distinct but connected challenges. The distinction came in the form of the pre-intervention situation in each. In Afghanistan, there was an ongoing civil war being contested inconclusively, but more importantly, the Taliban government was openly providing sanctuary for the renegade Al Qaeda terrorists and refused to cancel the refuge and turn them in, a refusal that flew in the face of virtually global demand. In Iraq, by contrast, there was no civil uprising, and while Saddam Hussein had drug his heels on the issue of weapons inspections, he had basically complied by the time the invasion occurred. The alleged connection between the two was the global war on terrorism (GWOT), but given the contrasting situations, there was great international sentiment to act in Afghanistan but not in Iraq.

The Intervention Response

In an international environment that has embraced human rights as a primary value, the new internal wars are the system's black eye, its not-so-well-kept dirty little secret. We are embarrassed at the slaughter of the innocents wherever the carnage occurs, although we feel more impelled to act in some cases than in others.

The pattern of international response has not been uniform to intervention questions. The international community, especially the major powers, has been willing to act forcefully in places like the Balkans, but not in Africa, for instance, where we have sought regional solutions that are probably a chimera. Similarly, the major powers heaved a sigh of relief when nearby Australia agreed to provide the bulk of the resources for the International Force in East Timor (INTERFET) in 1999. Intervention was supported in Afghanistan but not universally in Iraq.

When some sort of response is deemed unavoidable, the common mechanism for authorizing an international response has been to take it to the Security Council of the UN for a United Nations Security Council Resolution (UNSCR) under Chapter VII. The precedent for this route was Somalia, which in turn was the outgrowth of the successful use of UNSCRs in the Persian Gulf War. The effect, on an ad hoc basis, is to legitimize violations of states' sovereignty. But how?

First, because most of the world's countries are members of the world body, passing a resolution serves as a kind of statement of world opinion, a kind of legitimating statement that says an action has the support of the international community. The second, and more controversial, purpose of the use of UNSCRs is to create a kind of legal basis for intervention in civil wars. Intervention in civil wars violates international law and, especially when done without invitation, is clearly a violation of the sovereignty of the country where the intervention occurs.

The UN Charter, however, does authorize the UN to act in the name of peace. Articles 39 and 42 (both part of Chapter VII) create the authority. Article 39 states, "The Security Council shall determine the existence of any threat to the peace, breach of the peace, or act of aggression and shall make recommendations or decide what measures shall be taken . . . to maintain or restore international peace or security." Article 42 makes the military option explicit: "the Security Council . . . may take such action by air, sea or land forces as may be necessary to maintain or restore international peace and security." These provisions appear to refer to *international* rather than internal disputes. Earlier in the Charter, Article 2 (7) makes an ambivalent statement to that effect: "Nothing contained in the present Charter shall authorize the United Nations to intervene in matters which are essentially within the domestic jurisdiction of any state or shall require the members to submit such matters to settlement under the present Charter; but this principle shall not prejudice the application of enforcement measures under Chapter VII." One can use this language to justify intervening in a country's civil strife under two apparent circumstances: if there is a question about whether there is a domestic institution with jurisdiction, or if one determines that whatever is happening within a given country constitutes a threat to or breach of "international peace and security." The latter would appear to be the justification for Afghanistan and Iraq. The Taliban protection of Al Qaeda justified an Article 42 action; Iraq did not.

Why would the members of the UN go to all this trouble to justify interfering in internal matters? At least part of the answer has to be that it is a way to avoid the direct assault on national sovereignty that such actions involve. The UN Charter is quite explicit in its defense of the "territorial integrity or political independence of any state" (Article 2 [4]), or in other words, its sovereignty. The organization cannot directly admit that it is violating sovereignty without violating its own constitution, and its members, by signing the Charter, have also agreed to the sanctity of sovereignty. And yet that is exactly what the members do when they pass UNSCRs favoring intervention in internal wars and then dispatch their troops to foreign shores to enforce those decrees. Manipulating the Charter effectively finesses the underlying issue of the violation of sovereignty.

How long can the sovereignty issue effectively be skirted? As postwar experience with these interventions mounts, the answer would appear to be not indefinitely. The reason for this assertion is the length of the missions and the conflicts they produce with native populations, who over time decreasingly may see the UN peacekeeping missions as helpful rather than as an unwelcome intrusion.

What a decade's experience has shown is that interventions are more complicated and their success more difficult to attain than was believed when American and other UN forces waded ashore in Somalia. We have learned that it is relatively easy to end the violence by inserting well-armed peacekeepers into situations such as those in Bosnia, Kosovo, and East Timor (as well as Afghanistan and Iraq) and to keep the peace as long as the peacekeepers remain. We have also learned, however, that the presence of an intervening force in and of itself does not cause the formerly warring parties to settle their differences, so that the intervening forces can pack their bags and leave behind a tranquility that will result in continuing peace.

The effect is to create open-ended commitments where foreign troops are in place for a long time and eventually may be viewed as occupiers, even neocolonialists, rather than saviors or protectors. In extreme situations like Kosovo, the UN operation (including the deputized NATO military force) is dedicated to an outcome—Kosovo returning to the status of an autonomous region within the Yugoslav federation—that the vast majority of Albanian Kosovars oppose. When (or if) the hosts come publicly to oppose the continued presence of the outsiders, then it will become increasingly difficult to maintain the fiction that the intervening forces are not directly violating the sovereignty of their hosts.

CONCLUSION

The question of outside intervention has come into question in the United States and elsewhere most dramatically over Iraq. In the United States, the primary reasons for questioning have been political and practical. The issue has two facets. In the 2000 election campaign Republican George W. Bush came out strongly against the use of American forces in peacekeeping operations. The reason was practical: these deployments had become numerous and had placed a strain on declining manpower and financial resources that should be devoted to more traditional military priorities. The new president had been in office for fewer than nine months before the terrorist attacks of September 11, 2001, opened the window for intervention—possibly protracted—in Afghanistan and later in Iraq. President Bush even embraced state building in postwar Afghanistan, an idea he had previously rejected for other places like Kosovo. Questions of Afghan sovereignty were not raised in the deliberations, although the administration made a point of "restoring" Iraqi sovereignty in June 2004.

In discussions of intervention, the sovereignty question has never been raised very publicly. Does this mean there is a reluctance to open a Pandora's box of problems if the relationship is addressed directly? Are we afraid to raise a position that comes at odds with the more politically correct notion of humanitarian rights or other issues? Or is the question simply unimportant?

Whether we admit it openly or not, international intrusion into the domestic politics of states, no matter how objectionable or horrific the behavior of states may be, reflects a far different conceptualization of sovereignty than the one that reigned for the first 300 years of the modern state system. Had one asked in 1946 whether it was permissible to mount Operation Restore Hope in Somalia without the permission of the Somali government, the answer would have been overwhelmingly negative. The explanation would have been that such a mission would have been a direct violation of Somalia's sovereignty. The conception of sovereignty reflected in that argument, of course, would have been the traditional definition based in state sovereignty as an absolute and exclusive possession.

The situation has clearly changed in the interim. What we have witnessed is a de facto, indirect assault on the idea of absolute state sovereignty as a consequence of the rise in legitimacy of the idea of human rights and arguably in combating terrorism. As noted elsewhere in this text, the idea that all human beings have certain inalienable rights simply because of their humanity is a surprisingly recent development, one whose international expression can be dated to the post–World War II enunciation of the Convention on Genocide and the Universal Declaration of Human Rights in the latter 1940s. Interventions to thwart "evildoers" is of more recent vintage.

The effect of recent interventions has been to move the rationale for outside interference into alignment with the conceptualization of sovereignty based in the individual and the limited grant of individual sovereignty to the state. In terms of the meaning of sovereignty, there can be no rationale for violating state sovereignty other than saying that state sovereignty *is no longer an inviolable principle of international relations.* To make that assertion, in turn, it is necessary to locate sovereignty somewhere else, as in individuals and groups whose rights are being violated and to whose rescue international efforts are directed.

No state makes the justification of participation in UN or other peacekeeping activities or for intervention Iraq-style in these terms. Why not? The answer is simple and straightforward: no state is willing to admit the dilution of the concept of state sovereignty because to do so admits its own sovereignty is potentially diminished in the process; sovereignty is too much a bedrock of national jurisdiction to make such an admission. And no state will admit that its ability to control absolutely what occurs within its territory is not entirely its own but may be subject to internationally imposed limits. Nowhere is that sentiment more fiercely felt than in the United States.

Among the most jealous guardians of the doctrine of absolute sovereignty is the government of the United States. The idea that no outside force should have the ability to interfere in internal American affairs can be dated back certainly to the revolutionary period and the very negative view of governmental power that most of the supporters of the American Revolution held, and it remains an untouchable first principle, which, if breached, brings howls of protest. The result is schizophrenic but long-standing. The United States asserts the absolute nature of American national sovereignty, but has for a long time been willing in effect to ignore the sovereignty of others when it served our purposes. The numerous U.S. interventions in Central America and the Caribbean in the nineteenth and early twentieth centuries were nothing more than gross violations of the sovereignty of countries like Nicaragua, Panama, and Haiti. In some ways, the United States was simply acting as a large power in its "domain," the Western Hemisphere. Its profession of principles about sovereignty and its actions were, however, hardly consistent with one another.

The United States, of course, is not alone in this hypocrisy. The Russians (as Soviets), after all, invaded and occupied Afghanistan during the 1980s, a clear violation of Afghan sovereignty, and then turned around during the 1990s and used the absolutist rationale for sovereignty to argue that it was nobody's business but theirs how they dealt with the uprising in Chechnya while concurring in UNSCRs that violated the sovereignty of several other countries.

Afghanistan and especially Iraq bring life to this issue. Regardless of whether the U.S. invasion was justifiable on policy grounds (a debatable point), it was a clear violation of Iraqi sovereignty. The United States simply ignored that it was ignoring a principle that it holds dear when applied to interfering with the United States. Doing this is not unique to the United States, as power trumps principle in this situation: the powerful do what they can, and the weak endure what they must, to paraphrase the old saying. The United States forced Iraq to endure what it could not avoid.

The United States may decide to forego future interventions on pragmatic bases such as interests or costs, thereby making the erosive effect of such actions on sovereignty a moot point. The general international trend toward asserting the legitimacy of human rights and the need to punish terrorists and others who threaten American interests and the international order (by no means always the same thing), however, makes abstinence on these grounds unlikely. The alternate justification for abstinence is based in the effects on sovereignty. If international interference in the often chaotic affairs of states occurs, eventually the question of the impact on sovereignty will have to be confronted directly and decisions made by the international community generally how much of the principle of state sovereignty it is willing to jettison in the name of humanity. The outcome is yet to be determined.

 STUDY/DISCUSSION QUESTIONS

1. Is the idea of outside intervention in the civil wars of countries a viable, justifiable action by the UN or the international community more generally? Can you think of a circumstance in which such interference is or is not wise?

2. With which conception of sovereignty do you agree? In other words, are the rights of a state more important than the rights of individuals and groups within states? How would the international system be different without the supremacy of state sovereignty?

3. Does American participation in peacekeeping operations in countries torn by civil war violate American principles, such as our position on sovereignty? Or should the question of our participation be made on pragmatic grounds rather than principles? If you were in a position to do so, how would you advise President Bush when the next humanitarian intervention is proposed at the UN or elsewhere?

4. What would be worse for the relations among countries, a situation where sovereignty is overridden in cases of large-scale abuse of human rights or a situation where such abuses are ignored and the sovereign rights of states upheld?

5. The American intervention in Afghanistan in 2001 represents a direct violation of Afghan sovereignty, tempered by virtual global approval of the action. Do the circumstances justify this violation of sovereignty? Do we have to add terrorism to the list of permissible violations of state sovereignty? Apply the same analysis to Iraq.

READING/RESEARCH MATERIAL

Boniface, Pascal. "What Justifies Regime Change?" *Washington Quarterly* 26, 3 (Summer 2003), 61–71.

Cusimano, Mary Ann, ed. *Beyond Sovereignty.* Boston, MA: Bedford St. Martins, 1999.

Hashmi, Sohail H., ed. *State Sovereignty: Change and Persistence in International Relations.* University Park, PA: Pennsylvania State University Press, 1997.

Kantor, Arnold, and Linton F. Brooks, eds. *U.S. Intervention Policy for the Post–Cold War World.* New York: The American Assembly, 1994.

Lyons, Gene M., and Michael Mastanduno, eds. *Beyond Westphalia: State Sovereignty and International Intervention.* Baltimore, MD: Johns Hopkins University Press, 1995.

Mills, Kurt. *Human Rights in the Emerging Global Order: A New Sovereignty?* New York: St. Martin's Press, 1998.

Snow, Donald M. *UnCivil Wars: International Security and the New Internal Conflicts.* Boulder, CO: Lynne Rienner Publishers, 1996.

————. *When America Fights: The Uses of American Force.* Washington, DC: CQ Press, 2001.

Snow, Donald M., and Eugene Brown. *International Relations: The Changing Contours of Power.* New York: Longman, 2000.

WEB SITES

Organization promoting comprehensive debate on intervention and sovereignty

International Commission on Intervention and State Sovereignty at http://www.icis.gc.ca

Comprehensive collection of views on moral dilemmas of humanitarian intervention

Human Rights Initiative at http://www.cceia.org/themes/hrdwinter2001.html

Report of Stanley Foundation on humanitarian intervention

"Any Means Necessary" at http://reports.stanletfdn.org/UNND01.pdf

Reports on international security, sovereignty, and intervention

Pugwash Regional Conflict and Global Security Studies at http://www.pugwash.org/reports/rc/reclist.htm

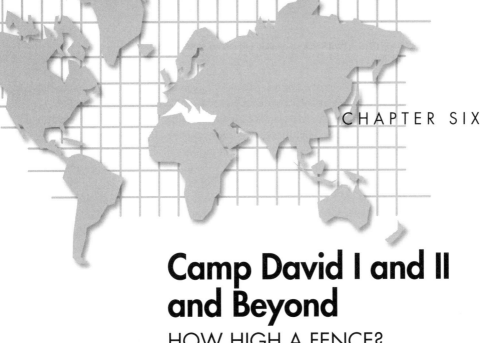

CHAPTER SIX

Camp David I and II and Beyond
HOW HIGH A FENCE?

PRÉCIS

The conflict between Israel and its Islamic neighbors has remained a central irritant in the international system for well over a half-century, and it does not appear to be moving toward any rapid conclusion today. In 1978, major progress was made in settling parts of the dispute when President Jimmy Carter brokered an agreement between Israel and Egypt to defuse the state of war between those two countries at Camp David, Maryland (Camp David I). In 2000, President Bill Clinton attempted to complete the process by bringing the Israelis and the Palestinians to the same place. Camp David II was unsuccessful, and its failure was followed by renewed violence between the two sides. After an interlude, President George W. Bush introduced his "road map" to reenergize the process in 2003. While this process made little progress, the death of Palestinian leader Yasir Arafat in November 2004 and the election of Mahmoud Abbas as his successor in February 2005 at least temporarily reenergized the process.

This case study looks at this process through two lenses. The first lens is a comparison between the two Camp David experiences and why one succeeded and one failed. The second lens is the structure of current differences that makes peace elusive: the issue of Jerusalem, the size and nature of the Palestinian state and how it will be physically separated from Israel, and whether the Palestinians have the right to be repatriated to their former homes in Israel. The positions of the two sides on each issue have proven too far apart to allow a solution.

Two meetings occurred twenty-two years apart, in 1978 and 2000. Each was convened by an American president at the presidential retreat of Camp David (named after Dwight Eisenhower's grandson) in Maryland's Catoctin Mountains a short helicopter ride from Washington. In both cases, the presidents, who happened both to be Democrats, locked away the participants and spent a considerable amount of time attempting to jaw-bone and cajole an agreement of enormous importance to the Middle East and world peace. The meeting in 1978 produced a groundbreaking peace agreement between Egypt and Israel that ended the cycle of war that had plagued the region for 30 years and began the peace process in the region that the 2000 meeting between Israel and the Palestinians was supposed to bring close to fruition. Because Camp David I succeeded in producing a groundbreaking accord, it was widely touted as Jimmy Carter's finest hour. Because Camp David II failed to produce a comprehensive agreement between Israel and the Palestinian state and ended with the two sides still at odds, the contribution of Camp David II to the legacy of Bill Clinton is more constrained. The aftermath of the 2000 failure has been an unrelenting return to the cycle of violence, with no short-term end in sight.

No two negotiations are ever identical, although there were clear similarities between these two events that we will explore in the pages that follow. Both centered on the Middle East and the reconciliation of Israel with its Islamic neighbors, for instance, and convening the second meeting at the site of the original was a conscious matter with considerable symbolic value. At the same time, Camp David I was negotiated in the atmosphere of the Cold War, the nature of which contributed to the purpose and urgency of the meeting, while Camp David II was conducted in a less intense geopolitical atmosphere. As well, the participants and issues were not the same; despite the participation of Israel in both, the Islamic side was represented by the president of Egypt, Anwar el-Sadat, in 1978 and the chairman of the Palestinian Liberation Organization (PLO), Yasir Arafat, in 2000. As a result, the motivations and aspirations of both the parties and the American mediators were not identical in the two cases.

Looming over both sets of meetings was the issue of Jerusalem, or more precisely, the Old City of Jerusalem. (In addition to the Old City, there is Israeli West Jerusalem and Islamic East Jerusalem outside the Old City's walls.) Because it is the site of some of the most significant holy shrines of the world's three largest monotheistic religions (Judaism, Christianity, and Islam), the dispensation of the fate of political control of Jerusalem has always been the most nettlesome and difficult problem dividing the principals in the region. The bottom line is simple: the Muslim neighbors of Israel will never accept total Israeli sovereignty over all of East Jerusalem and especially Muslim holy sites; and Israel will never accept total Muslim (in this case Palestinian) sovereignty over the Old City either. Tensions and emotions are high because Israelis were denied access to the Wailing Wall between 1948 and 1967, when East Jerusalem was part of Jordan, and because Muslims have effectively been denied access to shrines such as the Haram al Sharif ever since. Bridging this problem has so far proven illusive.

The Jerusalem issue also has great symbolic significance that provides a mask for other fundamental issues that divide Israel and the Palestinians and remain barriers to peace. Two stand out. One is the shape and size of an independent Palestine. The other is the fate of the Palestinians who fled Israel in 1948 and now seek repatriation; the shape of Palestinian economic and political development are as nettlesome as the fate of Jerusalem.

The Jerusalem quandary demonstrates a major principle of diplomacy: that you negotiate the issues on which you are least divided first, and leave the hardest questions for last. At Camp David I, Jerusalem was addressed and a general position was negotiated, but for political reasons the resolution never made its way into the final accords. At Camp David II, the rest of the agenda was negotiated and basically resolved; the meeting foundered on the hard rocks of East Jerusalem and repatriation.

This case study will examine the two meetings at Camp David. The focus will not be on the meetings themselves but instead on what they accomplished or failed to accomplish. As already stated, the contexts were different. What difference does it make that the Middle East was a major focal point of the Cold War competition in 1978, but not today? The actors and issues were different as well. In 1978, Anwar el-Sadat was forced to show enormous courage in recognizing Israel's right to exist in the face of almost universal rejection of that position in the rest of the Islamic Middle East. Was that different than the pressures on Yasir Arafat as the chief representative of the Palestinians in their quest for a sovereign state carved out of the West Bank of the Jordan River and the Gaza Strip?

We will proceed first by looking briefly at the two events, focusing on the issues that brought the parties together and how, in a general sense, they were resolved. With that factual base established, we will then turn to the main thrust of the case study, which is a comparison of the contexts in which the two meetings occurred and how those influences may have affected the outcomes. We will conclude with some extrapolation from the two meetings at Camp David on outstanding issues and their resolution—the prospects for a settlement of Israeli-Palestinian differences.

ISSUES AND OUTCOMES, 1978 AND 2000

Camp David I and II were conducted in considerably different atmospheres that manifested themselves in very different issues and proposed outcomes. Camp David I was the first formal discussion between Israel and any of the surrounding Islamic states, and much of its significance came from the fact that it occurred at all. The discussions did, however, produce a landmark agreement that had formed the foundation for the reconciliation of Israel with all of its neighboring states except Syria by 2000, when Camp David II was convened with the high hopes of bringing the Middle East peace process to a virtual close by creating the conditions for the Israelis and the Palestinians to resolve their remaining differences.

Camp David I

That there even *was* a first meeting at Camp David between the prime minister of Israel and the president of Egypt is one of the true miracles of twentieth-century diplomacy. The context in the region was about as unpromising for peace as anyplace in the world. During the thirty years since the creation of the state of Israel in 1948, the Jewish state and its neighboring Islamic states (Egypt, Syria, Jordan, and even Iraq) had fought four wars (in 1948, 1956, 1967, and 1973). All had resulted in Israeli victories, but that fact had done little to diffuse the stated Islamic purpose of destroying the Israeli state and returning the territory known as Israel to their Islamic brethren and former occupants, the Palestinians. An absolute and intractable hatred for Israel and its people was the only acceptable stance for the so-called Arab states (technically, a state is Arab only if its people can trace their ancestry back to the Arabian Peninsula). No state in the region diplomatically recognized the Jewish state or accepted its continuing right to exist.

The map of the region fanned these animosities. In the Six-Day War of 1967, Israel seized and occupied territory from each of its contiguous antagonists: the Golan Heights from Syria, the West Bank of the Jordan River from Jordan, and the Sinai peninsula and Gaza Strip from Egypt. Arab demands for the return of each piece of real estate were loud and unceasing; Israeli insistence that they must be retained on security and other grounds were equally adamant.

There was, however, incentive to change matters. In the wake of the 1973 Yom Kippur War, Egypt had expelled the Soviets and ridded themselves of their influence, thereby altering the geopolitical context. One of President Jimmy Carter's earliest initiatives toward the Soviet Union was to encourage discussions with them about a Middle East peace settlement. Although neither Egypt nor Israel liked the American-Soviet proposal, at least it got the matter on the table. In 1977, President Sadat made the bold move of flying to Jerusalem and meeting with Israeli Prime Minister Menachem Begin, thereby establishing a direct connection that led to bilateral meetings between the two countries. When those talks failed, the stage was set for Carter to bring the two leaders to Camp David.

The prospects for Camp David I were decidedly mixed, and the political stakes for Carter were very high. On the negative side was opposition to negotiations of any kind both within the Islamic world and in Israel. The fact that Sadat even met with the Israelis appeared a sign of the recognition of the Israeli state and thus met the uniform, unremitting opposition of leaderships and publics throughout the Islamic world. Israeli opposition came from the religious right in Israel but was moderated by the fact that Begin was the leader of the rightist Likud Party, where the greatest opposition to any accommodation with the Arab states resided (and still does). On the positive side, both sides had something to offer that the other wanted, so that a basis for a negotiated agreement was possible. Carter took a large political gamble by calling the meeting, because if the talks failed, his already low public opinion ratings would go even lower.

The talks succeeded because the leaders rose above the negatives and because they had things on which they could bargain and reach accommodation. In Israel, there was considerable ambivalence to dealing with Egypt. In the 1973 Yom Kippur War, the Egyptians had made some military progress for the first time before their ultimate defeat, a fact still fresh on Israeli minds. Many Israelis were reluctant to discuss giving back the Sinai Peninsula to Egypt, because that desert area provided a buffer against a new invasion by Egypt. On the other hand, Egypt was becoming militarily dependent on the United States, which would oppose another attack, and a growing number of Israelis were concluding that ending the state of siege of Israel imposed by its hostile neighbors might require exceptional efforts. Moreover, the Israelis recognized American pressure to negotiate an end to a military confrontation that had brought them to the brink of war with the Soviets in 1973.

Sadat faced similar ambivalence. The Islamic world uniformly opposed any dealings with the Israelis, and when an accord was reached, the Egyptians were isolated from the rest of the region and even had economic assistance cut off by Saudi Arabia. At the same time, having the Sinai and Gaza in Israeli possession was humiliating for the proud Egyptians, and Sadat reasoned that if he could negotiate a deal that also included movement toward a Palestinian state, a sort of talisman within the Islamic world, those misgivings would evaporate.

Thus, both sides had something the other wanted, and there was consequently the basis for negotiation. Israel badly wanted recognition of its legal existence and its *right* to exist, which Egypt could offer. The Egyptians wanted the Sinai Peninsula (including the small but significant oil industry that Israel had established there during the occupation) and the Gaza Strip back. To avoid or minimize the overwhelming backlash in the Islamic world, Egypt also required some guarantees regarding the status of Palestine and the Palestinians and Israeli willingness to address the Palestinian issue.

As has been well documented in places such as Jimmy Carter's memoirs, the negotiations were long, difficult, and, on several occasions, nearly failed. In the end, the historical enemies found enough common ground to agree on three basic matters that constitute the so-called Camp David Accord:

1. The withdrawal of Israel from the Sinai Peninsula;
2. A peace treaty between Israel and Egypt that included recognition of Israel;
3. A promise to resolve the Palestinian question in the form of autonomy for the West Bank and Gaza Strip, to become the basis for a Palestinian state.

The first two provisions were implemented routinely. The Israelis withdrew from Sinai in two steps, in 1979 and 1982, returning control to Egypt. The peace treaty between the two countries was signed in 1979.

The Palestinian question, which includes the fate of Jerusalem as its thorniest issue, remained contentious. While the Israelis agreed to enter into negotiations with representatives of the Palestinians and gradually have increased the degree of Palestinian autonomy in the West Bank and Gaza, the translation of that effort into a full-fledged sovereign Palestinian state lagged throughout the 1980s and 1990s. The failure to resolve the Palestinian question produced much frustration among Palestinians and other Muslims. It also provided the reason for something like Camp David II.

Camp David I did not go beyond these issues, leaving those problems that remained divisive to negotiations between the Israelis and the Palestinians. The fate of Jerusalem was omitted from the final declaration, even though it was discussed and the principles for a settlement were privately reached. The problem was, and still is, the mutually exclusive claims both sides have on East Jerusalem, positions inflamed by the religious shrines in the Old City. As Carter explained the 1978 situation in a *New York Times* op-ed piece shortly after the conclusion of Camp David II, "We knew that Israel had declared sovereignty over the entire city but that the international community considered East Jerusalem to be legally part of the occupied West Bank. We realized that no Israeli leader could renounce Israel's position, and that it would be politically suicidal for Sadat or any other Arab leader to surrender any of their people's claims regarding the Islamic and Christian holy places." Because the only possible solution involved compromises that one or both principals would have to renounce, language suggesting a solution was simply omitted rather than create political firestorms in Israel and Egypt that might singe both Begin and Sadat. Palestinian independence and self-determination and the fate of Jerusalem were deferred for another day.

Camp David II

The second Camp David meeting was between Israeli Prime Minister Ehud Barak (even though many of the compromises proposed by Barak were printed in the Israeli press shortly after the meetings ended, and both sides leaked invidious comments about the other) and Palestinian Authority President Yasir Arafat and was convened by President Bill Clinton in July 2000. The talks lasted more than two weeks, a considerably longer period than the original negotiations, both sides brought larger negotiating teams to the Catoctin resort than had been the case in 1978, and there was even a break in the proceedings to allow both sides to regroup. Considerable progress toward a comprehensive agreement was apparently made, but in the end, the efforts fell short. The public stumbling block in 2000 was Jerusalem, just as it had been in 1978. As the situation deteriorated in late 2000 and early 2001, the less public but in some ways more fundamental issues like the emergence of a sovereign Palestinian state and the question of Palestinians' "right" to return to Israel came to the fore.

In important ways, the agenda for Camp David II was made up of the outstanding issues from Camp David I. The major point of contention was the third point in the 1978 accords, the dispensation of the West Bank and Gaza and the fate of the Palestinians. In the minds of the Islamic states (and especially Egypt), the Israelis had agreed to a process that would lead systematically toward a fully sovereign Palestine located on the West Bank and in Gaza. For them, the "autonomy" contained in the 1978 agreement was only a stepping-stone on the way to independence. Israeli administrations, on the other hand, debated whether autonomy (giving the Palestinians control over, for instance, schools and local police matters) was not the end state, rather than a movement toward independence. Moreover, the Arab world viewed the process—whatever its purpose—as unduly slow, suggesting less than full Israeli adherence to the spirit of Camp David. The construction of Israeli settlements in the occupied West Bank added to tensions. A very rancorous political debate within Israel about whether there should be *any* concessions toward the Palestinians added to Muslim doubts about Israeli sincerity.

A breakthrough had occurred in September 1993. Meeting clandestinely under the auspices of the Norwegian government, representatives of Israel and the PLO agreed to mutual recognition in what became known as the Oslo framework. The PLO agreed to end its call for the destruction of Israel and to renounce terrorism. In return, Israel agreed to withdraw its authority from Gaza and the West Bank town of Jericho, turning both over to the Palestinians for self-governance. The deadline for a final agreement on Palestine was set for September 12, 2000. In 1994, Israel and Jordan agreed to a peace treaty that included a permanent border between them from which the Palestinian state would be forged. The peace process seemed to be moving toward a successful conclusion.

There remained a significant political problem on both sides. While polls indicated that the majority of Israelis and Palestinians favored a permanent settlement of the long conflict that included a Palestinian state, there were extremist elements on both sides who so hated and distrusted the others that they would go to any ends to subvert the process. In 1995, for instance, a Jewish extremist shot and killed Israeli Prime Minister Yitzhak Rabin for the avowed purpose of stopping the process. Although there were no instances of equal drama on the Palestinian side, terrorist acts by extreme groups have accompanied progress toward peace as well. Neither side demonstrated the political will or ability to suppress these elements dedicated to preventing a final accord.

By the time President Clinton invited Barak and Arafat to Camp David, there were four major outstanding issues facing the conferees. The largest and most public issue was the pace and extent of transfer of the West Bank from Israel to the Palestinian Authority. Both sides had their own formulas; as might be guessed, the Palestinians consistently maintained that more territory should be transferred faster than Israel proposed. Israeli settlements on the West Bank exacerbated the problem; although they do not occupy a large amount of territory, Israel insists on maintaining control, and the settlers themselves fear being abandoned by Israel to what they assume will be the not-so-tender care of the Palestinians. To Palestinians, the settlements' continued existence raised questions about whether the Israelis will ever relinquish control voluntarily. Moreover, the settlements are located on the most desirable real estate on the West Bank and Gaza—where most of the water supplies are.

The second issue was the timing of the declaration of Palestinian sovereignty and total independence. This issue was related to land transfer by the question of sovereignty over what. Arafat wanted to declare the Palestinian state as early as September 2000 (the expiration of the Oslo interim agreement) and threatened to do so unilaterally when the conference failed to reach an overall agreement. Although the September 2000 date was allowed to pass, the possibility that it might be invoked remained a potential threat for the Palestinian leader. Barak wanted to delay the declaration to avoid criticism from political elements in Israel that opposed *any* Palestinian independence.

The third issue that could not be surmounted was the status of East Jerusalem. It remained as immutable a problem as at Camp David I, the only major difference being that it became an open point of contention in the second meeting. The issues remain the same: both Israel and Palestine declare their sovereignty over the Old City. Israel claims all of Jerusalem as its capital, and Arafat insists upon East Jerusalem as the Palestinian capital. The positions are mutually exclusive, which means all parties will have to compromise to bring about a reconciliation and solution. The emotional significance of the holy sites—the Western Wall of the Second Temple (the Wailing Wall and Little Wall) to Jews, the place where legend has it Muhammad ascended to Heaven (the Temple Mount) to Muslims, the sites where Jesus was betrayed and resurrected (Gethsemane and the Church of the Holy Sepulchre) to Christians—makes compromise difficult.

Various proposals have been made across time to resolve the difficulty. The major principle that must be agreed to for all religions is that of guaranteed free access to all parts of the Old City by people of all faiths. In 1978, the proposal to accomplish that included acknowledgment that the city is holy to all three faiths, permitting holy places to be controlled by religious representatives and creating some governing body in which all three religions were represented to administer the city. At Camp David II, the United States argued for Palestinian sovereignty over the Islamic and Christian Quarters of the Old City, and Israeli control over the Jewish and Armenian Quarters. A second idea included giving the Palestinians sovereign control over several of the neighborhoods sur-rounding the Old City and administrative autonomy within the walls of the Old City. A third approach deferred the issue of Jerusalem for several years. None proved acceptable, and without an agreement on Jerusalem, no comprehensive agreement was possible.

The fourth issue, easily as difficult as Jerusalem, is the question of whether Pales-tinians who fled Israel in 1948 have a right to be repatriated into Israel. There are approx-imately 4 million Palestinians who might seek repatriation to an Israel that has a population of about 5.75 million, of whom slightly more than a million are already Mus-lim. In addition to the problems of absorbing such a large influx in a limited amount of space, repatriation threatens Israel's status as a Jewish state, an absolutely unacceptable possibility to the majority of Israeli citizens. As a result, Barak captured Israeli opinion when he declared in January 2001, "I will not accept under any circumstances the right of return of [Palestinian] refugees." Arafat was equally adamant that no final agreement is possible that does not include repatriation, because many Palestinians have long clung to the dream of returning to their former homes. Negotiating away that dream would be political suicide for any Palestinian leader.

INFLUENCES ON THE PROCESS

Why did the Camp David meetings of 1978 produce a major agreement promoting peace in one of the world's most volatile regions, whereas the effort in 2000 failed ultimately to reach such an accord? It may have been a human problem: Jimmy Carter may have been a more persuasive arbitrator than Bill Clinton, and Barak and Arafat may not have been able to reach the same level of statesmanship as Sadat and Begin. On the other hand, the differences may have had more to do with the structure and difficulty of the issues at the two meetings.

One way to think about the differences is in terms of the diplomatic strategy sug-gested earlier: concentrate on the easiest problems first, then attack the more difficult ones. This is not to suggest that the problems addressed and overcome at Camp David I were not difficult. They were, but as it turned out, they were resolvable. The more diffi-cult, arguably unsolvable, problems were left for Camp David II. They were not resolved—quite possibly because they could not be—leaving the situation in its contin-uing volatile state. The contrasting contexts of the two events and today highlight these dynamics, and the emotional issue of Jerusalem symbolizes more substantive differences.

Geopolitical Setting

The impact of the Cold War in 1978, and its absence in 2000 and beyond, is the most fundamental and obvious geopolitical difference in the two settings. Camp David I was, in a very real sense, the final scene of a Middle Eastern geopolitical play that had reached its most dangerous moment during the Yom Kippur War of 1973, at a time when the Arab-Israeli continuing conflict was also part of the Cold War geopolitical competition. The outcome of Camp David I itself contributed to a changed geopolitical setting for the future, and Camp David II was intended to put the crowning touch on the trans-formation of the geopolitics of the region. Its failure plunged the region back into chaos.

The Yom Kippur War of 1973 was a traumatic experience both for the region and for the global system. Locally, it was the first time the Egyptians had military success against the Israelis, to the point that early in the fighting Israel reportedly armed its small nuclear arsenal in anticipation of the need to attack its neighbors with those warheads. The Yom Kippur War also traumatized the Cold War international system. After the Israelis turned the tables on their enemies, they drove the Egyptians back to the Suez Canal, where the Egyptians were trapped with no way to get back across into Egypt; at the same time, Israeli forces were poised 80 miles from Cairo with no opposition in their way. In this situation, the Soviets announced their intention to drop Soviet paratroopers into the Egyptian lines to aid in their defense. Such an action made little military sense (lightly armed airborne forces not being of much utility against Israeli tanks and heavy artillery), but it did precipitate a major confrontation between the United States and the Soviet Union. In response, the United States signaled its resolve by going to highest alert status and prepared to counter intervene if necessary. During an incredibly tense 24 hours or so, American Secretary of State Henry Kissinger shuttled back and forth between Moscow and Tel Aviv, gaining assurances that the Israelis would let the Egyptians back into Egypt if the Soviets did not physically intervene. Ultimately Kissinger succeeded and the crisis passed.

In reviewing what almost happened, the conclusion was that the United States and the Soviet Union nearly confronted one another in a manner that could have escalated to a totally unacceptable nuclear war between them. Yom Kippur convinced the superpowers, and especially the United States, that another Arab-Israeli war that could lead to another nuclear confrontation was similarly intolerable, and that the possibility of such a future conflict had to be ended.

Between 1973 and 1978, the United States placed itself in a position to help broker peace in the region. In 1975, Egypt broke entirely with the Soviets. The United States quickly moved to replace Soviet presence and influence through bilateral economic and military assistance. The stage was thus set for the process that began with Sadat's visit to Jerusalem and ended in the Maryland mountains.

Geopolitics thus congealed to encourage the first Camp David meeting. The perceived need to defuse the Arab-Israeli conflict as a potential precipitant of World War III combined with President Carter's natural instincts as a peacemaker to give the United States considerable incentives to engage and encourage the process. Egypt's early success in 1973 meant that Sadat operated with a stronger hand than would previously have been possible, and that same experience reduced an overwhelming self-confidence among Israeli officials that any military confrontation with its neighbors would be a walkover.

The geopolitical situation had greatly changed by 2000. The Cold War was over, of course, and the peace process begun in 1978 had spread throughout the region. Egyptian-Israeli relations had totally normalized to the point that Israelis and Egyptians regularly flew back and forth between their capitals, and the peace process had spread to other countries in the region as well. Because progress was being made toward turning over parts of the West Bank to Palestinian control (although at a slower pace than the Palestinians wanted and faster than some Israelis wanted), there was not the same sense of urgency emanating from the geopolitical situation as had been the case before, although the formal expiration of the Oslo agreement on September 12, 2000, and the need for a permanent replacement agreement created a sense of some urgency. Arafat's threat simply to declare the Palestinian state in the absence of any agreement simply added to the concern (see below).

Camp David II was to accelerate and complete an ongoing process; Camp David I broke entirely new ground. Jimmy Carter was making peace to lessen the likelihood the region could trigger Armageddon; Bill Clinton sought to bring closure to a process in which he had been an active participant and to burnish his presidential legacy. The motivations of the two presidents, as well as the principals, were not quite the same.

The geopolitical situation changed again after 2000. The September 11, 2001, attacks refocused attention on the Middle East negatively, given that the region was the spawning ground of Al Qaeda. The failure of Camp David II, followed by the visit of Israeli Prime Minister Ariel Sharon to the disputed shrines in the Old City, sparked a renewed round of Israeli-Palestinian violence punctuated by Palestinian suicide terrorism and Israeli military retaliation. Because these two phenomena appear related, the new Bush administration abandoned the Carter-Clinton position of acting as an honest broker between the two sides, tilting decisively toward the Israeli position. The results included a reduced American ability to act as a go-between and a further polarization of the region that in turn made negotiations even more difficult.

Regional Situation

A major part of the changed geopolitical situation in which the two Camp David meetings occurred and since was the result of change in the region itself. In 1978, no Islamic state in the region (except Iran, which is not Arab at any rate) recognized Israel or its right to exist; all were, at least rhetorically, committed to the destruction of the Jewish state; and they all championed, once again at the rhetorical level, the cause of Palestinian statehood. Pan-Arabism, the drive to unify all Islamic peoples, was effectively defined as opposition to Israel.

In this situation, Israel was virtually totally isolated, a "Jewish state in an Arab Sea," as the saying went. Israel was, and still is, the only fully functioning democracy in the Middle East, and it also possesses the most advanced, diversified economy in the region. Petroleum wealth makes some Persian Gulf states richer than Israel, but the diversity of the Israeli economy made it the only state in the region that was economically competitive with the most advanced powers. Israel also possessed by far the most powerful military machine in the region, but the Israelis were, however, basically on their own in the region and the world. Most of the advanced countries kept Israel at arm's length, because their dependence on Middle Eastern oil made them reluctant potentially to alienate the oil-producing Islamic states.

The depth of the animosity between Israel and its neighbors cannot be overemphasized because it created an enormous chasm for President Sadat to leap when he went to Jerusalem and started the dialogue that led to Camp David. Sadat broke ranks in what had theretofore been a solid front against Israel; indeed, as the largest country in the coalition that had militarily opposed Israel, Egypt had *led* the opposition for much of the period of confrontation. It took enormous courage on his part to take the leadership for change, and he paid the price in terms of vilification and isolation within the Islamic world for having done so.

The situation had clearly changed by 2000. Israel had made peace with all of its historical opponents except Syria, and the change in regime in Damascus (the death of Syrian strongman Hafez al-Assad and his replacement by his son Mustafa) in summer 2000 raised the prospects of progress there at some future point. Egypt's Hosni Mubarak and Jordan's new King Abdullah had established good relations with Israeli Prime Minister Ehud Barak, and the process of handing over jurisdiction on the West Bank and Gaza from Israel to the Palestinian Authority had become an accepted and expected practice.

The emotional, adversarial nature of the situation thus clearly appeared to have abated a great deal. Except at the political extremes in both Israel and elsewhere in the region, expectations for continuation of the peace process was an accepted fact of life of the region, if one to which all Israelis and all Palestinians were not equally devoted.

All was thus not idyllic. There remained some residual animosity in places like Damascus, but the idea of a Muslim leader entering into negotiations with Israel has certainly lost its uniqueness or even controversy. One of the more notable visual images of the 1990s was Yasir Arafat reaching across the table and grabbing the hand of Israeli Prime Minister Yitzhak Rabin at a ceremony on the White House lawn on September 13, 1993, and Camp David II began with the playful videotape of Barak and Arafat jostling to see who would enter the lodge at the retreat first. Like Begin before him, the fact that Barak is a retired military hero insulated him from charges of being "soft" on the other side.

The problem for both sides was and is the political extremes. In 1978, distrust and suspicion of the motives of the other side was a mainstream emotion on both sides that made bold agreements all the more politically risky. By 2000, on the other hand, the majority of Israelis and Palestinians had embraced the idea of peace and had come to realize that sacrifices would be necessary to complete the peace process. Intractable opposition on both sides had been reduced to the fringes, the highly sectarian Orthodox right in Israel and their equivalent in Palestine. Since 2001, the situation has reverted, as both sides have polarized: terrorism-supporting elements have gained sway within the Palestinian movement, and hard-liners have gained influence in Israel. In a recent *Foreign Affairs* article, David Makovsky summarizes the atmosphere: "Israelis do not trust the Palestinian Authority (PA) to fulfill its security obligations and halt terrorist attacks, and Palestinians remain convinced that Israel will never voluntarily cede the West Bank."

Jerusalem

Jerusalem is the lightning rod that energizes all the worst fears both sides have about cooperation with the other. It is almost exclusively an emotional problem in the sense that there are, and have for some time, been reasonable and rational solutions that could solve the problem. The underlying principle has to be the unfettered ability of members of each religion to worship at its most holy places with no fear of interruption or harassment. Unfortunately, Jews have been excluded from their holiest shrines by Muslims, and followers of Islam have been denied free access to their holy places by Israelis. There is no reservoir of trust or good feelings from which to begin negotiations. The distrust and emotionalism blends with the other intractable issues like Palestinian repatriation to serve as a solid barrier to a final peace.

Various solutions, including turning the Old City into an international city, either on the model of Vatican City or possibly administered by an organization like the United

Nations, have been put forward from time to time. These proposals have always failed because they meant that someone other than members of the affected religions would have control, an intolerable situation.

A physical solution is possible, if the will to implement it is present. Some of the more promising—or less unpromising—suggestions include a physical division of the Old City and environs along sectarian lines. Under one proposal, Israel would have sovereignty over "the Jewish Quarter of the Old City, the entire Western Wall, and all the Jewish neighborhoods, new and old." (New and old refers to neighborhoods both inside and surrounding the Old City.) The Palestinians, on the other hand, would "be given

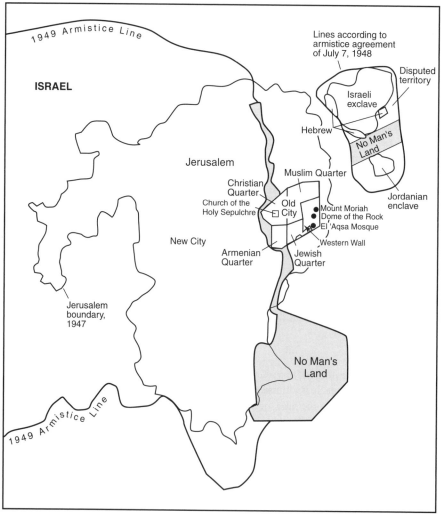

Map 6.1 Map of Jerusalem.

sovereignty over all outer Arab neighborhoods, virtually all the inner neighborhoods, and the Muslim, Christian and Armenian Quarters of the Old City." That leaves one holy site common to both Judaism and Islam, and a compromise solution proposes that "what the Muslims call the Haram (al Sharif) and what the Jews call the Temple Mount must be shared, with joint sovereignty."

As the accompanying map indicates, the effect is to partition the Old City: Israel maintains control of the Jewish population and sacred sites for Judaism, and the Palestinians get most of the rest. An important aspect, and one of enormous emotional importance for both sides, is that Jews can go to their shrines like the Wailing Wall and Muslims can approach shrines like the Haram al Sharif *without passing through a checkpoint controlled by the other religion.*

The tricky part is the proposal for joint sovereignty over the Temple Mount/Haram al Sharif. As the site of the first and second Jewish Temples and the site from which Muhammad ascended to Heaven, it clearly has enormous religious value to each side, and neither is going to accept any outcome that does not absolutely guarantee its continuing access. Finding common ground that will produce a trustworthy regime to meet the demands of Jew and Muslim will require the utmost political acumen and courage in the entire Camp David 2000 set of issues.

Beyond the Camp David Process: How High the Fence?

Palestinian violence beginning in 2000 (so-called Intifada II) and the Israeli election that brought Likud leader Ariel Sharon to power in February 2001 ended the Camp David process for now. Within days of Sharon's victory, a spokesman declared "everything in Camp David is null and void unless it was signed, and nothing was signed." Whether Sharon and Abbas can revive it remains an open question.

All three elements that had blocked progress have been addressed in ways that broaden the gulf between the parties and make renewed progress more difficult—or impossible. On Jerusalem, Sharon declared, the Old City is "the united and indivisible capital of Israel—with the Temple Mount as its center—for all eternity." On repatriation, he announced a renewal of the Zionist goal of Jewish immigration to Israel, a position that precludes the return of Palestinians to their former homes. On the Palestinian state, he says the issue is negotiable, but only on the basis of the 42 percent of the West Bank the Palestinian Authority currently administers, not the 95 percent offered by Barak. Abbas and the Palestinians cannot possibly accept any of these terms, leaving the situation at a stalemate that may be the only possible outcome until positions soften on one side or the other.

In descending order of intractability, these three issues (Jerusalem, the Palestinian state, and repatriation) frame the ongoing debate, and until there is some resolution to each with which both sides feel they can live, there can be no comprehensive solution that will bring the kind of lasting, durable peace that has not existed in the region in more than a half century. In the current atmosphere of animosity, distrust, and retribution, compromise on any of these issues seems impossible, and there are no active discussions being conducted face to face by the principals. Instead, Palestinians demonstrate, throw rocks, and occasionally dispatch suicide bombers into Israel to kill themselves and Israeli civilians. Politically, the Israelis refuse to negotiate with "terrorists," a position implicitly supported by the United States government. Meanwhile, the erection of the fence phys-ically dividing Israel from the Palestinians demonstrates the poverty of reason and, at least implicitly, utter despair over the prospect of reaching some form of mutual accommo-dation. In the absence of negotiated agreement, Israel's answer to the Berlin Wall may substitute for an agreed-upon settlement.

So where are we in the process? One of the ways in which the situation is different in 2005 than it was in 1978 and 2000 is the position of the United States. In the two Camp David meetings, the United States played two essential roles. It was, on one hand, the insistent convener of the negotiations, compelling both sides to the table and not allowing the talks to conclude without some agreement. The United States was able to act in this manner because of the second aspect of its role, that of honest broker. The major protagonists came to Camp David and stayed because each could trust the Amer-icans not to act prejudicially against its particular interests, giving the United States at least some leverage with each side.

Each of these roles has, to some extent, been reversed in the current context. The United States has tilted decisively toward the Israeli position, symbolized by the fact that during President Bush's first term in office, Israeli Prime Minister Ariel Sharon was a fre-quent visitor to the White House but no representative of the Palestinians (and notably Yasir Arafat) was extended an invitation. Beyond the personal disregard with which Bush was reported to hold Arafat, the reason for excluding the Palestinians was their alleged ties to terrorism, an allegation reinforced by Israel. (Abbas has been invited to the White House in 2005.)

Becoming an obvious partisan of the Israelis has effectively meant the United States cannot play either role it did in the past. The Palestinians no longer trust the United States government (a position widely held in the region), so that American entreaties to the Palestinians to negotiate would not resonate as they did before. Moreover, the United States could not, in the current policy atmosphere, possibly even pretend to play the role of honest broker.

Since 2001, the American role in this conflict has been much more limited and restrained than it was during the Clinton administration. After September 11, 2001, the United States' concentration of energies on the global war on terrorism meant that all other foreign policy priorities, including the Israeli-Palestinian conflict, were placed on the back burner. It was during this period of American inattention that the second *intifada* broke out, and some analysts maintain that American failure to act decisively to reactivate peace talks contributed to the spiraling out of control that currently marks the region.

The United States reentered the process in a limited way in 2003, when the Bush administration announced its "road map" for achieving peace, a set of guideposts to mea-sure progress toward settlement. The road map proposed three sequential steps toward peace. In step one in 2003, the Palestinians were to put an end to terrorism by Pales-tinians emanating from Palestinian soil, and the Israelis were to suspend the building of new settlement on the West Bank and Gaza. In step two (2004), a provisional Palestin-ian state was to be established. In step three (2005), "remaining differences" (the Bush administration's language) were to be settled and the Palestinian state established.

The road map has been far less than a success. The requirements for steps one and two (ending terrorism and suspending settlements, establishing a provisional Palestinian state) have only tentatively been met, without any particular expression of alarm or disappointment (the fact these steps were opposed by many supporters of Sharon may or may not be coincidental), and in their absence, there is clearly no forward progress toward the third step. In fact, the remaining differences raised in the third step are the same issues that prevented an agreement in 2000. The road map, in other words, proposed to return in 2005 to the situation in 2000, and it has failed in that.

Where are we on the issues dividing the two sides at this juncture? Clearly, there has not been forward progress on any of them, and in fact, the lack of progress has hardened exclusive positions at the extremes, making future progress all the more difficult. Moreover, the ongoing rampage of violence on both sides has deepened hatreds and animosities to the point that it is hard to imagine how members of the current generation of Israelis and Palestinians can ever embrace one another as neighbors and friends. Too many Israelis have been murdered by Palestinian suicide bombers and too many Palestinians have been slaughtered in bombing attacks by the Israeli Defense Force for there to be any remaining reservoir of goodwill between the two sides.

This glut of ill will, on which the endless cycle of attack and counterattack, initiative and revenge, feeds itself, creates a tremendous barrier to negotiation and compromise. This situation makes an extremely difficult process almost impossible. The issues dividing the two sides are indeed deep and difficult, if not impossible, to resolve. In the end, a de facto solution like the fence may be the only answer.

Each issue is further apart than it was in 2000, and the degree of mistrust and hatred that has been added to the mix since 2000 makes the prospects for narrowing the gap grimmer. In Camp David II, the Jerusalem question got as far as apportioning neighborhoods in the Old City, and the major remaining questions surrounded control of joint religious sites and the question of Jerusalem as national capitals for each. In an atmosphere of greater cooperation, some form of joint (or international) jurisdiction over the religious sites would have been possible (and almost was). At the same time, it should have been possible to divide Jerusalem politically so that Israel could claim one part of the city as its capital and Palestine another part as its capital. In the current atmosphere, such compromises have become practically impossible.

The question of the Palestinian state has similarly become more entrenched, a situation made more difficult by the American tilt toward Israel. The problem is largely one of Israeli domestic politics: Israelis have been split for decades on the "land for peace" issue at the heart of the settlement and thus the Palestinian state questions. Part of the Israeli electorate (historically supporters of the Labour Party) have been willing to compromise on the settlement issue in order to gain a permanent peace with the Palestinians, and their position was largely accepted in the Camp David II agreement. This position has always been fiercely opposed by the Israeli right (historically the supporters of the Likud Party) and especially the settlers themselves, who want to expand the settlements. After 2000, these elements at least temporarily gained control, and new settlements were begun, to the utter dismay of the Palestinians, who saw these movements as further evidence the Israelis would have to be driven from the settlements if the territory was to be reclaimed by Palestine (these new settlements, to repeat, tended to be on prime West Bank and Gaza real estate). It is difficult to imagine how an agreement on this issue is possible without evicting settlers from most of the post-2000 settlements, but doing so created a firestorm within Israel that will be politically hazardous for any Israeli government proposing or trying to implement it.

The real deal breaker in 2000 and today is repatriation. As noted, no Israeli government can possibly embrace the idea that Palestinians who fled their homes in Israel in 1948 can be allowed to return and reclaim them, on two grounds. First, those properties are now occupied by Israelis who have lived on and owned them for more than a half century. Any Israeli government that sought to evict these people to implement a peace agreement would be committing political suicide. Second, honoring the right to return potentially entails a demographic shift that would leave Jews a minority in Israel. While Israelis do debate whether Israel should be a secular or sectarian state, none of them believe it should be a state in which Jews are in the minority.

The issue is just as emotionally charged on the other side. Most Palestinian leaders have historically understood why Israel cannot embrace repatriation but do not accept Israeli insistence on renunciation of the right to return in principle. To enough Palestinians to matter, the right to return remains a goal—a dream—that they cannot and will not give up. Any Palestinian leadership that negotiated away the dream would be committing political suicide as surely as would any Israeli government. That problem, not the remaining 5 percent of the West Bank not ceded to the Palestinian state, was the deal breaker in 2000, and it remains intact.

In the absence of any progress—indeed in the midst of an intractable worsening of the situation—the Israelis have acted unilaterally (with the implicit support of the United States) to create a de facto settlement by dividing Israelis and Palestinians physically and in effect creating the basis for two sovereign political entities. The mechanism is "the fence," a concrete and barbed wire barrier being built the virtual length of the West Bank dividing the two peoples. Its intent and effect is similar to the "line of control" built by India to divide Kashmir into de facto Islamic and Hindu jurisdiction (see Chapter 12 for details), and the two are implicit admissions that a negotiated solution is impossible, leaving only forceful partition as an option.

The fence is clearly designed to serve Israeli interests. As Makovsky explains, these are "to reduce terrorism and to find a way out of the settlement morass that lets Israel keep a Jewish majority within its borders." As he explains, there is precedent for the fence as an antiterrorist device. A similar fence was built in Gaza in 1994, and "since early 2001, not a single Palestinian suicide bomber has infiltrated Israel from Gaza."

The idea of the fence clearly has more support among Israelis (and not all Israelis support the idea) than among Palestinians, on several grounds. First, there are the well-publicized anomalies created by the route of the fence, for instance, situations where the fields and farms of individual Palestinians are on one side of the fence, their homes on the other, and there is no easy way to get from one to the other. Second, many Palestinians have historically worked and earned their livings in Israel, and the fence makes it difficult and, in some instances, impossible for people to get to work and thus support their families.

There are more fundamental objections. The most difficult is exactly where the fence will go and thus what will be partitioned. The most controversial aspect of this is whether some of the newer Jewish settlements will be on the Israeli or Palestinian side of the fence. This is a volatile political issue in Israel (and especially within the settler community), but because the fence line will certainly define the parameters of an eventual territorial settlement, it is critical. As Makovsky puts it, "The (Israeli) planners must try to minimize Palestinian hardship, create incentives to bring Palestinian negotiators back to the table, and assure the contiguity of a future Palestinian state." Such foresight, not always evident in the region, is crucial to the future. The bottom line of the fence from a Palestinian viewpoint is that it is a humiliating demonstration of their impotence and inability to control their own destiny. If the Israelis ignore Palestinian sensibility, they will in effect be contributing to the nurturing of the next generation of terrorist bombers, who will almost assuredly find a way over or around the wall.

CONCLUSION

The two Camp David meetings represent signposts in the history of attempts to create a lasting structure of peace between Israel and its Islamic neighbors. Prior to Camp David I, the relationship was one of unremitting antagonism: no other state in the region recognized Israel's right to exist, and most were at least rhetorically committed to the proposition of driving the Israelis into the sea. Egypt's recognition of Israel and its right to exist broke that solidarity and ushered in a new era of normalization between Israel and it neighbors. The last link in the Camp David I chain, however, was the creation of the Palestinian state, and when Camp David II was unsuccessful in doing so, the situation began its process of reversion to the current situation of violence and counterviolence. Whether the reason for failure was the lack of skill or dedication of the participants or the difficulty of the issues remains a matter of contention.

Since 2000, the situation has reverted almost to the pre-1978 levels. Israel is condemned throughout the region for its intransigence on the Palestinian issue, and the United States, seen as Israel's staunch, partisan champion, is blamed as well. The two sides remain very far apart on the issues, and there is no force impelling them back to the negotiating table.

Will the Israeli-designed fence be the de facto solution to the problem? In the absence of powerful pressure to the contrary from the United States or other parts of the international community (which was not forthcoming as of summer 2005), the fence will define the geopolitical reality of the Israeli-Palestinian conflict. To this point, its impact has been to exacerbate tensions rather than to relieve them. How can (or can) that situation change so that division will form a positive rather than a negative influence? What can or should the United States do to promote that peace? The answers are not easy, but if they were, the problem would probably have been solved already.

STUDY/DISCUSSION QUESTIONS

1. How and why did the existence of the Cold War create a different atmosphere in the Middle East in 1978 from that in 2000? Assess the effects of the differences

2. What did Camp David I accomplish and fail to accomplish? How is it linked to Camp David II?

3. Why are the final status of Jerusalem, the Palestinian state, and repatriation so critical to any territorial settlement involving Israel and Palestine?

4. Look at the map of Jerusalem and the various proposals to divide it. Which proposal do you find most and least viable? Why?

5. Is a comprehensive peace settlement in the Middle East possible without resolving the Palestinian problem (including Jerusalem) to the satisfaction of all parties? Is such a solution adequate to end the problem between Israel and the Palestinians?

6. How can (or can't) the Palestinian repatriation issue be resolved to the satisfaction of all parties? Why do both sides feel as strongly as they do on this issue? Can there be peace without resolving the issue?

7. Is the fence the answer? If so, what kind of fence? How might the United States make a contribution to a fence all can embrace? Or can it?

READING/RESEARCH MATERIAL

Carter, Jimmy. "A Jerusalem Settlement Everyone Can Live With." *New York Times* (electronic edition), August 6, 2000.

——————. *Keeping Faith: The Memoirs of a President.* Fayetteville, AR: University of Arkansas Press, 1995.

Friedman, Thomas L. "Uniting Jerusalem." *New York Times* (National Edition), August 11, 2000, A21.

Hedges, Chris. "The New Palestinian Revolt." *Foreign Affairs* 80, 1 (January/February 2001), 124–138.

Hertzberg, Arthur. "A Small Peace for the Middle East." *Foreign Affairs* 80, 1 (January/February 2001), 139–147.

Lacey, Marc, and David E. Sanger. "With Legacy in Mind, Clinton Tried, Tried, and Tried Again, to Bitter End." *New York Times* (electronic edition), July 26, 2000.

Makovsky, David. "How to Build a Fence." *Foreign Affairs* 83, 2 (March/April 2004), 50–64.

Perlez, Jane. "Clinton Ends Peace Summit Saying it Is Deadlocked." *New York Times* (electronic edition), July 26, 2000.

Sadat, Anwar. *In Search of an Identity: An Autobiography.* New York: Harper and Row, 1978.

Sontag, Deborah. "Down from the Summit, Into Vale of Uncertainty." *New York Times* (electronic edition), July 26, 2000.

Viorst, Milton. "Middle East Peace: Mirage on the Horizon?" *Washington Quarterly* 23, 1 (Winter 2000), 41–54.

WEB SITES

Statements and background on Israeli-Palestinian issues, including Camp David II

The Middle East Peace Summit at http://www.mfa.gov.il/go.asp/MFA

Compilation of UN documents on Israeli-Palestinian conflict

The Question of Palestine at http://www.UN.org/Depts/dpa/qpal

Details on U.S. Mideast policy

Bureau of Near Eastern Affairs at http://www.state.gov/p/nea

Israeli documents on the conflict

The Israeli Ministry of Foreign Affairs at http://www.mfa.gov.il

Palestinian views of the conflict

The Palestinian Ministry of Information at http://minfo.gov.ps

PART 3

Economic Globalization

The spread of the international economy through increased world trade, commonly known as globalization, was one of the distinctive characteristics of the 1990s, and it continues to be a dominant force in the new century. Globalization, often combined with political democratization, provided much of the optimism of the early and middle 1990s, an optimism only partly dampened by the Asian financial crisis of 1997–98 and the virtual collapse of the Russian economy in 1998.

Optimism about the future evolution of the world economy remains high among many observers, but that optimism is now more tempered than it was in the 1990s. The sources of restraint about the future tend to focus on places and issues surrounding globalization that seem to counsel caution. The three case studies in this part all look at aspects of the globalization process that are troublesome, at least to some.

The first case, "The New Trinity of Globalism," looks at how the structure of the globalizing economy evolved during the 1990s in ways that masked some of the problems that emerged in that economy by the end of the decade, notably in East Asia. The model that drove the globalization phenomenon during the 1990s was the so-called American model or Washington consensus, and the case looks extensively both at that model and at how it was enforced through the triangular relationship between the United States, the International Monetary Fund, and the countries joining the global economy.

The second case, "Free Trade or Not Free Trade," looks at the substantive and organizational bases of free trade, the most basic underlying dynamic of the globalization process. The chapter begins with an examination of the institutional history of creating an international mechanism to support and enforce free trade, beginning with the 1940s advocacy of an International Trade Organization and ending in the 1990s with the World Trade Organization. The case then examines whether moving in this direction was a good idea for the world economy.

The third case, "Debating Globalization," looks at the impact of globalization—among other factors—on the world's fourth most populous country, Indonesia. Prior to the East Asian crisis of 1997, Indonesia was one of the most active Asian participants in globalization, despite having one of the world's most corrupt regimes. When the crisis hit Indonesia in 1997, the corrupt practices came to the fore and made the impact even more severe, including forcing the Suharto regime to resign. In the wake of that experience and related phenomena such as separatist movements in parts of the far-flung archipelago, Indonesia ponders its future. A major element in those deliberations is the relationship between Indonesia and the globalizing economy.

CHAPTER SEVEN

The New Trinity of Globalism

GEOPOLITICS FOR A NEW AGE?

PRÉCIS

The growing prosperity of the early and middle 1990s masked structural problems in the ways in which the global economy was evolving and produced competing "models" of integration into the so-called system of globalization. The euphoria of emerging political democracies in many of the countries joining the global economy was given a sharp jolt in 1997, however, when a financial crisis surfaced in Thailand and rapidly spread throughout the region, even infecting Japan and driving down market values on Wall Street. One major result was the triumph of the so-called American model of economic development over its chief conceptual rival, the Asian model.

This case examines the consequences of the ascendancy of the American model from two aspects. The first is the structure of the American model and the difficulties that acceptance of the American "rules" of economic activity creates for many countries seeking to join the system. The second aspect is the process by which the American regime is imposed and enforced. This process is conceptualized as a "trinity" in which American ideas are to a large extent enforced by the International Monetary Fund on the target countries that compose the third element in the trinity, as well as the impact on private investors.

The nineteenth-century Prussian military strategist and chronicler of the Napoleonic Wars, Carl von Clausewitz, described the preconditions for military success in terms of the relationship between three groups without whose mutual support a successful war

109

effort could not be mounted. The three societal groups were the government, the military (in his time, the army), and the people. Unless all three were of like mind in terms of support for a military effort, such an effort was doomed to fail. He referred to the necessary synergy between the government, army, and the people as a trinity (sometimes called the "Clausewitzian trinity").

The idea of a trinity may well be appropriate to describe another relationship that underlies some of the economic dynamics of international relations for a new century. That dynamic is the spread of the globalizing economy around the world and the desire of increasingly more parts of the world to join the emerging global system. This phenomenon is also known as globalism or globalization. The trinity, in this case, consists of the major elements and aspirants into the system: the United States, the International Monetary Fund (IMF), and those countries of the developing world that have either joined the global economy and want to expand their position in it or that aspire to "membership." Undergirding and providing the economic muscle to implement much of the effort and direction of the trinity is its "silent partner," the providers of private investment capital.

The relationships within the new trinity have significant elements of power involved in them, hence the reference in the subtitle to geopolitics. In essence, the United States, as the predominant economic power in the new economic order, wields considerable influence over global participation in the world economy through the enforcement of what has become known as the "American model" (or Washington consensus) of economic activity: countries that accept and embrace the American way of doing business (in a literal sense) have much greater success in joining the general prosperity than those countries that resist the American model. The nature of this power relationship became particularly apparent in 1997–98 as the global economy responded to the East Asian financial crisis. The existence and severity of that crisis was, especially in the United States, attributed to economic and business practices that were at odds with the American model and which, as a result, the United States insisted must be reformed to avoid a repeat performance.

The IMF enters the equation largely as the enforcers of the Washington consensus. The IMF is one of the charter members of the international economic organization created after World War II to restructure the international economic system in such a way as to avoid the economic crises that contributed to the war (see Chapter 8). The IMF's original role, and still one of its primary tasks, is as a currency stabilizer. Over time, and especially in the 1990s, it has expanded its duties to include being an evaluator of the health of the economies of various countries. In essence, the IMF rates the economic and financial practices of countries and their governments and provides them with ratings in terms of stability and thus attractiveness of a country for investment purposes. A good rating usually means investment will follow; a bad rating means it often will not. The criteria by which these evaluations are made resemble remarkably closely the values underlying the American model. Countries on whom the burden of conforming to IMF standards know full well that this is not a coincidence. Rather, they believe the system effectively reflects American control of the IMF and that the United States uses the IMF rating system to enforce its values in the international arena.

This evolving relationship represents an ongoing systemic problem that is not going away soon. To the extent that the coincidence of interests of the United States and the IMF produce burdens that developing countries must endure if they are to become active participants in the global economy, it will also remain a source of controversy and of resentment about the heavy-handedness of the United States in its role as the remaining superpower in the world.

The rest of this chapter will be devoted to exploring this new trinity, including the impact of IMF-enforced policies on developing countries that have evolved through the experience of the 1990s. We will begin by examining the nature of the problem, looking briefly at the evolution of globalism, the crisis in East Asia that brought the problem to a head in the late 1990s, and the competing American and Asian models of financial affairs. The evolution of the case to this point will serve as context for assessing the current status of the problem, focusing on the ways in which the American model influences the current problem and the controversy surrounding the role of the IMF. We will conclude with some assessment of how the controversy will likely evolve. Included in this discussion will be some assessment of the limits of the trinity in ordering the globalizing economy, thanks in no small measure to the activities of independent multinational corporations (MNCs) and other private investors. These private entities are in general agreement with the values of the members of the trinity, whose contributions provide the economic "grease" to make the trinity's gears mesh.

NATURE OF THE PROBLEM

The current condition of the globalizing economy is a product of forces that, for the most part, emerged in the 1980s and 1990s, although they can be traced back even further to the 1970s. There have been two primary lines of development that have combined to create this emergence. Technological advances have made possible a much more integrated and interactive economic condition than was heretofore possible, thereby making globalization physically possible. The adoption of policy emphases by the major economic powers has allowed the technological advances to be exploited in a global manner consistent with an underlying economic philosophy that has become the driving economic force in the world economy. All of this development has been remarkably rapid, changing, and fluid, resulting in global activity without a detailed framework within which to monitor the resulting floods of economic interaction. This amorphous nature of the system, in turn, came to a very public head with the economic crisis that centered itself in East Asia and created the perceived need for creating a uniformity in the global system that would minimize these kinds of problems in the future. How the international economic system evolved to the point of crisis and how the crisis stimulated the operation of the globalism trinity provides the heart of the case.

Technological and Policy Roots

The process of creating what is widely recognized as an integrating world economy is not a unique occurrence of the contemporary period. A century ago, there was the widespread belief in the emergence of economic interdependence among the major powers (principally in Europe and North America), which had produced a prosperity and economic interconnectedness that would, among other things, make war between them impossible or unthinkable. That vision, of course, was dashed by World War I, and many analysts who counsel caution about the current globalization point to the similarity between optimistic predictions about the salutary effects of global economic integration in 1900 and 2000.

No two periods of history are ever identical, and so the analogy between 1900 and 2000 would not be perfect under any circumstances. There are several significant ways in which twenty-first century globalization is different from its 1900 variant. First, economic integration in 1900 was limited to the most advanced parts of the world, notably the European countries that controlled much of the rest of the world through their colonial empires. Noncolonized but developing regions like Latin America were largely excluded from the process. The current round of globalization, on the other hand, is truly global; while some parts of the world are not as deeply involved as others (Africa, for instance), there are countries participating in and benefiting from the process in all parts of the world.

Second, the spread of the global economy today is proceeding in the absence of ideological division in the system. In 1900, Europe was still divided between authoritarian monarchies and empires and democratic states. This produced less similarity of outlook among countries, and eventually gave them enough to disagree about to engage in world war. Today, there are still remaining authoritarian regimes, but their number is dwindling and most are outside the globalizing economy (China, of course, is the notable exception). Instead, the overwhelmingly preponderant political ideology today is democracy, and democracy and economic advancement seem to be related to one another and to result in more peace and stability (a proposition discussed in Chapter 3 on the democratic peace). The fact that so many of the participants are political democracies, of course, also means they rely on popular consent in decision making on economic matters. Third, there was very little institutional coordination of economic activity in 1900, whereas today there is a robust nexus of international organizations like the IMF to provide a stabilizing force unavailable a century ago. Fourth, this round of globalization is occurring as part of the technological revolution that began in the 1960s and beyond and without which the globalizing economy as we know it would be impossible.

The Role of Technology. The great advances in technology that have emerged over the past one-third century or so have been the necessary preconditions for developing a truly global economic structure. Most of us now take these advances for granted, as if they have always been there. They have not, and their emergence has made the global economy possible.

Consider two economic possibilities present in the contemporary environment that were impossible as little as twenty years ago. One is the globalization of financial markets. Investors around the world can buy and sell stocks twenty-four hours a day by virtue of electronic access to stock markets around the globe. These transactions can involve the electronic movement of enormous amounts of capital instantaneously and without the ability of sovereign governments to interfere with, or in some cases even monitor, the volume and nature of transactions. This ability, in turn, creates an increased level of interest and concern about the quality of economic activity that is occurring worldwide. The interest of potential investors translates into a desire for accurate information about what is going on in national economies that forms much of the need for monitoring by impartial experts like the IMF. The fact that many investors rely on the IMF's assessment of a country's economic soundness provides much of the leverage the IMF enjoys with developing countries fearful a negative rating will cost them investment capital. It also means that private penetration of national economies by governments and especially private firms can occur routinely and create internationalization quite unthinkable before the electronic revolution.

The other example is the internationalization of production. This occurs in two ways. One is the movement of firms into countries with a favorable economic climate (low wages, favorable tax structures, etc.) to manufacture goods and produce services at lower prices than would be possible domestically. Apparel and toys are notably productive industries for this phenomenon at the lower end of the product chain, and Indian telemarketers demonstrates the service side of this phenomenon. The other method of internationalization occurs in the manufacture of complex products like automobiles and electronics. In this case, it is commonplace for multinational firms to contract in several countries for components of their products, which are then assembled elsewhere and sold at yet other locations.

These examples are no more than the tips of the iceberg. They represent phenomena that would have been quite impossible to imagine or implement before the telecommunications revolution. Buying stock in Tokyo requires instantaneous electronic access to the Tokyo stock exchange, subcontracting the sewing of shirts in China requires oversight and transportation capabilities that would have bee quite inconceivable at the turn of the last century, and coordinating the manufacture and transport of the parts necessary to build a sport-utility vehicle requires enormous electronic computing and communications capacity to ensure all the parts are at the right places at the right times.

The Policy Element. The technological revolution made the emergence of the globalizing economy physically possible, but it by no means made it inevitable. Harnessing economic forces to technological possibility required an additional element, the adoption of a policy framework wherein those possibilities could be maximized. The major elements of that policy framework turned out to be the removal of major restrictions on capitalist entrepreneurship within the major countries of the world, and the adoption of a global economic system that facilitated the interactions of economies of the world's countries. These two developments are sequential results of the 1980s and 1990s, although they have philosophical and policy antecedents in the 1970s and before. While the distinctions that will follow will be stated more clearly and more precisely than the messiness of real-world interactions, they are broadly illustrative of forces at work in the globalizing economy.

The 1980s was the decade when capitalist empowerment blossomed. With the battle between socialist and capitalist economics moving toward the total victory of capitalism following the collapse of communism, the unleashing of capitalist dynamics had two principal, influential proponents on either side of the Atlantic Ocean. Their messages were by no means original, but their ceaseless advocacy was influential in promoting change. In the United States, President Ronald W. Reagan campaigned on his slogan of "getting government off the people's back," and took steps to do so in the area of economic activity. In Great Britain, Prime Minister Margaret Thatcher led the charge, arguing the need for promoting capitalist activity through the TINA (There Is No Alternative) principle.

The initiative associated with Reagan and Thatcher had two major thrusts. One of these was *deregulation*, the systematic removal of restrictions on the way private companies did business. A chief target of deregulation was something called "industrial policy," the idea that the private sector and government should cooperate in setting economic priorities (some of which would be financed by government through things like research contracts). To the Reaganites, industrial policy was just the kind of governmental monkey to remove from private enterprise's back. This thrust was sharply at odds with the Japanese policy of extensive government intrusion in the economy that was widely credited with fueling the "economic miracle" of the 1950s–1980s but which came under fire in the 1990s. Other examples include removing restrictions on the price of airline tickets and deregulating long-distance telephone rates and providers.

The other emphasis was *privatization*, removing the government from performing certain economic tasks and turning these over to private enterprise. The idea behind this initiative was that private enterprises would provide the same goods and services at better quality and for lower prices than could government monopolies or regulated industries. Removing the long-distance telephone monopoly given to AT&T and thus creating a competitive long-distance industry is one example.

At the time, these trends were controversial, and as these principles are applied around the world to other national economies as part of the prerequisites for joining the global economy, they have met with varying degrees of resistance. When generally applied in Britain and especially the United States, they had an apparently dramatic effect on economies that had been suffering. During the early 1980s, the American economy was broadly believed to be in decline, but subsequently the economy revived dramatically. While one can (and economists do) debate how much the Reagan-inspired reforms had to do with this resurgence, the two phenomena certainly did coincide. What was left was to wed the fruits of technological possibility to policies that would allow the new system to go global.

If the 1980s witnessed the victory of the major elements of the economic philosophy of Adam Smith (whose *The Wealth of Nations* is considered the "bible" of capitalism), the 1990s was the decade when the basic ideas of David Ricardo, who in 1817 wrote *Principles of Political Economy and Taxation,* became relevant. The heart of Ricardo's theory of economics was the principle of *comparative advantage,* upon which he based his advocacy of free trade. The idea of comparative advantage was that producers should be encouraged to produce whatever they could produce at the lowest price and highest quality, and that those who could not compete should move their activities to areas where they did have a comparative advantage. On a global scale, interpretations of the Ricardian philosophy argue the result would be production and distribution to the maximum benefit of all.

While Ricardo's ideas may have been abstract and incapable of implementation in the early nineteenth century, the implications and applications of something like comparative advantage could occur in the 1990s. The technological revolution had made global commerce possible, and President William J. Clinton arose as the latest oracle of free trade, an idea with a long history in the United States (as discussed in Chapter 8). The heart of free trade is the progressive elimination of barriers to trade between countries, thereby allowing, at least in theory, for goods produced globally with the highest quality and lowest cost to move freely to market. Free trade advocacy became an international movement through mechanisms like the Asia-Pacific Economic Cooperation (APEC), an association of Pacific Rim countries, and the World Trade Organization (WTO). As developing countries in particular adopted the banner of free trade and began making their economies attractive to the form of capitalism advocated in the West, the globalizing economy took off.

The road to a global economy has not been without its dangers and pitfalls. To become a full-fledged "member" of the movement, countries have been required to adopt both capitalist principles and free trade and to adapt their economies to the dictates of both principles. This has been easier for some countries than others, depending on how closely the structures of their economies resembled those of the capitalist developed world—and especially the United States—how willing they were to make the associated changes, how well equipped they were physically and philosophically to undergo westernization, and how willing and able they were to use influxes of foreign direct investment from private sources. The amount and trauma of change was masked by the sheer momentum of change and prosperity associated with the first half of the "go-go-1990s." The bubble burst (literally!) in 1997 with the emergence of an economic crisis that began in Asia and threatened to spread worldwide.

The East Asian Crisis of 1997–98

The East Asian financial crisis was a complex set of phenomena that began in 1997 and spread throughout the region. It is difficult to generalize what caused it to occur and run its course, because it affected diverse countries of greatly varying size and economic structure differently. This complexity and restraints on space mean we can only speak generally about the crisis. Having said that, the financial crisis in Asia was basically the result of the globalizing economy growing too rapidly without an agreed framework of operating principles and rules to regulate its growth and to ensure that the system would remain stable.

It began in Thailand, where the local currency, the *baht*, collapsed on local and world markets. The collapse meant steep devaluation of the currency so that savings were worth much less than before and the number of *bahts* necessary to purchase goods rose sharply, all with negative impacts on the Thai population. The ensuing panic quickly spread regionally to Indonesia, Malaysia, and on to Hong Kong, South Korea, and even Japan. Much of the original crisis has been attributed to runaway current account deficits (the sum of trade deficits and the interest payments on foreign loans) that either could not be serviced or that could only be met with devalued currency that was worth only a fraction of its former value. It stopped when the contagion reached Wall Street, which experienced a one-quarter drop in the Dow-Jones, but quickly rebounded and stabilized within months.

It was not the first time in memory that the modern international economic system had gone into convulsions, and the lessons of the previous crises would be applied to correcting those aspects of the system that had contributed to the Asian problem. In 1982, an insolvency crisis had occurred in a number of Latin American countries, caused by excessive and often imprudent international borrowing that left several states on the verge of defaulting on their loans, mostly to private banks. After rescheduling and forgiveness of some of the loans, the lesson for the international economic system was to tighten criteria for foreign lending in the future. In 1994, the "peso crisis" in Mexico created the precedent for international intervention in the form of a massive bailout (American loan guarantees) tied to internal reform in Mexico. Although not international in nature, the American savings and loan (S&L) crisis of 1985, when a number of these savings institutions collapsed, mostly because of imprudent lending not open to public scrutiny, resulted in calls for more effective government regulation of the financial sector and improved means to protect investors. All these lessons would be applied in Asia and form part of the evolving system of which the IMF is a prominent part of the enforcement mechanism.

Whose fault was the crisis? As one might imagine in a situation where multiple billions of dollars were lost in a variety of countries, there was no shortage of finger pointing. The international financial community placed the blame primarily on the countries of East Asia for mismanagement of their economies. The governments of the affected countries, in turn, pointed the finger back at the West, arguing the real problem was the provision of foreign direct investment (FDI) in quantities excessive to needs and abilities to absorb it, what is known as overheating. Needless to say, both sides had a point.

The countries of East Asia clearly contributed to the problem. During the 1990s, there had been a debate of sorts about the virtues of the so-called Asian model of development versus the American model (or, as noted, the Washington consensus). A central difference between the two was that in several of the Asian countries, financial dealings were carried out in private, beyond the purview of the public and, for that matter, independent government regulators. This opacity, as it is known, was justified by traditional Asian cultural practices such as deference to elders, but its effect was to promote practices that are viewed in the West as corruption. Part of the fallout of the crisis was the demand for more public access to the financial sector, what is known as transparency.

One of the most blatant practices arising from opacity was "crony capitalism." In this arrangement, government officials would collaborate with bankers and entrepreneurs to decide how investment capital should be used, usually to the personal advantage of the groups making the decisions. One of the areas where this happened most blatantly was in real estate development. With a seemingly endless supply of foreign investment flowing in, large amounts were spent developing real estate, notably building huge, glittering office buildings that are a staple of the skylines of many Asian cities. In the process, the government officials authorizing the construction, the bankers making the loans, and the entrepreneurs doing the building would skim a little off the top for themselves. If one were a member of such an operation, the benefits were enormous.

The consequence in a number of places were so-called real estate "bubbles." Large office buildings would be commissioned and constructed, providing jobs and prosperity during the building stage but with little concern with who would occupy them, pay rent, and thus provide the revenue to repay the loans made to build them. The result has been a number of virtually unoccupied high-rise buildings in the region, where there are insufficient renters who can afford the rents necessary to pay off the loans and the builders are forced to default on their loans or the loans become nonperforming (which means that loan payments have not been made for a long period of time), thereby bursting the bubble. Those profiting during construction generally keep the money they received, and the financial institutions and their customers are left holding the bag.

Western countries and their own financial institutions have their share of the blame as well, mainly because of their contribution to the overheating of Asian economies that inflated the bubbles that eventually burst. Convinced of the growth potential in the region, lenders convinced themselves that there was a virtually endless amount of investment that could be absorbed, and that investors would reap substantial returns on their investments. The problem was that this belief created an excess amount of capital in some places, and in the zeal to utilize it, some honest (as well as some dishonest) mistakes in investing the money were made. There was simply more money available than there were productive uses for it. To make matters worse, when the crisis began to become evident, a number of foreign investors panicked and withdrew their investments, making the subsequent crashes of national economies worse than they probably would have been otherwise.

The Clash of Models

The Asian crisis brought to a head a debate that had been going on for a decade or more about which model of development was most appropriate in the new globalizing economy, the Western (which is to say American) model or the Asian (largely Japanese) model. As long as the global economy was growing positively and the prosperity was general, the debate was academic and did not seem to require resolving. When the crash occurred, one of its victims was the viability of the Asian model.

At its heart, the debate between advocates of the two models was about how to do business. Advocates of the Asian model pointed to the Japanese economic "miracle" and the derivative economic booms in other Asian countries (South Korea, Taiwan, China, Hong Kong, for instance) as evidence of the superiority of their way of doing business, *at least for them.* The heart of their contention was based in the opacity of economic activity, which was justified by cultural practices in many Asian countries. This collaboration among the principal actors in the economic system could result in substantial cooperation between government, industry, and the financial system. At the worst, the result could be the kind of corruption suggested already; but at best, the system had apparently fueled the Japanese economic miracle, reason enough to emulate and advocate the model.

In the Japanese case, the chief symbol of this collaboration was the Japanese Ministry of International Trade and Industry (MITI). The major mission of MITI was to coordinate the efforts of the major industrial sectors of the Japanese economy (electronics and automobiles, for instance) in order to maximize the trade potential of Japanese manufacturers in a manner remarkably similar to what was called industrial policy in the United States. This system appeared to be highly successful in the 1970s and 1980s and particularly in contrast to the situation in the United States, whose economy was stagnating during the same period. The MITI-led system was so successful that early in his first term, President Reagan suggested the creation of a Department of International Trade and Industry (DITI) for the United States, an idea he quickly jettisoned when he was told by aides that promoting industrial policy hardly constituted getting government off the people's backs.

In retrospect, the Japanese model probably received more credit than it deserved. MITI direction was fine as long as the economy was growing anyway and as long as Japan's chief competitor, the United States, was not yet making the structural adjustments to regain primacy. MITI direction stifled inter-firm competition within Japan and made mistakes, notably directing the Japanese electronic giants to adopt the wrong technology (analog rather than digital) for high-definition television (HDTV).

By the early 1990s, reform in the United States was producing a new and more robust American model. Part of the new model was based on the American experience in the S&L crisis, the outgrowth of which were reforms in the laws governing financial institutions, principally intended to make financial dealings more transparent and thus available to potential private investors, as well as guarantees to protect investor funds. The United States economy was booming under the new model, at a time when the Japanese economy, for a variety of reasons, was stagnating and even declining.

When the crisis broke in 1997 and spread through 1998, it became evident that a primary difference between the two models was that the Asian variant permitted, even encouraged, corruption and the misuse of investment funds. Because the Japanese system was no longer the "poster child" of economic efficiency and prosperity, cultural arguments were the remaining pillar of the Asian model, and the argument that Asians were simply different was insufficient.

APPLYING THE PAST TO THE FUTURE

The outcome of the Asian crisis provides a kind of case experience about how the international economic system may evolve in the future. Two primary lessons appear to have been learned. One is that a set of values must uniformly underlie the system and insure financial honesty (the American model). At the same time, the model must be enforced to ensure investor confidence, a role largely assigned to the IMF in the developing world. The result is the globalization trinity. This emergence represents an advancement of sorts because it will make international economic activity more uniform and predictable in those places that choose to accept the rules and become part of the system. Potential providers of foreign direct investment, for instance, can assume that certain rules and procedures are in place that will provide protection for their investments, making states that have adopted the model attractive. Conversely, countries that reject the model, or, more often, want to adopt some but not all the rules will find themselves less attractive in the competition for foreign investment, either of funds or of the location of industries in their countries.

The triumph of the American model provides the United States with considerable leverage in shaping the evolution of the developing economic order. As might be expected, this manifestation of American leadership and power is embraced in some quarters and opposed in others on grounds as emotional as American cultural imperialism and arrogance. Globalism itself is not a universally accepted value. Some people (and countries) do not benefit directly and have manifested their opposition through large, intense demonstrations such as the disruption of the World Trade Organization (WTO) meeting in Seattle in 1999. At the same time, American "soft power" (the appeal and attractiveness of American ideals) is a powerful force worldwide, and especially in many of the countries seeking to join the general prosperity. Inevitably, some of the animus that resides in developing countries about the imposition of the American model is directed at the third side of the trinity, the IMF, which helps impose the American model.

The American Model Applied

What we call the American model or Washington consensus is the composite of a set of economic practices. Schramm summarizes the dynamics: "The Washington consensus focuses on macroeconomic issues such as finance and trade, along with general institution building. Nations are urged to create good banking systems, reasonable interest and exchange rates, and stable tax structures. They are expected to privatize, deregulate, and invest in infrastructure and basic education." To the extent target countries comply, they make themselves attractive to private investors who provide the capital to energize growth.

While there is no public, official list of requirements or practices a country must adopt to conform to the model, *New York Times* foreign affairs writer Thomas L. Friedman, in his 1999 book, *The Lexus and the Olive Tree*, lays out in detail a representative list of the evolving rules of the system. Using the rhetorical device of putting on the "golden straitjacket" to depict conformance to these rules, he lays out the requirements for participation in the globalization system that arise from the American model.

The golden straitjacket is a list of criteria that countries must meet to make themselves attractive to outside investors who provide the capital that is the necessary underpinning for prosperity and thus participation in the global economy. This "electronic herd" of investors, as Friedman calls them, is composed of the "faceless stock, bond, and commodity traders" who, by controlling large amounts of investment capital, can make or break the developmental prospects for target countries. The electronic herd does not, by and large, have detailed expertise on the workings of the economies of all the countries of the world, but they do know what makes an economy attractive or unattractive to them. To make assessments about whether to invest their clients' funds, the herd must rely on the ratings of economies by private and public firms that specialize in rating economies. Amongst those organizations with the most prestige and access to information, of course, is the IMF.

While the IMF does not necessarily use the literal criteria of the golden straitjacket in its assessments of countries, the list of sixteen criteria is representative and provides a good glimpse at the character of the economic conditions that are demanded. As suggested, the criteria can be linked to the dual emphases of deregulation and privatization and free trade.

Ten of the criteria flow directly from deregulation and privatization. They are:

1. "Making the private sector the primary engine of its economic growth" (e.g., reducing practices such as industrial policy);

2. "Maintaining a low rate of inflation and price stability" (e.g., creating a stable macro-economic environment);

3. "Shrinking the size of its state bureaucracy" (e.g., reducing the cost of government);

4. "Maintaining as close to a balanced budget as possible" (e.g., reducing competition between government and the private sector over capital to borrow);

5. "Privatizing state-owned industries and utilities" (e.g., making these sectors competitive);

6. "Deregulating capital markets" (e.g., facilitating the unfettered flow of capital);

7. "Deregulating its economy to promote as much domestic competition as possible" (e.g., removing subsidies for state-owned enterprises or eliminating them altogether);

8. "Eliminating government corruption, subsidies, and kickbacks as much as possible" (e.g., making the system more honest and above board);

9. "Opening its banking and telecommunications systems to private ownership and competition" (e.g., promoting transparency); and

10. "Allowing its citizens to choose from an array of competing pension options and foreign-run pension and mutual funds" (e.g., reducing reliance on archaic government or privately run pension systems that stifle flexibility and limit individual investment choices).

The straitjacket also contains six criteria that are associated with the promotion of free trade. They are:

1. "Eliminating or lowering tariffs on imported goods" (e.g., reducing barriers to free trade);

2. "Removing restrictions on foreign investment" (e.g., cutting down barriers of foreign direct investment);

3. "Getting rid of quotas and domestic monopolies" (e.g., reducing artificial barriers to trade);

4. "Increasing exports" (e.g., specializing in goods produced at comparative advantage);

5. "Making its currency convertible" (e.g., removing restrictions on currency exchange to promote capital movement); and

6. "Opening its industries, stock, and bond markets to direct foreign ownership and investment" (e.g., ending economic isolationism).

Adoption or movement toward all these policies constitutes acceptance of the rules of the global economy.

Adopting the straitjacket in its entirety can be difficult, even traumatic, for countries whose traditional practices—such as high levels of secretiveness in business transactions that breed what Westerners regard as corruption—vary most from the rules. Some of these changes, moreover, have political or social bases that make necessary reform unpopular and thus difficult for governments to enact, in which case they resist, usually with negative economic effects.

The trauma is not limited to poor states outside the global economy. Take two prominent examples. China's booming economy has a giant albatross hanging around its neck in the form of a large number of *state-owned enterprises* (SOEs) that are holdovers from the Maoist period, as noted in Chapter 1. For China to put on the entire strait-jacket, the SOEs clearly should be jettisoned and replaced by more efficient private enterprises. But the government, which has been reasonably economically enlightened on most issues and recognizes the economic liability the SOEs represent, continues to balk at dismantling the inefficient SOEs. Why? The answer is the SOEs serve other purposes. For one thing, a number of them are owned by the Chinese military, which uses receipts from the SOEs to pay for part of the defense budget and to buy prestige for ranking officers. The regime needs the support of the military, which insists on maintaining the SOEs. At the same time, the SOEs provide pensions for their workers. Because China has no real social security system, putting the SOEs out of business would require creating a "social net" or leaving a large number of pensioners without support, a politically unsustainable idea.

Japan has a parallel problem. It has been a hallmark of the Japanese system that the bond between employees and companies is a lifelong proposition, where employee loyalty is rewarded by "cradle to grave" support by the company. The bond has been credited with contributing to superior Japanese productivity. But as the Japanese workforce grows older and the need for flexibility has become a characteristic of modern economies, this virtue is becoming a vice. The lifelong bond means companies have considerable sunk costs and obligations that cut into productivity, and it also means that "downsizing" segments of the workforce in certain declining industries (which has been argued as one of the reasons for American resurgence) is made very difficult by the commitments firms have made to their employees.

The IMF as Enforcer

The International Monetary Fund has a central role in enforcing the system that is represented by the rules of the golden straitjacket. As already noted, the relationship between the United States government and the IMF, while informal beyond U.S. leadership as a member, is close, if for no other reason than that the economic philosophies of both are similar. This should be relatively unsurprising; the IMF (and World Bank) are located in downtown Washington a short walk from the White House, and many of the same U.S. investors move back and forth between Wall Street and either the U.S. government or the IMF.

The IMF influences the evolving system in two basic ways. First, it loans money to countries that are caught in economic crises. As analyst David Hale puts it, the IMF is "the global lender of last resort during liquidity crunches." Thus, when insolvency is threatened, the IMF can make loans that will recreate some underpinning of support for a currency until the crisis passes. This is a major role it played in the East Asian crisis and represents its traditional role in stabilizing the international economic system. Second, the IMF dispenses economic advice to distressed countries. The advice it renders is often less than palatable, but the IMF can offer it more candidly than could, say, the United

States government, because as an international organization the IMF is more independent and nonpartisan. Countries that ignore IMF advice, however, are likely to get low ratings on their economic situation from the organization, which can scare away investors who rely on the IMF ranking. In effect, the IMF has money to lend and can influence the lending of others. It is a potent combination. The fact that the criteria it uses to rate economies closely parallels the American-based straitjacket adds to the controversy it raises when it seeks to influence governments to change their financial policies.

The wielding of IMF power has led to criticism of the organization. Although different critics draw different lists, the major criticisms can be condensed into three complaints. The most fundamental criticism of the IMF is that it has outstripped its mandate and assumed a role for which it was not designed. When the organization was created as part of the Bretton Woods system of international economic organizations after World War II, its major purpose was currency stabilization by promoting and supporting a system of fixed exchange rates pegged to the U.S. dollar. When the dollar was floated in 1971, that rationale faded, and the IMF turned to helping countries cope with temporary shortages of foreign exchange and more sustained trade deficits through granting IMF credits to shaky systems. In the 1990s, that role expanded even further, leading to the second criticism.

The second critique of the IMF is that it now includes major intrusions into national economies, a role that far supercedes its original mandate and brings it into direct conflict with some of its members. The IMF now places more emphasis on imposing major structural and institutional reforms with very strict adherence policies that must be followed if a country is to get help from the IMF, including its "seal of approval" for lending by private investors. Critics such as Martin Feldstein go a step further, accusing the organization of a kind of "cookie cutter" approach in its reviews. He maintains the IMF makes essentially the same kind of recommendations in all countries regardless of their individual situations: a macroeconomic policy of higher taxes, reduced spending, and high interest rates, for instance. These austerity policies often create short-term hardships for the populations on which they are imposed that make bad situations politically worse for regimes already under some political siege from the crises that brings the IMF to their door in the first place. These adverse effects have made some countries wary of the globalization process.

The austerity policies imposed by the IMF have a number of purposes, one of which forms the third criticism. One reason for imposing burdens is to assist foreign lenders in recovering their investments when the domestic economy undergoes trauma (sometimes at the expense of domestic investors being able to recover their own assets from failed financial institutions, one might add). The IMF's rationale for placing emphasis on recovering investor funds is that if investors run a great risk of losing their money if they invest it in developing economies, those funds will dry up or be diverted to less risky prospects.

The critics see it differently. Beyond the fact that the emphasis creates additional suffering in the target country is the matter of what is known as *moral hazard*. What this means is that if investors know they will be compensated regardless of the quality of their investments, they are in effect encouraged to make investments they might not make if their chances of losing their money was greater. Although it clearly is not the IMF's intent to encourage risky investment, the very generous safety net provided by the IMF creates this moral hazard that could lead to even worse investments with even more tragic economic consequences. Moreover, the practice clearly aligns the IMF with the "fat cat" investors of the developed world—and especially the United States—thereby reinforcing the suspicion that the IMF in operation is little more than an appendage of the American government.

The Role of Investors

The globalism trinity would be little more than an academic exercise were it not for the impact of corporations, individuals, and other private entities like banks on whom the trinity's actions have direct impact. The purveyors of the bromides that compose the Washington consensus—the elements of the straitjacket—provide advice that is often politically and economically unpalatable to the target countries at which the advice is directed. Why take advice that hurts?

The answer, of course, is that taking the advice makes countries attractive to those who can provide the foreign direct investment without which economic expansion is impossible. The United States and the IMF may provide a fraction of the capital necessary for development, but the vast majority of it comes from private sources motivated by investment and profits from that investment. In many cases, these investors do not possess the detailed knowledge about specific foreign economies to make totally informed judgments about where to (and where not to) put their money, and thus they must rely on advice from sources like the IMF (as well as private firms specializing in these matters). Target countries understand that private investment capital is the life blood without which development is unlikely to occur and that much of that capital's availability is based on acceptance of IMF advice. In those circumstances, target countries realize they have little choice but to accept IMF Washington consensus-based advice, whether they like it or not.

CONCLUSION

The subtitle raises the question of whether the process of expanding participation in the globalizing economy represents a new form of geopolitics for the post–Cold War world. In a sense, of course, using economic might and incentives to gain what countries want has always been one of the geopolitical tools that states have employed. The "economic instrument of power" has always been part of the foreign policy "quiver" of those states with powerful economies. Are things any different now?

In some ways, they clearly are. For one thing, the globalizing economy *is* a more pervasive phenomenon than was the older system of international economics. More countries participate in the global system, levels of trade are up everywhere, the number of nonparticipants that desire "membership" is on the increase, and foreign investment is increasingly worldwide. What is also different is that much of the dynamic for this increased penetration of world economies is by private investors and firms. If one of the characteristics of geopolitics is its association with promoting the policies of states (which has traditionally been the case), then a major geopolitical question surrounds whether states can sufficiently control economic matters to harness them to national ends. The promotion of the American model through IMF assistance in fashioning the rules of which the golden straitjacket is one depiction is a geopolitical application of American economic power, but if private investors did not accept judgments based on these rules in making investment decisions, their impact would be much more constrained.

A second evidence of the greater difference of this round of globalization is its universality. Thanks to influences as diverse as global television and student exchange programs, there are advocates of joining the globalization system in virtually every corner of the world, and this fact creates in all countries a level of demand for the fruits of the system. In many places, there are also opponents, who mostly want to cling to the virtues of an earlier era or who are either frightened by the prospect of change or see the consequences as undesirable (see Chapter 9). But there is also a growing class, usually relatively young and well educated, wearing western clothes and equipped with cell phones and laptop computers, eager to lace up the straitjacket and join the prosperity.

A third difference is the greater impact that the globalization system has on the behavior of countries in other policy areas. In 1999, for instance, China began saber rattling against Taiwan when its elections threatened to produce a new president committed to total political independence of the island from the mainland. Before globalization, this might have become an important military crisis, but the concern quickly dissipated. The likelihood of Chinese military action was dismissed on decidedly nonmilitary bases: the fear that such action would interrupt the considerable level of Taiwanese private investment in the Chinese economy (estimated in the $30–40 billion range) and fear that there would be economic repercussions, especially the suspension of trade with the United States that is a vital part of the Chinese economy.

Finally, there is the unique position of the United States in the evolving system. The enormous economic strength of the United States, the fact that the new system is based heavily on American economic and political values, and the open desire of many to emulate the United States (at least materially) place the United States in the central position in the new system. The fact that the United States is able, at least informally, to enforce its values and to "force" other countries to adopt its rules as enforced by instruments like the IMF produces an enormous responsibility and geopolitical presence. That position also creates resentment in some quarters as the new trinity permeates more and more of the global system. The major question is whether a new geopolitics based on this new trinity is a permanent or transient phenomenon. The terrorist attacks of September 11, 2001, at least temporarily pushed globalization to the back burner. The final question is whether it will return in as vibrant a form as it had in the 1990s.

STUDY/DISCUSSION QUESTIONS

1. The technological revolution was a necessary but not sufficient condition to produce the global economy. What political phenomena were necessary to create that economy? How do they create a changed environment?

2. The East Asian crisis had a major part in the evolution of the globalizing economy toward the model represented by the Washington consensus. Explain that contribution and the direction it helped impel the evolving system.

3. Thomas L. Friedman's golden straitjacket creates a kind of operational checklist of what states and regions must do to join the globalization system. What are the principal elements of the straitjacket? Does adoption create a homogenized system where all members are essentially the same? Is that good or bad?

4. Some countries and areas resist parts of the straitjacket, as the Chinese and Japanese examples suggested. What kinds of countries feel impelled to accept or reject the straitjacket?

5. This case is based on the relationship between the parts of the globalization trinity (the U.S. government, the IMF, and developing countries). Explain and assess how this relationship works, and especially the relationship between the U.S. government and the IMF and why this creates some level of resentment within countries that aspire to join the global economy.

6. A major characteristic of the new global system is the extent to which it is "privatized" and not controlled by governments. What are the consequences of privatization? Are they good or bad? What is the crucial role of private investors in the process?

7. Is the globalization system the geopolitics of the post–Cold War world? Or is it just a further element in the calculation of geopolitics? What are the consequences of your conclusions for international relations?

READING/RESEARCH MATERIAL

Feldstein, Martin S. "Refocusing the IMF." *Foreign Affairs* 77, 2 (March/April 1998), 20–33.

Friedman, Thomas L. *The Lexus and the Olive Tree: Understanding Globalization.* New York: Farrar, Straus, Giroux, 1999.

Hale, David D. "The IMF, More Than Ever." *Foreign Affairs* 77, 6 (November/December 1998), 7–13.

Kapur, Devesh. "The IMF: A Cure or a Curse?" *Foreign Policy* 111 (Summer 1998), 114–131.

Keohane, Robert O., and Joseph S. Nye Jr. "Globalism: What's New?" *Foreign Policy* 118 (Spring 2000), 104–119.

———. *Power and Interdependence.* 2nd ed. Glenview, IL: Scott Foresman/Little Brown, 1989.

Luttwak, Edward. "From Geopolitics to Geo-Economics: Logic of Conflict, Grammar of Commerce." *National Interest* 20 (Summer 1990), 17–24.

Schramm, Carl J. "Building Entrepreneurial Economies." *Foreign Affairs* 83, 4 (July/August 2004), 104–115.

Snow, Donald M. *The Shape of the Future: World Politics in a New Century.* 3rd ed. Armonk, NY: M. E. Sharpe, 1999.

Spero, Joan Edelman. *The Politics of International Economic Relations.* 4th ed. New York: St. Martin's Press, 1990.

WEB SITES

Overview of the IMF role in the East Asian crisis

Factsheet: The IMF Role in the Asian crisis at
http://www.imf.org/external/np/ext/facts /asia.htm

Leading think tank on economic issues, including trade and globalization

Economic Policy Institute at http://www.epinet.org

Think tank propounding free trade and warning against protectionism

CATO Institute at http://www.freetrade.org

Arguments for and against globalization

The Globalization Guide at http://www.globalisationguide.org

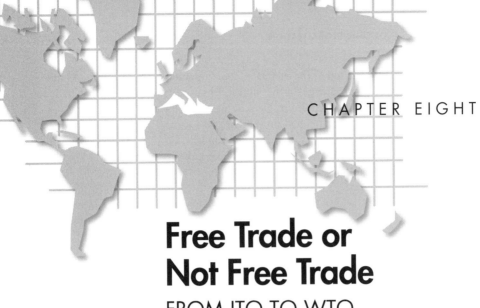

CHAPTER EIGHT

Free Trade or Not Free Trade

FROM ITO TO WTO AND BEYOND

PRÉCIS

Free trade is and for a long time has been a controversial concept, as has its institutionalization in the form of an intergovernmental organization. In this case, we begin by looking at the question of promoting free trade historically, from the early post–World War II advocacy of an International Trade Organization at the Bretton Woods conference through the creation of the World Trade Organization in 1995. As events like massive demonstrations against the WTO in Seattle in 1999 indicate, this institutionalization remains controversial.

Because of this controversy, we then ask the question of whether free trade is a good idea. This in turn leads to breaking the question into two aspects, the desirability of free trade as an idea and phenomenon, and what kind of institutional structure is most desirable for promoting and enforcing free trade. The case concludes by combining the two aspects and comparing them.

Trading goods and services has been one of man's oldest forms of interchange with other peoples and communities. In ancient times, the purpose of trade was generally to acquire goods that either did not grow or could not be produced locally, such as the importation of exotic fabric like silk or spices. As the ability of political communities to span greater distances in shorter periods of time increased, trade expanded both in extent and in terms of what was and was not traded. The modern issue of trade probably congealed over whether to import goods and services that were also produced domestically.

That question is near the top of the agenda in contemporary discussions of trade and is manifested in most disagreements on the subject, from questions of barriers to trade to environmental impacts of importation versus domestic production.

Whether to allow the unfettered movement of goods and services internationally (free trade) or to place restrictions of one kind or another on that flow is a central element in contemporary international relations. The removal of barriers to trade was the centerpiece of the economic globalization movement of the 1990s, one of the engines designed to draw countries into closer collaboration by entwining them in the global prosperity that was burgeoning during that decade. The global economic downturn of the turn of the millennium and the rise of the global war on terrorism has taken some of the luster from the free trade issue and relegated it to a less prominent place on the international political agenda. Yet, while our attention is diverted elsewhere, globalization continues, and proponents and opponents continue to fight over whether to expand or constrict free trade arrangements.

The debate about trade has a long intellectual and political history. The basic poles in the debate have always been between those seeking to expand trade (free traders) and those seeking to restrict trade (protectionists). Nestled between the extremes are those who advocate freer, but not necessarily totally free, trade (who often portray themselves as fair traders). While the industrial revolution was raging in Europe and later North America, the need to nurture nascent industries from outside competition militated toward restriction, largely under the intellectual banner of mercantilism. By the nineteenth and twentieth centuries, the banner of capitalism propelled free trade into the debate. During the period leading to World War II, protectionism ran rampant in a Great Depression–riddled Europe, and economic restrictions were partially blamed for the bloodiest war in human history. The "lessons" of interwar economics, in turn, helped frame the international political debate and its institutionalization, the topics of this case.

There has always been a lively debate in the United States on the issue of trade that has been intertwined with the debate over the extent of American political interaction with the world. Part of the reason for the American Revolution, after all, had to do with restrictions on colonial trading (principally from the port of Boston) by the British, and one of the underlying disagreements between North and South that led to the American Civil War was the southern preference for importing European goods in return for their cotton and the northern preference for high tariffs on imported goods to protect infant northern industries from foreign competitors.

The economic aspect of the debate has been, and is, asymmetrical, so that proponents on one side or the other tend to talk past one another, meaning interchange often devolves into monologues. The arguments for free trade tend to be mainly abstract, impersonal, and macroeconomic. Free trade is said to be beneficial because it unleashes basic economic principles like comparative advantage that make overall economies (national or international) stronger and economic conditions within and between countries more vital. Anti-free trade arguments, on the other hand, tend to be specific, personal, and microeconomic. Cries to restrict trade tend to be posed in terms of the adverse impact that opening up trade opportunities has on individuals. Trade is not about economic theories; it is about people's jobs and livelihoods. Fair traders seek a compromise somewhere between the extremes, advocating selective trade reductions in conformance with the principle of free trade but minimizing negative microeconomic impact.

The argument over textiles illustrates the asymmetry in this debate. To pro-free traders, moving clothing manufacturing overseas, where labor costs are lower, makes perfect economic sense. Consumers benefit from lower clothing prices, the economies of new textile producers are stimulated, which in turn allows them to buy things produced in the United States, and uncompetitive American textile manufacturers redirect their efforts to other production areas where they can compete successfully (produce better products at lower costs). Moreover, all consumers benefit because goods are produced at the lowest possible costs, and the savings are passed along to consumers. Moving the manufacture of clothing overseas, in other words, means Americans can buy their clothes more cheaply than they could from domestic producers with higher labor costs in this labor-intensive industry. In the end, it is a macroeconomic win-win situation with the added benefit of drawing countries closer together, thus promoting greater cooperation and reduced international tension.

From the anti-free trade viewpoint, these abstractions are unconvincing; to them, the effect of moving textile manufacturing overseas is to cost American textile workers their jobs. It is a concern centered on the impact on individuals, not on abstract phenomena. Thus, when free traders extol the removal of barriers and anti-free traders deride that possibility, they are, in a very real sense, not talking about the same thing. In this particular case, fair traders would favor some reduction in barriers to trade, but with limits to minimize individual displacement (scheduled reductions over a period of time, for instance) combined with retraining programs to equip displaced workers to enter alternative industries.

The debate is intensely political at both the domestic and international levels. At the level of American national politics, the asymmetry is reflected between branches of the federal government. Historically, the executive branch of government, more concerned with the overall health of the economy and somewhat more removed from the impact on specific individuals or groups (as opposed to the whole), tends to be more free trade–oriented and macroeconomic. Members of Congress, whose constituents are the people whose jobs are endangered when foreign goods and services are allowed more freely to enter the country, thus tend to be more microeconomic and opposed.

At the international level, the debate tends to get muddled with preferences for the general orientation toward political interactions with the world. Broadly speaking, two positions have dominated the American experience (and that of other countries as well to some extent). *Internationalists* generally advocate a maximum involvement of the United States in the international system; in a world where the United States is the remaining superpower in the system, this means advocacy of the United States playing a prominent leadership role working with other countries. Advocacy of free trade and globalization is a natural extension of that political preference to the economic realm.

The other position, *isolationism*, advocates a much more restrained level of American involvement in the world. This position reached its institutionalized zenith during the period between the world wars, when "splendid isolationism" sought to keep the United States entirely separated from world, and especially European, politics. The belief that the United States could remain aloof from world affairs was, of course, punctured permanently by Pearl Harbor, and its successor ideology, *neoisolationism,* advocates a restricted level of U.S. interaction from the world, but not total rejection of the world outside American boundaries. In its pure form, isolationists are also protectionist, because protectionism limits international economic interactions. This preference is expressed most forcefully in terms of protecting American jobs and industries from foreign intrusion, a sort of America-first advocacy.

The problem with the conjunction of the political and economic positions is that they have never been as compatible in practice as they are in theory. During the first half of the twentieth century, the United States attempted to remain politically isolationist, but at the same time was aggressively internationalist in the economic realm. This theme of participation in the global economy while remaining politically uninvolved goes back to the entreaties of George Washington in his farewell address, where he called for friendly relations with all countries but "permanent alliances" with none. Thomas Jefferson, in his first inaugural address, reflected the same theme, warning against "entangling alliances." The United States, in other words, should be free to trade with all while remaining resolutely neutral politically.

The terms of the debate thus are not purely economic. Pro-trade advocates of the 1990s, for instance, argued that the globalization process of which free trade is an underpinning produces political as well as economic benefits. As noted in Chapter 1, one of the major reasons for promoting trade with China is to draw that country more intimately into the global political system. At the same time, anti-free trade arguments have expanded to include strictly noneconomic concerns ranging from environmental degradation to compromises of sovereignty.

This introduction frames the structure of the case, which has three purposes. The first, and major, purpose is historical, tracing the process whereby free trade has been institutionalized in the international system since the end of World War II. That process has crystallized the principal reasons for advocating and opposing free trade, a discussion of which supports that evolution and is the second purpose of the case. Finally, we will attempt to apply this institutional framework and the positions of the two sides to the current, ongoing debate on the issue.

INSTITUTIONALIZING TRADE

The genesis of the contemporary debate over free trade comes from the period leading to World War II, the traumatic impact of the world's bloodiest war, and the determination to attempt to do a better job than had been done at the end of World War I to restructure the international system so that the situation would not recur. Part of the blame for the war was attributed to economic conditions that had arisen in the 1930s (during the Great Depression) that had produced economic chaos that worsened conditions and made the descent into the maelstrom of global war more likely.

Economic nationalism and protectionism were deemed to be among the chief culprits during the interwar period. As the Great Depression took hold across Europe and North America, governments scrambled to minimize the effects on their own economies and peoples. One way to do this was to attempt to protect national industries from ruinous foreign competition, and the vehicle was the erection of prohibitively high trade barriers to keep foreign goods and services out and thus to keep domestic industries (and the jobs they created) alive. The erection of tariff and other barriers resulted in retaliation and counterretaliation that brought European trade to a virtual standstill. At the same time, currency fluctuations and devaluations became commonplace as a means to prop up failing enterprises. The resulting destabilization was felt especially strongly in Germany, which faced stiff reparations repayment requirements exacted at the Versailles Peace Conference that ended World War I. Unable to meet reparations schedules with foreign exchange from trade that had dried up, the German economy spun out of control as the depression hit that country harder than any other (pictures of Germans literally pushing wheelbarrows full of currency to buy necessities like bread and million mark postage stamps were symbols of the time). Beyond the horrible economic privations that these practices created, they also fueled the animosities and hatreds that made the slide to war easier. In that atmosphere, Adolf Hitler arose, promising, among other things, to restore prosperity.

The process of rebuilding the world after World War II began early during the war, largely through British and American collaboration. The purpose was to ensure that the mistakes made in 1919 were not repeated and that the structure of postwar peace would prevent a recurrence of the war. Politically, this collaboration produced thoroughly internationalist constructs such as the United Nations Charter and the North American Treaty Organization. Economically, it produced a series of agreements to restructure the global economy, a construct known as the Bretton Woods system.

The Bretton Woods System and Free Trade

Encouraged and cajoled by the governments of Great Britain and the United States, representatives of forty-four countries met in the White Mountains resort town of Bretton Woods, New Hampshire, in July 1944 to plan for the postwar economic peace. The site, at the picturesque Washington Hotel at the foot of Mount Washington, was chosen for both its splendor and its isolation (the site was accessible by a single two-lane highway). At Bretton Woods, the conferees hammered out a series of agreements that produced international economic institutions that have endured into the twenty-first century and have become staple parts of the system of globalization.

The conferees agreed that the heart of the 1930s economic problem was protectionism, manifested in such international financial and economic practices as large fluctuations in exchange rates of currencies, chronic balance of payments difficulties experienced by some countries, and prohibitively high tariffs. All of these practices had contributed to restriction of international commerce, and the conferees agreed that a major antidote to these practices was the encouragement of much freer trade among countries. This explicitly free trade preference was held most strongly by the United States delegation to Bretton Woods (the British, seeking to protect the series of preferences for members of the Commonwealth through the Imperial Preference System, sought a more restrained form of trade restriction reduction). This preference, coming from the Roosevelt administration, had some opposition domestically from some conservative members of Congress (a dynamic suggested earlier) and from private organizations like the U.S. Chamber of Commerce (a close ally of American businesses and hence protectionism).

The Bretton Woods process was more successful in confronting some of its priorities than others. Two international organizations were created, the International Monetary Fund (IMF) and the International Bank for Reconstruction and Development (IBRD or World Bank). The IMF was originally chartered to deal with the problem of currency fluctuations by authorizing the granting of credits to shore up weak currencies, thus contributing to economic stabilization. As pointed out in Chapter 7, the IMF has gradually widened its purview to a variety of other economic matters. The World Bank, on the other hand, was to assist in economic stabilization by granting loans originally for reconstruction of war-torn countries, and later for the development of the emerging third world.

The priority of freeing trade did not enjoy as successful a fate. While Bretton Woods produced two organizations, it failed to see the third pillar of its vision institutionalized, an international organization devoted explicitly to the promotion of free trade. Instead, that process became gradual and convoluted, not reaching fruition until the 1990s. The length of time involved is, in important ways, a testimony to the endurance and strength of the anti-free trade position, especially in the United States.

The Road from Bretton Woods to the WTO

Although there was a clear sentiment for the institutionalization of a free trade–promoting international organization at Bretton Woods, there was enough opposition to the idea both internationally (British misgivings about infringements on its Imperial Preference System relationship with the Commonwealth) and domestically to keep such an organization from being part of the Bretton Woods package. That did not mean, however, that there was not active enthusiasm for the creation of an International Trade Organization (ITO).

The problem was that the proposal to create the ITO ran into the familiar ambivalence of American politics as they relate to foreign affairs. For nearly half a century, the United States found itself alternately championing and opposing the creation of an organization to promote free trade, depending on whether free trade or anti-free trade elements held sway in the decision process.

During and shortly after the war, the idea of the ITO largely existed within the executive branch of the American government, and more specifically the U.S. Department of State. When Harry S. Truman succeeded Franklin Delano Roosevelt as president in 1945, he adopted advocacy of the ITO as his own project. The Truman administration took the leadership role in proposing a United Nations Conference on Trade and Development in 1946, a major purpose of which was to draft a charter for the ITO. That proposal was, however, opposed by powerful elements in the U.S. Congress, and as a result, a meeting was held in Geneva, Switzerland, in 1947 to lay out the principles of a General Agreement on Tariffs and Trade (GATT) as an interim, partial solution to the free trade issue. The proposal for GATT was to be a temporary "fix" while the treaty to create the ITO was being honed and perfected. A meeting was scheduled for Havana, Cuba, in 1947 formally to propose the ITO.

Then American domestic politics got in the way. ITO, like other free trade institutions since, would have done two things of varying controversy. The first of these was to provide an institutional basis to promote the reduction of barriers to trade. Although there were objections to the proposal on this basis from protectionists and others, this was the less controversial aspect. The second, and more divisive, purpose was to create an instrument with jurisdiction and authority to enforce trade agreements, including the capability to levy enforceable penalties against sovereign governments. Opponents of ITO and its successors complained that this enforcement provision represented an unwise infringement on American sovereignty, a position that resonated with both opponents and some proponents of the principle of tree trade.

The ITO proposal was undermined by political actions in the United States in 1948. A coalition of powerful elements in Congress led the way. The major elements in this array against the ITO included conservative Republicans backed by protectionist agricultural and manufacturing interests seeking to protect American goods from foreign competition, liberal Democrats who viewed the ITO document as too timid an approach to promoting free trade, and conservatives who feared the sovereignty infringement that ITO enforcement provisions represented.

This Congressional array faced a Truman administration that favored ratification of the ITO statute but which was unwilling to expend scarce political capital in the process. Competing in the foreign policy agenda was the North American Treaty Organization (NATO) proposal. As an initiative to create the first peacetime alliance in American history, NATO was also a controversial concept. The Truman administration reasoned that it could muster support for one or the other of the treaties, and that of the two, NATO was the more critical (the Cold War was heating up at the time). At the same time, 1948 was a presidential election year, and underdog incumbent Truman feared that spirited advocacy of a controversial idea like the ITO could become a negative campaign issue. Thus, the Truman administration backed away from its advocacy of the ITO, and the proposal died. The United States had both enthusiastically endorsed and helped develop the charter for the ITO and then destroyed it, yet another evidence of American ambivalence toward international involvements.

The demise of ITO elevated the GATT to a more prominent and permanent position than had been envisioned by those who had originally proposed it. GATT survived as the banner carrier for international fee trade from 1948 until the WTO came into existence in 1995. Those who opposed free trade in principle or effect were unenthused by the GATT, but felt less threatened by it than by the ITO.

The reason GATT was less objectionable than ITO was that it lacked the second characteristic of the ITO, an enforcement capability. The GATT, in effect, was not an organization at all, but rather a series of negotiating sessions (called "rounds" and normally named after wherever a given round's first session was held) among the sovereign members. The result of these sessions was to create international agreements on different free trade issues, but these were less threatening than the ITO. For one thing, because the GATT was not an organization and thus lacked more than a modest staff, it had no investigating capability. Moreover, the GATT was never granted any enforcement authority, and all of the agreements reached during GATT negotiations had to be ratified by all participating countries before the provisions affected them. Thus, those who feared institutionalizing free trade on sovereignty grounds had little to fear from the GATT process.

Although it lacked the foundation of a permanent international organization, the GATT was not useless. Indeed, the outcomes of the various rounds did produce a series of principles and practices that have been incorporated into the WTO. At heart, the principal thrust of GATT action was centered on the *most-favored nation* (MFN) principle: the idea of providing to all trading partners the same customs and tariff treatment given a country with the greatest trade privilege—the most-favored country. Thus, if one country lowers its tariffs on a particular good to another country, it should extend that same tariff treatment to all GATT members. John Rothgeb argues that the GATT experience can be categorized around four distinct principles flowing from the most-favored-nation precedent. They are: *nondiscrimination* (the promotion of MFN status among all countries regardless of status); *transparency* (the unacceptability of secret trade restrictions and barriers); *consultation and dispute settlement* (resolution of disputes through direct negotiations); and *reciprocity* (the idea that all members should incur balanced obligations).

The last, or Uruguay, round of the GATT included among its proposals the establishment of the World Trade Organization (WTO). In a very real sense, the WTO is the ITO reincarnated, because it combines the two basic elements of the ITO again within a permanent international organization: the promotion of free trade, *and* mechanisms to enforce trade agreements and the legal authority to penalize members of the organization who violate international trade agreements.

When the WTO was first proposed in 1993, it did not produce the same volume of objection that the ITO did in 1948. The same basic opposed interests, if with different representatives, were against the WTO. Protectionists disfavor the principle of free trade; in 1948, these were mostly business-related Republicans, but in 1993 they were mostly union-supporting Democrats. Some again objected on the grounds that the organization was too timid—in this case the objectors were principally environmentalists concerned the WTO would not aggressively protect the environment. Others raised objections on the grounds of infringements of national sovereignty. These problems are discussed in the next section.

The WTO statute was ratified by the United States Congress on December 1, 1994. It was not submitted as a treaty (requiring the advice and consent of two-thirds of the Senate) but instead as an economic agreement under the provisions of so-called *fast track* procedures (now known as trade promotion authority). Treating the WTO as an economic agreement meant it had to pass both houses of Congress, but with only a simple, rather than a weighted, majority. Designating it under fast track (a provision to facilitate the passage of trade agreements) meant there were limits on Congressional debate on the matter and that it could only be voted up or down in its entirety (the authority to amend it was removed). The date is important because it came after the November 1994 off-year elections but before the newly elected Congress was inaugurated (qualifying it as a lame duck session). Critics wailed at the timing and procedures (some maintained, for instance, that had WTO accession been presented as a treaty it never would have gotten a two-thirds majority), but their cries of "foul" were in vain. Nearly fifty years after its principles were first proposed, institutionalized free trade became reality in 1995.

The WTO has now been in existence for more than a decade. Its membership has increased from approximately 70 countries in 1995 to 147 as of April 23, 2004 (according to its Web Site). In addition, 30 nonmember countries participate in the organization (observers have five years to apply for full membership), including Russia, Iraq, Saudi Arabia, and Vietnam, among others. The headquarters, including the secretariat, are located in Lausanne, Switzerland. The WTO has established itself as a leading international economic organization in the process.

Its brief tenure has also been filled with controversy and a great deal more visibility than functional international organizations (those that deal with a specific policy area rather than generalist organizations like the UN) usually attract or desire. In some ways, the acceptance of or opposition to WTO reflects the status of globalization, whose central principle of free trade it exemplifies. When the Charter came into effect in 1995, globalization was at its apex and the new WTO only activated its most ardent opponents. By the end of the decade of the 1990s, on the other hand, globalization was less in vogue, and the WTO had become more controversial. This controversy became extremely public during widespread and highly destructive demonstrations at its 1999 convention in Seattle, Washington, leading the organization to hold its 2001 meeting in Doha, Qatar, and its 2003 meeting in Cancun, Mexico, presumably more easily secured locations that would attract less attention.

IS INSTITUTIONALIZED FREE TRADE A GOOD IDEA?

This is really two separate but related questions, and there is disagreement on both aspects. One aspect has to do with whether free trade itself is a worthy goal, and it has as a subtext the question whether free trade *as it is currently defined and being pursued* is a good idea. One can, for instance, believe that the general principle of removing barriers to trade is a good idea, but disagree that the overarching implementing principle of removing "barriers to trade" should override other principles, such as the promotion of human rights. The other aspect of the question is whether free trade advocacy and implementation should be institutionalized, and that question has the subtext of whether the WTO *as it is currently organized and with the authority it has* is a good idea. Many of those who believe in free trade as a principle and accept the idea that it needs some institutional base, for instance, disagree with the structure of the WTO and advocate a more open, democratic structure for the organization.

The WTO has become a lightning rod on the free trade issue. Those who oppose free trade, generally on the basis that its effects are not as desirable as its advocates suggest, clearly oppose an advocating institution, and especially one with mandatory authority to impose its values on individuals and countries. Proponents of free trade generally support the idea of an institutional base from which to promote their advocacy, but may or may not like the structure they have. To make some reasonable personal assessment on the issue of free trade requires unraveling and reaching some personal conclusions on each aspect.

Free Trade or Not Free Trade?

The generalized defense of free trade has already been made and need not be repeated in detail here. Free trade is the international application of the Ricardian principle of comparative advantage. By removing barriers to the movement of goods and services across national boundaries, the most efficient producers of goods and providers of services will come to predominate the markets in the areas of their advantage, to the benefit of consumers who will receive the best goods and services at the lowest prices from these providers. Presuming all countries can find products or services at which they have such advantages, all will find markets, and the result will be a general and growing specialization and prosperity. The application of free trade internationally is the handmaiden of the process of economic globalization, because the result should be the gradual widening of participation in the global economy, as more and more countries find and exploit areas where they have or can develop a comparative advantage (often with the assistance of public and private advisors and investors, as discussed in Chapter 7).

Freeing trade has the added benefit of promoting a more cooperative, peaceful environment, according to its champions. The major conceptual vehicle for this dynamic is *complex interdependence*, the idea that as countries become increasingly reliant upon one another for the goods and services that they need, their ability and desire to engage in conflict, and especially war, becomes more remote—either because the desire to fight is decreased by proximity and acquaintance or because the intertwining of economies makes it impractical or impossible to fight.

This argument is, as noted earlier, abstract and intellectual. It argues that free trade improves the general lot of peoples, and thus increases the prosperity of individuals: "a rising tide lifts all boats," to borrow a phrase. As an abstract matter presented in this way, it is difficult to argue with the virtue of free trade, and only a few try. At a slightly less abstract level, proponents of free trade also point to largely macroeconomic indicators, especially from the middle 1990s, that demonstrate growth in the global economy and within individual countries, phenomena they attribute to free trade–driven globalization. Once again, at these levels of analysis, there can be little argument with the benefits. However, when these statistics are applied at more specific levels like those of individuals or even sectors of economies within countries, then the case is not as clearly positive.

The major objections to free trade come not from these abstract principles but from the way they are applied. In the current debate about free trade, many of the objections go back to the conjunction of free trade and the values of market economics in fact if not in theory. It is the effect of the kind of free trade that the advocates put forward that is the problem.

Without seeking to be comprehensive, two examples can be put forward. One regards the question of intellectual property rights. The protection of things like patents, copyrights, and trademarks has long been controversial, because some countries ignore these intellectual property rights. Pirating music and selling it well below market costs (and not paying royalties to the artists) has been an obvious case in point for some time, but the practice of stealing protected ideas and the like is certainly not new. Historically, China has been an especially egregious violator of intellectual property rights, and one of the major accomplishments of bringing China into the WTO has been to force China to renounce these illegal practices.

Protecting intellectual property rights seems an uncontroversial idea, and it is covered by the WTO Agreement on Trade-related Aspects of Intellectual Property Rights (TRIPS), under which signatories agree to honor patents, copyright protection, and trademarks. Who can disagree with the idea of TRIPS?

The answer is a large number of people in the developing world. Among the intellectual property rights protected under TRIPS are the patents and copyrights held by the large, predominantly Western, pharmaceutical companies that give individual companies effective monopolies on particular medications. The result is that the pharmaceutical companies set the prices of particular drugs and other medications, often at high levels (a familiar issue within the United States as well as internationally). The justification for these practices is to provide sufficient capital for the high research and development costs associated with producing new drugs for the treatment of future diseases and maladies.

The objectionable effect of this application of TRIPS is that it effectively denies access to critical medications to those who cannot afford the prices charged by the pharmaceutical companies, and that encompasses a large part of the world. The most frequent example cited is the availability of HIV-AIDS medication in Africa (also discussed in Chapter 15). Virtually no country in the developing world can afford the prices charged by those who hold the property rights to these medications, leaving them with two choices. One is to develop generic drugs based on the protected formulas at much lower cost to patients. The other is not to treat the diseases and allow people to suffer. The first solution falls under TRIPS and is prohibited; the WTO has threatened sanctions against those who attempt this solution, leaving the second option. The pharmaceutical companies realize this consequence is a major public relations disaster and have sought compromise solutions (lower costs), but the issue remains. As the AIDS pandemic spreads in influential countries like India and China, the pressure on WTO will undoubtedly increase.

A second example regards the effect of institutionalized free trade on the economic development of poor countries. Because of the basis of free trade in the most-favored nation (MFN) principle, opponents argue that poor countries that are members of the free trade regime are vulnerable to be flooded with goods and services across the range of economic activity. Virtually by definition, poor countries lack comparative advantage in producing anything, so that their inability to protect nascent economic activities means that indigenous development will be systematically undercut by the free trade regime and domestic industry and thus development will be retarded. The net impact of being exposed to MFN has been, according to critics, to contribute to greater economic inequality between the rich and poor countries, the very opposite of what the proponents of free trade argue.

For the "turtles," as Thomas Friedman labels the countries that cannot compete in the free trade environment, there are two options, as in the example above. One is to stay outside the WTO framework, since the principles and rules only apply to members. Notably, almost all the countries that have not joined WTO are extremely poor, and although the WTO has tried to develop outreach programs to these nonmembers, they have not been successful at overcoming these objections. The other alternative is to join the WTO and suffer the consequences of assault on the domestic economy in the hopes that doing so will help "lift" the national boat.

The WTO: Problem or Solution?

The WTO is the final fulfillment of the dreams of the planners of the post–World War II global economy who convened at Bretton Woods. Freeing trade was a central part of the remedy they saw for the international economic ills associated with protection-ism and its contribution to the war. When the idea was first presented, American objec-tions prevented the first institutional form, the ITO, from coming into being. In 1995, the proponents succeeded, but the controversy remains. Is the WTO the answer, or is it the problem?

Assessing whether WTO helps or hinders the progression of free trade can be bro-ken into three separate questions. The first has to do with the kind of free trade that the WTO advocates. To its opponents, the WTO is little more than a handmaiden to the large multinational corporations (MNCs). Global Exchange, a Web-based research orga-nization that is critical of the WTO, calls in an "unaccountable, corporate-based gov-ernment" that reflects the values of the MNCs at the expense of virtually everyone else. At least to some extent, this should come as little surprise. The globalization process of which free trade is an implementing device is based in the promotion of capitalist, free market economics—made up predominately of corporations. Moreover, as pointed out in Chapter 7, much of the economic resources on which the spread of globalization is based is in the form of foreign direct investment (FDI) by private sources, and entities like international banks and multinational corporations provide most of the FDI. Because they do so out of a profit motive and not from a sense of philanthropy, it stands to rea-son that these entities would have an interest in helping to shape the philosophies and policies the WTO promotes. As indirect evidence of the success of the MNCs in this regard, it might be remembered that corporations within the United States were major opponents of the ITO because of protectionist motives, but have by and large been equally strong supporters of the WTO.

The advocacy of free trade and the promotion of its implementation through the WTO thus entails two substantive judgments. One is whether there is an alternative eco-nomic philosophy that could be attached to free trade that would make it more palatable to those who oppose the idea or its consequences. Is there some alternative to a market-economy based, free trade–driven globalized economy? The second judgment flows from the first: if there is no acceptable alternative underpinning (and none is obvious), are the positive outcomes of institutionalized free trade better or worse than the absence of such a system? The analogy of the rising tide and the boat are sometimes used to frame these questions. Pro-free traders admit that not everyone benefits equally from free trade, but that everyone does benefit to some extent and thus everyone is better off under a free trade regime (the tide lifts all boats). Opponents argue the benefits are so inequitably dis-tributed that gaps are actually widened to the point that some are left relatively worse off (some boats get swamped).

The second question revolves around the structure of the WTO itself. To reiterate, the WTO has two basic functions: the promotion of free trade and the enforcement of free trade agreements. The first purpose has been expanded into areas like TRIPS and the General Agreement on Trade in Services (GATS), which adds the international flow of services to the traditional emphasis on removing barriers to the movement of products to the WTO charge, but remains the basis of what consensus there is around WTO.

The enforcement mandate is and always has been the more controversial aspect of WTO. The mechanism for enforcement was agreed upon during the Uruguay round of the GATT in the form of the Dispute Settlement Understanding (DSU). Under the DSU, the WTO is authorized to establish and convene the Dispute Settlement Body (DSB). The Geneva Briefing Book describes the considerable authority of the DSB, "which has the sole authority to establish such panels to adjudicate disputes between members and to accept or reject the findings of panels and the Appellate Body, a standing appeals body of seven independent experts. The DSB also…has the power to authorize retaliation when a member does not comply with DSB recommendations and rulings."

These powers are not inconsiderable and include the power to identify alleged violations, to convene and prosecute those alleged violations, and then to issue binding rulings and penalties and to enforce those penalties, ostensibly without recourse to an outside, independent source of appeal (since the appeals are internal to the process). The membership of these panels is chosen by the WTO itself, and, according to Global Exchange, "consist[s] of three trade bureaucrats that are not screened for conflict of interest."

To critics that span the ITO-WTO debate, a chief objection to this arrangement is its effect on national sovereignty. The rulings of the DSU process have the effect of treaties on the countries against which they are levied, which means that they can overturn the effect of those laws. This is particularly a concern in the United States, where, as noted, there is particular sensitivity over intrusions on state sovereignty. In the specific case of WTO rulings, these have disproportionately affected the United States. According to the Geneva Briefing Book, "From the advent of the WTO, in January 1995, until October 1, 2003, the United States has been a party in 56 out of 93 WTO dispute settlement panel reports and 36 out of 56 Appellate Body reports." While the source does not indicate how many of these involved judgments against the United States, it is likely that at least some of them did.

The third question regards what unforeseen consequences the institutionalization of free trade has had, and whether those consequences are acceptable. As one might expect, most of the unforeseen outcomes that have been identified are negative and are expressed most vocally by opponents of the process and its outcomes. Two in particular stand out as examples: the alleged antilabor bias of the WTO, and its negative environmental impacts. Unsurprisingly, these two arguments have been raised by two of the most prominent and visible opponents of the WTO, neither of which was evident in the 1940s but are today. Both touch upon the dual questions of whether free trade or the way it is institutionalized is the problem.

Opposition to free trade on the basis of being antilabor contains both elements of objection. Free trade is, of course, the culprit among those people working in industries and services that do not enjoy comparative advantage and can only compete if protected by some form of trade barrier. The textile industry cited earlier is a prime example. Labor unions also object that the way the WTO operates to remove barriers to trade provides incentives for corporations to move their businesses to place that engage in unfair labor practices, everything from low wages and benefits to child labor, thereby creating an unfair environment within which to compete. Moreover, they believe that the corporatist mentality they say reigns supreme within the WTO encourages foreign direct investors to nurture and create these unfair practices as ways to create comparative advantage. These allegations are parallel to older domestic arguments about union busting and scab labor practices. The fact that these are extremely emotional issues among trade unionists helps explain the depth of their animosity toward the WTO and the prevalence of trade union-ists in anti-free trade, anti-WTO demonstrations.

Environmentalist objection to free trade and the WTO are parallel. The need to establish conditions of comparative advantage drives some countries to rescind environ-mental regulations that add to the cost of production (dumping hazardous chemicals used in processing materials into the environment rather than rendering these chemical harmless before release), thereby making their industries more competitive than indus-tries in the United States that must meet environmental standards that add to produc-tion costs. Critics cite cases in Latin America (especially Mexico), where environmental standards have indeed been relaxed or done away with to attract industry.

The environmentalist objection is also applied directly to the WTO. Environmental-ists contend that most corporations resist environmental restraints philosophically and only accede to environmental regulation reluctantly and unenthusiastically. Because the WTO is alleged to be largely controlled by corporate interests and reflects corporate values, envi-ronmentalists are thus predisposed to be suspicious of the organization on those grounds. Environmentalists are also generally conspicuous at demonstrations against the WTO.

CONCLUSION

Advocacy or opposition to free trade and its institutionalization is not an easy or straight-forward proposition. At the abstract, theoretical level of international macroeconomics, the case for free trade is very compelling, and it is not surprising that many of the defenses of free trade spring from these theoretical arguments. At the applied level of the impact of free trade on individuals and groups (the microeconomic level), the proposition is more ambiva-lent. Certainly, individuals as consumers benefit when comparative advantage produces goods and services at lower cost and higher quality through free trade than from less effi-cient, protected domestic industries. Imagine, for instance, the impact on Christmas gift spending if all goods from China were eliminated. At the same time, removing protection can terminate employment for those in the less efficient industries, and although the the-ory of comparative advantage says that people so displaced should find alternative employ-ment in more competitive fields, this is almost always easier said than done.

The question of institutionalizing free trade is a related but not synonymous mat-ter, because one can reasonably take one of three positions on the desirability of free trade per se: one can favor free trade unconditionally, one can oppose it equally uncondit01on-ally, or one can favor free trade some but not all of the time, a position we have called *freer (or fair) trade*. For the "pure" positions, the answer to whether some organization should be established to promote and enforce free trade is fairly straightforward. If one believes free trade is comprehensively desirable, then a free trade–promoting institution is clearly a desirable instrument to that end (although the kind and extent of enforce-ment capability may be debatable). Conversely, if one opposes free trade across the board, then it would be nonsensical to support any instrumentality that promotes or enforces a rejected idea.

That leaves the "freer traders," who support expansions in trade through the reduc-tion of barriers to trade, but who believe there should be exclusions or limitations on the extent and degree of trade promotion. Such an advocacy attempts to finesse the dichotomy between free trade and protectionism by advocating some of both, depending on the context. This position is politically tenable as well, because it allows general support for free trade (which, in the abstract, most people favor) with restrictions to protect politically significant victims of free trade.

The advocacy of freer trade leads to three questions that can be applied to the dual thrusts of free trade and its institutionalization. The first is, "How free should trade be?" The general criterion for answering the question is how much of the benefits and costs of free trade is one willing to bear, and the answer one determines will, in turn, vary with the level of personal benefit one (or one's group or country) derives from various levels of free trade.

The second question is, "What kinds of values should underlie a free trading system and, especially, the institution that supports and promotes it?" If the current free trade–based system of globalization is founded on the values of market-based, capitalist economics, as it at least partly is, this leads to one form of organization based in pure economic competition where the less government regulation exists, generally the better. If, as alleged, the WTO is dominated by people with these values and interests, then the *kind* of free trade system that evolves and is institutionalized will reflect those values. On the other hand, if one enters values such as equity ("fair trade") and social consciousness (environmentalism) into the values underlying a free trade system, it probably looks different from the current system.

The third and final question is, "What kind of enforcement mechanism is most desirable?" The answer, of course, begins with the level of enthusiasm one has about free trade in the first place: the more enthusiastic one is, the more enforcement one is likely to favor. But the answer also incorporates how one has answered the second question: one's enthusiasm for enforcement may depend on what kinds of values are being enforced and whether one supports those values. In a favorite example cited by critics of the current system, the American ban on tuna fishing with mile-long nets that also ensnare and kill dolphins was overruled in a judgment by the WTO to an action brought by Mexico that said the law, when applied to American territorial waters, was a barrier to trade. Does a free trade regime need to lead to that kind of conclusion?

The question implied in the title "free trade or not free trade?" turns out to be more complicated than the simple dichotomy suggests. Whether, or to what extent, free trade, its advocacy, and its institutionalization are desirable are not simple matters, but involve questions and sub-questions, the answers to which are not always as easy as they may seem at first blush. But then, that is why the question has endured for more than a half-century and will undoubtedly remain on the agenda for the foreseeable future.

STUDY/DISCUSSION QUESTIONS

1. What is free trade? Why is it an issue, both historically and in the contemporary context? What are the basic disagreements about the desirability of free trade? What basic positions do people take on the trade issue?

2. Describe the process of institutionalizing free trade from the Bretton Woods conference of 1944 to the ratification of the World Trade Organization in 1995. Why

did the International Trade Organization fail to come into existence in 1948 but the WTO succeed in 1995? What was the role of the General Agreement on Trade and Tariffs in this evolution?

3. What are the principal arguments for and against free trade? How do the disputes over intellectual property rights and the impact of free trade on development of the poorest countries illustrate this debate?

4. What are the major controversies surrounding the WTO? What values does it promote? What powers does it have? How do labor and environmental objections illustrate this controversy?

5. Answer the three questions posed in the conclusion: How free should trade be? What kinds of values should it promote? What kind of enforcement mechanism is most desirable? After determining your personal answers to these questions, do you consider yourself a free trader, an anti-free trader, or somewhere in between (a fair trader)? Why?

READING/RESEARCH MATERIAL

Barshefsky, Charlene. "Trade Policy in a Networked World." *Foreign Affairs* 80, 2 (March/April 2001), 134–146.

Bauman, Zygmunt. *Globalization: The Human Consequences.* New York: Columbia University Press, 1998.

Dierks, Rosa Gomez. *Introduction to Globalization: Political and Economic Perspectives for a New Era.* Chicago: Burnham, 2001.

Friedman, Thomas L. *The Lexus and the Olive Tree: Understanding Globalization.* New York: Farrar, Straus, Giroux, 1999.

Landau, Alice. *Redrawing the Global Economy: Elements of Integration and Fragmentation.* New York: Palgrave, 2001.

McBride, Stephen, and John Wiseman, eds. *Globalization and Its Discontents.* New York: St. Martin's Press, 2000.

"Measuring Globalization." *Foreign Policy* (March/April 2004), 46–53.

O'Connor, David E. *Demystifying the Global Economy: A Guide for Students.* Westport, CT: Greenwood Press, 2002.

Panagariya, Arvind. "Think Again: International Trade." *Foreign Policy* (November/December 2003), 20–29.

Park, Jacob. "Globalization after Seattle." *Washington Quarterly* 23, 2 (Spring 2000), 13–16.

Rothgeb, John M. J. *Trade Policy: Balancing Economic Dreams and Political Realities.* Washington, DC: CQ Press, 2001.

Schaeffer, Robert K. *Understanding Globalization: The Social Consequences of Political, Economic, and Environmental Change.* Lanham, MD: Rowman and Littlefield, 2003.

"World Trade Organization." *The Geneva Briefing Book.* Lausanne, Switzerland: World Trade Organization, 2004.

WEB SITES

The text of GATT online

GATT at http://farnsworth.mit.edu/diig/NII_info.gatt.html[

Critical views of the World Trade Organization

Global Exchange at http://www.globalexchange.org/campaigns/rulemakers/
    topTenReasons.html

Summaries of international trade law

International Trade Law Monitor at http://itl.irv.uit.no/trade_law/

The home page of the World Trade Organization at http://www.wto.org/Welcome.html

Information on worldwide trade

Global Trade Watch at http://www.citizen.org/pctrade/tradehome.html

CHAPTER NINE

Debating
Globalization
THE CASE OF INDONESIA

PRÉCIS

In the new century, some of the enthusiasm for globalization that was so prominent during the 1990s has faded. Part of the reason is that the world's economy has slowed since the later part of the 1990s, and especially in the wake of the East Asian financial crisis of 1997, introduced in Chapter 7. At the same time, the results of adopting globalization as a value have had mixed results in some states. As a consequence, some states and peoples are viewing globalization and their part in it more cautiously than they did a decade ago.

No state represents more fully the mixed impact of globalization than Indonesia, the world's fourth most populous state. Indonesia was an enthusiastic recruit to globalization in the early 1990s, but when the impact of the East Asian crisis washed onto its shores, it set into motion a political and economic crisis on the archipelago that only recently began to settle down. Although not all of Indonesia's problems can be blamed on globalization, the global economy contributed to that spiral that began the process of change and has manifested itself in political alterations and crises that include secessionism and terrorism. As a result, Indonesia is reassessing its relationship to the global economy.

Until the East Asian economic crisis of 1997 (described in Chapter 7), the spread of the global economy worldwide seemed an inexorable process, a bandwagon heading to prosperity and political freedom onto which virtually every country in the world sought to climb. But as the crisis devastated economies that turned out to be much more fragile than was realized before the problems began, enthusiasm dampened somewhat, especially when the International Monetary Fund (IMF) created tough conditions on the affected economies to guarantee their long-term recovery and viability. In some instances, the IMF imposed political and economic burdens that added to the woes caused by the crisis itself. As a result, unbridled, nearly blind adherence to globalization has given way to somewhat greater restraint about participation in the world economy, which was suddenly revealed to have a down side in addition to the great boom of the 1990s. The result, at least in some places, has been a debate over globalization and the extent to which countries will participate in the global economy.

No country was more greatly affected by the negative forces of the late 1990s than Indonesia. In addition to the economic ruination that accompanied the 1997 crisis itself, the country experienced the fall of a long-standing authoritarian regime—widely considered one of the most corrupt in the world—and has been hounded by charges of excesses by the military in the face of secessionist movements on several islands and more recently terrorism and the devastating tsunami of 2005. Indonesia is thus in the midst of a period of national trauma. It is a country that is blessed with great natural wealth, but the archipelago was hit hard by the collapse of the currencies of most of the states of Southeast Asia in 1997. The economic chaos surrounding the crisis in turn energized a latent opposition to the Suharto regime that had ruled since 1966, leading to Suharto's resignation in 1998. Shortly thereafter, the country was further rocked by the uprising in East Timor, which was accompanied by allegations of widespread atrocities against East Timorese separatists allegedly abetted and supported by elements in the Indonesian military. The seeds of separatism have spread to other parts of the island country. Dealing with terrorism has more recently been added to the Indonesian agenda. The result has been great questioning about the future of the Indonesian state.

Indonesia is thus in a state of deep national reexamination about the future of the Indonesian people and state. Prior to the events unleashed in 1997, Indonesia had been part of the network of prosperous states of East Asia that had enthusiastically entered the globalizing economy through membership in organizations such as the Asia-Pacific Economic Cooperation (APEC) and the Association of Southeast Asian Nations (ASEAN). Like many of its neighbors, Indonesia seemed a "poster child" for the virtues of globalization and a model for other states that aspired to participation in the globalizing system.

And then the economic crisis of 1997 burst the bubble and revealed a very different, and far less happy, reality about Indonesian prosperity. The Indonesian economy was clearly rocked, and the reverberations coincided with traumas in the political system as well. The question that many Indonesians had to ask themselves is how much of their trauma was simply coincident with the problems of globalization and how much was caused by globalization. In the middle of the 2000s, that question remains unanswered.

The economic crash revealed, or highlighted, other sources of tension and instability that had been glossed over during the prosperity that Indonesia enjoyed during the early 1990s. During that period, Indonesia embraced globalization and the world embraced Indonesia. The signs of trouble were there to be seen, but they tended to be ignored or downplayed in light of what appeared to be perpetual expansion and prosperity. And then the crisis hit. During 1998, the Indonesian economy experienced sharp contractions in economic growth accompanied by high inflation rates, massive bank failures, and extremely high interest rates. The economic bad times, in turn, resulted in finger-pointing against the regime of President Suharto and the massive corruption for which it was infamous. Amidst extensive criticism of cronyism and the accumulation of great personal wealth for the benefit of his family, Suharto, who had been elected to a fifth six-year term in 1996, resigned on May 21, 1998.

Even though the economy began to stabilize by the end of the year, Indonesia's woes were by no means over. The province of East Timor, occupying roughly one-half the island of Timor in the southern part of the archipelago, held a referendum on independence on August 30, 1999, and the citizens voted overwhelmingly (78.5 percent) for secession from the Indonesian state. The vote prompted vicious attacks against East Timorese by pro-Indonesian "militias," marauding armed bands that, at a minimum, the Indonesian military was unable to suppress. At worst, it was widely believed that elements in the army supported the actions and had helped organize, equip, and encourage the offenders. In the end, fighting was only ended when an Australian-led UN peacekeeping force (the International Force in East Timor or INTERFET) landed in East Timor and established order.

This jackhammer sequence of events has caused a basic reassessment of the future within Indonesia that centers on Indonesia's place in the economic globalization system. During the 1990s, Indonesia embraced globalization with something of a vengeance. The result during the first half of the decade was great prosperity and even the hope among some younger Indonesians, whom *New York Times* correspondent Thomas L. Friedman calls the "globalutionaries," that involvement in the global economy could provide the engine for political and other reform. Moreover, the prosperity glossed over the other very real problems that beset the country. Indonesia's good times proved to be ephemeral indeed.

Post-crisis Indonesia is reassessing itself, and the outcome is uncertain. The economic crisis, followed by the imposition of tough standards by the IMF to correct the situation (see Chapter 7 for a discussion of the IMF's role generally), have left some Indonesians wary of the country's location in the global economy and anxious to place their participation in a more distinctly Indonesian context. That ambivalence continues. The fall of Suharto has ended the long reign of corrupt, authoritarian rule. After a transition period, Suharto was replaced by the daughter of the "George Washington" of Indonesia (Achmed Sukarno). Megawati Sukarnoputri was elected president by the legislature on July 26, 2001, and was replaced by a 55-year-old former general, Susilo Bambang Yudhoyono (known locally and hereafter referred to as SBY), who was elected by popular vote (the first Indonesian leader to do so) in September 2004 (he was inaugurated in October 2004).

What happens in Indonesia is important both within its own boundaries and beyond. As the world's fourth most populous country (with a population estimated in July 2004 at slightly less than 238 million people living on a land mass slightly less than three times the state of Texas), Indonesia is a tremendous potential market for the region and globally; as by far the largest country in Southeast Asia, it is a regional power of importance. Moreover, the archipelago sits astride the Indian and Pacific Oceans, and the Straits of Malacca that flow between the Indonesian island of Sumatra and Malaysia carries more than 40 percent of the world's shipborne commerce, making a stable Indonesia desirable for global commercial activity. Moreover, the outcome of Indonesia's choices for the future will almost certainly have a ripple effect in other, smaller countries in the region facing similar economic and political situations.

This construction of the problem suggests the method by which the case will proceed. We will begin with a sketch of the Indonesian past in a general sense, but also focusing on the three dimensions of the current crisis—economics and the relationship to globalization, the political transition, and the geopolitics of trying to hold the country together in the face of secessionist and terrorist threats. With the past as background, we will then examine the post-1997 choices available to Indonesia, which it will likely choose, and what difference those choices make for Indonesia and the region.

INDONESIA: A THUMBNAIL SKETCH

Like all countries, Indonesia has unique qualities that are the result of a combination of historical, geographical, and other factors that form the context in which its current debate over its relationship to globalization is taking place. The discussion therefore begins by looking at those factors that help shape Indonesia's view of the future.

Indonesia is the world's largest archipelago. It is composed of more than 13,600 individual islands, about 6,000 of which are inhabited. The major islands include Sumatra, Java (one of the most densely populated land masses in the world, at more than 2,000 people per square mile), parts of Borneo and New Guinea, and the Maluccas, among others. The capital, Jakarta, is on Java, where the majority of the Indonesian population resides.

The archipelago has a very long history. Anthropologists have found human remains (*Java man*) that are among the oldest in the world. The country, which is approximately 88 percent Muslim, attracted the attention of Islamic traders in the 1400s, and they were followed by the Portuguese, British, and the Dutch in the sixteenth century. After a period of posturing, the Netherlands established domain over the heart of what became known as the Dutch East Indies (which had formerly been called the Spice Islands) through the Dutch East Indies Company. Dutch colonial rule remained until World War II, when Japan invaded and occupied the country after their defeat of an Allied fleet in the Battle of the Java Sea in 1942. During the war, the Dutch helped organize a resistance to Japanese rule in Indonesia that became the basis of the independence movement against the Netherlands after the Japanese surrendered in 1945. Under the leadership of Achmed Sukarno, who became the first president of Indonesia, the Indonesians fought the reimposition of colonial rule until they prevailed and the Dutch granted independence.

Indonesia achieved its independence on December 27, 1949. After a period of transition, Sukarno gained and gradually consolidated power in the country, ultimately dissolving the country's parliament in 1960, declaring Indonesia a *guided democracy*, and having himself declared president for life in 1963. Sukarno's rule was marked by general mismanagement of the economy, as he devoted great resources to meaningless projects that served as monuments to himself but did little for the economy, and he gradually moved away from the West, seeking closer relations with the People's Republic of China.

Opposition to Sukarno gradually grew, particularly as the Indonesian Communist Party came to gain greater influence in institutions such as the country's labor unions. In

1965, a cabal of army officers accused of links to the communists staged an attempted coup that was put down by a countercoup led by General Suharto. In 1966, Sukarno was forced to relinquish much of his authority to Suharto, and in 1968, Suharto was named president for the first of his terms that ended with his resignation in 1998.

The reign of Suharto lasted for three decades, and may still have continued beyond that had it not been for globalization and the East Asian financial crisis of 1997. His government was certainly less than democratic or even democratizing, supported and sustained primarily by an alliance between the Indonesia military and supporters and cronies of the president. Economically and politically, Indonesia had the reputation of being one of the most corrupt countries in the world. The Berlin-based independent agency Transparency International Inc. (founded by former World Bank official Peter Eigen) ranked Indonesia the fourth most corrupt country in the world in its 1999 Corruption Perceptions Index (it rated only Cameroon, Nigeria, and Azerbaijan as being more corrupt than Indonesia).

The Suharto regime was, however, very much a Cold War artifact. When Suharto replaced Sukarno, he did turn the country solidly anticommunist. He outlawed the Indonesian Communist Party, suppressed communists throughout the country, and brought Indonesia into the Western security and economic system. During the height of the Cold War, this reorientation of Indonesian foreign policy was adequate to win favor in the West and to cause the West to look the other way at Indonesian governmental malfeasance and expansionism. Among the more egregious examples of ignoring Suharto's excesses was implied American acceptance of the violent annexation of East Timor in 1975.

The Suharto regime began to lose favor, as did a number of other leaders around the world (Zaire's Mobutu Sese Seku, for instance), with the end of the Cold War. With no communist threat against which to be an apparent bulwark, there was a more critical, less accepting view of authoritarian regimes generally and the Indonesian regime more specifically in the world at large. When the economic bubble burst in 1997, the Suharto regime found itself with few friends internally or externally in much the same way the world treated Mobutu when his regime began to crumble.

The situation kindled the debate over the future of Indonesia. It is an illustrative case both because of the size and importance of the country and because other states have or will attempt to make the transition from twentieth-century authoritarianism to some different form of twenty-first-century arrangement, all within the framework of a relationship with the globalizing economy. To see how this may occur in the Indonesian case, we will thus look at each of the three dimensions of the crisis identified earlier—economic, political, and geopolitical—as preface to the ongoing debate and its possible outcomes.

The Economic Legacy

The economic and political legacies of the half-century of Indonesian independence can be separated only artificially, because what are now viewed as problems in both areas fed upon and reinforced one another. The "Chinese-dominated business class," as the *CIA Factbook* describes it, operated a classic form of *crony capitalism* (where collusion among economic entities was carried out for personal advantage and at the expense of public goods) that could only have flourished with governmental blessing or at least implicit approval. At the same time, rampant *nepotism* at the highest governmental levels allowed the Suharto family to own major segments of and to benefit from the civilian economy. In turn, this activity required the assistance or at least the indulgence of the private business sector.

The result was that Suharto's *new order* produced what has been described as "one of the most corrupt regimes that East Asia has yet produced." Because of Indonesia's considerable natural resource abundance (the country produces between one-third and two-fifth's of the world's supply of liquefied natural gas or LNG, for instance), the result of corruption was not necessarily the systematic impoverishment of the population. Rather, the underlying governmental and economic rot was obscured by Indonesia's participation in the global economy and the general prosperity that attached to that economy in the 1980s and 1990s. Indeed, during the 1990s, Indonesia had one of the fastest growing economies in the world, with an average growth in GDP per capita around 7.5 percent. With this appearance of economic dynamism, the outside world looked the other way at the signs of gross corruption and malfeasance, emphasizing economic growth and ignoring institutional and other sources of weakness.

The East Asian crisis revealed that Indonesia's prosperity, like that of many of its neighbors, was a classic economic bubble ready to explode when pricked. High rates of foreign direct investment (FDI) were revealed to have been spent on unproductive projects, overextended banks collapsed as the *rupiah* plunged, and economic chaos ensued when panicky foreign and domestic investors removed their assets from Indonesia as rapidly as possible. The result was economic stagnation reflected in a flat economic growth rate and high inflation marked by exorbitantly high interest rates in 1998, which began to come down only in 1999.

The corruption of the system both allowed the bubble to form and made matters worse when it finally burst. In a manner reminiscent of the other East Asian countries, the chief culprits were in the financial sector and encompassed both private entrepreneurs and governmental officials. Indonesia lacked a strong banking system, and especially regulation of the activities of banks that would insure the soundness of lending decisions and the accountability of financial officials to investors. The financial regulatory system, which one analyst has described simply as "decrepit," could thus not provide protection for the savings of average citizens who put their money in those banks and counted on the banks to protect them. Further, Indonesia lacked a bond market that could serve as an alternative conduit for savings by average Indonesians, who did not have access to overseas outlets to invest their money. The result was an opacity in the financial sector (transactions could be conducted secretly, with little or no accountability to savers) that encouraged the growth of crony capitalist networks of bankers, businessmen, and supposed governmental regulators, making decisions from which they benefited but those whose money was spent did not.

The Suharto family was in the middle of this system. In order to gain protection from government regulation and access to funds, members of the extended Suharto family became prominent entrepreneurs in the system, effectively wedding crony capitalism and nepotism. When a project was approved to develop an Indonesian-made automobile (a project that never reached fruition), the exclusive franchise was awarded to a Suharto family member, and support for developing the project was funneled through the financial system, with significant amounts of money ending up in Suharto family pockets. Although reliable estimates are difficult to find, the post-Suharto government has decided that the family looted the national treasury of at least $500 million.

All of this activity did not go unnoticed, but until 1997, little was done to stop it. From outside the country, there was little desire to embarrass a longtime ally, even if economic rating services warned about the dangers of investing in the Indonesian economy. Similarly, there were Indonesians, mainly those younger and better educated (often in the West), who recognized the corruption and wanted to see something done about it. The problem for them was how to bring about reform in a self-contained and self-reinforcing system that could reform itself only at the personal expense of the reformers themselves, an unlikely prospect. Moreover, the Indonesian economic system was grounded in an authoritarian state that supported the status quo. In fact, the Indonesian Army had shown little reluctance to squashing dissent against the regime, leaving political dissent a physically risky form of enterprise. Indonesian politics thus reinforced the economic system.

Indonesian Politics

The combination of cronyism and nepotism in the Indonesian economy could only be sustained in a political atmosphere where criticism and exposure of corrupt—and ultimately economically debilitating—practices could be suppressed. In Indonesia, the development and continuation of these practices was made possible by an authoritarian political system originally devised by Sukarno and his followers, then refined by Suharto and his supporters after he seized power. In the post-Suharto Indonesia, charges of corruption in early 2001 against President Abdurrahman Wahid, the first freely elected Indonesian leader in forty-five years, suggests the practice may still continue (and ultimately led to his removal from office). Wahid was replaced by Megawati Sukarnoputri and ultimately by SBY. But during Suharto's reign, while the symbols of representative government were present—an elected parliament and the periodic reelection of Suharto as president—the system rested on political repression enforced by the national police and, when necessary in the face of major disturbances, the Indonesian military. Such actions were generally justified under Suharto as means to deal with subversives (especially communists) and later separatists.

Corrupt government reinforced a corrupt political system. With government officials part of "iron triangles" with financiers and businessmen from which all three profited, the result was a system of purposely weak regulation and oversight, where policymakers and policy implementers protected rather than exposed practices that would ultimately be ruinous when the economic bubble burst. The practices were known both inside and outside Indonesia, but any attempt to expose them would bring the system down upon the head of the exposer.

Younger, more Westernized, Indonesians were particularly frustrated by the system, but they did not know how to reform it. Thomas L. Friedman describes this group as "educated 20- and 30-year-olds . . . [who] wanted to get rich, but without having to be corrupt, and they wanted democracy, but they didn't want to go into the streets to fight for it." Seeing that the chances for reform from within the country were negligible and unwilling to engage in violent revolution from below, their solution was *revolution from beyond*, integrating Indonesia into the global economy, which would force the Indonesian economy to adopt the non-corrupt practices of the global economy as a way to force reform of the domestic economy and political system. The conscious attempt by citizens of the target country to use globalization as the tool to bring about reforms is one of the defining characteristics of the Indonesian case.

Authoritarian rule is on the wane in Indonesia, although one observer, Patrick Smith, warns, "A working democracy is still distant in Indonesia." One of the remaining vestiges of authoritarianism in the country is an Indonesian military that has always played an active part in the country's politics and that retains the ability to affect the outcomes of reform efforts. Much of the military's remaining claim to a part of the post-Suharto political action is the effort to keep parts of Indonesia from leaving the federation.

The 2004 elections may be a sign of hope for the future. SBY was elected without significant charges of corruption of the electoral process, and in his inaugural address, he promised, "Indonesia will be a democratic country. Open, modern, pluralistic and tolerant. We will try hard to form a clean and good government."

The Geopolitics of Separatism and Terrorism

Although the core of Indonesia is the Dutch East Indies and the vast majority of the population share the religion of Islam, not all of the Indonesian states share these unifying characteristics. Rather, there are areas that either have been forcefully added to the Indonesian state over time or retain specific grievances against the government in Jakarta. As a result, there have been several active separatist movements within the archipelago

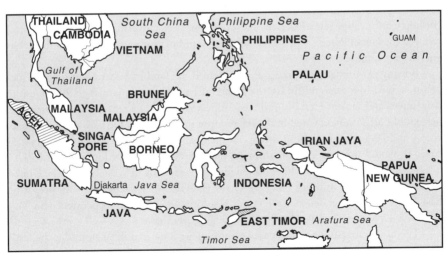

Map 9.1 Map of Indonesia, featuring East Timor and Aceh.

that remained latent during the Suharto period but surfaced publicly during the latter 1990s. For most of Indonesian history (certainly during the Cold War), the outside world ignored these rebellions, because good relations with the Suharto regime was deemed more important than support for secessionists. The organized violence that sought to intimidate the East Timorese so they would not vote for secession and the successful, internationally supervised removal of Indonesian forces from East Timor raised international awareness of the other claims against Jakarta.

The situation in East Timor is both exemplary of the other claims and unique in its own right. East Timor was neither a part of the Dutch East Indies nor an original part of the Indonesian state. Rather, the half of the island of Timor (located about midway between Java and New Guinea and several hundred miles north of Australia) that constitutes East Timor is a former colony of Portugal. When Portugal relinquished the last of its colonial empire in 1975, East Timor was among the former possessions to receive its independence from the mother country.

Freedom did not last long. Indonesian troops forcefully entered the country in December 1975 with the tacit approval of the West (and notably the United States), and Suharto declared it a province of Indonesia. Indonesia forcefully annexed the overwhelmingly Catholic country in 1976 (an action condemned by the United Nations) and began a brutal campaign of assimilation of the East Timorese people into Indonesia. Amnesty International, among other organizations, estimates that as many as 100,000 East Timorese (of a total population of about 700,000) were killed by security forces during this period, and a "transmigration" program brought tens of thousands of Muslims from West Timor and other parts of the country into East Timor.

A low-level campaign for independence sprang up in East Timor—the Revolutionary Front for an Independent East Timor (Fretilin)—but the Indonesian army managed to keep the lid on the problem until the 1990s. In 1991, East Timor returned to international attention when Western journalists witnessed Indonesian troops killing up to 270 unarmed East Timorese civilians in the capital of Dili. In 1996, two East Timorese (Bishop Carlos Filipe Ximenes Belo and exiled political spokesman Jose Ramos Horta) received the Nobel Peace Prize, and they added to publicity about the plight of the beleaguered East Timorese.

Bowing to international pressures, President B. J. Habibie, Suharto's immediate successor, agreed to a referendum on the future of East Timor in January 1999. Despite harassment and violence led by "militias" suspected of being aligned with the army, 98 percent of East Timorese voted in the referendum monitored by the UN and global television, and 78.5 percent of those voting cast their ballots for independence. When Jakarta could or would not suppress the militias, the Australian-led UN force (INTERFET) intervened to restore order as the Indonesian army sat idly by in West Timor. The United Nations Transitional Authority in East Timor (UNTAET) was charged with preparing East Timor for independence. East Timor was formally granted independence on May 20, 2002, an action approved by the Indonesian government.

The other currently active separatist movement is located in Aceh under the leadership of the Free Aceh Movement (GAM), which has been fighting the government since 1989. Unlike East Timor, Aceh is a Muslim province located in the extreme northwest corner of Sumatra. Because Aceh is located closer to the Middle East than any of the other parts of the archipelago, Acehnese consider their territory "the front porch of Mecca." Aceh was the closest part of Indonesia to the epicenter of the earthquake that caused the tsunami of 2005, and its capital city, Banda Aceh, was the most devastated part of the archipelago.

The Acehnese complaints with Jakarta are economic and political. Economically, Aceh contributes more to the central government than it receives in return, prompting a demand for economic parity in the form either of lower taxes or greater services. The lopsided economic balance arises because 40 percent of the liquefied natural gas to which allusion has already been made comes from off the coast of Aceh. Considering themselves to be more pious than most Indonesians, the Acehnese demand greater religious freedom and also want to see an end to military suppression in their region by the Indonesian army. Tensions increased in late 2000, when a popular Acehnese nationalist, Tengku Safwan Idris, was assassinated in Banda Aceh. Idris had been appointed by former President Habibie to investigate unrest in Aceh. Periodic fighting between GAM and the Indonesian army continued through 2004. Other uprisings include that in Papua (Irian Jaya), which has been ongoing since 1969, and several potential conflicts in the Molucca Islands and on Borneo, where native Dayaks went on a rampage against Madurese immigrants who had been forcefully relocated into traditional Dayak lands.

Terrorism has been added to the list of Indonesian woes. Because Indonesia is the world's largest Muslim state by population and suffers instability that makes effective control of its far-flung reaches problematic, Islamic radical groups have descended on the archipelago. Indonesia now follows only Pakistan in its hosting of so-called *madrassas* (religious schools that have been linked to terrorism), and elements related to Al Qaeda have entered the country as well. The result has been to add Indonesia to the "crescent of crisis" stretching from Israel to Indonesia.

The terrorism problem became public when a group calling itself Jemaah Islamiyah (with reported links to Al Qaeda) detonated a bomb at a resort hotel in Bali on October 12, 2002, that killed 202 people from twenty-one countries. The group's leader, calling himself Imam Samudra (his real name is Abdul Azis), and several others were tried and convicted of the attack in June 2003, but in July 2004, Indonesia's Constitutional Court invalidated the convictions on the ground that the terrorists were tried under a statute passed after the commission of the crime. On August 9, 2004, Jemaah Islamiyah apparently detonated a bomb outside the Australian embassy in Jakarta, killing 9 Indonesians and wounding 180, after authorities received a telephone demand for the release of imprisoned members of the terrorist organization and especially accused leader Abu Bakar Bashir. The new government refused to accept the demand, and the cleric's trial began October 20, 2004. Jemaah Islamiyah has also been accused of a hotel bombing in Jakarta in 2003 that killed twelve, making the group an ongoing problem.

WHERE IS INDONESIA GOING?

The events of the latter 1990s and beyond—the financial crisis, the downfall of the authoritarian Suharto regime, and the emergence of secessionist and terrorist movements—have broken old patterns and left decisions to be reached about the direction that Indonesia will take in the new century. The first and most central concern will be the relationship of the country to the global economy, because the recovery of the Indonesian economy would probably moderate the other problems. Indonesia was one of the most enthusiastic converts to globalization during the early 1990s, but the financial crisis hit Indonesia hard, collapsing banks and other financial institutions and sending many Indonesians (there are estimates of as many as 40 percent of the population) below the official poverty line. IMF-imposed requirements for recovery have faced significant opposition (see below).

What may prove in the long run to have been a benefit of the 1997 crisis is that it swept from power the thirty-year-long Suharto dictatorship. Opposition to the regime and its corruption had been simmering below the surface of Indonesian politics for a long time, but the army's alliance with Suharto and its consequent willingness to suppress dissent violently, even ruthlessly, had kept that opposition out of view and on the fringes. When it became clear that the depth of the 1997 crisis was in large measure the fault of the government—or at least made worse by corrupt practices—the days of Suharto were numbered. The problem, of course, was that a half-century of despotic rule has left Indonesia with neither democratic, participatory institutions nor traditions, and the process of post-Suharto democratization has been slowed by this legacy.

Finally, there is the question of the territorial integrity of the country, an issue also integrally related to the future of the Indonesian armed forces that have been the violent glue of Indonesian unity in the past. Whether East Timorese independence will act as a significant lightning rod for others in the far-flung archipelago or as a fairly isolated incident has yet to be determined. Acehnese separatism continues, and terrorism has been added to the mix. Whether Indonesia will be held together by force or will splinter further remains a choice both for the Javanese-dominated majority and the various minorities.

Reevaluating Globalization

There are two contradictory positions with regard to Indonesia's future participation in the globalizing economy that stand out, and given Indonesia's immediate past, both of them are understandable. Neither argument calls for outright rejection of the world economy, although there are probably those who would favor total isolationism from the world system, at least for a time. Rather, there is disagreement about the degree of enthusiasm Indonesia should show toward taking its place in the world economy. In its most pure sense, it is a debate between the globalutionaries/westernizers and a group known in Indonesia as the *reformasi.*

Those elements in Indonesia committed to transforming Indonesia into a full participant in the global economy (and for most of them, into a fully functioning political democracy as well) view the post-Suharto era as an opportunity of sorts. Certainly, no one advocates more of the economic pain that has been inflicted on the country by the crash and the subsequent restructuring that is being forced on the country. Having said that, the crash did cause the autocratic Suharto regime to collapse, thereby creating the possibility for reform that would have been served by the "revolution from below" that the globalutionaries, as described earlier by Friedman, could not bring themselves to carry out.

Not all Indonesians are quite so certain about the virtue of a headlong flight into the embrace of globalization. The more conservative *reformasi*, rather, see the fall of Suharto's

New Order as an opportunity for a process that Patrick Smith calls "national reinvention," including questioning "the very ideals the West urges upon the world—democracy, liberty, equality, self-determination, modernization, progress." Instead, many Indonesians who are less Westernized than the globalutionaries see the need to assert Indonesian autonomy as more desirable than the homogenization of the Indonesian culture with the Western world that appears to be part and parcel of joining the globalization system.

Considerable problems remain. The CIA's *World Factbook* for 2004 listed the following economic problems still plaguing the country: alleviating widespread poverty, reforming the banking system, addressing cronyism and corruption, and rectifying a "generally poor climate for foreign investment." All of these conditions were present in the 1990s, and they are still present despite the IMF's attempts to infuse the values of the Washington consensus (see Chapter 7) on the system. New president SBY said in his inaugural that his government would "stimulate the economy" and "increase productivity," but offered no specific initiatives.

The intrusion of Western economic values into Indonesian affairs is the source of controversy within the country. Many Indonesians believe they uncritically embraced globalization in the early 1990s, only to get burned in 1997. The counter argument to this belief is the assertion by the globalutionaries that the reason Indonesia suffered was because it adopted the trappings of globalization but not the essential underpinnings of a truly globalizing country, notably openness and honesty in the financial sector. The veneer of globalization covered the rotten core of an essentially corrupted economic system; when the veneer was cracked by the reverberations from the *baht* crisis, the effect swept across the region and engulfed Indonesia, revealing how rotten the core was.

Which side of the argument one finds compelling is a matter of perspective that reflects the ambivalence many developing states have about globalization. Essentially, Indonesia has three options as it confronts its future relationship within the global economy. One option is to embrace the globalutionaries, swallow the bitter medicine of reform and austerity the IMF insists is necessary for its health to be restored, and then plunge headlong into the global economy. In an environment where the globalizing economy remains prosperous and vibrant, that strategy probably yields the greatest economic gains for most—but certainly not all—Indonesians. The other side of that choice is that there are no guarantees that the events of 1997 will not repeat themselves; also, the embrace will almost certainly necessitate abandoning some social and economic practices and institutions that are uniquely Indonesian.

The second option is joining the globalizing economy, but with a distinctively Asian flavor, what some call the "Asian model." There are clear incentives to exercise this option, largely on cultural grounds. Joining the West entails becoming like the West, and groups like the *reformasi* are concerned about this erosive effect on Indonesian culture and society. As Smith once again argues, a strong thread of Indonesian opinion believes that, "amid great material change, traditional morals and hierarchies must be maintained." The problem is that adherence to aspects of the Asian model that allowed opacity in the financial sector caused the problem in the first place, and that one of the traditional morals turned out to be the "traditional" corruption and nepotism that made the crisis worse than it might otherwise have been.

If Indonesia opts for resistance to the requirements of the global community, its effective third option may be a minimal participation in the global economy. Such a course would almost certainly leave Indonesia poorer than and isolated from its neighbors who accept the strictures of the IMF and other international agencies, and it would certainly be opposed by the westernizers and globalutionaries, who favor participation in the global economy as a way to make Indonesia more like the developed world.

For the time being, at least, Indonesia has apparently chosen a variant of option two. It remains tied to the globalization system through its continued membership and participation in the major globalization-promoting international organizations, including the Asia-Pacific Economic Cooperation, the Association of Southeast Asian Nations, the World Bank, the International Monetary Fund, and the World Trade Organization. At the same time, Indonesia withdrew from its IMF development program at the end of 2003. In doing so, it issued a "White Paper" committing the government to maintaining the sound macroeconomic policies established under the IMF guidelines. Withdrawal from the IMF program apparently was intended to allow more uniquely Indonesian solutions to the range of microeconomic issues that have plagued the country in the past and that remain barriers to economic growth and foreign investment. Physical recovery from the tsunami places greater strains on the economy.

Political Reformation

As already noted, Indonesia has less than a rich democratic tradition, and the absence of Western-style democracy is one of the parts of the distinctly Eastern, Indonesian culture that those who have benefited from the traditional system have sought to continue. The traditional autocratic nature of the political system forged in the wake of independence was strengthened by the alliance between the government and an Indonesian military that has long been politically active in support of the traditional system. In the past, challenges to the authority of Jakarta have been opposed and upon occasion even ruthlessly crushed by the army. The question is whether this situation will continue in the future with a democratically elected president at the helm of state.

The answer clearly crosses the line from politics into the economy. There are clear connections between economic globalization and political democratization. Virtually all the countries at the heart of the global economy are or are becoming democratic, and it can be argued that economic capitalism (the economic philosophy of the globalizing economy) and political democracy are both expressions of the same underlying commitment to individual freedom to choose, arguments discussed in Chapter 3.

If democratization and participation in the global economy are linked, then the decision either to become a full-fledged part of the global economy or a partial participant will also help determine the political path for the country. Overcoming the legacy of corruption and mismanagement at the highest levels is clearly part of the problem. The government of Megawati Sukarnoputri attempted to walk a tight line here. The decision by her government to withdraw from its IMF program signaled both a commitment to globalization and a recognition of the realities of domestic politics. The direction her successor takes will have an important, even critical, impact on the future.

National Integrity

The recently concluded events in East Timor are inconclusive about whether Indonesia will remain a cohesive unit or whether other areas of the far-flung island chain will spin away by seceding from the union. The situation in East Timor was unique and the loss of the territory does not threaten the economic or political integrity of the country directly; nonetheless, it does potentially provide a precedent that other areas of the country might seek to exploit in the future. The successful conclusion of Timorese separatism has neither triggered a spate of new secessionist movements nor reduced separatist movements in Aceh, Irian Jaya, or elsewhere, and these movements reverberate throughout the Indonesian system and add to the general uncertainty surrounding Indonesia's future. The Indonesian military has been particularly opposed to secession and has historically used its power to repress separatist movements. It also tends to equate democratization with the freedom to organize seditious movements. At the same time, the kind of campaign that it waged clandestinely to suppress East Timorese separatism clearly blew up in its face, and the military knows that any similar action will be subject to intense international scrutiny that very much limits the choices it can exercise. In addition, it now has homegrown terrorists to deal with.

Whether a concern over the relationship between democratization and separatism will provide sufficient weight to slow processes of political and economic integration into the evolving world system remains to be seen. It is, however, a concern that does not influence the process in many other countries debating globalization but lacking similar divisive forces.

CONCLUSION

Indonesia continues to struggle in the transition from its past to the future. In late 2000, two apparently related incidents provided dramatic, and highly symbolic, evidence of the content and direction of Indonesia's travail. On August 31, 2000, the government convened a trial against former President Suharto, who was summoned to answer charges he had stolen $571 million from the government during his years in office and distributed the money to family and friends. Beyond the emphasis on rooting out corruption in the government, investigators hoped to recover all or most of the embezzled funds. Suharto, claiming he was too ill to answer the summons to court, did not appear, to the dismay of his opponents.

The government attempted to begin the trial two weeks later, on September 13. Suharto again pleaded ill health and failed to appear again, but in addition, a powerful car bomb exploded outside the Indonesian Stock Exchange in Jakarta, killing fifteen people and injuring more than forty. There were immediate accusations that supporters of Suharto had engineered the explosion to divert attention from the former president, and his youngest son (known as Tommy Suharto) was arrested by police in an attempt to insure that a repeat performance did not occur. The symbolism of an attack on the most prominent symbol of Indonesia's flirtation with the globalization system did not go unnoticed. Neither did the fact that the successor government of President Wahid would pursue charges against the leading symbol of the country's corrupt political past. The fact that the Indonesian parliament voted 393 to 4 to investigate allegations of corruption against Wahid in late January 2001 further indicates the pervasiveness of the problem of corruption and the desire to root it out. From this political chaos, the current regime emerged. The fact that his successor, Megawati Sukrnoputri, a truly popular figure in much of the country, was defeated in the 2004 election by a relative unknown (at least before the campaign) offers some hope for the emergence of popular democracy.

Where is Indonesia headed? Will the country make the successful transition to globalization and democracy or will it sink back into autocracy and backwardness, a kind of island Myanmar (Burma)? What will the future mean for the centrifugal forces at play in parts of the country?

Indonesia may not face meaningful choices. Unless something dramatic occurs to change the direction of the global economy—an enormous worldwide depression, for instance—Indonesia may have no choice but to jump back on and ride the wave, especially because all of its neighbors in APEC and ASEAN remain essentially committed to globalization. Moreover, acceptance or resistance to Westernization is largely generational in Indonesia, as it is elsewhere. The young, well-educated professionals—the globalutionaries—are committed to full participation in the world order. While their success is not preordained, time is probably on their side.

There is, of course, the matter of Indonesia's special problem, the centrifugal force of areas like Aceh, Borneo, and Irian Jaya. The real problem in these diverse areas is, and has been, the treatment the people of these areas have received from the central government in Jakarta, and especially from the military. Whether separatism will continue to mount or where it might occur is probably a matter of the success or failure of reform. Would a truly democratic central government, for instance, have permitted the brutal suppression of the East Timorese by government forces? In a prosperous, open Indonesia, would Acehnese demands for a more equitable distribution of government resources and firmer guarantees of religious freedom not receive a more sympathetic hearing? Would a return to the growing prosperity of the early 1990s heal some of the wounds and moderate some of the centrifugal forces in the country?

Like other countries in the region, Indonesia was badly burned by the East Asian financial crisis of 1997, and the country continues to strain under the restrictions placed upon it by the international community that are designed to reform and strengthen the Indonesian economy. Given the trauma the country has undergone, it should not be surprising that at least some Indonesians are reluctant to jump unconditionally back into the globalization system. On the other hand, many Indonesians believe strongly that the country's problem was that it adopted only part of the globalization system before, providing a veneer that obscured the ugly innards of a highly secretive, corrupt system that ultimately undermined the globalization effort. Whether the *reformasi* or the globalizers will prevail in the unfolding debate over the participation of the world's fourth most populous state remains to be seen. The outcome is, of course, important for Indonesia and its large, strategically located population. But it could prove important in a broader context as well. Within the region are the two most populous countries in the world, and each faces deep divisions of its own. Will the fate of Indonesia presage the future for other countries like China, India, and possibly others?

STUDY/DISCUSSION QUESTIONS

1. Why is Indonesia an important country to study in terms of its transition to the globalization system? How will the outcome of the Indonesian experience affect its region and beyond?

2. The East Asian financial crisis of 1997 had an enormous impact on Indonesia and its region. How was Indonesia in particular affected economically, politically, and geopolitically?

3. One of the effects of the 1997 crisis was to cause a serious collapse of the Indonesian economy and a subsequent debate over the future of Indonesia's participation in the global economy. What are the major arguments in that debate? Who holds which positions? How do they differ?

4. Indonesia's experience with globalization contributed to the political crisis of 1998 that brought down Suharto. How were politics and economics connected in the crisis? What is the relationship between politics and economics in the globalization process more generally, and how does this affect the future of Indonesia?

5. At least partly because it is a far-flung archipelago, Indonesia has a number of centrifugal forces that are unique to it. What are the sources of separatism, and what can the Indonesian government do to dampen these tendencies?

6. Based on the information provided, draw two distinct futures for Indonesia on the three dimensions discussed, one negative and one positive. Which future do you prefer? Which one do you think Indonesia will follow? Why?

7. If you were an Indonesian, what lessons do you think you would draw from your country's globalization experience? Would you choose the path they apparently have? Why or why not?

READING/RESEARCH MATERIAL

Bilveer, Singh. "Civil-Military Relations in Democratizing Indonesia: Change Amidst Continuity." *Armed Forces and Society* 20, 4 (Summer 2000), 607–633.

Emmerson, Donald K. "Will Indonesia Survive?" *Foreign Affairs* 79, 3 (Summer 2000), 95–106.

Friedman, Thomas L. *The Lexus and the Olive Tree: Understanding Globalization.* New York: Farrar, Straus, Giroux, 1999.

Pei, Minxin. "Will China Become Another Indonesia?" *Foreign Policy* 116 (Fall 1999), 94–109.

Ravich, Samantha. "Eyeing Indonesia Through the Lens of Aceh." *Washington Quarterly* 23, 3 (Summer 2000), 7–20.

Smith, Patrick. "What Does it Mean to Be Modern? Indonesia's *Reformasi.*" *Washington Quarterly* 22, 4 (Autumn 1999), 47–64.

WEB SITES

Official U.S. government view and facts

Central Intelligence Agency, *The World Factbook 2004* http://www.odci.gov/cia/publications/factbook

Overview from a respected English journal on Indonesia

Economist Intelligence Unit, *Country Overviews* 2004 http://www.eiu.com

Federation of American Scientists, *U.S. Arms Clients Profiles, Indonesia* http://fas.org/asmp/profiles/indonesia.htm

Ratings on corruption in countries around the world

Transparency International, *1999 Corruption Perceptions Index* http://www.transparency.org

Basic information on Indonesia and its foreign affairs

Department of Foreign Affairs of the Republic of Indonesia at http://dfa-deplu.go.id

PART 4

The Altered Face
of Security

Along with globalization, some of the most dramatic changes in the post–Cold War environment have occurred in the areas of national and international security. The Cold War security system was overshadowed by the prospect of nuclear war between the superpowers, a cataclysmic possibility beside which other problems paled in comparison. Certainly, there was no shortage of other problems; it was just that they were subordinate to avoiding a possibly nuclear World War III.

Although a nuclear inferno is still a physical possibility, it is now considered far less likely to occur. This change has allowed consideration of some old problems that existed before the end of the Cold War but that received less concern then, but especially of some matters that have arisen since the Cold War ended. Much of the change is connected to technological possibilities that did not exist before, which have turned on their heads the traditional patterns of warfare.

The cases selected for this part of the book reflect this continuity and change. Chapter 10, "Future War," looks broadly at what warfare may look like in the future and how well our anticipation of the future of war in the past century affects our confidence about judging the shape of war in a new century. The focus is on the contrasting impact of military technology on two eras: the period between the two world wars and the present. Planning in the 1920s and 1930s produced differential refinements in thinking about conventional, European-style, or symmetrical warfare. In contrast, technology today has produced such imbalances between the most capable militaries and others that planning must concentrate on unconventional, or asymmetrical, warfare.

The other two cases deal with problems that have their sources before the end of the Cold War. National missile defense, the subject of Chapter 11, "When National and International Politics Collide," is a possibility that first appeared in the 1960s, reappeared in the 1980s, and forms one of the major emphases of the American Bush presidency in the new century. The case focuses on the evolution of this policy thrust, but with the added concern that the American policy initiative to build a defense system is fundamentally opposed by nearly all the major powers, creating a tension about which priorities are best served in this area.

Chapter 12, "Who Cares about Kashmir?" examines a basic problem of Indo-Pakistani relations that dates back to the partition of the Indian subcontinent in 1948. The princely states of Jammu and Kashmir have been points of contention ever since, but now the problem has been made more dangerous by the addition of the "new teeth" of nuclear weapons on each side. The case looks at how this new "variable" may affect Kashmir in the future.

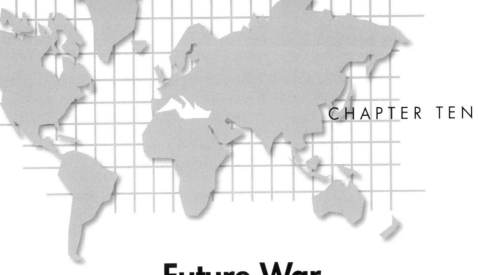

CHAPTER TEN

Future War

FROM SYMMETRICAL TO ASYMMETRICAL CONFLICT

PRÉCIS

Anticipating the nature of future conflict and preparing for that form of combat has always been a primary responsibility for those charged with national and international security. This is a difficult process involving extrapolation of the past into the future.

The difficulties in preparing for future wars is the central theme of this case study. It is presented in a comparative fashion. The first part of the case deals with preparation for what became World War II during the two decades after World War I, the interwar years. The basic problem was extending the prospects of war between two similar groups of countries fighting in a similar manner, what we call symmetrical warfare. The second part of the case looks at the contemporary military planning problem. Unlike the gradual changes in warfare that faced the World War II planners, contemporary planners face a world increasingly dominated by asymmetrical warfare, where competing sides fight in a dissimilar manner under different rules and with ever changing concepts and execution. This part of the case describes asymmetrical warfare, the reasons it is important, its major characteristics, and some examples.

Anticipating and preparing for the next war is an age-old problem that has concerned politically organized entities throughout history. Whether states or other political organizations thought about the problem as a means to plan to attack or to defend, knowing who one's enemies are and how they are likely to provide a menace can mean the difference between victory and defeat, even survival or destruction. Understanding the threats present in the environment and acting appropriately to defuse them can also lead to the avoidance of war, clearly the best outcome.

Why political groups prepare for and go to war will not concern us directly in this case study. Certainly, why one prepares does have a bearing; preparations to deter attack or to defend are different from preparations to act aggressively, although that distinction may or may not have significant meaning for a potential adversary. But regardless of motivations, there are hardly any societies that have not felt the need to address the problem posed by future threats.

It is, and always has been, a difficult problem. Future wars, by definition, are projections into a period of time that does not yet exist and that, by definition, we cannot know entirely in advance. Will the same kinds of weapons be available in the future as there were in the past? If there are new weapons, what will they be like, how will they be used, and what will be their effect? Who will have the new weapons, and who will not? How will weapons balance affect patterns of war? For that matter, who will the enemy be? Where will I have to fight the next adversary?

Because we cannot precisely know the answers to any of these questions in advance, the result is a condition of uncertainty that becomes a major part of the operational universe of the military planner. These uncertainties produce an environment laced as well by an aura of conservatism and seriousness. It is conservative because reckless innovation and lack of preparedness can lead to vulnerability that can have potentially devastating consequences. It is serious because the wrong decisions—the failure to prepare properly or adequately—can literally endanger national existence. Because of these potential consequences, there is a built in propensity to over prepare—to anticipate more threats than realistically exist. Conservatism and the seriousness of making mistakes also predispose planners to emphasize ways of doing things that have worked in the past—to stay "inside the box"—rather than to embrace change and its uncertainties. The result is a tendency to prepare "to fight the last (most recently concluded) war."

Despite the apparently benign environment during the 1990s (and in some sense, because of the tranquility) that was shattered by the terrorist attacks in 2001, the problem of gauging the future of war is especially acute today. There are some clear reasons why many states are grappling seriously with the future. For one thing, the period that marked the Cold War also marked the "long peace" of the second half of the twentieth century. Because much of the preparation that states undertake in planning for war is in fact an extrapolation of their most recent experience, our useful experience, at least in the desperation of a major war that threatens national existence and thus forms what is known as the "worst case," is now more than a half-century old. What is the continuing relevance of the most recent experience to the future?

It depends. One of the most important aspects of preparing for future war is anticipating against whom one is likely to have to fight. Although many Americans sought to ignore the warning signs during the 1930s, it was pretty clear that World War II would find the United States on one side and countries like Germany and Japan on the other (at least retrospect suggests that structure of the conflict). During the Cold War, it was absolutely clear that the enemy against whom we had to prepare was the Soviet Union and its communist allies. The structure of the system dictated the content of the planning process.

Not all planning has such a clear focus. In August 1990, Iraq invaded and quickly conquered Kuwait. This act of aggression would ultimately bring together a coalition of more than twenty-five states, none of whom had given much if any thought to the possibility of war with Iraq as little as a few months before the invasion occurred. The lesson was that some problems can be easily anticipated; others cannot. The completely unanticipated terrorist attacks of September 11, 2001, redouble the point.

There is another factor that influences the process today that was a lesser concern in the past: technological change. In the historical past, warfare generally did not change greatly. As chroniclers of war like the Brodies (see the readings) have suggested, with the exception of an occasional innovation like the catapult or gunpowder, warfare during much of the second millennium did not change a great deal, and most of the changes were gradual and incremental rather than revolutionary and dramatic. Once in a while, a traditional enemy might fashion some new weapon—such as the crossbow—that would make accepted ways of conducting war dangerous or suicidal. At the same time, an outsider might present a military problem with which a society had no idea how to cope— the massed mounted cavalry of Genghis Khan's Golden Horde, for instance. But generally, the problem of physical preparation remained relatively the same.

The Industrial Revolution and its adaptation to warfare in the nineteenth century accelerated the impact of technology, and its impact has grown steadily ever since. Our twentieth century past involved applying inventions like the internal combustion engine to warfare. The twenty-first century looks at a battlefield environment more reminiscent of science fiction motion pictures than of warfare in the past. New and deadly possibilities like chemical and biological agents applied to war add further to the uncertainty of a future where tomorrow's enemies, like the Iraqis in Kuwait in 1990 and the Iraqi resistance of 2004, are more difficult to anticipate.

All of the past millennium was dominated by a style and philosophy of warfare that was heavily Western and that culminated in the way World War II was fought, what we now call symmetrical warfare (where both sides fight in the same manner and basically by the same rules). However, since early in the post–Cold War world, that situation has changed. Arguably, warfare is changing fundamentally from the confrontation and clash of mass armies to a more asymmetrical form: weaker foes seek to negate Western styles with non-Western variants on war where the two sides are dissimilar in organization and purpose and do not fight honoring the same rules and conventions. September 11, 2001, may be remembered as the harbinger of this change in the nature of warfare.

Thus, the problem of preparing for future war boils down to three basic considerations. The first is the *conflict environment*, and the main factor in that environment is the nature of the adversaries one may encounter in the future, including why and how one may have to fight them. In the past, war was between the organized armed forces of other states. Contemporary conflicts often pit traditional armed forces against so-called non–state actors, forces with no territorial base or governmental affiliation. The second consideration is the *physical structure of warfare*, which consists of the means available for adversaries to fight each other and the degree to which the means available are appropriately adapted to achieve military ends. In the contemporary era, the means are widely disparate for different foes, creating the basis for asymmetrical approaches for the disadvantaged. The third concern is determining *against whom one might have to fight* in a major power environment that was remarkably tranquil for more than a decade, that has not witnessed a major war in more than a half century, and where possible enemies are difficult to anticipate in conventional ways.

Military technology is a major influence in these calculations. Between the world wars, new technologies were "weaponized" by both sides, and more efficient applications were rewarded. The competition, however, was essentially over who could harness the same technologies to becoming "best" at symmetrical warfare. Today, technological levels have become so imbalanced that the nonpossessors of modern technology have no reasonable chance engaging the opponent symmetrically and must fight asymmetrically to have any prospect of success.

These observations form the rationale for the rest of the case. In the following pages, we will examine the problem of preparing for future war through two "mini-cases." The first will be historical—how planners in the 1930s prepared for the likelihood of a second major war in the first half of the twentieth century. Looking at the three basic categories of concern, the conflict environment was, or could have been, fairly clear, but the physical structure of conflict was not. While some argued that war with the Soviets was more likely than war with Germany or Japan and others felt it could be avoided altogether, the combatants were basically locked in by the latter part of the 1930s. Although the last major war was only twenty years in the past, the planners had to grapple with adapting to a number of weapons—tanks, for instance—that were introduced during the Great War (as World War I was known at the time) but not used to maximum effect, and to a number of uniquely new technologies adapted for military use—ultimately atomic weapons.

Planning for the wars of the twenty-first century is more difficult. For one thing, there are no obvious major, conventional adversaries in the system, due in large measure to the ideological harmony among the major powers in the current international system. The answer to the question, "preparing to fight whom?" is especially fraught with uncertainty regarding who to prepare to fight and how to prepare to fight them. At the same time, the long gap between major wars has allowed the accumulation of a large number of militarily relevant technologies that have greatly enhanced the conventional capabilities of those who possess them. Some of the electronically based innovations have been employed in "shooting galleries" like the Persian Gulf War and Operation Iraqi Freedom in 2003, and the primary lesson these victims seemed to have learned is not to fight the West (especially the United States) on its terms. The imbalance in symmetrical capabilities has in effect done two things: it has made the development of asymmetrical, technology-negating methods the primary dynamic of the present, and it has arguably rendered symmetrical warfare archaic, because no one will fight that way.

PLANNING TWENTIETH-CENTURY STYLE: ANTICIPATING WORLD WAR II

Imagine the world from the viewpoint of a military planner in 1919, shortly after the end of World War I. The bloodiest military conflict in human history to that point had just been concluded. It had been a war that had been poorly anticipated; as late as the early 1910s, there was still the widespread belief that economic interdependence had rendered war between the major powers functionally impossible or at least highly unlikely.

Although there were some who decried the fact that major war had been absent from Europe for more than forty years, few believed that there were any differences worth fighting over.

The Great War had started almost accidentally, as the assassination of Archduke Franz Ferdinand of Austria and his wife by Bosnian terrorists had activated a string of alliance commitments that brought the major combatants into confrontation. As the crisis grew, little was done to defuse it. Some attribute that failure to mediocre leadership in the major capitals (see Stoessinger in the readings). There was even positive sentiment for war, based on the belief that European youth had gone soft in the interim since the last large European conflict, the Franco-Prussian War of 1870. A war, so the argument went, would infuse Europe with a reinvigorating discipline and sense of national duty and sacrifice.

The greatest tragedy was that Europe had so poorly anticipated the kind of war that it was going to get. From warfare in the nineteenth and early twentieth centuries, there were two models available about what war in the future would be. One model was that of the Franco-Prussian War, where lightning strikes by offensively oriented armies led to rapid and decisive warfare. The Franco-Prussian War lasted only a little more than six weeks before the French surrender to Germany, and losses on both sides were minimal by contemporary standards.

The other model combined the experiences of the American Civil War and the Russo-Japanese War of 1904–05. Both these wars, conducted forty years apart, were extremely hard fought and costly in terms of blood, and both featured the increasing dominance of defensive tactics over the offense. Indeed, around Petersburg, Virginia, in the winter of 1864–65, and the Asian battlefields of the Russo-Japanese War, trench warfare, which would ultimately become the grisly symbol of World War I, was even present.

The planners had these two models to choose from, and they chose the wrong one as the harbinger of World War I. They dismissed the American Civil War, which one German observer described at the time as "two armed mobs chasing one another around the country, from which nothing can be learned." It was a war between amateurs and hence unlike one conducted between the professional armies of Europe. The Russo-Japanese precedent was similarly dismissed because the combatants were either Asian or Eurasian, and hence considered inferior to European troops.

Preparations and predictions reflected the belief that the war would be short and decisive. In the wake of defeat in the Franco-Prussian War, French General Ferdinand Foch developed the strategy of *offensive a outrance* (offensive to the extreme) as the guiding principle of the French military. In Imperial Germany, Count Alfred von Schlieffen, chief of the general staff, devised a plan for a rapid "right hook" through the Low Countries that would roll up the French forces in a manner not dissimilar to 1870. In Berlin, the Kaiser exhorted troops leaving for war in the summer of 1914 that they would be back before the first leaves fell from the trees in the fall. Everyone anticipated a short, decisive, and relatively bloodless reprise of the Franco-Prussian War.

All of these projections were, of course, erroneous, and planners looking at the scene in 1919 could only shake their heads at the wreckage and begin to plan for the future, hoping to fashion a system that would prevent a future war, or, failing in that, assuring that the conduct and outcome would be very different than what they could survey from the last war. That meant examining the likely environment in the future and the physical structure of the next war.

Largely lost in the bitterness surrounding the environment in 1919 was rebuilding a durable peace that would make a repeat unlikely. In retrospect, World War I had been avoidable if the combatants had tried to avoid it, but they did not. Woodrow Wilson had sought a durable peace through the League of Nations, but U.S. Senate rejection of the peace treaty and vindictive, bitter sentiments in Europe and elsewhere pushed war avoidance to the back burner.

Conflict Environment

The conflict environment facing military planers and political leaders in 1919 bore both similarities to and differences from the prewar environment. The map, for instance, had changed somewhat, but the major players were still intact. The Austro-Hungarian Empire and Ottoman Empire had disappeared from the map, and the Russian Empire had been refashioned as the Soviet Union. Germany was disarmed and had contrition forced upon it by the terms of the peace treaty, but it would rise again in the 1930s to great power status. France and Great Britain were physically and financially exhausted by the war, and both sought to retreat from major commitments and recover. In the Pacific, Imperial Japan was showing signs of the militarism that would lead to its expansion and the road to war in the Pacific. The United States, of course, was in the process of its retreat into "splendid isolationism."

The geopolitical environment was not entirely unlike the prewar environment. Germany was prostrate and held down by provisions of the Versailles Treaty officially ending the war, but Franco-German animosity remained, and the geopolitical question that had dominated Europe since the Napoleonic Wars, which country would dominate the continent, had clearly not been permanently resolved. The major innovation in the system was the new League of Nations, the twentieth century's first attempt at organizing the peace around an international organization.

Although it is easier to make projections with the assistance of "20/20 hindsight," the geopolitical environment in which conflict might emerge had to be basically familiar to planners in 1919. One might or might not have been able to project with precision what country or countries one might have to fight sometime in the future, but the next war was likely to be between the major European states fighting in familiar ways. Force planning, in other words, was likely to be an extrapolation from the geopolitical past rather than any major deviation from that past. It may have been more difficult to anticipate the growing rivalry between the United States and Japan over the Pacific region, although some historians have argued that war between the two countries was probably made inevitable by American colonization of the Philippines in 1898, because the Philippines archipelago was a clear barrier standing in the way of Japanese expansion in East Asia.

Physical Structure of Warfare

World War I had been a technologically interesting event, as a number of new weapons based on technologies developed in the years leading to the conflict were introduced to the battlefield. As is so often the case, the new technologies were often not employed in the most effective way that they could be, nor were they employed in support of warfare as they would be in the future. For military planners in the years between the world wars, the task was to assess these innovations and how they might be better utilized in a future war. Most tragically, planners did not anticipate the greater lethality of the new technologies and the quantum leap in carnage they would produce.

Although it risks some oversimplification, there were two categories of innovation introduced between 1914 and 1918. One of these was in firepower, and it was represented by two kinds of weapons in land warfare. World War I, for instance, introduced rapid-fire weapons to the battlefield. Modern military rifles of the kind issued to average soldiers could fire up to 20 bullets per minute, an enormous increase over older weapons that could fire only a few shots in that period. More dramatically, the first reliable machine guns were introduced; they could fire as many as 200–400 rounds per minute. These weapons were, however, heavy; the machine gun and its mount weighed about 100 pounds, meaning it had to be placed in a stationary position, generally with entrenchment or some other form of protection for the machine gunner. The other innovation was improvement in heavy artillery. The artillery pieces employed in World War I could fire large shells over long distances at the rate of 6–10 shots per minute. As the name implies, their weight made them largely immobile, and the result was that large-scale artillery exchanges took place as each side tried to silence the other's big guns.

The tactics associated with the war did not adequately compensate for this change in firepower. The offensive orientation that both sides had adopted before the war put them on the attack as the doctrinally proper way to fight. When the trench lines hardened (and were aided by other innovations such as razor sharp concertina wire), attacks against these rapid-fire weapons systems were nothing short of suicidal. Planners of strategies like the *offensive a outrance,* however, remained wedded to their ideas, and sent wave after wave of increasingly cynical, disillusioned young men to their deaths at the hands of the machine gunners.

The other innovation was in transportation, inspired by the invention and application in warfare of the internal combustion engine and the storage battery. The internal combustion engine produced three vehicles of war: the truck, the tank, and the heavier than air airplane. The battery made the submarine possible. Each changed the nature of warfare, although with different effects.

The truck served two functions. First, it provided a way to transport troops and supplies to the battlefield. It increased military flexibility because trucks could go anywhere there were roads. In the setting of the trenches that stretched unbroken from the Alps to the North Sea, the purpose of trucks was to move personnel and materiel to weak spots in the trench line—in other words further to reinforce the advantage of the defense.

The tank was first introduced into the war by the British in 1916. Its promise was as a weapon system that could smash through German trenches and open spaces through which troops could advance, thereby breaking the deadlock and recreating movement on the front. The tank did not, however, fulfill its promise in World War I. The early tank designs were very slow, leaving them vulnerable to artillery fire, and their treads often came off, leaving them immobile sitting ducks. At that, tanks were to be the centerpiece of Plan 1919, a strategy devised by British General J. F. C. Fuller to have tanks spearhead a breakthrough against the Germans in 1919. The plan was never implemented, because the war ended in 1918.

Finally, the internal combustion engine made feasible flight by heavier than air flying machines. The airplane was introduced into the war with little advance indication of what its role would be. The first air warriors were used as observers, flying over enemy positions and performing reconnaissance missions. Gradually, airplanes became engaged in air-to-air combat and some limited bombing, but their impact on the war's outcome was minimal.

Finally, the storage battery made the submarine a plausible naval weapon. Their major purpose was attacking Allied shipping across the Atlantic, and especially between the United States and the Western Allies. Fortunately for the Allies, the Germans manufactured relatively few U-boats, because the Kaiser was discouraged from putting his resources into so-called "commerce raiders" by the writings of American naval strategist Alfred Thayer Mahan. Instead, the Germans concentrated on building large battleships (as Mahan suggested they should), the largest of which were the dreadnaughts, which remained bottled up in the North Sea, while the submarines were able to slip through the British naval net and wreak havoc on Allied shipping.

Interwar Planning

Each of these innovations underwent reevaluation during the interwar years, and with revisions of hardware and tactics, became part of the backbone of the military machines that prepared for and fought World War II. In the case of each technology, there would be some disagreement about what those roles would be, and only the crucible of war itself would validate some ideas and invalidate others.

Military planning incorporating the new technologies affected all three media on which warfare could take place: on land, in and under the water, and in the air. Land warfare, especially as it would be applied again in Europe, came to reemphasize the offense in warfare through mobility. The fruits of the internal combustion engine led the way, as tanks, armored personnel carriers, and the like became the spearheads of land campaigns, with infantry acting in a supportive role to armor rather than the other way around, as had been the case in World War I. At the same time, rapid-fire weapons developed further, so the average infantryman could carry a semiautomatic machine gun into battle rather than having to mount it in an entrenched position. The idea of the defense did not disappear; the Maginot Line, the single deadly flaw of which was that it did not extend all the way to the North Sea, was testimony to the legacy of the first war.

Some of these developments were anticipated in World War I. German General Oskar von Hutier experimented with highly mobile special forces that infiltrated Western trench lines by avoiding the most heavily defended areas and attacking isolated places instead. Fuller's Plan 1919 similarly relied on the mobility as well as punching power of tanks crashing through German trench lines. Neither materially affected the outcome of the war in 1918. These ideas would, however, bear fruit in World War II.

Some countries anticipated these possibilities and planned accordingly better than others. The German general staff was at the forefront, developing principles of mobility and movement into what became known as *blitzkrieg* (lightning war). Other countries, notably France and Poland, continued to rely on mounted cavalry and gave inadequate attention to mechanization of the war machine. When war came, those who had failed to understand the change in warfare suffered the most. On the battlefield, the leaders who understood and accommodated these changes best were generals like the German Erwin Rommel and the American George S. Patton.

Naval warfare was transformed as well. Prior to World War II, naval warfare was typically between surface combatants, where the object was to attack and sink the opponent and where the largest and most heavily armed vessels normally prevailed. Certainly that had been the case in World War I, where the largest battleships, the dreadnaughts, were the crown jewels of the world's navies.

Technological advancements also rendered battleships highly vulnerable and increasingly obsolete. The battery systems (and internal combustion engine for providing propulsion on the surface and for recharging the batteries) that made submarines practical in the first war were improved considerably, and the torpedo-armed submarine became a long-range platform that could lurk beneath the surface and put the largest battleships at mercy.

More fundamentally, the airplane transformed the way naval warfare would be fought in the second world conflagration. As early as the 1920s, air power enthusiasts like the American "Billy" Mitchell were arguing that airplanes could be used to attack and sink surface ships. When he demonstrated the feasibility of attacking a battleship by flying a bomber with its bomb bay open over a battleship and taking a picture of the vessel, the process of transformation was underway. In the years between the world wars, the centerpiece in naval warfare ceased being the battleship and became instead the aircraft carrier. In World War II, carrier-based aircraft became the principal weapons of naval warfare, with other ships relegated largely to the role of protecting the carrier from attack (a principle that remains largely intact today).

The enthusiasts of the airplane were among the most active and ambitious planners between the world wars. People like Mitchell, the Italian Guilio Douhet, and Great Britain's Hugh Trenchard led the way, arguing that the ability to attack from the air would ultimately make other forms of warfare obsolete. In the future, they argued as part of what became known as the theory of strategic bombardment, it would not be necessary to defeat an enemy's army or navy to attack the homeland; aircraft would simply fly over the battlefield and attack the enemy with impunity. When this idea was embellished with the notion of attacking so-called "vital centers" (targets which if destroyed would compromise the enemy's ability to make war, such as oil refineries), the air warrior's claims were complete.

The airmen's claims proved to be excessive, and the supremacy of air power remains a contentious issue. Air power eventually did reduce Germany's war industries to rubble, but the detractors counter that Germany had essentially lost the war anyway by the time bombing succeeded in destroying Germany's vital centers. In the Pacific, the atomic bombing of Hiroshima and Nagasaki by the U.S. Eighth Air Force relieved the United States of the need to launch a resisted invasion of the Japanese home islands, but that relief was at a terrible cost in civilian deaths.

The atomic attacks provide a vivid example of the other major controversy introduced by the air power theorists. Prior to the concentrated bombings of the enemy's homelands, the laws of war made it illegal to direct purposeful attacks on noncombatant civilians. Certainly those rules had been violated on occasion, but attacking the vital centers of military productions inevitably entailed large civilian casualties, euphemistically referred to as "collateral damage" (objects inadvertently destroyed in the process of attacking a military target). The fire bombings of Tokyo by the Americans and Dresden by the British during the war are particularly vivid instances of this practice. It remains controversial to this day, as indicated by the reaction to the bombing of Belgrade, Yugoslavia, by NATO in 1999 to put pressure on the Milosevic regime to end its suppression of Albanian Kosovars.

Determining Opponents

The coalitions that would ultimately fight World War II did varying jobs of "sizing up" their potential opponents. The Japanese understood that their expansion would ultimately bring them face-to-face with the United States, but they underestimated the ultimate power the United States would bring to bear against them. Similarly, Hitler underestimated the task of subduing the Soviet Union. Had his hatred for Slavs been less consuming, he might have maintained an uneasy accommodation with the Soviets, in which case the war might have ended very differently. On the Allied side, none of the major powers prepared adequately for war, and when it came, they had to build up their capabilities, thereby almost certainly prolonging the fighting.

PLANNING TWENTY-FIRST–CENTURY STYLE: ANTICIPATING FUTURE WARS

The process of anticipating and planning for war during the first one-half of the last century has a certain comfortableness and familiarity about it. For the most part, wars were fought for traditional reasons between traditional adversaries in basically familiar ways. The same basic coalitions, after all, fought both world wars in Europe, with only the war in the Pacific between the United States and Japan adding novelty to the cast of characters and motivations. The basic function of planning was the adaptation of new technology to its most efficient ends. In effect, the planners were fine-tuning and adapting a style of warfare with which they were familiar and comfortable—symmetrical warfare. The Cold War was a further refinement of these same ideas centered on American- and Soviet-led coalitions.

But those conditions are not so clearly evident today. If we put ourselves in the shoes of a military planner in the year 2005, the continuities of the past are not clear. Both elements of the planning process, the conflict environment and the physical structure of warfare, have changed, and the composition of likely enemies to be deterred or, if necessary, fought, continues to evolve and be the source of controversy.

Two major factors have changed things: the end of the Cold War and the rise of new forms of opposition. The collapse of the Cold War left the United States as the only traditional military great power. American technology-based power has continued to grow absolutely and relatively to other states and no new opponent has replaced the Soviet Union as an opponent; the result is a chasm in military power between the United States and the rest of the world. As that power has increased, however, it may have lost some of its relevance. American conventional military capability has become so overwhelming as to be unchallengeable. No one can or will fight the United States the way the United States is prepared to fight. The rise of new opposition emerges in this context. Middle Eastern, fundamentalist Islamic opposition to Western values cannot confront the West head on, and has reverted to less direct, more traditionally Eastern forms of asymmetrical warfare that are rapidly adapting to American responses. The terrorism of September 11, 2001, and the Iraqi resistance may be the future with which planners must contend.

Conflict Environment

Traditional geopolitics has clearly taken a beating since the end of the Cold War. A situation in which two politico-military alliances face one another is the stuff of traditional calculation, but that basis has evaporated. The first victim of the end of the Cold War has been the operational environment for military planning, a structure of adversarial relationships that provides concrete military problems against which to prepare. At least among the major military members of the international system, that structure has utterly disappeared.

In some ways, this is a considerable improvement over the past. It means that for now, at least, there is virtually no likelihood of major war between the most powerful countries of the world on the scale of the world wars and made more potentially devastating by the addition of nuclear weapons in the arsenals of antagonists. Certainly the tools for such a war are still available, but it is difficult to conjure the circumstances that would ignite such a conflagration. There are a few places in the world, for instance the Indian subcontinent, where adversaries might become involved in a war of fairly large proportions, but none of those places would raise the distinct likelihood of drawing in other major actors on opposite sides and thus widening the conflict to anything like the scale of World War III (the major planning case of the Cold War).

The conflict environment is different in two distinct ways. First, the imbalance in conventional capability between the United States and the rest of the world is so great that no one is likely to confront the United States in large-scale conventional warfare. Positively, this means the danger of massive twentieth century-style warfare has virtually disappeared for the time being. It also means, however, that those who oppose the United States must devise new ways to do so. This innovation is the second new characteristic of the environment: the adoption and adaptation of asymmetrical ways to negate the advantages of overwhelming military capability and the emergence of new categories of opponents, such as non–state actors. Asymmetrical approaches are not—quite purposefully—easily countered by conventional means and require new strategic approaches. This problem is progressive, because the core of asymmetrical warfare is constant adaptation, meaning the problem is never exactly the same from instance to instance. Moreover, traditional warfare is directed at state-based political opponents, and it is not clear how one subdues an opponent who lacks such a base.

Asymmetrical warfare is different from conventional war not only in the military manner in which it is conducted. It is also different in terms of the problems for which it is conducted, how those who carry it out think and act, and the motives of the asymmetrical warrior. Asymmetrical warfare is not only militarily unconventional, it is intellectually unconventional as well. Asymmetrical warriors do not organize as standing armies and march out on fields of battle where they would be slaughtered. Instead, they often lack any clear military hierarchy, are prone to use ambushes or acts of terror to achieve their goals, and may act from motives that seem strange, even bizarre to outsiders.

The United States' first major encounter with asymmetrical warfare was in Vietnam (we had previous limited experience in places like the Philippines at the turn of the twentieth century, but on a much smaller scale). Vietnam mixed symmetrical and asymmetrical characteristics. In terms of its purposes, it was quite conventional: the North Vietnamese and their Viet Cong allies sought to unify Vietnam as a communist country, and the South Vietnamese and the Americans sought to avoid that outcome. The purpose of war, therefore, was familiar—for one territorially based political entity or the other to impose its will on the other. In terms of conduct, however, the war was unconventional. The North Vietnamese concluded early in the American phase of the war that they could not compete with the United States in symmetrical warfare because of the visible superiority of American firepower. Instead, they reverted to tactics of harassment, ambush, and attrition, the purpose of which was to produce sufficient American casualties to convince the American people that the cost of war was not worth the projected benefits. Had the North Vietnamese fought the war according to the established rules of warfare, they would certainly have been defeated. In that circumstance, their only hope was to change the rules and fight in a way that minimized American advantage and gave them a chance. It worked.

The heart of asymmetrical warfare is not a set of tactics or strategies but instead is a mindset. The potential asymmetrical warrior always begins from a position of military inferiority, and the problem is how to negate that disadvantage. Thus, the first concern for the asymmetrical planner is to devise ways to shrink that disadvantage. If the enemy has overwhelming firepower capable of inflicting great casualties on concentrated bodies of combatants, the first thing to do is to avoid massing one's forces in ways that would lead to their slaughter. Instead, it is better to hide in ambush and attack and kill isolated elements of the enemy force. If that does not work, try something else.

Adaptability is at the heart of asymmetrical approaches to warfare. Vietnam was a primer for those who may want to confront American power, but an organization like Al Qaeda or the Iraqi resistance to the American occupation in Iraq could not succeed simply by adopting Vietnamese methods (for one thing, there are no mountainous jungles into which to retreat after engagements). Instead, the asymmetrical warrior learns from what works and discards what does not. Iraq is a case in point.

In 1990–91, Iraq attempted to confront the United States conventionally and was crushed for the effort. Iraq apparently learned from this experience that a future conflict with the United States, the prospect for which was faced after September 11, 2001, could not be conducted in the same manner as before without equally devastating results, which included the decimation of Iraqi armed forces.

What to do? The answer, largely unanticipated by the United States, was to offer only enough resistance to American symmetrical force application to make the Americans think they were prevailing, while regrouping with important parts of the military structure to resist an occupation that they were powerless to avoid. Thus, the limited form of irregular warfare (ambushes, car bombings, and suicide terror attacks) became the primary method of resisting the Americans, aimed apparently at the same goal the Vietnamese attained thirty years earlier—convincing the Americans that the occupation was not worth the costs in lives lost and treasure expended.

Whether or not this was some carefully modulated plan formulated in advance of the invasion by the Iraqis is not the point (and it is a point for which inadequate evidence is available, anyway). What is hardly arguable is that the United States did not take into account such an asymmetrical response in planning the invasion in the first place. In post-invasion analysis, the argument is frequently made that American planning was flawed in, among other ways, its failure to allocate sufficient troops to the effort. The criticism somewhat misses the point. The troop numbers *were* clearly adequate for a symmetrical invasion and conquest, which is apparently all that was anticipated. But the troop levels were (and are) arguably inadequate for a protracted resistance to occupation, which was an asymmetrical response that was apparently not anticipated. If the dynamics of symmetrical and asymmetrical warfare are what has been argued here, then one can maintain that some planning for asymmetrical possibilities should have been included in planning for the war. If asymmetrical actions are likely in the future (and the success of the Iraqi resistance has to be encouraging to potential asymmetrical warriors), it is necessary to look at the physical dynamics of these kinds of situations.

Physical Structure of Warfare

What is absolutely clear about the future of warfare involving the United States is that we are uncertain about its face. Part of the reason is the changing nature of the face of war. As argued, a primary characteristic of future conflict is that it is itself changing. If Vietnam was a prototype, it was not an example that would be repeated. Rather, the experience in Vietnam became the base line from which others would adapt, changing the problem the next time we encountered it. Similarly, the next asymmetrical challenge will incorporate elements of Iraq, but it will not be identical. Preparing for the next war has become very perilous.

The other problem is finding a conceptual frame for organizing looking at the future. Writing in 1995, then U.S. Army Chief of Staff Gordon Sullivan and Anthony M. Coroalles analogized the problem to "seeing the elephant," a phrase borrowed from the American Civil War (the idea of what the initial exposure to combat was like from descriptions by others being like having an elephant described). They wrote, "Our elephant is the complexity, ambiguity, and uncertainty of tomorrow's battlefield. We are trying to see the elephant of the future. But trying to draw that metaphorical elephant is infinitely harder than drawing a real one. We don't know what we don't know; none of us has a clear view of what the elephant will look like this time around."

We have learned some of the language to describe the new elephant, if not the dynamics of asymmetrical warfare. Lawrence Freedman, writing in *Foreign Policy*, quotes an American Marine officer in Iraq as reporting, "The enemy has gone asymmetric on us. There's treachery. There are ambushes. It's not straight-up conventional fighting." In other words, it does not conform to the accepted rules of symmetrical warfare.

In trying to determine the shape of the new elephant of asymmetrical warfare, one can begin by looking at predictable problems that the asymmetrical warrior will present in the future. With no pretense of being exhaustive, at least five stand out. Undoubtedly more will evolve.

First, political and military aspects of these conflicts will continue to merge, and distinctions between military and civilian targets and assets will continue to dissolve. The asymmetrical warrior will continue to muddy the distinction for two reasons. One is that he is likely to see conflicts as pitting societies against societies such that there is no meaningful distinction between combatants and noncombatants. A second reason is that imbedding conflict within the fabric facilitates removing some of the advantage of the symmetrical warrior. Urban warfare, for instance, can only be waged symmetrically by concentrating firepower intensity on areas where civilians and opponents are intermingled, meaning such applications of firepower create maximum civilian casualties for which the symmetrical warriors are blamed (Israeli attacks against Palestinian neighborhoods where accused terrorists hide is an example). If fighting can be reduced to the street-by-street, door-to-door level, much of the symmetrical warrior's advantage is undercut.

Second, the opposition in these kinds of conflicts will increasingly consist of non–state actors often functioning out of non–state motivations. International terrorist organizations act this way (see Chapter 16 for a discussion), acting in places that may grant them no or only implicit permission to act, where the terrorist's goals may have nothing to do with policies of the host government. As suggested already, this creates a problem of response for the symmetrical warrior. Who does he go after? Who does he attack and punish? If the asymmetrical warrior remains in the shadows (or the mountains or desert) and the government plausibly denies affiliation or association, then the lever of using force against the opponent is weakened, and the symmetrical warrior is left ungrounded.

Third, the opposition posed by asymmetrical warriors will almost certainly be protracted, even if the tempo and intensity of opposition varies greatly from situation to situation. The reason for protraction flows from the weakness of the asymmetrical warrior compared to his symmetrical foe. Because direct confrontation is suicidal, the alternative is patient, measured application of force not designed to destroy the enemy (which the asymmetrical warrior is quite incapable of performing) but instead to drag out the conflict, testing the will and patience of the opponent. The United States first saw this dynamic in Vietnam and may be seeing it again in Iraq. The antidote is recognition of the tactic and a considerable degree of patience, generally not the long suit of the United States.

Fourth, these conflicts will often occur in the most fractured, failed states, where conditions are ripe for people to engage in acts of desperation that include things like suicide bombing. In situations of high desperation and deprivation, the systemic problems will be extraordinarily difficult to address and rectify. The problem of addressing the problems is recognizing the multifaceted nature of the problem and needs of the people. The difficulty of rectifying these problems is having the patience and level of physical (including financial) commitment to remove the festering conditions that give rise to violence in the first place. The situation in Afghanistan is probably an excellent example of this kind of problem.

Fifth, we have only seen the tip of the iceberg of what asymmetrical warfare will look like in the future. The problem of Iraq is more than overcoming the Iraqi resistance, it is a matter of defeating and discrediting its methods so they will not form the basis for the opposition of others in the future. From the vantage point of potential asymmetrical warriors, the resistance has already been successful enough that parts of it will be imitated. Can anyone doubt the next asymmetrical warriors will come armed with improvised explosive devices (IEDs) to be lobbed at symmetrical opponents? Or that hostage-taking and execution will be employed to force occupiers out of the next occupation? The trick is figuring what else will be learned from the experience to be countered and what new and unique elements will be added.

Determining Opponents

Virtually by definition, asymmetrical warfare will take on a variety of forms in the future. Asymmetrical warfare is, after all, an approach rather than a method, and some variant will occur whenever a technologically inferior force confronts an opponent so superior that it cannot be confronted directly. In this section we will look at three current variants. One is hybrid symmetrical-asymmetrical conflicts, of which Afghanistan is a prime example. Quasi-military situations involve attacks on states generally by non–state actors, whereas internal wars involve factions within a state. Each poses a different planning problem. Hybrids are likely to be confused as symmetrical wars, quasi-military situations are likely to be overly militarized, and internal wars raise vexing questions of interests and solutions.

Symmetrical-Asymmetrical War. One of the most difficult aspects of dealing with asymmetrical war situations is recognizing them for what they are. The United States faced this recognition problem in Vietnam in the 1960s and concluded, after the first major encounter between American and North Vietnamese regulars in the Ia Drang Valley, that the war was conventional, a symmetrical conflict between two similar foes that could be prosecuted in a conventional manner.

The problem was that the strategy of the Vietnamese was not unidimensional, but instead contained both symmetrical and asymmetrical elements. After the battle of the Ia Drang, the North Vietnamese concluded they could not match American firepower on the conventional battlefield and switched their method of fighting to guerrilla-style warfare, one of the classic forms of asymmetrical warfare. Their purpose was to harass and drain the Americans sufficiently to cause them to give up the fight as unwinnable at acceptable cost. After the United States abandoned the war, the North Vietnamese returned to conventional, symmetrical warfare against a South Vietnamese opponent that they could defeat conventionally.

The Vietnam War spawned a great debate within the United States about whether it had been a conventional (symmetrical) or an unconventional (asymmetrical) conflict. The answer, it turns out, was that it was both, and the lesson seemed to have been that the United States (and anyone else) would have to be prepared to adapt and fight either conventionally or unconventionally (in Vietnam, the United States never successfully developed and implemented an effective counter asymmetrical warfare strategy). American experiences in Afghanistan and Iraq suggest the United States continues to confuse this hybrid form of warfare.

In 2001, the United States entered an altogether symmetrical civil war between the Taliban government of Afghanistan and a coalition of opposition clans known collectively as the Northern Alliance. Both sides relied heavily on guerrilla warfare tactics, but because both sides used the same rules, the situation was symmetrical. The role of the United States was to aid in the overthrow of the Taliban government, which was providing sanctuary to Al Qaeda—an extension of the war on terrorism. The American military role was to provide strategic airpower against the Taliban forces facing the Northern Alliance. The tactic was successful, because the Taliban could not abandon their lines and take cover without ceding vital territory to the rebels. As a result, their forces were decimated, their government was forced to flee, and victory was proclaimed. Stephen Biddle, writing in *Foreign Affairs* in 2003, concluded that "the war as a whole was much more orthodox, and much less revolutionary, than most now believe."

Yes and no. Biddle is correct that the overthrow of the Taliban was essentially a victory for symmetrical arms, but that phase was not the entirety of the war. After their defeat on the conventional battlefield, the Taliban and their Al Qaeda allies (the real objects of U.S. policy) retreated to the rugged Afghan mountains and began the second phase of the war, an unconventional campaign that continues to this day. The war thus became asymmetrical, and the Taliban and other clans opposed to the central government now control the vast majority of Afghan territory. The third phase of the overall effort, to establish a peaceful Afghan state through state building, has hardly begun.

The Afghan precedent is important, because it demonstrates that modern war is more than simply crushing the organized armed forces of an opposition country. In fact, conceptualizing contemporary war in conventional military terms, as in Afghanistan, oversimplifies how one views the problem and leads to incomplete responses. In many ways, the American effort in Iraq is quite similar: a crushing symmetrical warfare victory followed by a long, inconclusive campaign against an asymmetrical opponent whose existence and methods were apparently unanticipated. Yet, this hybrid form of war, partly symmetrical and partly asymmetrical, is likely to be a prominent part of the future pattern of warfare in developing world countries, for the simple reason that it appears to work.

Quasi-Military Situations. A second set of circumstances where military force may be employed in the future is in quasi-military unconventional roles and missions. Some of these are outgrowths of the struggles between the haves and the have-nots within developing countries and finds vent in things like terrorist acts either within the society or against outsiders, with the objects normally being the major powers (the African embassy bombings against the United States in 1998, and most dramatically, the attacks against New York and Washington, DC, in 2001). Others are extensions of the general decay of some of the failed states and often manifest themselves in activities such as criminality (the "war" over control of the diamond field in Sierra Leone, discussed in Chapter 14, is an example). Attempts to deal with the prospects of potential WMD attacks also fit into this category. What these phenomena share is that they are only semi-military, even quasi-military, in content.

The Western, and specifically American, problem with Usama bin Laden illustrates the problem of terrorism. For a variety of reasons that he has publicly stated (see examples in Chapter 16), bin Laden blames the United States for a large number of the problems afflicting the Middle East and is consequently devoted to inflicting as much pain and suffering on the United States and Americans as he can through the commission of acts of terror committed by his followers and associates (many of whom were trained in camps in Afghanistan originally built by the American Central Intelligence Agency to train the Afghan resistance to Soviet occupation during the 1980s and that became the core cadre of Al Qaeda). The campaign to eradicate Al Qaeda since 2001 has in fact decimated much of the ranks and leadership of the original organization, but it has also spawned a series of spin-off, copycat, and affiliated organizations that make the terrorist threat much more hydra-headed than it was before (this problem is discussed in Chapter 16). These successful actions have, by and large, been the result of intelligence and law enforcement efforts.

Is dealing with the Usama bin Ladens of this world a military problem? In the 1980s the United States "made war" on drugs, although many argued at the time that the analogy was flawed, implying as it did that the problem was indeed military in nature and thus something on which to make war. Is terrorism similarly military, and can the international system "make war" on terrorists? The answer is ambiguous. There are certainly aspects of dealing with terrorism that have a military cast, but there are also aspects that do not. Counterterrorist acts intended to punish terrorists (the cruise missile attacks against bin Laden's training camps in Afghanistan in 1998 and the military campaign of 2001 to topple the Taliban government) may employ military means, but dissuading terrorists from acting or penetrating and dismantling terrorist groups is not so clearly military. The problem of dealing with WMD is analogous: threats or acts of retaliation against biological or chemical attacks contain military aspects, but it is not clear that stemming the motives that lead states to acquire these capabilities is military.

The other problem is dealing with the criminalization of societies in states broadly described as failing. In the contemporary world, there is no better example than Colombia, where elements associated with the illicit narcotics industry have destabilized that country to the point of making Colombia virtually a lawless land. Worse yet, Colombia's criminalization appears to be spreading across the border and infecting neighboring countries like Venezuela. There is a danger of greater or lesser severity (because the phenomenon is fairly new, it is hard to gauge which) that effectively criminalized countries will also destabilize their neighbors. More or less predictable consequences include migration of those who can afford to do so out of the country and the dangers of living in a lawless society.

Internal Wars. The third kind of environment in which asymmetrical warfare will certainly occur is in the *new internal wars* of parts of the developing world. These wars became a prominent part of the landscape of violence in the 1990s after the end of the Cold War. Although overshadowed by the conflicts spawned by responses to terrorism since 2001, these wars will continue to produce "opportunities" for the application of force by countries around the world, generally for the purpose of ending the violence. During the 1990s, major international efforts were made in places such as Somalia, Bosnia, Kosovo, and even East Timor, while similar outbreaks were ignored in places such as Rwanda and the Democratic Republic of Congo (former Zaire).

There are several characteristics of these situations that make them problematic as sites for the application of force, especially by major powers. Many of these characteristics are shared by terrorist and other asymmetrical warriors. Six of these are worth mentioning in the current context.

First, they will always display dramatically the gaps in capability between opponents. Generally speaking, the protagonists in these civil conflicts will be armed with little more than hand-carried weapons or light artillery, will be loosely organized militarily if they are organized at all (the participants will generally be "fighters" as opposed to trained "soldiers"), will engage in hit-and-run attacks and terror directed at the civilian population, and will not stand and fight against organized military units intervening to stop the killing. By contrast, intervening forces will be technologically sophisticated, firepower-intensive, and will emphasize high mobility and an emphasis on air power. Because the countries where these wars occur will often be equatorial and mountainous, many of the advantages of the technologically superior will be of dubious benefit.

Second, the decision to become involved in these situations will always be difficult for outside parties, because generally the potential peacemakers will have few if any concrete, geopolitical interests in the situation important enough clearly to justify intervention. Most of the time, vital interests will be absent for the major powers in these situations unless a former colonial power is involved, and the answer to the operational question, "how will my interests be affected by any possible outcome?" will be "not very much."

Third, there is a growing consensus in the developed world that involvement where important interests do not exist must be relatively bloodless to be tolerable. This idea was especially evident during the NATO intervention in Yugoslavia, where particular attention was paid to ensuring that Allied pilots engaged in the bombing campaign were not shot down and killed. The absence of casualties has been a major factor in Allied efforts in Bosnia and Kosovo as well. Strategies that begin with the avoidance of casualties as a first requirement, of course, severely limit the kinds and quality of military action that can be undertaken.

Fourth, the absence of major interests also dictates that interventions will be multilateral affairs, where coalitions of intervening states provide "burden sharing" by major actors and the problem of the "free rider" (the actor that does not participate in but benefits from an action) is avoided. Although the situation is not an internal war, criticism of the minimal coalition recruited by the United States in Iraq offers some insight into this problem. If it appears that the United States is shouldering a disproportionate burden, the political ability to mount or sustain an operation may be questioned. The other side of this problem is that coalition actions are generally militarily inefficient and sometimes fraught with major operational problems. In the NATO Kosovo Force (KFOR) operation, for instance, all the national units report to their home defense ministries before accepting orders from the mission command, and occasionally those orders are refused.

Fifth, there will always be international pressures, generally under the rubric of something like *humanitarian interests,* to mount an effort to ease these situations. Whether it is the distended bellies of the starving children of Somalia, the concentration camp–like detainment centers in Bosnia, or the feckless refugees of Kosovo, these situations will always be marked by gut-wrenching scenes of human misery that are difficult to ignore and that trigger a strong inclination to respond in some manner to ease the suffering. This instinct is made all the stronger when the human suffering is recorded and disseminated by global television, as it often is.

Sixth, the outcomes of these missions are highly problematical. International involvement in the internal affairs of countries predates the post–Cold War period (UN interventions in Cyprus and the Belgian Congo during the 1960s, for instance), but those earlier instances did not produce a pattern or a "model" for how to drop in and "solve" these problems. If the goal of intervention is both to stop the fighting and to reasonably assure peace and tranquility after the mission is completed (which it usually is), it can fairly be said that no humanitarian intervention has unqualifiedly succeeded. Some may, but none have. There is a suspicion, especially held within military establishments, that these kinds of operations are probably doomed to long-term failure and thus should be avoided.

CONCLUSION

Planning for the wars of the future has always been a difficult business. During man's bloodiest century, the twentieth, the problem of seeing into the future and determining what kinds of wars to prepare for has clearly evolved. As the first part of this case study demonstrated, the exercise was more linear in the first half of the century: the protagonists remained relatively constant, and the major problem was adapting the emerging weapons technologies to their most efficacious applications. Planning for World War II was not that much different from planning for World War I. Only the scale of violence escalated.

Planning for the future wars of the twenty-first century does not offer the same apparent continuities. The Cold War structure and military planning problem was familiar and represented the kind of continuity that World War II planners faced; the structure of who provided the opposition was the major difference. But the collapse of the communist world and the threat it presented has fundamentally altered the landscape of possible future violence. There are few concrete, compelling, state-based enemies (or even potential adversaries) that provide the grist for planning grounded in concrete problems. Instead, we face a shifting set of shadowy potential opponents, the nature of whom and the threats they pose being largely speculative and ever changing. Who will the next terrorists be, and where and why will they strike? Will they attack with exotic WMDs, and what can be done to prepare for that contingency? How will their experience in the last war temper their approach to the next war and thus complicate our counter asymmetrical warfare strategy problem? *Should* we interfere in the fratricide that has become so common in so much of the developing world? The answers to these questions are not at all clear. What is clear, however, is that these are characteristics of the environment in which future war will occur. They all seem more compelling today than they did before September 11, 2001.

STUDY/DISCUSSION QUESTIONS

1. The past case of military planning between the world wars and the case today offer points of similarity and contrast. One of these is in the nature of planning—for the familiar in the 1930s and the unfamiliar now. Discuss these similarities and differences. Which would be a more comfortable planning environment?

2. Put yourself in the position of being a military planner looking at weapons for the future based upon the experience of the past. What kinds of military capability would you like to have to deal with the universe you see ten or fifteen years in the future?

3. What is asymmetrical warfare? Contrast it to symmetrical warfare. Why has it arisen as the major military problem of the twenty-first century? Is it likely to continue to be the dominant problem?

4. Should it be a major priority of the most advanced countries to involve themselves in trying to ameliorate internal violence in the developing world? If so, what kind of criteria should be adopted to guide involvements? If not, what should we prepare for?

5. Predict where and in what kind of conflict the United States is most likely to be fighting ten years from today. Try to devise the basic principles for a counter asymmetrical warfare strategy to deal with that future.

READING/RESEARCH MATERIAL

Biddle, Stephen. "Afghanistan and the Future of Warfare." *Foreign Affairs* 82, 2 (March/April 2003), 31–46.

Brodie, Bernard, and Fawn M. Brodie. *From Crossbow to H-Bomb: The Evolution of Weapons and Tactics on Warfare.* Bloomington, IN: Indiana University Press, 1965.

Fukuyama, Francis. *The End of History and the Last Man.* New York: Free Press, 1992.

Gannon, Kathy. "Afghanistan Unbound." *Foreign Affairs* 83, 3 (May/June 2004), 35–46.

Johnsen, William T., et al. *The Principles of War in the 21st Century: Strategic Considerations.* Carlisle Barracks, PA: U.S. Army War College, 1995.

Lind, William S., et al. "The Changing Face of War: Into the Fourth Generation." *Marine Corps Gazette,* October 1989, 22–26.

Metz, Steven. *Strategic Horizons: The Military Implications of Alternative Futures.* Carlisle Barracks, PA: U.S. Army War College, 1997.

Scales, Major General Robert H. Jr. *Future War: Anthology.* Carlisle Barracks, PA: U.S. Army War College, 1999.

Snow, Donald M. *When America Fights: The Uses of U.S. Military Force.* Washington, DC: CQ Press, 2000.

Snow, Donald M., and Dennis M. Drew. *From Lexington to Desert Storm and Beyond: War and Politics in the American Experience,* 2nd edition. Armonk, NY: M. E. Sharpe, 2001.

Stoessinger, John. *Why Nations Go to War,* 7th edition. New York: St. Martin's Press, 1997.

Sullivan, General Gordon R., and Anthony M. Coroalles. *Seeing the Elephant: Leading America's Army into the Twenty-First Century.* Boston, MA: Institute for Foreign Policy Analysis, 1995.

Van Creveld, Martin. *The Transformation of War.* New York: Free Press, 1991.

WEB SITES

Research projects on national security issues conducted by the RAND Corporation for the U.S. defense establishment

National Security: Research and analysis at http://www.ran.org/natsec_area

Reports on future trends in terrorism

Federal Research Division: Terrorism studies at http://www/loc.gov./rr/frd/terrorism.htm

Leading organization studying military matters

The International Institute for Strategic Studies at http://www.iiss.org

Alternate visions of defense issues

Stockholm International Peace Research Institute at http://www.sipri.se

CHAPTER ELEVEN

When National and International Politics Collide
THE CASE OF MISSILE DEFENSE

PRÉCIS

The question of defenses against ballistic missiles has been a recurring theme in international relations. It has tended to focus on the United States, which, because of its superior technological base, is the country most likely to be able to field such a system (if anyone ever can), and on the status of American efforts to build a missile defense. Proposals to do so have arisen periodically, culminating in the advocacy of a national missile defense (NMD) by the current Bush administration. The first elements of a missile defense were scheduled to be ready in Alaska by the end of 2004.

The thrust of this case is two-fold. It offers a comparison of the current NMD with previous American programs designed to defeat a missile attack. The analysis is theoretical (Is a missile defense desirable?), technological (Is a missile defense possible?), and historical (How do programs compare across time?). The case then looks at missile defense as a transnational issue whereby the actions of one state (the United States) could adversely affect the actions of other states, possibly making the world less secure than it was without the program. This goal is accomplished by looking at the objections that a number of former American adversaries (notably Russia and China) and allies have made to the NMD proposal.

One of the more common scholarly and policy concerns during the Cold War era was the question of the effects that national security decisions made by individual states or groups of states had on other—especially adversarial—states or on the international system as a whole. Much of the concern centered on armaments decisions that states made: what would the effect of fielding a particular kind or quantity of weapons systems have on friends, allies, or adversaries?

This problem was captured in a number of concepts that fell collectively into the analytical category of *arms racing*. While the literature on arms races is extensive and complex and thus beyond our detailed consideration in this case study, two concepts—each developed specifically to describe aspects of arms racing in the Soviet-American nuclear relationship—capture the heart of this concern as it applies to a contemporary international issue.

The first concept is the *action-reaction phenomenon (ARP)*, a notion at the core of arms racing. The basic idea here is that a particular decision to deploy a weapons system (an action) will trigger a response by the adversary at whom it is aimed to counter the original action (the reaction), which in turn may trigger another reaction and so on. At the end of the process, either or both parties may or may not be better off in a security sense (be or feel more secure).

This concept leads to the second and related concept, the *security dilemma*. In this construct, a state may take an action to improve its own security that has the effect of making the object of the original action feel more insecure than before, forcing that state to take counteraction to restore its sense of security. In extreme, the net result can be to leave the initiator less secure than before the original action or, even worse, to leave the entire international system less secure than before the original action.

These kinds of concepts and problems largely disappeared from the public dialogue after the end of the Cold War. The military confrontation rapidly receded with the demise of half the competition. Especially in the area of nuclear weapons, questions of threats and insecurities became subdued, and virtually all countries radically reduced their defense spending in an apparently more benign security environment. The old concepts seemed archaic, a part of history.

These concerns may have been revived with the announced intention of the American Bush administration to field a national missile defense (NMD) when the efficacy of a deployment is demonstrated (or even before such a demonstration). The decision, when it is made, will be the result of largely domestic political decisions about what strengthens U.S. security. This action will, however, almost certainly trigger a reaction from an international community virtually unanimous in its opposition to the American initiative. In some cases, the responses by states may be so strong as to raise the possible negative consequences of the security dilemma.

The international reaction to missile defenses resembles what are known as transstate issues in a political regard. International opposition to the prospects of missile defenses comes from a variety of concerns, such as their feasibility, cost, or, more importantly, their impact on the stability of the international system. There is, for instance, the fear that an American deployment of a missile shield would force China to expand its small nuclear missile force to be able to penetrate the American shield, thereby avoiding having the Chinese force left impotent (a classic action-reaction phenomenon with security dilemma ramifications). In turn, a Chinese expansion could have ripple effects elsewhere in Asia, with the net result that the international security system is left more unstable than would be the case in its absence.

The advocates of missile defense in the United States, on the other hand, focus almost completely on what they believe will be the salutary effects on the security of Americans provided by the planned ability to intercept small missile attacks by rogue states (now designated "states of concern" by the U.S. Department of State). These rogue states are also among those targeted as part of the global war on terrorism (GWOT), creating a linkage between missile defense and responses to terrorism. The prospect of negative international, systemic effects of the unilateral American actions is either ignored or denied by NMD advocates.

In fact, the national missile defense issue may also fall broadly into a new category of transstate issues, what Asia-Pacific Center for Strategic Studies analyst Paul Smith has called *transnational security issues* in a recent article. Citing examples such as transnational crime and terrorism and transnational migrations and even disease flows, he generally defines his concept as "threats that cross borders and either threaten the political and social integrity of a nation [*sic*] or threaten that nation's inhabitants." A transstate launch of a terrorist missile (one of the problems that NMD is designed to negate) would clearly fall within the purview of such a problem. The same would be the case should a rogue state like Iran obtain a few intercontinental-range missiles and target them on the American homeland.

The missile defense plan is hardly new. In the United States, an interest in developing and deploying a defensive system against attacks by nuclear-tipped (or, for that matter, nonnuclear) missiles delivered by its enemies is at least as old as the missile age itself. Before there had even been a successful test-firing of an intercontinental-range missile, the theoretical problems of defending against such a missile had been solved; the only problem, which continues to plague similar efforts in the twenty-first century, is making that knowledge operational by developing a functioning, effective missile defense system.

The intellectual and emotional lure of an antimissile capability is obvious. The ballistic missile, when it was introduced, was an *indefensible* weapon system. What that means is that there were not at the time, and still are not today, effective ways to avoid being destroyed by a ballistic missile launched against a target. The reason is the extraordinary speed at which ballistic missiles travel—in the intercontinental varieties at rates of 15,000 miles or more per hour. The problem of intercepting and destroying a launched missile drew the analogy from then-candidate John F. Kennedy in the 1960 presidential campaign of "hitting a bullet with another bullet," clearly a daunting task. The *Berliner Morgenpost* newspaper (quoted in *World Press Review*) revived the analogy on July 12, 2000, asking, "whether a system where a bullet must hit another bullet in flight can ever be made functional." The analogy, of course, suggests that missile defense is a nearly impossible task, an inference often intended by critics of the concept.

In the absence of reliable missile defenses, the only way to avoid being destroyed by missile attacks is to avoid those attacks from occurring in the first place. In the latter 1950s, as missiles began entering the arsenals of the United States and the Soviet Union, and later Great Britain, France, and to a much more modest degree China, this recognition created a lively interest in the idea of *deterrence*, which evolved to mean dissuading an adversary from attacking with nuclear-tipped missiles for fear of the consequences in retaliation. While the system of deterrence coincided with the absence of nuclear war (or other war directed against the United States using missiles), embrace of the concept of deterrence as the basis of national existence has always been tentative. The reason is that deterrence could fail, leaving us completely vulnerable, and thus there has always been sentiment for building a system that could protect the homeland even in the event of an attack from some foreign enemy.

Enthusiasm for missile defenses has never much extended beyond the United States. Part of the reason is technological: even if one doubts (as leaders around the world do) that missile defenses are possible, the United States is less unlikely than other countries to be able to develop them due to its scientific and technological base. Moreover, it is universally agreed that the development and deployment of a missile defense system would be terribly costly, probably beyond the practical means of any country but the United States. Missile defense, if it is possible, is a luxury only the Americans can obviously afford.

When the missile defense issue remains at the abstract level of American research and testing programs with no particular likelihood of deployment and no overt champion, the international community overlooks the American advantage. These opponents do not raise other objections to American unilateral deployment or what are viewed as paternalistic, probably insincere American offers to share the missile shield with others. At these times, missile defense remains almost exclusively a domestic political issue within the United States. The poles of that debate are, on one side, the irresponsibility of not trying to protect American citizens from attack by hostile states, and the impracticability and expense of a feckless enterprise on the other.

Whenever the United States has announced the potential decision to field one form of missile defense or another, the matter has quickly become an international issue as well as a domestic concern. The current NMD advocacy is the third time the issue has been raised, and each time it has followed a similar script. Thus, when the U.S. government continued testing of the national missile defense system in 2000 and announced that if testing was successful, deployment could begin as early as 2003, the reaction was predictable. If anything, the collision of national and international concerns was intensified by the election to the presidency of Republican nominee George W. Bush, an ardent supporter of deploying the system.

International reactions were predictably negative, as they have been each time the United States has approached the threshold of a missile defense deployment. In many ways, the domestic and international debate of 2000 was little more than a replay of the 1960s and 1970s, when the U.S. government proposed and actually began to deploy a defensive system largely against the threat from a newly nuclear China. It resurfaced again in the debate over the Anti-Ballistic Missile (ABM) Treaty of 1972 and regarding the Reagan Strategic Defense Initiative (SDI) in the 1980s. In each case, those favoring missile defense failed to carry the day, not so much because there was general international opposition but because they could not demonstrate that the system could work or was worth the expense it entailed and because the opposition could raise the further objection that fielding the system would destabilize a deterrence system based in the ABM Treaty, from which the United States withdrew in 2002.

The current controversy is the latest chapter in the national-international debate over missile defenses. While it shares a common lineage with the rounds of debate about previously proposed programs, it is different in at least two ways. The first and most obvious is that it occurs outside the context of the Cold War. The clear difference is the focus and rationale for defenses. The answer to "defenses against whom?" was easy to answer during the Cold War; it is neither easy nor obviously compelling now. The other difference is the larger, and more uniform, international opposition to the idea. During the Cold War, American allies could not openly complain about the idea of defense against a known, robust Soviet enemy (although they could complain about whether or not they would be protected by the defenses). Freed of that tether, they can now raise more concerns about the systemic influence of missile defenses that they always held but were reluctant to articulate.

Thus, the nature of the national-international policy debate over missile defense has broadened since the last time it arose. The question is whether the generally negative tone of international reaction to the prospect of a U.S. missile defense system, which most see as an international-system destabilizing action propelled by domestic American politics, will affect the outcome more this time than before.

Answering that question will be the burden of the case. Because the current debate resembles others that preceded it, we will begin by looking at the previous American missile defense initiatives and their outcomes, particularly in terms of the relative weight of domestic and international concerns. We will then move to the current debate, summarizing the American aspect and dwelling at some length on responses and criticisms from outside the United States. The relative weight of the two aspects of the debate will form the basis for some conclusions couched in concepts like the ARP and the security dilemma that NMD has helped to reintroduce into the international security environment.

MISSILE DEFENSE IN THE PAST: HISTORY AND PRECEDENTS

The issue of missile defenses has gone through three distinct phases, each of which reflected two major schools of thought and advocacy. These phases reflect similar dynamics: a growth in missile defense technology that emboldened its champions and growing criticism among its detractors of those proposals domestically and internationally. The domestic criticism has not changed greatly over time. Centered on feasibility, cost, and the effects of missile defenses on deterrence, it emerged in the 1960s and has remained so constant as hardly to constitute a variable. Indeed, one is struck by the fact that the same critics from the 1960s and 1970s are making the same arguments today.

What has changed is the gradual internationalization of the missile defense argument, which has intensified and spread over time to the point that the only states that currently openly support the idea are the United States and Israel, the latter facing a real potential threat of the kind NMD is supposed to solve and which expects to develop its own NMD based on the American system. A quick summary of two of the three historic phases of the debate, the Sentinel/Safeguard proposal of the 1960s and the Strategic Defense Initiative of the 1980s, demonstrates this evolution and provides the context for understanding the relative place of the NMD proposal in the international and domestic political framework.

The Sentinel/Safeguard System

The spotted history of ballistic missile defense in the American political debate got its start in the middle 1960s in a manner strikingly similar to the circumstances surrounding the national missile defense debate in the new century. The stimulus was the threat posed by the incipient Chinese nuclear force, which caused the Johnson administration to propose to deploy a light missile defense of U.S. (and especially California) cities, an objective modified and eventually abandoned by the Nixon administration. Thus, Sentinel/Safeguard was a domestic political response to a potential international threat; when the system was cancelled in the middle 1970s, the reasons were almost exclusively domestic.

The impetus for Sentinel, the original system, must be seen in the context of the international politics of its day. At that time, the People's Republic of China was viewed as an intractable enemy of the United States, one with which the United States had had no formal diplomatic relations since the Chinese mainland fell to Mao Zedong and his communist supporters in 1949. In 1964, the Chinese had successfully obtained nuclear weapons capability and had begun a modest missile-testing program. In 1966, the Chinese had embarked on the highly militant Cultural Revolution, and Mao had even opined publicly that China—due to the size of its population—was the only country in the world that could survive a nuclear war. In addition, the PRC was an open supporter of North Vietnam in the war the United States was waging in Southeast Asia. China appeared to be, indeed, the "Yellow Peril," and an increasingly implacable and threatening power that deserved the attention of the American defense establishment.

Chinese international militancy and possession of nuclear weapons created pressure within Congress and the Joint Chiefs of Staff for an American missile defense response. It came in a speech by Secretary of Defense Robert S. McNamara in September 1967, where he intoned, "There is evidence that the Chinese are devoting very substantial resources to the development of both nuclear warheads and missile delivery systems. Indications are they will have…an initial intercontinental ballistic missile capability in the early 1970s, and a modest force in the mid-70s."

On the basis of this assessment of what was a *potential future* threat, the Johnson administration announced in December 1967 its intention to erect a missile defense system it called Sentinel around major U.S. cities to protect them from the Chinese menace. When construction began, however, it met widespread public opposition, especially from the places it was being deployed and was designed to protect (much of which was the result of the fact that interceptors themselves were nuclear weapons that no one wanted in their communities). Aside from the question about the effectiveness of the system that has always plagued missile defense proposals, there were objections that the defensive missiles might pose as much of a threat to the American population as the Chinese missiles. Moreover, it was argued that the sites where the missiles were placed might themselves become targets, thus increasing the likelihood of such attacks.

These domestic pressures caused the Nixon administration quietly to dump the Sentinel program, replacing it with another light missile defense it called Safeguard. The major difference between Sentinel and Safeguard was where it would be located. Instead of stationing antimissile missiles around populated areas, Safeguard would be erected around intercontinental missile silos in remote areas far from urban areas. The strategic rationale for the deployment was that protecting missiles from attackers would mean more American forces would survive a nuclear attack and be available after such an attack to retaliate against the aggressor. In turn, the knowledge of that increased availability would contribute to deterrence by promising a more devastating retaliation. The practical political reason was that no voter's backyard would—figuratively, of course—be dug up to place a nuclear missile in it. There was ultimately one Safeguard site built and made operational: in Grand Forks, North Dakota, in 1975. Because of "technical difficulties," the site was only active for a few months, after which it was quietly deactivated. The cost to taxpayers was about $5 billion.

The current proposed NMD system bears an eerie resemblance to Sentinel/Safeguard. The first and most obvious similarity is that both are responses to potential, rather than actual, threats to the United States. China posed no nuclear threat to the United States in 1967; it was presumed that it would in the near future. What may be instructive is that the estimates of the threat at the time proved to be gross overestimations of what in fact evolved. According to the prestigious International Institute of Strategic Studies (IISS) in London, the first Chinese nuclear missiles appeared in 1993 or 1994, when the PRC deployed about fourteen ICBMs and twelve sea-launched ballistic missiles (SLBMs). The 1999 Chinese nuclear threat consisted of twenty ICBMs and twelve SLBMs (the latter with a modest range of 2,150 miles, far out of range of the American homeland), according to IISS. In other words, the threat against which Safeguard/Sentinel was supposed to deal has not yet emerged more than one-third of a century after the deployment decision was reached. Will the potential threat against which NMD is proposed be similar? In this first case, domestic American politics drove the program from birth to death, and the parameters of the debate—the moral entreaty to protect citizens from a nuclear inferno versus whether a missile defense was feasible—are familiar in the current debate over NMD as well.

The domestic politics of missile defense affected and was affected by one major international factor, the negotiation and adoption in 1972 of the Anti-Ballistic Missile (ABM) Treaty as part of the Strategic Arms Limitation Talks (SALT) discussions between the United States and the Soviet Union. The Soviets always opposed missile defenses, at least partially because they recognized their own technological base was inadequate to produce a workable system. While the Soviets were skeptical of the American ability to field an effective ABM in the 1970s, they did not want to encourage the American technological community to investigate the prospects and thus insisted on a very limited deployment in the treaty. Originally under the treaty, each side was allowed two sites: one around the national capital (Sentinel, in other words) and a second around a missile site at least 1,500 kilometers from the capital (Safeguard). When Sentinel was abandoned, an amendment to the treaty reduced the number of permissible deployments to a single site. Many argued that the ABM Treaty became the bedrock of stable deterrence and the NMD system would force the United States to withdraw from the treaty, sparking security dilemma concerns. The Bush administration denies the importance of the ABM Treaty, with Secretary of Defense Donald Rumsfeld dismissing it as "ancient history." President Bush withdrew the United States from the treaty in 2002, as noted.

The Strategic Defense Initiative

Ronald Reagan's Strategic Defense Initiative (SDI) was announced as part of a March 1983 speech in which he declared his intention to develop a missile defense screen that would render nuclear-tipped missiles "impotent and obsolete" by providing a blanket defense against even the largest of attacks on the United States—specifically an all-out Soviet attack. Reagan reasoned that, by denying the Soviets the ability to destroy the United States with its nuclear forces, such a defense would make the maintenance of such forces irrelevant and would lead eventually the Soviets to join in his ultimate goal, nuclear disarmament.

The Reagan proposal, which was quickly nicknamed "Star Wars" by a White House press corps reporter (much to the president's annoyance), was clearly more ambitious than Sentinel and Safeguard. The earlier versions were "thin" defenses, the purpose of which was to deflect a few warheads launched at the American homeland by China or some other state with a very small arsenal of weapons. The SDI proposed a very thick shield that was analogized to a geodesic dome or umbrella defense that could deflect or destroy a Soviet launch of 10,000–12,000 warheads in a concerted attack.

The SDI was both similar and different from Sentinel/Safeguard. Its similarities included the fact that it came from the same prodefense scientific and military community that had favored Sentinel/Safeguard (Reagan, as the governor of California, was an early enthusiast of the Sentinel protection of California cities from Chinese attack) and the fact that it was produced with little regard to international reaction, which was overwhelmingly negative. Its differences included the fact that it was a response to a concrete rather than a hypothetical threat and that it was conceptually and technologically much more ambitious than its predecessor.

The knotty problem of Star Wars was not its vision, but its realization. Sentinel and Safeguard were designed to deflect very small, "manageable" threats, and they both failed to accomplish their task (a major factor in their demise). The SDI, on the other hand, faced an enormously large and complicated mission. While relatively few could argue that the goal of SDI was not praiseworthy, how could technology produce a system that could deflect thousands of enemy missiles when the same technological base had failed to design one that could shoot down a handful?

The answer lay in a very complex, technologically sophisticated system known as a "layered" defense, made theoretically possible by technological developments during the intervening decade. Laser battle stations in space would receive information of a Soviet attack from sensors and satellites in space and then attack and destroy rising missiles and their reentry vehicles, backed up by ground-based interceptor antimissile missiles that would "mop up" whatever Soviet forces survived the defenses in space (a vision reintroduced by President George W. Bush as part of a potential NMD design). At one point, it was estimated that the computer program necessary to manage the system would be between 30 and 100 *million* lines long; estimates of cost ranged from $500 billion to two trillion dollars over a ten-year deployment period. Ultimately, a combination of projected cost and suspicion that such a system could never be built successfully subverted the project.

International criticism was largely confined to the Soviet Union, and it changed over time. American allies complained that the system would protect the United States but not them (Reagan promised to extend the shield to the European allies), and some analysts worried that there could be destabilization of the nuclear balance while the system was being put in place (e.g., the Soviets might be tempted to destroy the system before it could be made operational and leave their forces "impotent and obsolete"). Mostly, however, the Soviets provided the intellectual objections. Because these were within the Cold War framework, they tended to be confined to the propaganda level.

Soviet attitudes reflected the succession crisis going on within the Soviet Union during the heyday of the SDI. In 1983, that process had begun with the death of Leonid Brezhnev, and the successors to Stalin were giving way to the leadership of Mikhail S. Gorbachev. In the early years of SDI, the Soviets painted the defensive system in dire, confrontational tones, viewing it as a potential offensive, rather than defensive, system (the analogy with the "Death Star" of the 1980s *Star Wars* movies was often drawn). After Mikhail S. Gorbachev came to power, and especially after he brought Soviet physicist Andrei Sakharov out of internal exile, the tone changed as the new Soviet leader became convinced that the SDI would never be fielded and that Reagan was sincere in his desire to use the SDI as a tool for disarmament, a goal with which Gorbachev was sympathetic.

SDI was almost exclusively the vision of Ronald Reagan, and it did not survive his tenure in office. President George H. W. Bush maintained the SDI as a research program within the Strategic Defense Initiative Office (SDIO) with gradually decreased funding. When President Clinton became the chief executive in 1993, he allowed the project to lapse quietly to a shell that eventually became the basis for a return to a more modest system, the NMD.

The National Missile Defense (NMD)

In the American defense community, advocates of missile defense have consistently demonstrated that they do not give up or go away, they simply regroup. Although the SDI "umbrella defense" proposal fell to the combined suspicion that it would not work and would cost too much, the more general proposition that defending against ballistic missiles was desirable never left the American political dialogue and, indeed, was aided by events that occurred during the 1990s.

The first event was the use of Russian *Scud* missiles by Iraq during the Persian Gulf War of 1990–91. Although American Patriot antiaircraft missiles were apparently effective in defending against the attacks by the Iraqis, they also increased interest in *theater* missile defenses (TMDs, antiballistic missiles designed to shoot down battlefield and short-range missiles) for two reasons. First, the fact that the Iraqis had employed the weapons against both civilian and military targets indicated a willingness for so-called *rogue states* like Iraq to do so again in the future and thus buttressed the "need" to be able to defend. Second, it was presumed that in the future the missiles available to potential attackers would be more sophisticated and difficult to intercept, thereby justifying efforts to fashion more effective defenders. The result in the United States was passage of the Missile Defense Act of 1991, with an emphasis on TMD.

The current NMD advocacy was revived by two events in 1998. First, a blue-ribbon panel chaired by current U.S. Secretary of Defense Donald Rumsfeld issued a report arguing that rogue states like Iran and North Korea could well be capable of fielding offensive missiles within five years, rather than the fifteen years or so in the future that was commonly assumed in the defense community. As if to accentuate and validate this prediction, the North Koreans test fired a *Taepo Dong I* rocket over Japan, raising fears they were intent on producing an intercontinental-range missile in the upcoming years. The national missile defense proposal thus entered the American dialogue and would soon become part of the international stage as well.

Like all the proposals that preceded it, NMD entered the scene in the midst of controversy, with domestic and international supporters and opponents. The cast of characters and their positions were familiar to anyone who had followed the earlier debates, although the nature of the threat and the pretensions of the system were different. In many ways, the NMD is a return to the debate over Sentinel/Safeguard, both in terms of the threat it addresses (a potential threat) and the capability it proposes (a limited system).

NMD is the successor of something called Global Protection against Limited Strikes (GPALS). It is much closer in concept to Safeguard/Sentinel than it is to SDI. As Walter Slocombe, the Clinton administration's undersecretary of defense for policy, explains, it is "designed to counter a few tens" of incoming missile reentry vehicles, not a massive launch. The justification for this more modest shield is twofold: it is designed for the size of attack a rogue state can contemplate in the foreseeable future, and its more modest requirements make it more plausible to design and operate. Its opponents reject both these claims. As John Pike of the Federation of American Scientists and a consistent opponent of missile defenses over the years puts it, NMD is "a system that won't work against a threat that does not exist."

Advocacy and opposition are strong and polarized. Bush administration advocates and their civilian supporters tend to make five supporting assertions. The first is that the threat from the rogue states (Iran, North Korea, and Iraq have been the most frequently cited examples) is real and must be dealt with now, before their missile capabilities become operational and pose a more ominous threat. Second, possession of NMD will insure that the United States will be willing to act forcefully in regional conflicts, since it will not be vulnerable to missile attacks (or their threat) from the rogue states. Third, the supporters say the protection will be extended to allies and others (such as Russia and Israel), thereby widening its appeal. Fourth, they argue that the cost of NMD is a "small price" to pay for a system that will protect the United States from nuclear and other exotic (e.g., chemical and biological) attacks delivered by missiles. Fifth, they argue the system is not designed against Russia and China and thus should not worry them (which, we will see in the next section, they believe is not quite the case).

The opponents are equally detailed in their concerns. Many of the four most frequently voiced objections to NMD reflect the reverse of the claims of the advocates. First and foremost, opponents argue that the feasibility of the system has not been demonstrated even in a testing program designed to maximize the likelihood of success. Further, Richard Garwin, a longtime critic, maintains the current system would fail miserably against any kind of countermeasures (efforts to confuse or disable the defenses) that would certainly be part of any attack. Second, the critics disagree with cost estimates, saying they will almost certainly escalate beyond current projections and citing inflation in the price tags for Safeguard/Sentinel and SDI as precedents. Third, they argue that we are (or at least should be) working politically to improve relations with both Iran and the Democratic People's Republic of Korea (North Korea), and that is a better way to deal with the problem than building provocative defenses.

Fourth, they have taken exception to the assertion of the generally benign effect that defenses will have on the international scene. The Russians, they point out, are opposed to missile defenses and that erecting them over Russian objections could affect bilateral relations between what remain the two nuclear superpowers (Russian opposition to the American invasion of Iraq, for instance). Similarly, the Chinese fear the effect of NMD on the deterrent ability of their currently small nuclear force. American allies, on the other hand, have shown very little enthusiasm about the project, and despite overtures from Rumsfeld and other Bush administration officials, their support cannot be taken for granted.

It is at this level that the national and international political imperatives collide. The essence of the arguments put forward by the advocates of NMD is that these defenses are in the American national interests because they will protect American citizens from attacks by the rogue states. Critics, as noted, dispute whether the defenses will protect anyone from anything, but they also raise potential negative international effects as well. Internationally, the American determination to build NMD in the face of opposition from most countries is seen as evidence of disturbing, unilateralist trends in American foreign policy.

INTERNATIONAL REACTIONS

Part of the international objection to NMD deployment by the United States arises from the sense of American *unilateralism*, the perception that the United States takes actions without thinking about the broader repercussions of the international system. Yoichi Funabashi, chief diplomatic correspondent for the Tokyo newspaper *Asahi Shimbun,* warns of potential unforeseen effects "if the United States proceeds with its own NMD deployment while disregarding the international implications of such an action." A July 13, 2000, editorial in *Le Monde* of Paris concurs, with an added dimension: "The American disregard for the reactions of the international community reminds us, if we needed a reminder, that we are in the middle of an election campaign. This is a time when foreign policy means little."

Aside from this general objection of unilateral action, specific states have had different reactions to the NMD proposal. Israel stands out as a strong supporter of the project, on the presumption that the technology will be shared with them, thereby increasing their ability to deal with the rogue states that confront them. Otherwise, all the major states have more or less major objections. These states include Russia, China, India, and American allies. Whether these objections, which are not necessarily universally held in each capital, will have an important bearing in the deployment decision will help determine whether national or international imperatives turn out to be pivotal in the deployment decision. The NMD has been lowered among U.S. priorities since 2003, largely based on budgetary constraints associated with the Iraq war, thereby muting criticism. A new NMD thrust would surely rekindle opposition.

Russia

During the Cold War, the then Soviets uniformly opposed American missile defense proposals. While their official reasons for doing so were generally couched in terms of the adverse effect on deterrence, at least part of their reasons for wanting to scuttle the projects was technological: the Soviets knew they did not have the scientific manpower or computer power to tackle missile defenses without diverting enormous resources needed for other priorities. Although the Soviets did deploy and the Russians maintain a suspect ABM system (*Galosh*) around Moscow, that perspective holds for Russia today—in some ways even more vividly than it did when their Soviet predecessors were seeking to undermine SDI.

The chief official objection the Russian government had to NMD deployment was its effect on the ABM Treaty of 1972. To advocates of arms control generally around the world, the ABM Treaty has been considered the cornerstone of post–World War II nuclear arms control, because it sanctified the system of mutual deterrence between the two superpowers by denying them the ability to field defensive forces that might threaten retaliatory capabilities and thus lower inhibition to starting a nuclear war. Indeed, the ABM Treaty has been regarded by many as the *heart* of nuclear deterrence, making any threat to its continuation emotionally and intellectually wrenching.

The U.S. and Russian governments disagreed on the effect of NMD on the treaty. The U.S. government argued that the ABM Treaty is the product of a very different security environment and that, given the nature of the contemporary environment, the treaty is largely obsolete. The Russians disagreed vociferously. As Sergei Ivanov, secretary of Russia's security council, put it at a conference in Munich in February 2001, "The destruction of the ABM Treaty will result in the annihilation of the whole structure of strategic stability and create the prerequisites for a new arms race." Something had to give, and there was little movement on the disagreement when Bush and Russian President Vladimir Putin met for the first time in June 2001 in Slovenia. Putin subsequently agreed in principle to NMD testing that violates the treaty, and then grudgingly acceded to American withdrawal from the treaty. (The Russians actually had little choice but to accede, since the treaty contained a provision allowing the parties to withdraw with six months' notice.)

The Russian attachment to the ABM Treaty had other bases. Paramount among them is the need to engage in further nuclear force reductions as a way to save monetary resources desperately needed in other areas of the Russian economy, including the military. The Russian parliament (the *Duma)* ratified the Strategic Arms Reduction Talks (START) II treaty during the summer of 2000, which reduces the number of warheads in the Russian arsenal (as well as the United States) to about 3,500 and thus reduces maintenance costs. The Russians are known to want to complete START III, which will likely reduce the number to about 1,500 warheads apiece, allowing further needed savings. This need ultimately left the Russians in a weak negotiating position on the ABM Treaty, since they could not threaten to back out of arms reductions talks the Americans favored. At a slightly lower level of concern, the Russians also worry that continuing research by the Americans on the missile defense problem could lead to a "strategic breakout" that could produce a comprehensive system of the SDI variety that would render their deterrent force "impotent and obsolete," to borrow the Reagan term.

The result has been a political standoff. When the Duma passed START II, one of its specific conditions was continuation of the ABM Treaty. If the ABM Treaty were somehow breached, then ratification of START II is rescinded and so are the needed plans for force reduction and the diversion of funds to other uses. Vladimir Putin, the Russian president, has consistently tied adherence to the treaty to progress in START III, despite Bush administration attempts to change his mind. Putin has also stated that a unilateral U.S. decision to deploy NMD could result in increases in Russian offensive forces, a countermeasure with anti-START ramifications. Such a decision could not fail to strain American-Russian relations. Yet, when Bush announced the American intent to withdraw, the Russians were profoundly silent on the issue, acceding with as little fanfare as possible.

The outcome of the NMD thus has the potential to affect adversely the relations between the successors to the Cold War rivalry and still two of the world's most powerful states militarily. There are three possible NMD/ABM Treaty outcomes. The United States could abandon NMD deployment. This would be the outcome preferred by the Russians and probably most other countries in the world. The United States could continue discussions with the Russians about altering the treaty so that it will accommodate a larger, more robust NMD deployment than currently is allowed. Finally, the United States could exercise its rights under the treaty and withdraw, as it has done. This allows the United States to deploy as large an NMD as it wants without violating any treaty obligation. It would also maximize international enmity and reactions toward the project. Choosing the latter would be an effective slap in the face for the Russians. Opposition to American presence in Iraq may be part of their payback.

China

If Russia worries that a breakout could leave its nuclear deterrent impotent against the United States somewhere in the future, China has the same fear about the effects of the current proposed system. Although China is today not the avowed object against which the NMD proposal is designed, as it was in the 1960s, the prospect of the deployment of such a system has a direct effect on the small Chinese nuclear force and its deterrent ability.

The Chinese are on record that they would never initiate nuclear war, thus having disavowed any possibility of launching a first strike against an opponent. The current small size of its force reinforces this statement, since a Chinese first strike could not destroy an opponent and would certainly invite a much larger retaliation. Rather, China maintains its force for retaliation in opposition to a first strike against it, promising to punish an aggressor by means of retaliation should it be attacked.

How can China argue it has a credible deterrent given the small size of its arsenal (as noted earlier, twenty ICBMs and about a dozen SLBMs)? The answer, of course, is that it cannot sustain the argument credibly against an adversary with a large, capable arsenal: its ICBMs are at fixed sites that could be targeted by an aggressor, and its submarine-launched missiles are highly unreliable and have a short range. Thus, the retaliatory capacity of the Chinese force is sometimes referred to in the defense community as a "strategic fiction."

The proposal for NMD, however, upsets and undermines that fiction in Chinese minds. China argues that, even in the event of a nuclear aggression against it, a few of its missiles might survive and be available for a retaliatory mission. If the initial attack was by the United States and it had an operational NMD, the remaining Chinese force after the initial attack would be the exact kind of force with which the NMD is designed to cope. The prospect that a Chinese retaliation could be picked off by the NMD would, in the words of retired American Rear Admiral Michael McDevitt, restore Chinese "nuclear vulnerability without a retaliatory recourse" and leave China in a position where it could be subject to "nuclear blackmail." The most common scenario in which the United States might threaten China would be a renewed Taiwan crisis (which occurs periodically) that somehow spun out of control.

For these reasons, China much prefers that the United States maintain the status quo and refrain from NMD deployment. *Renmin Rabao*, the Communist Party daily newspaper published in Beijing, made the case that presumably reflects official policy in a July 7, 2000, editorial: "U.S. deployment of the NMD system, a plan aimed at strengthening its own offensive and defensive capacity while blunting other countries' offensive weapons, is an act of sheer selfishness and hegemonism. Going against the main trend of the times, the United States will inevitably end up self-injured. The whole world, including the United States, will never be at peace."

One can argue that the concern contained in this statement is overblown, but nonetheless, an American decision to deploy NMD does put China in a strategic policy bind. If China believes the "strategic fiction" of a retaliatory capability is sufficiently important, one possible, even likely, response would be to modernize and expand its nuclear forces to the point that they would be capable of overwhelming the NMD after an American attack, a possibility that has been hinted could occur. Doing so would come at the expense of modernizing other elements of Chinese military forces (as noted in Chapter 1, "China Rising," military upgrading is one of the "four modernizations" begun in the 1970s), a process to which the regime is dedicated. At the same time, an enlarged Chinese force could be viewed as a threat to some of its regional neighbors, notably India, thereby setting off a ripple effect.

India

Along with Pakistan, India is the newest avowed member of the nuclear weapons "club" (discussed in Chapter 12). The Indian nuclear program is much older than its recent emergence in 1998 would suggest; India detonated what it maintained was a "peaceful nuclear explosive" in 1974, and it is generally conceded that India has been a potential nuclear weapons possessor ever since. While the impetus for going overtly nuclear in 1998 has largely been seen in the context of Indo-Pakistani relations and Indian nationalism, the original—and continuing—obsession of Indian military planners has been China and the Chinese nuclear force. Anything that potentially affects the nature of Chinese nuclear capability is therefore also a concern to India.

India considers itself to be in a uniquely vulnerable geopolitical situation. As possibly the most steadfastly neutral country in the world, India does not fall under the nuclear "umbrella" (protection) of any nuclear weapons state, meaning India is on its own to deter potential nuclear opponents. At the same time, its geographic position is such that it is one of the "few countries [that] confront the multitude of missile threats that India does," according to Brahma Chellaney, a former consultant to India's National Security Coun-cil. Among the actual or potential nuclear states that do or might menace India are China, Pakistan, Iran, and Iraq.

To the Indians, however, the real problem is China, a country it fought border wars with in the 1960s and which it considers a natural enemy. The Indian fear of NMD derives from the fact that it might cause China to expand its nuclear forces, as suggested above. Were that the case, India fears the result might well begin a new arms race in Asia. Because India's nuclear deterrent could be undermined by a larger Chinese force, the Indi-ans fear they might have to expand their own forces to restore deterrence, a process that could spiral into a classic action-reaction phenomenon that would, in the end, leave nei-ther more secure. At the same time, an expanded Chinese force would presumably also be modernized, and the Indians fear that China might be tempted to sell its old missiles to Pakistan to help pay for modernization.

Moreover, the Indians believe the threat to which NMD is a supposed response is itself overblown, particularly given the potential cost of deployment. Chellaney, for instance, refers to the Clinton justification of the system as a "cry wolf" approach to the problem, suggesting the threat really does not exist. Moreover, the Indians realized the ABM Treaty will be a certain victim of deployment, and given the symbolic importance of the ABM Treaty, Chellaney concludes, "NMD's biggest casualty will be international arms control."

The Allies

The proposal to field an American missile defense has not had a tremendous impact on allies in Europe and Japan, since neither area will be directly affected by the protection or costs (at least not initially). In both cases, however, there are residual concerns that suggest to them that NMD is not a good idea.

European concerns have been muted in some measure because they take the threat less seriously than do the Americans. As Francois Heisbourg, a professor at the French *Institut d'Etudes Politique*, argues in an article summarizing European attitudes toward NMD, Europe has "a more laid-back attitude" toward the rogue states and the threats they pose or may pose in the foreseeable future. Nonetheless, there are at least four con-cerns that NATO allies do raise.

One concern is the opportunity cost associated with developing and deploying the system. Regardless of what NMD ultimately costs, the bill will come at the expense of other investments the United States might have made and which, given their assessment of the threat, the allies think would probably be spent on better allocations of resources. Some Europeans question the strategic impact of erecting a defense against a country like North Korea, which Heisbourg describes as "a famine-ridden Asian backwater with a yearly GDP [gross domestic product] representing one month's worth of Wal-Mart sales." Euro-peans worry as well about the adverse impact NMD could have on Western relations with China, which have expanded greatly in the economic realm, and also what a European-based NMD might look like sometime in the future, should Europe decide to join an NMD regime. Moreover, European leaders believe maintenance of the ABM Treaty is more important than any gains in security that might derive from an NMD deployment.

The Japanese perspective is somewhat different. Japan is, obviously, geographically close to one of the rogue states (North Korea) against which the system is directed, and Japanese policy has been influenced by what it refers to as the three "security shocks" of the 1990s: Chinese missile tests over Taiwan, the North Korean missile tests over Japan itself, and the explosion of nuclear weapons by India and Pakistan. Each of these events alters the strategic equation in Asia in the Japanese mind, if not in altogether predictable ways.

According to Funabashi, the proposed missile defense system has an impact on five areas of Japanese interest:

1. *Impact on extended deterrence.* The Japanese have long relied on the American nuclear deterrent. Their fear is that the United States might retreat behind the missile shield to "fortress America."

2. *Differing perceptions of North Korea.* Many Japanese feel the level of concern the United States is demonstrating over the North Korean missile threat is exaggerated and might upset diplomatic approaches that could lead to more realistic solutions to the problem.

3. *Connection to theater missile defense (TMD).* While Japan downplays the *strategic* threat posed by North Korea (its ability to target the United States), they do worry about the prospects of short-range missiles and fear American preoccupation with NMD will lead to a deemphasis on TMD, which is important to them.

4. *Russian and Chinese reaction.* Japan realizes that both these large and powerful neighbors oppose NMD and wonders what the negative effects of supporting the United States on NMD will be for their relations with the Chinese and the Russians.

5. *Long-term architecture in Asia.* Were the NMD to become a comprehensive system covering Asian countries including Japan and Taiwan, the Japanese worry about the ramifications for dealing with China.

CONCLUSION

As the preceding discussion suggests, the debate over further development and deployment of a national missile defense system is more than a domestic American political issue, even though most of the discussions within the United States have stressed American rather than international effects. The problem of missile defense has much of the *structure* of a traditional arms issue, bearing a resemblance to arms racing issues that roiled the Cold War, including earlier considerations of missile defenses. The similarity is fairly clear on three grounds.

First, missile defense meets the criterion of being a problem with both national and international ramifications, which can best be dealt with by the concerted efforts of a number of states. If the solution to deploying missile defenses is not to deploy them, of course, that could be done by a unilateral American decision. If, on the other hand, the problem of missile proliferation that is the reason for a missile defense initiative is included, then the underlying problem can only be solved by the abstention of possible missile proliferators as well. Whether that goal is best accomplished by negotiations that result in agreement to abstain or defenses to hedge against proliferation is at the heart of the international debate about defenses.

A second way in which missile defense resembles earlier arms race issues is its abstract nature. The problem that missile defenses seek to overcome is a *potential*, not an actual, capability, although one can argue about when (or if) the threat will become real. Many traditional arms race issues—including the debate over Sentinel/Safeguard—are similar, and with a similar effect. The international problems caused by missile defenses are abstract, somewhere indefinably in the future, problems that may or may not materialize. If, in other words, one could argue powerfully and convincingly that erecting missile defenses will have immediate and strong deleterious effects on the international security environment, the debate would be changed to a greater international dialogue. The fact that this argument cannot be made allows, for instance, the Bush administration to try to "jawbone" opponents without the threat of short-term repercussions.

Third and finally, we return to the basic concern, which is the clash between national and international interests. If the arguments about defenses have merit, whatever decisions are reached will have opposite effects on the two levels. If missile defenses work and are deployed, American national security—narrowly defined as the protection of the homeland—will be arguably strengthened, but at the expense of adverse international reaction that may destabilize the international environment because of the actions it causes other states to take (the security dilemma). Conversely, a decision not to deploy may leave the international system tranquil, while leaving American national security less secure. Who is the more important winner or loser with either outcome?

The whole issue of missile defense has been relegated to the back burner by the war on terrorism and the U.S. military involvement in Iraq. As long as these problems continue to occupy the attention and resources of the United States, forceful advocacy of NMD and the hostile reaction of the international community will remain muted.

But missile defenses will not remain in the shadows forever. The emphasis of the American government on containing the behavior of rogue states and even terrorist possession of ballistically delivered weapons of mass destruction ensure missile defenses will remain on the GWOT and homeland security agendas. If that is not enough, the sheer resilience of NMD advocates ensures the issue will not die. Thus, the collision of national and international politics remains on the horizon.

STUDY/DISCUSSION QUESTIONS

1. What is the nature of traditional arms race, including ARP, the security dilemma, and transstate security issues? How does the national missile defense (NMD) proposed by the United States fit into that definition?

2. How are the Sentinel/Safeguard and NMD system proposals similar and how are they different? What lessons, if any, can be learned from the earlier deployment that apply to the newer proposal?

3. How did the Reagan Strategic Defense Initiative (SDI) differ from Sentinel/Safeguard, which preceded it, and NMD, which followed it? How did those differences make SDI simultaneously more and less appealing?

4. What exactly is the NMD? What is it supposed to do, and how? Why does it clash with the ABM Treaty, and why is that important to critics both in the United States and elsewhere?

5. Why do Russia, China, India, and American allies object to the NMD plan? Are their objections reasonable? What are the consequences of those negative assessments?

6. Would the negative reactions that could occur in places like Russia, China, and India if NMD is deployed leave the world a more or a less secure place than it is now?

7. Given your assessment of these effects, should the United States pursue or abandon the NMD program, or should it withhold final judgment until the threat materializes or workable NMD designs are demonstrated?

READING/RESEARCH MATERIAL

Guertner, Gary L., and Donald M. Snow. *The Last Frontier: An Analysis of the Strategic Defense Initiative.* Lexington, MA: Lexington Books, 1986.

Ivanov, Igor. "The Missile Defense Mistake: Undermining Strategic Stability and the ABM Treaty." *Foreign Affairs* 79, 5 (September/October 2000), 15–20.

The Military Balance. London: International Institute for Strategic Studies.

"Misguided Missile Defense." *World Press Review* 47, 9 (September 2000), 4.

The *Washington Quarterly*, a respected foreign policy journal associated with the Center for Strategic and International Studies, devoted much of its Summer 2000 edition (vol. 3, 3) to the argument over missile defense. The pertinent articles and their authors follow:

Chellaney, Brahma. "New Delhi's Dilemma," 145–154.

Funabashi, Yoichi. "Tokyo's Temperance," 135–144.

Hadley, Stephen J. "A Call to Deploy," 95–108.

Heisbourg, Francois. "Brussels's Burden," 127–134.

McDevitt, Michael. "Beijing's Bind," 177–186.

Nacht, Michael. "The Politics: How Did We Get Here?" 87–94.

Pikayev, Alexander A. "Moscow's Matrix," 187–193.

Slocombe, Walter B. "The Administration's Approach," 79–86.

WEB SITES

Complete online source of NMD information

National Missile Defense: What Does it All Mean? At http://www.cdi.org/hotspots/issuebrief/default.asp

Technical analyses, testimonies, and other documents criticizing NMD

Global Security: Missile Defense at <u>http://www.ucsusa.org/arms/0missile.html</u>

Developments and links to official documents, governmental sources, and nongovernmental sources

Arms Control and Non-Proliferation: Missile Defense at <u>http://usinfo.state.gov/topical/pol/arms/nmd</u>

A wide variety of documents on missile defenses and proliferation

Ballistic Missile Defense at <u>http://fas.org/ssp/bmd</u>

News, briefings, and other resources favoring NMD

Missile Defense at <u>http://www.defenselik.mil/specials/missiledefense/inner.html</u>

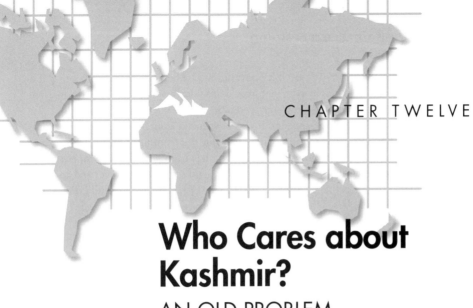

Who Cares about Kashmir?

AN OLD PROBLEM
WITH NEW TEETH

PRÉCIS

There are some politico-military problems that are so deep and fundamental that they appear to be incapable of solution and thus linger on for a very long time. The situation between Israel and its neighbors depicted in Chapter 6 is that kind of conflict. The struggle between India and Pakistan over control of the strategically and emotionally important princely state of Jammu and Kashmir (Kashmir for short) is another. Given the depth and diametrical opposition of the various sides, it is a truly irresolvable conflict.

This case develops the problem in two ways. The first is historical, looking at the evolution of the problem from the partition of the Indian subcontinent after World War II to the present. The second, and more fundamental, purpose is to look at the prospects for ending the fighting and coming up with a peaceful solution with which all parties can live. This involves examining the underlying interests of the major players and their desired outcomes. Why do India and Pakistan believe control of Kashmir is vital to their national interests? Why do some Kashmiris believe that independence is the only acceptable option? The basic problem is that the outcomes preferred by each antagonist are absolutely opposed by the others, creating an intractable situation parallel to that between the Israelis and the Palestinians.

It is a war being fought literally at the top of the world, in a land that is home to some of the world's tallest mountains and most awesome vistas that have earned it the nickname the "Switzerland of the East." The battlefields are the high Himalayan Mountains, often at altitudes of 16,000–17,000 feet above sea level where the air is so oxygen-poor that normal military activities by combat forces are physically impossible to perform even were it not for the icy, snow-covered, rugged terrain. Given the conditions, much of the fighting consists of long-range artillery duels between the contending sides. The front moves periodically in one direction or the other, but the frontier never seems to move very far. At varying levels of intensity, the fighting has been going on for more than a half-century, with no conclusive end in sight to the grim struggle for power and control.

The place is the northern tip of the Asian subcontinent, where India, Pakistan, Afghanistan, Tajikistan, and China meet in the world's tallest mountain range. The *CIA Factbook* calls it "the world's most highly militarized territorial dispute." Forming the geographic cap for the new country of India when independence came to the subcontinent, the point of contention is the princely state of Jammu and Kashmir (hereafter Kashmir), a territory about the size of Utah annexed by India when the subcontinent was subdivided in the latter 1940s by Great Britain as it dissolved its long-held colonial empire there. Because the population of Kashmir is about 70 percent Muslim, the new government of Pakistan never recognized Indian control and has, through Kashmiri "freedom fighters" whom India accuses of being agents of the Pakistani government (a charge denied by Pakistan), been contesting sovereign political control ever since. On at least two occasions, Kashmir has been a major battleground in wars between India and Pakistan. The rest of the time, Kashmir is the site of a low-level war of attrition with considerable explosive potential for the region and potentially beyond.

Why highlight a seemingly parochial dispute over some physically awe-inspiring but economically impoverished territory very far from the center of the international political scene? On the face of it, the answer to who cares about Kashmir would seem to be not much of anyone except the people who live there. Such a conclusion, however, would not be warranted.

What has revived, or for much of the world, created international interest in Kashmir, quite simply, are the "new teeth" demonstrated by India and Pakistan in 1998 when they both exploded nuclear weapons and thus made official the spread of the nuclear arms race to that part of Asia. Kashmir is the most likely flashpoint that could lead to wider war between India and Pakistan, and dealing with the Kashmir problem was one of the major reasons that former President Clinton traveled to the subcontinent in early 2000. Prior to leaving on that trip, he referred to Kashmir as "the most dangerous place in the world today."

Defusing the Kashmir conflict as a means to help lower the likelihood of nuclear war on the subcontinent would seem enough reason to establish its importance, but there is more. On one hand, the outcome of the dispute, particularly if it resulted in independence for Kashmir or attachment to Pakistan, would provide a significant territorial precedent in the region in at least two ways. Indian possession of Kashmir has been compared to Chinese possession of Tibet (which is not far away physically). At the same time, Kashmir's secession could provide encouragement for other areas within India (or even Pakistan) with centrifugal tendencies.

In addition, there is another significant aspect of the Kashmir situation for the study of international relations. In a world where American power seems to be a factor nearly everywhere, the crisis also demonstrates the limit of the United States to influence events.

The United States has always had very limited influence on the subcontinent and especially with the government of India, a lack of affinity that might seem strange between the world's two largest political democracies. Part of the problem is that the United States has been more interested in improved relations with China, and that fact has "tilted" U.S. policy more toward China's ally, Pakistan. India, in turn, felt the necessity to be closer to the Soviet Union during the Cold War to counterbalance China, and especially after the Soviets took a leading role in mediating the outcome of the 1965 Indo-Pakistani War. Even with the Cold War over, however, U.S. influence on the subcontinent, and especially with India, remains minimal. The U.S. de facto alignment with Pakistan over the 2001 war in Afghanistan (in which India has also offered assistance) has increased American visibility and presence in the region. Any long-term change in influence remains to be seen. Unlike in so many other crisis situations around the world, the United States is not clearly an important "player" in resolving the tensions over Kashmir. We will speculate on why this may be the case in the conclusions.

The Kashmir conflict is an extremely intractable situation that has proven very difficult—to this point impossible—to resolve, and it may remain so. To understand both the nature of the problem and the barriers to its solution, we will begin by looking at the historical basis of the disagreement and how it has evolved, including the effects that "nuclearization" has had on it. Next we will examine the interests of the various parties to the dispute, and how those interests have served to preclude particular outcomes. We will then look at a series of options for settling or managing the dispute and the political and other barriers to implementing them. Finally, we will conclude with some assessment of where the dispute may head in the future.

EVOLUTION OF THE PROBLEM

Kashmir became an international problem with the breakup of the British Raj (the British colonial administration) on the subcontinent after World War II. Before World War II, there were several independence movements on the subcontinent. One of these, the Muslim League, headed by Muhamad Ali Jinnah, represented the interests of the Islamic minority on the subcontinent, while the interests of the Hindu majority were represented by the Indian Congress, headed by Mohandas Gandhi. During the period between the world wars, the activism was sufficient to force the British to pass the Government of India Act of 1935, promising independence for the subcontinent. That process was interrupted by the outbreak and conduct of World War II. After the war, the situation would return and have to be faced.

Subdividing the Subcontinent

After World War II ended, a high-level British delegation under the leadership of British war hero Lord Mountbatten was dispatched to the Indian subcontinent. Its purpose was to subdivide what had been a single colonial unit (the *Raj*) into independent units that represented some reasonable form of self-determination along ethnic and communal lines. The problem was that the subcontinent before (and after) colonialism is an incredibly diverse physical and political place, made of numerous nationalities and religions that

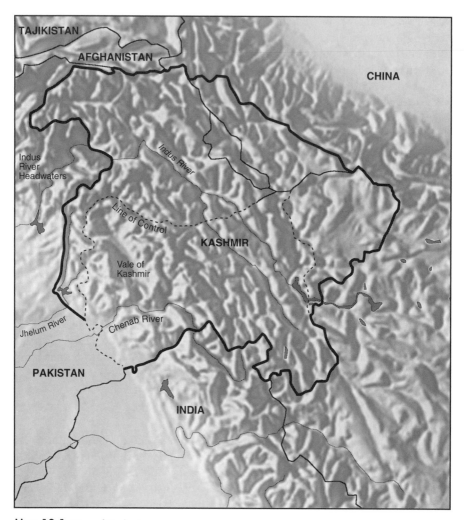

Map 12.1 Map of Kashmir.

have, through history, been more or less antithetical to one another. To get some feel of the extent of this diversity, 562 "princely states" had to decide their political destiny for partition to be complete.

The basic form of partition was conceptually simple enough. The subcontinent would be divided into a predominantly Muslim state (Pakistan) and a Hindu state (India). The basic criterion for drawing the map between the two would be territorial: areas that were overwhelmingly Muslim would become part of Pakistan, and predominantly Hindu areas would accede to India. For a variety of ethnic, cultural, religious, and historical reasons, such a basic subdivision was both necessary and sensible.

No political boundary line could perfectly partition the two groups, and as a result, at independence several million Muslims were left in India and vice versa, causing a panicked migration across the borders that remains the largest such event in human history (most of this occurred in the Punjab region of western India and West Pakistan) and resulted in high levels of tension and fighting there as populations migrated from one side of the frontier to the other. In addition, the principle of territorial majority also meant that the Muslim state would be divided into two physically distant parts of Pakistan, the Punjabi-dominated West Pakistan and Bengali-majority East Pakistan separated by 1,000 miles of Indian territory. In 1971, East Pakistan splintered away from Pakistan to form the independent country of Bangladesh.

The princely states were given two choices. They could accede either to India or to Pakistan; it was understood that they could not choose independence. Further, states that were not predominantly Muslim would become part of India. Based on religion and other factors, most had little difficulty reaching a decision under what was known as the Transfer of Power. In the vast majority of cases, accession to one state or another was accomplished either through popular vote or by an act of accession by the government of the princely states and India or Pakistan. The Transfer of Power guidelines did not specify which method would be used.

The accession process went well for all areas except Jammu and Kashmir, which, along with Janagadh and Hyderabad, had not decided their fate when the Transfer of Power took place on August 15, 1947. All three states eventually became part of India over the protests of Pakistan; of the three, Kashmir has remained the major point of contention since 1947.

The situation in Kashmir was the mirror image of that in Jungadh in the Punjabi western part of the subcontinent. In Jungadh, 80 percent of the population was Hindu, but the region's ruler was a Muslim. At the insistence of the Indian government, the issue of accession was submitted to a plebiscite, and the population voted overwhelming to become part of India. This line of action would not provide a precedent when it came time to decide the political fate of Kashmir.

In Kashmir, the demographics and geopolitics were reversed: about three-quarters of the population of four million in 1947 were Muslims, while the ruler of the state was a Hindu, Maharajah Sir Hari Singh. The maharajah's instinct was to press for independence, but this option was unacceptable to any of the other parties. In 1947, Muslim "freedom fighters" invaded Kashmir to force union with Pakistan, and the fighting became part of the general war on the subcontinent between India and Pakistan that broke out in October of that year. Unwilling to submit the fate of Kashmir to a referendum he knew he would lose, the maharajah reluctantly acceded to joining India in 1948. The state of Pakistan refused to recognize the accession and demanded a referendum that was authorized by the United Nations in 1949. The Indian government refused to hold the referendum, maintaining Kashmir had legally become part of India by intergovernmental agreement. The basis for the ongoing dispute was established by this action by India.

The Bases of Dispute

On the face of it, the case for allowing Kashmir to be a part of Pakistan rather than part of India would appear to be a strong one. Writing in 1991, Alastair Lamb summarizes these bases of the Pakistani claim to Kashmir: "First, the State of Jammu and

Kashmir was a region with an overwhelming Muslim majority contiguous to the Muslim majority region of the Punjab, which became part of Pakistan. Second, the economy . . . was bound up in what was to become Pakistan. Its best communication with the outside world lay through Pakistan, and this was the route taken by the bulk of its exports. Third, the waters of the Indus, Jhelum, and Chenab [rivers], all of which flowed through Jammu and Kashmir territory, were essential for the prosperity of the agricultural life of Pakistan."

These reasons are emotional, pragmatic, and geopolitical. Clearly, the desire to have coreligionists united with their religious brethren is a deeply emotional question that has helped fuel continued Muslim activism over the decades of the conflict and that formed the original rationale for partition. Particularly given that India insisted on popular self-determination in other cases where Hindus were in the majority, it contributes to the ongoing sense of distrust and hatred between the people of the country and the Pakistanis, which, among other things, precluded a meeting between heads of states of India and Pakistan between 1947, when partition occurred, and 2000, when such a meeting finally took place. The pragmatic, economic argument, of course, has been overcome with time, as the commercial patterns that formed its base in the 1940s have been supplanted with a reorientation of the Kashmiri economy toward India.

Although it is less often emphasized, the geopolitical argument about the Indus rivers, which contains an emotional element as well, may be the most sustaining part of the Pakistani contention other than religious kinship. The basis of this importance is the enormous reliance of Pakistan on the waters from these rivers to sustain Pakistani agriculture, which depends on irrigation using the waters of the rivers, a dependence brought dramatically home when India interrupted the flow of waters in 1948 during harvest time and almost destroyed a vital crop harvest.

As the accompanying map shows, essentially all the river water flowing into Pakistan has its source in the mountains of Kashmir. Of a total of six rivers, three (the Indus, Jhelum, and Chenab, collectively known as the western rivers) flow directly from Kashmir to Pakistan, while the other three (known as the eastern rivers) flow from Kashmir into the Indian state of Rajasthan, and then into Pakistan. Before the partition of the subcontinent, the Indus river system had formed part of the oldest irrigation system in the world, providing irrigation waters for what would become Pakistan and India. When the Mountbatten mission provided its final plan for partition, the boundary line cut through the irrigation system, leaving ambiguous which states would continue to have access to the waters.

The crisis that brought home to Pakistan the vitality of control of the headwaters of the rivers in Kashmir occurred in the spring of 1948. The Indian government, arguing it needed the extra water to sustain Hindu immigrants who had fled from Pakistan into Rajasthan, cut the flow of the eastern rivers for six weeks at a critical period just prior to harvest, nearly ruining the crops in Pakistan that relied upon the rivers. Although the flow was restored after international intermediation, a Pakistani government already suspicious of Indian intentions took the lesson to heart that access to the water could never be interrupted again.

The issue is clearly an emotional one for the Pakistanis as well. Pakistan's need for water from the rivers is undeniable; most of the Punjab region of Pakistan (West Pakistan) is very arid, with an average annual rainfall in the 10–15 inch per year range (about the same as eastern Colorado), and a good deal of that falls in a spate during the monsoon season. Without a reliable source of irrigation water during the year, much of Pakistani agriculture is at peril. The geopolitics of Pakistani survival and prosperity are clearly at work.

Recognizing this problem and attempting to solve it, the International Bank for Reconstruction and Development (IBRD or World Bank) helped India and Pakistan negotiate the Indus Waters Treaty of 1960. The provisions of the agreement included dividing claims to the waters so that India received all the water from the eastern rivers (a fraction of the total flow), while Pakistan got all the water from the western rivers. Hydroelectric dams were built in Kashmir to create reservoirs that would allow control of the flow of the rivers into Pakistan, and canals were built to redirect water from the western rivers to irrigate parts of Pakistan formerly supplied by water from the eastern rivers.

This agreement would seem to have solved the water problem, but it has not. Because the headwaters of the western rivers continued to rise in Indian-controlled Kashmir, the Pakistanis continued to worry about another interruption and thus insist on de facto control of those headwaters by Azad Kashmir (Free Kashmir) rebels. Their position is more emotional than rational in this regard because the geography of the mountains through which the water flows makes it physically impossible to divert any of the water into India without boring tunnels through the mountains to redirect the flow, and such a diversion goes well beyond Indian physical or financial assets.

The Indian position on Kashmir is more straightforward. As far as India is concerned, there is no conflict over the status of Kashmir, because that was settled in 1948 with Kashmir's accession into India. Thus, the fracas that flares from time to time is strictly an internal matter, although one that is aggravated by what they see as illegal Pakistani interference in support of "rebels" and pro-independence freedom fighters or terrorists (depending on what side one is on) that India considers as agents of Islamabad.

The Indian position has a geopolitical side as well. Part of their reason for insisting upon continuing control of Kashmir is based in geography. Located as it is literally as the "cap" of India, Kashmir also sits astride historic invasion routes into India, notably from China (which occupies a small part of Kashmir known as Aksai Chin). A Kashmir controlled by a Pakistan in official or informal alignment with China poses a very real military threat to India. At the same time, the idea of Kashmir breaking away from India has precedential value for India, as it does for China over Tibet. There are any number of Indian states with varying levels of secessionist inclinations, and the government of India worries that a breakaway by Kashmir could encourage other similarly inclined areas to follow the lead.

STATUS OF THE PROBLEM

The dispute over Kashmir sporadically breaks out into more or less intense violence, with even the "peaceful" interludes marked by some intercommunal fighting and terrorist attacks. Kashmir was a major object of the first war fought between the two countries shortly after independence was granted in 1947, a conflict that ended on January 1, 1948, with a United Nations mandate to hold a plebiscite that never, in fact, occurred, as already noted. In 1965, war broke out again between India and Pakistan at a barren area along the border between West Pakistan and India known as the Rann of Kutch; initial Pakistani success in that encounter emboldened them to try to seize Kashmir, making it what turned out to be the inconclusive focus of the war. In 1971, war broke out again, and although its major focus was the secession of East Pakistan to form Bangladesh, much of the tension during the conflict centered on Kashmir as a potential second front in that war.

Kashmir has thus been a major focus in each of the three full-scale wars fought between the two subcontinental powers since their independence. A truce line drawn after the war in 1971 gave de facto control over portions of western Kashmir to the Pakistanis and their Kashmiri brethren, thereby creating a lull in the violence for a time. Kashmiri dissidents under the banner of Azad Kashmir resumed the armed struggle in 1988, and regular Indian and Pakistani units began exchanging fire in 1990. Although violence was suspended in summer 2000 as part of the first-ever meeting between the heads of state of the two countries, tensions remain high and terrorist attacks continued to be reported in 2001. Inconclusive talks have continued into 2004.

The potential for resumption of the fighting thus remains. It is not, for instance, entirely clear what the relationship is between the Pakistani government and Azad Kashmir, and hence the degree to which the Pakistanis can control the actions of their "allies." If Indian descriptions of that relationship are to be believed, Azad Kashmir is no more than a puppet organization of the Pakistanis, who recruit, equip, train, and even provide some of the "freedom fighters" that make up the force. Pakistan, of course, vehemently denies these charges, maintaining that the rebels are an independent body seeking independence for Kashmir, possibly with the long-term intention of union with Pakistan. As a result, the possibility of renewed violence remains as long as relations between India and Pakistan continue to be problematical.

Part of the problem is that the status quo, while minimally acceptable, pleases neither side. The "line of control" or truce line established in 1971 provides de facto Pakistani control over most of the western portion of Kashmir, giving them (through Azad Kashmir) physical possession of the headwaters (or sources) of the western rivers of the Indus system. Because Kashmir remains legally a part of India, however, that possession is not as firm as Pakistan would like, given the dependency Pakistan has on the irrigation waters from the river system for survival. Moreover, some of the hydroelectric dams created by the settlement of the Indus Waters Treaty to provide electricity and to store monsoon rains for later use are also in the zone. India, on the other hand, maintains physical control of the mountainous regions and thus the geopolitically important passes along their border with China. The fact that part of their sovereign territory is effectively outside their sovereign control is annoying to the Indian national ego and creates the motivation to alter the line of control.

The issue of Kashmir was revived in international consciousness by the public display of nuclear weapons capability by India and Pakistan in 1998. On May 11 and 13, India conducted five underground nuclear tests in the desert of Rajasthan, announcing the reason for the tests was growing concern about the Chinese nuclear threat (see the discussion in Chapter 11) and alleged nuclear cooperation between China and Pakistan. On May 28 of that year, Pakistan also exploded five devices underground at the Chagai test site. Following a protest by the United States government and the threat to suspend economic assistance, Pakistan conducted another test on May 30.

One of the interesting aspects of the Kashmir dispute and its nuclear extension is the impotence of the United States to affect the situation one way or the other. One of the hallmarks of the post–Cold War 1990s has been American global activism in brokering peaceful settlements of international disputes, often through the personal efforts of President Clinton. The most notable instances of this success have been in negotiating agreements on aspects of the Arab-Israeli conflict (not including Palestine) and in Northern Ireland.

But the United States has been notably unsuccessful in influencing events on the subcontinent. The United States was, for instance, not even informed ahead of time about the nuclear tests by either India or Pakistan (partly because both countries knew the United States would object), and American intelligence was apparently caught completely off guard and failed to predict the explosions. When Clinton visited the subcontinent in April 2000, going first to India and then to Pakistan, he was largely unsuccessful in moving along the peace process. Besides "photo ops" in front of the Taj Mahal and other Indian sites, he made little headway with the Indian leadership on the nuclear weapons question and was virtually given the cold shoulder by the leaders of Pakistan. Given the centrality of the United States in other parts of the world, this void means, in Shankar Bajpai's words in *Foreign Affairs*, "there are no positive pressures whatsoever in Indo-Pakistani relations."

PROSPECTS FOR RESOLUTION

Why has the conflict over Kashmir been allowed to fester for more than a half-century? One possible explanation is that the issues involved are so intractable and the possible outcomes so emotionally charged that none appears acceptable, a situation not unlike the Palestinian question in the Middle East. Another possibility is that resolution of the matter is insufficiently important for the parties to make the necessary sacrifices to achieve closure. Yet a third possibility is that there has been no outside force that has the level of interest or leverage involved to mount an effective effort to mediate the differences.

The Problem Reformulated

Until 1998, some combination of intractability, insufficient local interest, or outside interest or leverage explained why the dispute was not resolved. But things have changed. Most notably, the explosion of nuclear weapons has added Kashmir to the list of conflicts in the world over which a nuclear war might begin. Whether the public demonstration of nuclear capability by the two major regional powers has made any war between them more or less likely is an open question, and one for which a case can be made in either direction. What that demonstration *does* mean is that nuclear war between them is now physically possible. Moreover, the aspect of the Indo-Pakistani relationship that has most often resulted in war has been over Kashmir; the kind of war the next battle over Kashmir could become would seem to make resolution more important than before, both to the principals and to the international system as a whole.

There is precedent for international involvement. In the 1973 Yom Kippur War between Israel and her Islamic neighbors, there were two incidents that raised the fear that the situation could escalate to nuclear weapons use, with unforeseeable consequences for the rest of the international system. First, when Israel suffered serious military setbacks early in the fighting, the Israeli government allegedly authorized the arming of Israel's nuclear arsenal (which Israel neither admits nor denies it possesses). The arsenal presumably could have reached and destroyed the capitals of all of Israel's adversaries, thus raising the stakes had such attacks occurred. Later in the war, when Israel's military fortunes had improved significantly, the Israelis trapped an entire Egyptian army with its back to the Suez Canal but no way to get across and escape, and the Israelis threatened to destroy that army "in detail." The Soviet Union at that point threatened to drop Soviet paratroopers into the Egyptian lines to help in their defense. Neither Israel activating its nuclear forces or the Soviet threat to intervene triggered a nuclear war, but the knowledge they could have helped energize, especially within the United States government, a determination that the Arab-Israeli crisis could not be allowed to devolve again to a point where the result could be a general nuclear war that would threaten the international system itself. The seeds of the Middle East peace process were really born in the desperation of the Yom Kippur War.

Now Kashmir has potentially achieved a similar status within the structure of international problems. But does settling the differences over Kashmir have the same perceived urgency in 2005 that settling the Middle East crisis had in the 1970s?

The answer is mixed. There are certainly dissimilarities. What made the situation so volatile in 1973 was that the United States was clearly aligned with one side (Israel) whereas the other nuclear superpower was a benefactor of the Islamic states. Thus, the possibility of being drawn into the fray simply because one's "friends" became entangled was a very real prospect. Because we had never been to the brink of nuclear war in this manner before, the dynamics of escalation were unknown (as they basically are today). At the same time, both the Soviets and the Americans had some ability to influence the behavior of their client states. The United States, for instance, was able to restrain the Israelis from destroying the trapped and largely defenseless Egyptian army.

Neither of these conflicting factors is present on the subcontinent today. With the end of the Cold War, there are clearly no client states to draw the superpowers into the conflict on opposing sides. This fact may actually make the probabilities of war greater, however, because the major powers also cannot as easily restrain the principal actors. At the same time, the prospects of being dragged inadvertently into a war that has gone or threatens to go nuclear would seem to be reduced; the same escalatory potential is missing.

There is one point of commonality, and that is *uncertainty*. The simple fact of the matter is that nuclear weapons have never been used in war when both sides possessed them and could use them against their enemies. Over the years of the nuclear age, we have devised "rational" constructs about how countries should act in different nuclear situations, but given our total lack of experience in the circumstances surrounding the nuclear escalation process, they remain no more than elaborate, articulate speculations.

That means the answer to the question, "what happens to the rest of the world if India and Pakistan engage in a nuclear exchange during the next Kashmir crisis?" must be, "there is no way to know." Rationally and analytically, the prospect of escalation to the system as a whole would seem to be fairly remote; what the major—including nuclear—powers *probably* would do would be to marshal as much international pressure as possible to end the nuclear fighting at as low a level of death and suffering as possible. That would make sense, if sensibility were to prevail.

But we do not know that would happen. Everyone might act calmly and rationally, or they might not. What we *do* know for certain is that the most certain way to avoid finding out the answer is to avoid there being another war over Kashmir that could escalate to nuclear exchange. Thus, the search for a suitable option to resolve the dispute takes on added meaning when the "new teeth" are present.

There is yet another possible effect that nuclearization of the subcontinent could have on the Kashmir issue. It is also possible to argue that the overt possession of nuclear weapons will have a calming, sobering, and even stabilizing effect on both India and Pakistan. Both countries are now fully aware that *any* war in which they might face one another is a potential nuclear exchange with incalculable consequences for both of them. This realization forces either side to include in its decision process the question of whether any objectives in any contemplated conflict are worth the risk of nuclear escalation, no matter how small that risk might appear to be in any given situation. It might or might not have much or any impact in any particular encounter, but it is also true that no two states, both of which possess nuclear weapons, have ever fought one another. That may be the result of coincidence rather than of the weapons. But it is nonetheless true and can lead to the conclusion that nuclear weapons will stabilize rather than destabilize the subcontinent in the future. Some evidence to support this possibility is continuing negotiations between the two sides on the issues that divide them.

Options for Resolution

The possibility that another war over Kashmir could escalate to a nuclear exchange may make resolution a more important priority although, as noted above, it may also make a renewed war less likely, since both sides presumably recognize what could happen now and may avoid actions with escalatory potential. Regardless of which of these arguments one makes, the clearest way to avoid finding out if Kashmir has nuclear dynamics is to settle the problem in such a manner that the reversion to war is no longer a real prospect—if it is possible to find such a solution acceptable to the parties.

A variety of schemes for settling the problem have been put forward over time. Not all have been formal proposals, nor have any of them enjoyed widespread support. What has bedeviled all the proposals is that none have, to date, been acceptable to the three principal groups to the conflict: the Indians, the Pakistanis, and the Kashmiris. The crux of the difficulty is that each interested party sees the outcomes in absolute and mutually exclusive terms, as a kind of zero-sum game in which one side's gains are inevitably the other side's losses. The Indians optimally want to reassert their sovereign authority over all of Kashmir. The Pakistanis and Kashmiris want that sovereignty reversed, either by accession of Kashmir to Pakistan (the Pakistani preference) or independence for Kashmir (the preference of at least some Kashmiris). None of these outcomes has been acceptable to the others.

The proposals for settling the dispute have generally followed these preferred outcomes. In *The Crisis in Kashmir*, Sumit Ganguly has summarized seven proposals, three of which would reinforce India's continued claim of sovereign control, two of which represent compromises where each side receives some but not all of what it wants, and two of which support the Pakistani/Kashmiri desire to remove Indian sovereignty. In addition, we will explore an eighth outcome, which is a more or less permanent stalemate that results in continuation of the status quo.

The Pro-Indian Options. The three pro-Indian options involve changing the political composition of Kashmir in such a manner that some semblance of pro-Indian legitimate control can be manifested. One possibility, which violates current Indian law and thus cannot be formally advocated, is called *ethnic flooding*. The idea here is to encourage massive Indian immigration into Kashmir to tip the population balance to the Indians, thereby allowing something like a plebiscite in which the new Indian majority might prevail and legitimize Kashmir's status as an Indian state. Because 70 percent of the seven million current citizens of Kashmir are Muslim, this would require a very large influx of people who would patently not be welcomed by the current citizenry, particularly after the reasons for their migration became known. Implementation of the strategy would require amendment of the Indian constitution, a provision of which (Article 370) prohibits, among other things, the sale of immovable properties in Kashmir to non-Kashmiris. The provision, unless rescinded, would virtually prohibit Hindus from establishing homes in Kashmir. Moreover, it is impossible to imagine that organizations like the Jammu Kashmir Liberation Front (JKLF), which seeks independence for the state, would sit idly by while the population flood occurred.

The other two pro-Indian solutions involve military actions the purpose of which would be to destroy the armed resistance to Indian rule. Each strategy is based on a precedent that India has employed elsewhere in the country to quell dissent, although the situations from which the precedents derive are arguably too different to be applicable. Also, it is hard to imagine that Pakistan would accede to the reduction and destruction of groups with which it has had, at a minimum, close relations for a half-century. Military solutions, in other words, almost certainly increase the risk of more general war on the subcontinent, with all the dangers that might entail.

One military solution is the *mailed-fist strategy*. Like ethnic flooding, this option, which is the most bellicose of any, has not received any formal endorsement within the Indian political system. The idea, based on a strategy used earlier to pacify the Punjab, would require greatly increased military action against the dissidents, the purpose of which would be to crush the armed resistance completely, as was done to the Sikhs in the Punjab. With the rebels defeated and removed from the scene, the idea is that elections could be held that would hopefully endorse Indian hegemony. History suggests that Kashmiri resistance to such a campaign would be considerably greater than that which occurred in the Punjab, making the possibility of success more problematical.

The other military solution, applied in India's northwestern region in the 1960s and 1970s, is a *wear-down strategy* of attrition. The idea in this case is that a patient strategy of military pressure may literally wear down the dissident Kashmiris by using "superior military might," according to Bajpai, to the point that they simply tire of the contest and fade away. This suggestion runs in the face of a long-term, tenacious opposition within Kashmir that has shown considerable resilience over a long period of time. It is even arguable that India, which has plenty of other problems of its own, including a large population segment not all that interested in the fate of Kashmir, might actually be more vulnerable to this strategy than the Kashmiris (public opinion turning against the campaign as it did to the United States in Vietnam).

Compromises. As in any situation where all parties have strong claims to the object at hand, compromise is always an attractive possibility, especially if a compromise can be arranged whereby each party can argue that it prevailed. This is especially the case in an emotionally charged situation where almost any concession will be viewed by some partisans as an unacceptable sellout of a deeply held preference. Finding a solution that represents a compromise with which all feel they can live has proven elusive to this point.

Two ideas, one territorial and one jurisdictional, have been put forward. The territorial solution involves *cessation of the Vale of Kashmir to Pakistan*. This region is in the western part of Kashmir, thus contiguous to Pakistan, and it is also the region through which the rivers flow (the Jhelum in particular traverses the valley). The tradeoff would be Pakistan's relinquishing claims to other parts of Kashmir, and notably the mountainous areas so important to Indian security. It is a solution with conceptual ties to Israel relinquishing the West Bank as part of the price of peace with the Palestinians. The problem is that it is politically unacceptable.

There are several objections to this compromise raised by the various parties. First, it is argued that formally ceding *any* part of Kashmir to Pakistan after a half-century of resistance to just such an outcome would be political suicide for any Indian government that might suggest it. Doing so might be interpreted in Islamabad as a sign of Indian weakness, which was a perception that many Indians believe contributed to Pakistani aggression into Kashmir in 1965. Further, the concession might embolden Pakistan to try to annex all of Kashmir. The solution would also be unacceptable to the JKLF, which will accept nothing less than total independence for the province. There is also the objection that the concession would be morally unacceptable for India, since it would involve abandonment of pro-Indian citizens who are residents in the valley.

The other proposed compromise, little more than a fuzzy suggestion at this point, is *shared sovereignty*. The basic idea here would be somehow to come up with a scheme whereby India and Pakistan would jointly control Kashmir, presumably with some participation by the Kashmiris themselves. Details of how this might work—for instance, would there be parts of the country administered by one country and parts by the other?—have not been talked through, and it is difficult to imagine how two countries with as long and bitter a relationship of animosity could suddenly agree to the extraordinary levels of cooperation that any form of joint administration would require. There is also the question of whether Kashmiri separatists would agree to anything less than full autonomy.

Pro-Pakistani Solutions. The last two solutions favor Pakistan or Kashmir. One of these is to hold a *plebiscite* to let the Kashmiris decide their own fate. This was, of course, the solution favored by the United Nations in 1948, and it has been endorsed in subsequent UN resolutions as well. The Pakistanis would clearly be most enthused about this option, particularly if the options for voters were limited to those available under the Transfer of Power guidelines crafted in 1948: union with Pakistan or union with India. The problem is that independence for Kashmir has entered the discussion and would be advocated by a large number of natives of Kashmir (and probably opposed by Pakistan). Short of a campaign of ethnic flooding that preceded a vote, the Indians would oppose any form of plebiscite, because regardless of whether the voters favored union with Pakistan or independence, they would clearly vote for disunion with India.

The final option is *Kashmiri independence.* This idea is opposed by everyone except those Kashmiris who want an independent state. The Indians and Pakistanis oppose the creation of such a state for geopolitical reasons: India would lose control of strategically vital territory in the north of Kashmir, and Pakistan would lose control of the equally vital headwaters of the Indus rivers. In addition, both countries have other regions whose continuing desire to remain part of India or Pakistan is suspect. The creation of an independent state of Kashmir could only serve as an encouraging precedent for separatists elsewhere on the subcontinent. Even neighboring China joins the chorus on this point, because the success of Kashmir's independence movement might also encourage similar sentiments in Tibet.

Perpetual Stalemate. None of these solutions seems especially promising, and it may be that the situation is so intractable and the unwillingness of the parties to compromise so deeply set that no mutually acceptable outcome is possible. Because the imposition of a solution by military force is largely ruled out by the nuclear possibility, Kashmir may be a problem that cannot be solved but instead only managed in a way least objectionable to the most people.

The situation may be analogous to the Palestinian impasse that derailed the Camp David process short of peace in 2000 (see Chapter 6). The Palestinians and Israelis could not agree on two of the issues dividing them (repatriation of Palestinians to Israel and control of Jerusalem) because the positions each held were diametrically opposed and uncompromisable. There was ultimately no room to negotiate.

The triangular relationship between the Kashmiris, Pakistanis, and Indians over the political control of Kashmir may be similar. All three sides have irreconcilable positions about who should be sovereign, and none is willing to compromise its preferred outcome. Even if the Kashmiri separatists and Pakistan could somehow reach agreement (the only possible compromise), the Indians would disapprove and block implementation.

Thus, managing a perpetual stalemate based on the status quo established in 1971 may be the only attainable solution. While de facto control of the headwaters provides less security for Pakistan than sovereign control, it is better than Indian control. India wants the whole issue to go away, but it will not; at least in this scenario India controls the invasion routes. The Kashmiri separatists, who are incapable of seizing independence, at least do not have their hopes snuffed out altogether. It is by no means the best solution; but it may be the best *possible* solution.

CONCLUSION

Two things have change about the Kashmir situation since the latter 1990s: the nuclearization of the subcontinent in 1998 and the opening of discussions between the Indians and Pakistanis on a variety of matters dividing them, including Kashmir, in 2002, talks that continue to be held. The two phenomena are related. The "new teeth" added to the relationship have dampened any bellicose sentiments both sides hold due to the sobering possibility of escalation to nuclear war. That prospect, in turn, has produced the realization that those disagreements most likely to lead to war need to be contained or resolved. Kashmir heads that list, and while resolution remains as elusive as ever, at least the two sides are talking.

Despite ongoing talks and symbolic events like a 2003 cricket match between the Indian and Pakistani national teams, the situation continues to be intractable. Each of the sides has distinct positions that have survived for more than fifty years, when Kashmir was annexed to India over the protests of Pakistan and Kashmir's ethnic majority of Muslims. The Indian accession was of shaky legality and was and continues to be condemned by the United Nations as a rather clear violation of the principle of self-determination that was supposed to dictate the political affiliation of the princely states at the time of partition. Still, accession to India remains a fact.

Positions have hardened, and circumstances have changed. The longer Kashmir has been part of India, the more Indians think of it as Indian territory; as a result, ceding Kashmir (or even a part of it) to Kashmir would be a politically heinous crime on the order of giving New Mexico back to Mexico. No Indian politician or government could survive such an event, and the prospect is made all the more impossible by probably well-grounded fears that such an action would encourage other dissident groups in other parts of the country to attempt to follow suit out of the Indian state. Moreover, the transfer might be seen as an act of weakness by the hated Pakistanis, and if the territory ceded included the passes between India and China, could be a geopolitical disaster. Any compromise by India would require an enormous act of political courage by any Indian politician proposing it.

The Pakistani position is equally hardened. Pakistan has made itself the principal advocate of Muslim Kashmiris for more than a half century and is no more likely to abandon that position than are the Indians to turn their backs on Kashmir's Hindu minority. Politically, the Pakistanis have less to lose by movement toward a settlement, because any solution is likely to come at physical Indian expense (giving away sovereign control over some of Kashmir), which is a net gain for Pakistan. As long as pro-Pakistani elements have power over the regions of Kashmir that control access to water, the status quo is tolerable if not optimal. The only outcome (other than the reassertion of Indian hegemony over all of Kashmir) that could cause Pakistan potentially to suffer would be independence for Kashmir.

The independence movement is one important way things have changed in the Kashmir situation. As stated earlier, independence for the princely states was ruled out as an option by the British when the subcontinent was divided. It is still opposed by all parties except the Kashmiri separatists, notably the JKLF. Any settlement that does not give at least some consideration to separatist demands may well be resisted violently within Kashmir itself by those who see Kashmiri independence as the only acceptable outcome.

Finally, there is the matter of outside efforts to achieve a lasting peace in the region. Such efforts were minimal during the Cold War, from a combination of lack of interest and fear of embroiling the area as yet another Cold War battleground. Cold War reluctance has given way to concern with the possibility of nuclear war on the subcontinent. Is the need to remove Kashmir from the list of potential nuclear battlegrounds sufficiently great to make an attempt to mediate the dispute more attractive than it was in the past? Does the international effort in Afghanistan make the region more geopolitically important than before?

There is precedent for an international effort about Kashmir: the Indus Waters Treaty of 1960. In that instance, the principal outside mediator was the World Bank, which negotiated a division of the waters that provided India with secure access to the waters of the eastern Indus rivers to irrigate Rajasthan and Pakistan with control of all the western rivers, including diverting some of that flow to irrigate areas previously watered by the eastern rivers. Hydroelectric and storage dams to produce power and regulate the flow of the rivers were an added incentive.

The bank's efforts succeeded because it was able to provide funding from a group of interested countries who were willing to foot the bill for the projects that made the agreement possible. In that case, everyone could view themselves as winner: India got the eastern rivers, and Pakistan got total control of the western rivers, plus funds for diversionary canals to move water to areas historically serviced by the eastern rivers and the dams. The benefits for each outweighed the political costs of consorting with the historic enemy. The World Bank was able to transform the situation from a zero-sum to a positive-sum outcome.

Would a parallel effort work to settle the dispute in Kashmir? If so, who would lead it? As noted at the beginning of this chapter, American lack of clout in the region is one of the distinguishing characteristics of the conflict. Should the lead role go to some other state, such as the old colonial power, Great Britain? Is there enough interest in settling the problem to produce the funding for some kind of solution, some way to escape the current zero-sum mentality? More fundamentally, is there some mutually acceptable solution that will still the guns at the top of the world?

STUDY/DISCUSSION QUESTIONS

1. There are four possible long-term outcomes to the crisis in Kashmir: continued union with India, annexation to Pakistan, partition between India and Pakistan, or Kashmir independence. Compare and contrast each. As an outsider with no vested interest in the outcome, which would you recommend?

2. The problem with each possible outcome is the objection that other interested parties have to each solution. Using the four options in Question 1, to whom is each outcome unacceptable? Weigh the objections. Which have the most and least merit?

3. Assume the role of an outside mediator. What would be the position on settling the dispute from which you would begin negotiations? What concessions would you have to be prepared to make to reach a compromise solution? What would be the costs of a solution?

4. Think of yourself as an outsider viewing the problem. How much difference does the possession of nuclear weapons by India and Pakistan make to you? Does the addition of nuclear weapons create enough interest for you to become involved? If, as is likely, a settlement will require lubrication with outside funds, how much is a settlement worth?

5. The other possibility is that nuclear weapons actually stabilize the situation by making both sides realize the consequences of escalation. Defend and critique the ideas that nuclear weapons make negotiating a settlement more and less important to the subcontinent and the international system at large.

6. Eight potential solutions were suggested as possibilities for solving the crisis over Kashmir. Rate them by two criteria: desirability and practicality, for each party. Is there any basis for optimism? Does perpetual stalemate emerge as the least objectionable solution?

7. Is there any way to create a positive-sum atmosphere in the Kashmir conflict that parallels the Indus Waters Treaty in 1960 and allows agreement to be reached?

READING/RESEARCH MATERIAL

Bajpai, K. Shankar. "Untangling India and Pakistan." *Foreign Affairs* 8, 3 (May/June 2003), 112–126.

Ganguly, Sumit. *The Crisis in Kashmir: Portents of War, Hopes of Peace.* New York: Cambridge University Press, 1997.

Jha, Prem Shankar. *Kashmir 1947: Rival Versions of History.* New Delhi, India: Oxford University Press, 1996.

Krasner, D. Stephen. *Sovereignty: Organized Hypocrisy.* Princeton, NJ: Princeton University Press, 1999 (see especially Jose Joffe, "Rethinking the Nation-State").

Lamb, Alastair. *Kashmir: A Disputed Legacy, 1846–1990.* Hertingfordbury, UK: Roxford Books, 1991.

Schofield, Victoria. *Kashmir in the Crossfire.* London, UK: I. B. Tauris and Co., 1996.

WEB SITES

Oldest and most widely circulated newspaper of Kashmir

The *Kashmir Times* at http://www.kashmirtimes.com

Annotated, current record of electronically distributed sources on Kashmir

Kashmir Virtual Library at http://www.clas.ufl.edu/users/gthrusby/kashmir

Views on the situation from Pakistan
Islamic Republic of Pakistan: Kashmir at http://www.pak.gov.pk/public/kashmir
Views on the situation from Kashmir government, India
Jammu and Kashmir at http://jammukashmir.nic.in
Organization publicizing Kashmir's desire for independence
Kashmiri American Council at http://www.kashmiri.com
Sociocultural events, political events, and current affairs on Kashmir
Kashmirnet at http://www.kashmir.co.uk

PART 5

Transnational Issues

The book concludes with a discussion of a relatively recent emphasis in international relations, something called transnational issues (technically they are transstate or transsovereign issues, since states must deal with these issues, but the term transnational has become conventional in describing them). These issues are defined as problems that transcend international borders in ways over which governments of individual states have little control and which, generally, cannot be solved by the actions of individual states working alone.

In most of the literature, the discussion of transnational issues focuses on a few familiar problems such as various environmental difficulties, the human condition (human rights or the rights of certain groups of people), and man-made problems like drugs, to name the most obvious. In an attempt to broaden and extend the discussion, this part addresses three different areas that meet the criterion of transnational issues or that attempt to address transnational issues that are not so commonly found in the literature.

Chapter 13, "Warm and Getting Warmer," examines one of the most serious and controversial transnational issue, global warming and efforts to deal with it. The issue is controversial in two ways not dissimilar to the issue of free trade. One controversy surrounds the international effort to control global warming and has centered on the Kyoto Protocol of 1997. The other controversy surrounds the nature and severity of the problem and thus what needs (or does not need) to be done about it. The two come together around the question of whether the Kyoto Protocol is needed.

The second chapter in the section, Chapter 14, looks at the transnational issue of resource scarcity in the new century. One such issue is water scarcity, especially in the Middle East, from which the chapter takes its title, "Let Them Drink Oil." Two other mini-cases look at different aspects of scarcity: the problems associated with exploiting the petroleum and natural gas reserves of the Caspian Sea and the tragedy of attempting to exploit the diamond wealth of Sierra Leone. The purpose of the cases is to suggest different transnational resource problems in the future.

Chapter 15, "Worse Than the Bubonic Plague," is a case study of the AIDS pandemic in Africa. Beyond the reiteration of the enormous social and physical consequences of the problem (projections suggest more people will die from AIDS than perished in the bubonic plague of the Middle Ages), local and world attention (or inattention) will be presented as a model for how the international system deals with the problem that "disease knows no frontiers" (the motto of the World Health Organization), with particular emphasis on the possibility of an Ebola virus epidemic.

Finally, Chapter 16, "Understanding and Organizing a Post–September 11, 2001, World," looks at the problem of global terrorism over three years after the attacks of 9/11. The case will concentrate on how the terrorist problem has changed and grown since 2001, what creates and motivates terrorists, and what can be done about the problem in the future, including suggestions for a comprehensive strategy for what the Bush administration calls the Global War on Terrorism (GWOT).

CHAPTER THIRTEEN

Warm and Getting Warmer

GLOBAL WARMING AND THE FATE OF THE KYOTO PROTOCOL

PRÉCIS

Global warming represents one of the most pure, yet controversial, transnational issues. It is a pure issue because it is clearly a problem that cannot be solved by the individual efforts of states but must be done collectively if it is to be done successfully at all. It is controversial because there is substantial disagreement both about the nature and severity of the problem and over the structure and content of proposed solutions to climate change that is the clear byproduct of global warming.

This case study looks at the problem from two related vantage points that are similar in structure to the case on free trade in Chapter 8. The first vantage point is an examination of the controversial process surrounding international efforts to deal with global warming, the lightning rod for which has been the Kyoto Protocol of 1997 and attempts to implement that treaty (which have largely focused on the United States as a prime opponent of the initiative since its 2001 withdrawal from the protocol). The second is on the nature and extent of the problem and thus what does and does not require controlling. The two emphases are related because the nature of the problem has a clear relationship to the kinds and extent of remedies that are proposed for it.

The issue of global warming—the extent to which the climate of the Earth is gradually increasing in temperature due largely to human actions—is one of the most controversial, divisive, and yet consequential problems facing international relations in the twenty-first century. No one, of course, favors a gradual or precipitous change in global climate because the consequences could be catastrophic. Having said that, amateurs and experts, some disinterested and some self-interested, disagree on almost everything about the phenomenon. Some question whether global warming exists at all, while others predict apocryphal consequences unless drastic measures are taken to curb the contributors to warming (mostly the burning of fossil fuels in support of a broad variety of human activities). There are significant differences on the parameters of the problem (exactly what will be affected and how much) and on the quality of the science underlying claims on either side (especially when extrapolations are made far into the future).

Regardless of how serious the problem is, global warming is clearly a classic, full-blown transnational issue. As Claussen and McNeilly put it, "Climate change is a global problem that demands a global solution because emissions from one country can impact the climate in all other countries." Global warming, in other words, will be curbed internationally or not at all.

The underlying dynamic, if not its seriousness, can be easily stated. Global warming is the direct result of the release of so-called greenhouse gases into the atmosphere in volumes that are in excess of the capacity of the ecosystem to eliminate them naturally. Although there are a number of these gases, the vast majority of the problem comes from the burning of fossil fuels such as petroleum, natural gas, coal, and wood. Burning these fuels releases carbon dioxide, methane, and nitrous oxide (what the Kyoto Protocol calls the "three most important" contributors) into the air in large quantities. The natural method of containing the amount of carbon dioxide (which is the major culprit) in the atmosphere is the absorption and conversion of that gas in so-called carbon sinks, which separate the two elements (carbon and oxygen) and release them harmlessly back into the atmosphere. In nature, the equatorial rain forests have been where these sinks have historically done most of the work.

The problem of excessive carbon dioxide comes from both sides of the production and elimination process. The burning of fossil fuels, which are essential for much energy production and thus economic activity worldwide, has increased steadily over the last century (and at current rates will continue to do so). Thus, there is more carbon dioxide in the atmosphere than there used to be, and because carbon dioxide has a half-life of roughly a century, that which is emitted today will be around for a long time. At the same time, the cutting down of trees in the rain forests has reduced the number and quality of natural sinks, thereby reducing nature's ability to capture and convert carbon dioxide into innocuous elements.

The cumulative effect is that there is more carbon dioxide in the atmosphere than there used to be, and it acts as a greenhouse gas. What this means is that, as heat from the sun radiates off the Earth and attempts to return in adequate amount into space to maintain current climate, carbon dioxide acts as a "trap" that keeps the heat in the atmosphere rather than allowing it to escape. The effect of this blanketing is to keep excess heat in the atmosphere, and the result is a warmer atmosphere and the phenomenon of global warming—net increases in atmospheric temperatures in specific locales and worldwide.

Responsibility for causing global warming and thus primary liability for doing something about it is also controversial. Significantly, the problem has become a mainstay of the global debate between the more industrially developed countries mostly located in the Northern Hemisphere and the less developed countries, many of which are located in the Southern Hemisphere. One aspect of this debate has to do with causation of the problem and hence responsibility. Because fossil fuel burning is at the heart of warming, clearly much of the problem was created in the North, which has already gone through an industrializing process for which fossil fuel–based energy was and remains an important component. From the vantage point of developing countries that aspire to the material success of the developed countries, this creates two points of contention. On one hand, they view developed countries as the cause of the problem and thus believe those countries should solve the problem by reducing emissions or by other means. At the same time, developed countries ask them to refrain from the same kind of fossil fuel–driven growth that they underwent, because doing so will simply worsen the greenhouse gas effect. The call for self-abnegation (under the banner of "sustainable development") by those countries that were fossil fuel self-indulgers strikes many in the developing world as hypocritical, to say the least.

This North-South dimension is undeniable and critical to any solution to the global warming problem. At the most obvious physical level, both the developing and developed world have to contribute to any solution: the developed world by reducing its emissions to something like sustainable levels and the developing world by minimizing the destruction of carbon sinks that are the natural form of abatement of excess gases.

At the political level, the debate over global warming, like virtually all transnational issues with a developed–developing world context, gets tied inextricably into the debate over development and the obligations (if any) of developed countries to assist in the development of the less developed countries. The dialogue takes on a tit-for-tat character. Developed countries insist that efforts aimed at economic development be conducted within the context of sustainable development, by which is meant developmental processes that do not use more of resources than can be restored by development. In the case of greenhouse gases, fossil fuel consumption should not exceed the ability of carbon sinks to absorb it. These self-imposed limits were not constraints on the already developed states, of course, and developing states insist that their compliance with such restrictions be accompanied by developmental assistance both to speed growth and to help underwrite compliance with sustainable-growth requirements. Thus, the issue of global warming becomes something of a pawn within a wider international debate.

The Kyoto Protocol of 1997 (so named after the city where it was finalized) is the most visible symbol of this process and has become the lightning rod of the procedural and substantive debate over global warming. The Kyoto Protocol is a very technical, complicated document (see the next section), the heart of which is a series of guidelines for the reduction of emissions by various countries according to a timetable established in the document. The requirements of the protocol have raised controversy because of the differential levels of reduction they impose; this has been especially true of the United States. Support for or opposition to the Kyoto Protocol has also become, in many quarters, emblematic of how one feels about the issue of global warming.

This introduction has laid out some of the basic underlying issues about global warming and the Kyoto Protocol as its symbol. In the next section, we will briefly examine the process by which the international community moved to the formalization of the effort to contain and reverse global warming. Because the urgency (or even the need) to engage in such a process depends on whether the problem exists, positions on global warming are then presented. The case concludes by looking at the prospects for global warming and the institutionalization of efforts to contain it.

THE ROAD TO KYOTO—AND BEYOND?

Although the Kyoto Protocol is the most visible symbol (or target, depending on one's perspective), it was in fact an evolutionary step in a process that was begun well before the Protocol was adopted and has continued to evolve since. Kyoto became the lightning rod for support or opposition because it provided the most comprehensive set of regulations and guidelines that had occurred to that point; in a very real sense, the rhetoric of global warming turned into a concrete plan and program in 1997.

Several points can be made about the road to Kyoto by means of introduction. First, concern about climatic change had been going on for a long time before the Protocol was adopted, and the formal international process that resulted in the document began almost twenty years earlier. Second, the document and its requirements are complicated and technical, making a detailed description impossible within the confines of this case format. We will, however, discuss the highlights, including those that the Bush administration has found most objectionable. Third, the United States has had a special role in the evolution of this process, as is so often the case in international initiatives. In this case, the United States has, as in the case of the International Criminal Court, vacillated on the issue, with one administration serving as a major architect and its successor reversing that position completely, in some ways reflecting domestic constituencies within the United States. At the same time, the United States is the world's largest producer of greenhouse gases, and thus the Kyoto Protocol's provisions have questionable effectiveness in attacking the problem of global warming in the absence of American participation. Fourth, the protocol is now more than seven years old, and there are critics who maintain that it is based in science that has been overcome by events, meaning its provisions are of declining relevance.

The Kyoto Process

The chronology of global warming as a formal international concern is described by the United Nations Framework Convention for Climate Change (UNFCCC) Secretariat in a 2000 publication, *Caring for Climate*. According to that document, the first step in the process occurred in 1979, when the First World Climate Conference was held. That meeting brought together international scientists concerned with the effects of human intervention in the climate process and the possible pernicious effects of trends that they observed. This meeting also provided the first widespread recognition of the greenhouse gases phenomenon, which was largely known only within the scientific community before then.

Although not directly related to global warming, interest in atmospheric degradation and its effects on the human condition was further publicized in 1987 by the Montreal Treaty dealing with chlorofluorocarbons (CFCs). The problem of CFCs was their relationship to ozone depletion and notably the emergence of holes in the ozone layers over the North and South Poles (that, it was argued, contributed to the melting of polar ice caps). A more specific problem than carbon dioxide, the CFC problem was the result of several chemicals mostly used as aerosol propellants in consumer goods (e.g., hair sprays) and for air conditioning systems (e.g., freon). The treaty negotiated a gradual elimination of CFCs and served as a model for the more ambitious pursuit of an agreement on global warming.

The international momentum began to pick up in 1988 with two events. First, the United Nations General Assembly adopted a resolution, 43/53, urging the "protection of global climate for present and future generations of mankind." The resolution was sponsored by Malta. In a separate action, the World Meteorological Organization (WMO) and the United Nations Environmental Programme created the Intergovernmental Panel on Climate Change (IPCC) and charged this new body with assessing the scientific evidence on the subject. As requested, the IPCC issued its First Assessment Report in 1990, unsurprisingly concluding that the threat of climate change was real and worthy of further study and concern. Also in 1990, the World Climate Conference held its second meeting in Geneva, Switzerland, and called for a global treaty on climate change. This call in turn prompted the General Assembly to pass another resolution, 45/12, which commissioned negotiations for a convention on climate change to be conducted by an Intergovernmental Negotiating Committee (INC). This body first met in February 1991 as an intergovernmental body. On May 9, 1992, the INC adopted the UNFCCC, which was presented for signature at the Rio De Janeiro United Nations Conference on the Environment and Development (the Earth Summit) in June 1992. The requisite number of signatures was obtained in 1994, and the UNFCCC entered force on March 21, 1994. The process leading to the Kyoto Protocol was thus officially launched.

One of the express features of the UNFCCC was an annual meeting of all members of the convention (which numbered 188 in 2002), known as the Conference of the Parties (COP). The first COP was held in 1995 in Berlin. The third COP was held in Kyoto, Japan; the result was the Kyoto Protocol.

The Protocol

The Kyoto Protocol is a complicated document (the entire treaty can be found in the Web Sites section of this chapter), the details of which go beyond present purposes. Several elements can, however, be laid out to provide a summary of what the protocol attempts to do and, based upon those purposes, the objections that have been raised to it.

The overarching goal of the Kyoto Protocol, of course, is a net reduction in the production and emission of greenhouse gases and thus the arrest and reversal of the adverse effects of climate changes caused by these gases (as a sort of baseline, the Intergovernmental Panel on Climate Change predicts a rise of 1.4 to 5.8 degrees Centigrade in global surface temperatures during this century if present trends continue). For this purpose, the protocol identifies six gases for control and emission reduction. As noted, the protocol specifies three of these gases as "most important": carbon dioxide (CO_2), methane (CH_4), and nitrous oxide (N_2O). This importance comes from the large relative contribution of these gases to the problem: carbon dioxide accounts for fully one-half of "the overall global warming effect arising from human activities" in UNFCCC's language, followed by 18 percent for methane and 6 percent for nitrous oxide. For the United States in 2002, the percentages were 83 percent carbon dioxide, 9 percent methane, and 6 percent nitrous oxide, according to David Victor. The other three specified categories, the "long-lived industrial gases," are hydrofluorocarbons (HFCs), perfluorocarbons (PFCs), and sulfur hexafluoride (SF_6).

The goal of the protocol is a global reduction in the production of targeted gases of 5 percent below the baseline year for measuring emissions, 1990, by the period 2008–12. The baseline year establishes how much each developed country contributed to emission levels. These levels are then used for two purposes: to determine how much reduction each targeted country must accomplish and to provide a measuring stick for determining when the protocol comes fully into effect. For determining these contributions, the protocol further divides the countries of the world into three different categories (what it calls Annexes) in terms of the obligations that are incurred.

Because the source of greenhouse gases is fossil fuel consumption (gasoline, coal, and natural gas) for energy production for economic activity and transportation, it comes as no surprise that the countries most clearly identified and targeted are those in the developed world, and indeed, Annex I contains these countries. Using 1990 baseline figures for CO_2 emissions as its yardstick, these countries are listed by the amount of emission they produced and the percentage of the world's total emissions this amount represents. Leading the list by a wide margin is the United States, which was responsible for 36.1 percent of global emissions. Aggregated as a whole, the European Union followed with 24.2 percent, followed by the countries of the Russian Federation with 17.4 percent and Japan with 8.5 percent (for a total of 86 percent of global emissions). The next largest polluter after these was Australia with 2.1 percent.

The countries in Annex I are subdivided into two subcategories in terms of determining contributions to greenhouse gas reductions. Most of the countries are full members and must use the 1990 baseline figures to determine the amount of their reductions. Because 1990 was a year of transition in the status of the countries of the communist world, these countries (including the Russian Federation and other former Soviet republics and Eastern Europe) were designated Economies in Transition (EIT) Parties, which meant they could choose a different baseline year against which to measure their reductions.

The protocol also created two other Annex categories. Annex II contains all the members of the Organization of Economic Cooperation and Development (OECD) but excludes the EIT countries (it is, in other words, the Annex I countries minus the old communist world). Countries designated in Annex II are "required to provide financial resources to enable developing countries to undertake emissions reduction activities and to help them adapt to adverse effects of climate change," according to the UNFCCC. The final category are Non-Annex I countries. These are the developing countries whose economies are not yet well enough developed to contribute meaningfully to global warming (although some of them could become part of the problem in the future) and are thus excluded from participating in reduction activities. This category contains some significant economic powers (South Korea, for instance) and the world's two largest countries in population, China and India, whose potential contribution to the global-warming problem are enormous.

The baseline for Annex I countries provides the specifications for reductions of emissions levels. These differ by country. Switzerland, most Central and Eastern European countries, and the European Union are targeted at 8 percent reductions (individual EU countries have different standards to reach the total); the United States target is 7 percent; and Canada, Hungary, and Japan have 6 percent targets. Russia, New Zealand, and the Ukraine are ordered to stabilize their emissions at 1990 levels, and Norway, Australia, and Iceland can actually increase their emissions levels.

The baseline serves an additional function. Rather than creating a standard for coming into effect based on how many countries ratify the protocol (which is the standard method by which international treaties take effect), the standard for the Kyoto Protocol is the percentage contribution to the baseline of all countries that ratify. The standard set is 55 percent of emissions. This fact reflects the truly transnational nature of global warming by saying that reduction can only be meaningful if most of the real pollution falls under the protocol. It also reflects the enormous importance of American participation in the protocol: American ratification means 36 of the necessary 55 percent is accomplished; conversely, American refusal to participate means that only 64 percent of emissions can fall under the protocol if all other Annex I parties accede. The 55 percent threshold was reached in 2004 without American accession; the protocol took effect for the signatories on February 16, 2005.

If all these provisions are not complicated enough, the protocol adds another source of complications in terms of what UNFCCC calls "three innovative mechanisms" for meeting goals by means other than straight reductions. These are joint implementation, the clean development mechanism (CDM), and emissions trading. Each mechanism deserves at least brief mention, if only to illustrate the convoluted nature of the entire process.

Joint implementation (technically emission reduction units in the protocol) allows Annex I countries to gain credits against their emission-reduction quotas by undertaking projects with Non-Annex I countries either to help those countries reduce their emissions or to increase carbon sinks. The CDM provides emissions credits for Annex I countries that invest in projects in Non-Annex I countries, especially in the private sector, that contribute to emissions reductions or in other ways that support the general principle of sustainable development (developmental projects that do not add to pollution of the environment). Emissions trading allows countries that exceed (purposely or as the result of a downturn in their economies) their emissions goals in effect to sell that excess to Annex I countries, which can then apply the excess purchased toward reaching their own required reductions.

As this discussion suggests, the mechanisms and procedures included within the Kyoto Protocol process are indeed complicated and intricate, creating very different requirements for different states and categories of states, as well as complicated means of compliance through the addition of the "innovative" methods discussed directly above. As a result, it should not be surprising that this process has also resulted in a certain level of controversy. That controversy, in turn, centers on the United States, which has emerged as the most vocal and important opponent of the protocol.

American and Other Objections

Because of both the extent of American contribution to greenhouse gas emission (about 25 percent of all the affected gases as opposed to 36 percent of carbon dioxide) and the related formula for implementing the Kyoto Protocol, American participation in the effort is virtually a sine qua non for the global warming effort to succeed. When the movement began, the United States was an enthusiastic participant in the process leading to Kyoto, and the Clinton administration was among the early signers and supporters of the protocol and its implementation.

But that position changed when the Bush administration entered office. During the 2000 campaign, Bush favored legislation that would require power plants (one of the major sources of carbon dioxide, along with transportation vehicles) to reduce their emissions by adding "scrubbers" to emissions leaving plants and entering the atmosphere. After he assumed office, he quickly changed course, siding instead with power industry opponents and announcing on March 13, 2001, that he no longer favored U.S. participation in the Kyoto Protocol. In the process, the administration publicly stated that it would not send the treaty signed by Clinton to the Senate for ratification. As a result, the United States remains the most important country in the world that is not a party to the protocol and thus does not consider itself subject to its requirements, although it remains a party to the UNFCCC.

American objections to the protocol tend to focus on two basic themes. The first is cost and burden to the United States. Although some other countries have higher percentage reduction quotas than the United States, the mathematics of bearing 7 percent of 36 percent of the total required reductions is odious, in the view of opponents of the treaty. In addition, U.S. emissions were already 15 percent above the 1990 level by the end of the millennium and, according to Victor, rising at 1.3 percent per year, thereby demanding further reductions. Thus, the United States is being asked to do too much proportionately to the rest of the world. This is particularly true of the burden that would fall on the power and transportation industries in the United States, which would be forced to take actions to reduce most of the carbon dioxide reduction requirements. In the view of administration and other critics, compliance would be economically ruinous in terms of the additional expenses of doing business and the loss of comparative advantage to industries in other countries that are not regulated by these requirements and the additional costs they add to production. Conformance to Kyoto standards that do not apply to everyone else thus imbalances the "playing field" of economic competition in unfair ways.

This leads to the second objection, which is the exclusion of developing countries from the requirements of the protocol. In most cases, this exclusion is innocuous, because most of these countries either do not or will not contribute meaningfully to greenhouse gas in the foreseeable future, when circumstances could be much different due, in part, to the effects of the protocol. At the same time, there are exceptions to that basis for exclusion, as already noted.

The Bush administration has directed its criticism of developing-world exclusion principally at two countries: China and India. China, it is alleged, is becoming a major greenhouse gas emitter (some estimates maintain it is already the second-largest emitter in the world), and that this situation will continue and intensify as China further develops (thereby requiring additional energy) and as China continues to promote automobile ownership among its huge population base. India does not pose quite as urgent a threat, but with a population roughly the size of China's and an emerging technological and industrial capacity, the sheer magnitude of the country's potential suggests it should be part of the solution before it becomes an overt part of the problem. The contrary argument that inclusion of these countries would impede their ability to develop and become competitive economies is simply further evidence of the unfavorable set of rules the protocol creates.

A third, more contemporary objection to the protocol is that it is essentially dated. The protocol is now more than seven years old, and the march of technology and change may have simply outgrown its provisions. John Browne, writing in a recent *Foreign Affairs*, summarizes this argument: "First, Kyoto was simply the starting point of a very long endeavor. Second, we have improved, if still imperfect, knowledge of the challenges and uncertainties that climate change presents….Third, many countries and companies have had experience reducing emissions that have proved that such reductions can be achieved without destroying competitiveness of jobs. Fourth, science and technology have advanced on multiple fronts. Finally, public awareness of the issue has grown."

A fourth objection, related to the third, is that the protocol and all its provisions are simply too complicated and unwieldy to be administered in any enforceable, objective way. The various "innovative" ways of substituting means of compliance discussed earlier are a case in point. This complexity suggests to some critics of the protocol that the effort should be scrapped and a new, comprehensive approach grounded in contemporary realities should replace it (this argument is often made by administration supporters with energy industry credentials). Environmentalists argue this argument is essentially a cop-out to avoid implementing greenhouse gas emission standards. As Fred Krupp, executive director of the private advocacy group Environmental Defense, puts it, "It is bad for America's interests for the United States to be seen as the rogue nation of greenhouse gas pollution. By simply opposing the Kyoto Protocol rather than seeking to improve it, the administration would have effectively blocked the only binding international agreement for fighting global warming, while offering no alternate path to protect the planet."

Finally, there is an objection from the other end of the spectrum that says the fatal flaw of the Kyoto Protocol is not that it requires too much of countries and the world but that it requires too little. In this argument, the problem is not the degree of sacrifice demanded, but the need to cut greenhouse gas emission much more drastically, in the range of 50 percent rather than the roughly 5 percent demanded in the Kyoto Protocol.

Just how compelling these arguments surrounding the Kyoto Protocol are and thus how vital universal compliance with the document should be is a matter of conjecture. As might be guessed, American objections to Kyoto are at least partially grounded in an assessment of the consequences of greenhouse gas contamination that is significantly less dire than the estimates made by those who argue the problem is serious and pressing. For that reason, it is necessary to at least raise some of the questions that occur in the debate about global warming.

Warm and Getting Warmer: But How Much?

There are at least three related factors that make a calm, rational debate over the extent and consequences of global warming difficult to conduct. The first is the absence of immediate consequences of whatever change is occurring. Over the past quarter century or more, climate change in the form of warming has indeed been occurring worldwide, but the effects have been so gradual and generally miniscule that either they have gone unnoticed by most people or they have not been easily attributable to the phenomenon. Were there dramatic events that could be associated with climate change (or equally convincing absences of predicted changes), it would be easier to make the case one way or the other. But such immediate effects have not, by and large, occurred—even if they are predicted by many scientists who believe some apocryphal event is inevitable somewhere in the not too distant future.

Second, there is abundant scientific disagreement about the parameters of the problem and its solution. Some of the disagreement is honest, some possibly self-interested (as noted); but for every dire prediction about future consequences, there is a rebuttal from another part of the scientific community. This debate often becomes scientifically shrill and accusatory, leading to confusion in the public about what to believe (which, of course, both sides accuse the other of trying to create). In this confusion, the citizenry has a difficult time making reasoned assessments and consequent demands on policy makers to adopt standards.

Third, almost all the projections are sufficiently far in the future to allow considerable disagreement and to discourage resolution. While one can argue the scientific evidence to date is very strong one way or the other on various consequences of warming, the actual consequences are distant enough that the extrapolation is subject to sufficient variation that scientists can take the same data and reach diametrically opposed conclusions. These extrapolations are often 50 or even 100 years in the future, when most of the people at whom they are aimed will not even be alive to witness or be held accountable for them. Is it any wonder there is difficulty mobilizing the population in these circumstances?

An example may help here. One of the effects of global warming universally cited by advocates of regulation is the melting of the polar ice cap as surface temperatures rise. The result of this melting will be to increase the volume of water in the oceans and make the oceans rise (this has already happened to some degree). In the long run, this rise will risk inundating very low-lying areas, submerging them and making them uninhabitable (see below for some projections).

But this is abstract to most people. What if there was a real example with which people could relate? For instance, the furor over Hurricane Charley in July 2004 revealed how dangerously low-lying most of Tampa Bay was. A large part of the waterfront of Tampa, for instance, lies at five feet or less above sea level, making it a prime candidate for eventual inundation during the next century, when some projections say sea levels will rise *more than* five feet. Does that prediction alarm citizens of Tampa Bay, or will it take some violent occasion (such as the surge that was predicted had Charley come ashore at Tampa Bay) to convince people to take the problem seriously? It is not an easy case to make.

Getting Too Warm?

The fact that global climate is changing is not contested on any side of the debate over global warming. The Intergovernmental Panel on Climate Change (IPCC) has investigated the extent to which this has happened in the past and has concluded that the average surface temperature of the Earth increased by about one degree Fahrenheit during the twentieth century and "that most of the warming observed over the past 50 years is attributable to human activities." (Much of the IPCC material in this section is from the 2001 report of Group I-III of the IPCC, cited in the suggested readings.) Extrapolating from trends in the past century, the IPCC predicts additional warming of 2.2–10 degrees Fahrenheit (1.4–5.8 degrees Centigrade). The primary culprits are the greenhouse gases cited in the Kyoto Protocol that result from deforestation (and its destruction of carbon sinks), energy production from the combustion of fossil fuels (natural gas, oil, and coal), transportation (primarily cars and trucks, but also trains and other modes), cattle production (methane gases), rice farming, and cement production.

A variety of effects have been observed and attributed to these changes. In some areas, birds are laying eggs a few weeks earlier than they used to, butterflies are moving their habitats further up mountains to avoid lowland heat, and trees are blooming earlier in the spring and losing their leaves later in the fall. While any of these changes can be dismissed as of low relative concern, there are more fundamental changes alleged with more obvious consequences. Warming, the IPCC II reports, shows that snow accumulation is decreasing worldwide, as is the global supply of icepack. At the same time, glaciers are retreating worldwide (some of the most dramatic American examples are in places like Glacier National Park in Montana), sea levels and ocean temperatures have risen, and rainfall patterns in many regions have changed. In addition, there is evidence that that permafrost is thawing in the polar regions, that lakes are freezing later and thawing earlier, and that even some plant and animal species have declined and may disappear due to changes in climate.

If these trends continue, the results could be dramatic. As an example, tropical diseases that have heretofore been confined to tropical lowlands could spread to previously impervious areas such as plateaus and mountains and might even extend to temperate regions of the globe that have previously been too cool for them to survive. Although there is widespread disagreement on the details, it is likely that a large number of fragile animal and plant species will become extinct (one study estimates between 15 and 37 percent in some regions will be vulnerable).

Some of the most dramatic examples involve the effects on coastal regions. The projected problems arise from both the gradual rise of oceanic levels and the warming of ocean waters. Both are a concern because of the large and growing portion of populations residing in coastal locations (it is, for instance, a major demographic reality in the United States that the population is gradually moving out of the central parts of the country toward more temperate coastal regions).

The extent of these effects, of course, depends on the amount of change caused by global warming. IPCC II data project an average rise of between 6 and 36 inches in sea levels by 2100. Using the higher figure, the impact on some countries would be dramatic. A 36-inch rise would inundate territory in which 10 million people live in Bangladesh alone, forcing their relocation to scarce higher land. The same increase would cover 12 percent of the arable land of the Nile River delta in Egypt, which produces crops on which more than seven million people are dependent. Some estimates suggest the island country of Vanuatu in the South Pacific would simply disappear under the rising waters. Worldwide, it is estimated that 45 million people would be displaced.

Warming of ocean water could also have dramatic effects. A warming of the ocean's waters could, for instance, affect ocean currents that now influence climate in various parts of the world. The Atlantic Gulf Stream, for instance, could be affected by warmer water coming from polar regions, changing patterns for the coastal United States and Europe. As an example, Gulf Stream effects that tend to keep major hurricanes off parts of the American coast (e.g., the South Carolina Lowcountry) could be diverted, resulting in a new pattern of hurricane, tornado, and storm patterns. Large-scale changes in patterns of ocean circulation are possible worldwide. The cumulative effect, according to the IPCC, could be "a widespread increase in the risk of flooding for human settlements (tens of millions of inhabitants in settlements studied) from both increased heavy precipitation and sea level rise." (IPCC II)

Not So Fast

Scientists disagree about the accuracy of these projections and the direness of the consequences that they project. There is little disagreement about the historical record (e.g., the amount of climate change in the last century) because that is based on observable data that can be examined for accuracy, although there is some disagreement on the precise causes of change (e.g., scientists affiliated with the power industry tend to downplay the impact of energy production). Where there is disagreement is on projections of trends and effects extrapolated into the future. The large source of this disagreement is the result of the fact that projections are not based on observations of effects in a future that has not yet occurred, but are instead based on projections of historically grounded observations (and hence scientific inference) into a future, the exact dimensions of which cannot be known or entirely predicted. Extrapolation becomes more uncertain the further predictions are cast into the future, and thus there is an increased level of disagreement the further into the future one goes. Because the deleterious effects of global warming are argued to be cumulative and thus more serious the further into the future one projects, the bases for lively, at times acrimonious, discussions are thus built into the debate.

Without delving into great detail, there tend to be three criticisms of global warming scientists that can be phrased in terms of questions. The first is the factual content of the warnings: how much effect will global warming have? A corollary question is how much those effects will accumulate under different assumptions about natural and manmade adjustments to these effects. Third, how difficult are the solutions?

These are good questions that, depending on how they are answered, define both the dimensions of the problem and the urgency and forms that dealing with it should take. The question of how much is clearly the driving dynamic here: if the amount of change will be great and the consequences large and damaging, that makes the problem urgent so that sacrifices to solve it are both urgent and important.

The problem, of course, is that there is disagreement on these matters. Take, for instance, the projections on how much average surface temperatures will warm in this century if action is not taken. As noted, they range from one to ten degrees Fahrenheit, and that is a considerable range in terms of the consequences to the world and mankind. If the actual figure is at the upper end of that spectrum, then things like snowpack, glacier, and polar icecap melting will be considerable, with oceans rising at the upper limits of predictions (around three feet). Parts of Tampa Bay and New Orleans, among other places, will be under water unless levees are constructed to keep the water out, and Vanuatu may become the next Lost City of Atlantis (an analogy often made by global warming scientists). On the other hand, if the rise in mean surface temperature is closer to or at the lower extreme (a degree or so), then the consequences are probably far less dire.

Who knows which part of the range is correct? The answer is that with any scientific certitude, no one does. The amount of warming is necessarily an extrapolation into a future that does not exist, not an observation of something that does. Clearly, it is in the interests of those who either do not believe in the more severe projections or who would be most adversely affected by concerted efforts to reduce emissions to believe in the lower projections and thus to deny the more severe reactions. At the same time, those who believe the problem to be dire have an interest in accepting the higher estimates, either as a hedge against uncertainty (if one plans for the worst, then anything less may be more manageable) or because of a sincere belief in the higher numbers.

The layman is left wondering. Because the effects are not immediate and unambiguous, the average person has little way of answering the second question: what does all this mean? Are we headed for an environmental catastrophe if we do not do something to slow, stop, or reverse global warming? The scientists on both sides of the issue are passionate and self-convinced, but they have not, by and large, made a case to the world's publics that is compelling, understandable, and convincing—one way or the other. In a world of more instantly consequential problems, it is hard to bring one's self to develop the passion that the advocates, regardless of scientific credentials, have on the issue.

This raises the third question, which brings the concern full circle and returns us to the Kyoto Protocol: what should we do about the problem? The immediate answer, of course, is that it depends on how bad the problem is. Most of the world has accepted the basic science of those warning about the more dire consequences of not solving the global warming problem, and the United States remains virtually alone among major powers (and greenhouse gas emitters) in denying or downplaying the problem and resisting the Kyoto solution. Admittedly, the major source of official U.S. objection is not to the veracity of global warming science, but is instead directed at the differential obligations for solving it that Kyoto prescribes: reductions with economic consequences that would make the American economy less competitive and the exclusion of developing world countries with large pollution potentials from regulation. If, however, the American government fully accepted the direst projections of the consequences, these objections would probably pale in comparison to the dictates of solving the problem. Implicitly or explicitly, American opposition to the Kyoto Protocol also reflects a belief the problem is not great (or, more minimally, that the solution can be deferred without significant consequences).

There is, of course, a hedge in answering the third question that reflects a deep American trait in viewing problems. That hedge is a belief that technology will somehow find a way to ameliorate the problem, either by finding a way to decrease the emission of greenhouse gases or to increase the ability to absorb and neutralize those gases and their consequences. That is the position often taken by the American energy and transportation industries, and it is an approach that has worked to solve other problems at other times. Whether adherence to that belief is a blind leap of faith or a sound scientific prediction is, like so much of the debate over global warming, a question of perspective.

CONCLUSION

No one disagrees that global warming is taking place or that its effects are not pernicious to some degree. There are no pro-global warmers. However, there is, as we have seen, considerable reluctance to attack and eradicate the problem, especially in the United States, where participation in the effort is absolutely critical to its solution. Why?

The answer lies in two phenomena, one only hinted at to this point and one discussed more fully. One problem is the contrast between the short term and the longer term regarding global warming and its effects. In the short term (say the next ten–twenty years), it is not absolutely clear that there will be major negative worldwide or local events that can be attributed unambiguously and consensually to global warming. As a result, the problem lacks urgency to the average citizen, who in turn is not pressing his or her elected representatives to take forceful actions to reduce greenhouse gases. At the same time, however, those who warn about the prospects of global warming are, quite correctly from their viewpoint, insisting that remedial actions need to be taken now to avoid disastrous effects in the longer term. These actions include personal and societal sacrifices on the altar of cleaner air, including reductions in omissions from power plants, automobiles, and the like, which will incur costs that will be passed along to all of us. We are, in other words, being asked to sacrifice at a time when we will not be able to see the beneficial effects that warrant our sacrifices; instead, we are asked to sacrifice today to serve an abstract future.

The longer view reverses this perspective. According to those most concerned with the damaging effects of global warming, the failure to act in the short run condemns those who will experience the negative effects. As cities are inundated a hundred years from now, for instance, it will likely not be difficult at all to convince people they need to make those sacrifices as the water laps at their front doors, but by then it may be too late to take the corrective actions that should be taken now to prevent that future fate.

Can we reconcile these two contrasting perspectives? In the abstract, we can. If we *knew* that the failure to take action today would condemn those who follow (or if we are young enough, ourselves) to a specific negative fate, then we might be able to agree to make those sacrifices. That reconciliation flies in the face of the second phenomenon, uncertainty of the nature of the future and a consequent reluctance to act when we are not entirely certain why we need to act.

The first part of this difficulty has been discussed extensively already and need not be reiterated. The simple fact is that there is indeed disagreement about the parameters and severity of the global warming problem, and those who are reluctant to counsel sacrifices that would be politically unpopular can and do use that uncertainty to justify inaction. Those who warn of global warming counter the irresponsibility of ignoring what they are convinced is inevitable, but such arguments fall on at least partially deaf ears in the absence of incontrovertible evidence that the warnings are true.

Until that undeniable evidence is produced, there is precedent to believe we will simply defer the problem. In some ways, the global warming problem and its solution are like deficit spending. No one believes spending more than we take in is good and responsible policy, and everyone knows in the abstract that sometime in the future, someone else is going to have to pay off the debt that is being accumulated as we operate literally on borrowed money. At some point, we will have to "pay the piper," but exactly when this will occur and what exactly the piper will exact are matters of disagreement that help us justify not taking the corrective action of balancing budgets. Why should we expect global warming to be any different?

At the beginning of the case study, global warming was described as a true transnational issue, and one with unique aspects. That uniqueness has at least three significant angles. First, global warming is truly a global issue that affects the entire planet and can only be solved by essentially universal actions by the world's countries. This observation accentuates the role of American opposition to the Kyoto Protocol; if global warming is indeed the problem it is advertised to be, the United States will bear unique responsibility globally if we fail to address and solve it. Second, responding to global warming will have direct impacts on two of the most important motors of the global economy, energy production and use and transportation. Disruptions to either or both of these industries could have catastrophic economic effects for the world generally. The problem of global warming, in other words, is important to the well-being of all. Third, global warming is the only environmental-change problem that intensifies or is intensified by other major environmental problems. Rising water levels affect the ability of the Earth to produce food, and desertification is increased by warming, to cite two problems created. The effects of global warming are, in other words, pervasive.

How warm is the world getting, what does that matter, and what should or must be done or not done about it? These are the questions that we have asked throughout this case study, and they are all questions that have potentially vital answers for the good of all of us individually and collectively. What, then, are those answers?

STUDY/DISCUSSION QUESTIONS

1. Describe the global warming problem. What causes it? What are the short-term and long-term consequences of global warming?

2. Describe global warming as a North-South political and climatic problem. Who bears responsibility for creating and solving the problem?

3. Describe the process leading to the Kyoto Protocol. What are the major provisions of the protocol? Which provisions are most controversial? Why?

4. Why does the United States have a unique place in the global warming and Kyoto Protocol process? What are the major U.S. objections to the protocol? Why can the protocol not be effective without American participation in its implementation?

5. What are the major claims made by those who believe that global warming is a major worldwide problem? How do skeptics counter these assertions?

6. Explain the major dilemma of the global warming debate in terms of short-term and long-term effects. Are the prospects sufficiently dire that you believe we should endure short-term sacrifices to guard against long-term dangers?

7. Why is global warming unique as a transnational issue? Explain.

READING/RESEARCH MATERIAL

Ackerman, John T. "Global Climate Change: Catalyst for International Relations Disequilibria." Ph.D. diss., University of Alabama, 2004.

Anderson, Terry, and Harry I. Miller, eds. *The Greening of U.S. Foreign Policy.* Stanford, CA: Hoover Institution Press, 2000.

Beyond Kyoto: Advancing the International Effort Against Climate Change. Arlington, VA: Pew Center on Global Climate Change, 2003.

Browne, John. "Beyond Kyoto." *Foreign Affairs* 83, 4 (July/August 2004), 20–32.

Claussen, Eileen, and Lisa McNeilly. *Equity and Global Climate Change: The Complex Elements of Global Fairness.* Arlington, VA: Pew Center on Global Climate Change, 2000.

Diehl, Paul R., and Niles Peter Gleditsch, eds. *Environmental Conflict.* Boulder, CO: Westview Press, 2001.

Gupta, Joyeeta. *Our Simmering Planet: What to Do about Global Warming?* New York: Zed Books, 2001.

Intergovernmental Panel on Climate Change. A Report on Working Groups I–III. *Summary for Policymakers—Climate Change 2001.* Cambridge, MA: Cambridge University Press, 2001.

Luterbacher, Urs, and Detlef F. Sprinz, eds. *International Relations and Global Climate Change.* Cambridge, MA: MIT Press, 2001.

Michaels, Patrick J., and Robert C. Balling Jr. *The Satanic Gases: Clearing the Air about Global Warming.* Washington, DC: Cato Institute, 2000.

Pirages, Dennis C., and Theresa Manley DeGeest. *Ecological Security: An Evolutionary Perspective on Globalization.* New York: Rowman and Littlefield, 2004.

Schelling, Thomas C. "The Cost of Combating Global Warming: Facing the Tradeoffs." *Foreign Affairs* 76, 6 (November/December 1997), 8–14.

Victor, David G. *Climate Change: Debating America's Options.* New York: Council on Foreign Relations, 2004.

Wirth, Timothy. "Hot Air Over Kyoto: The United States and the Politics of Global Warming." *Harvard International Review* 23, 4 (2002), 72–77.

WEB SITES

Assessment of state of environment

Yale Center for Environmental Law and Policy at http://www.ciesin.columbia.edu/indicators/ESI

Text of Kyoto Protocol at http://unfccc.int/resource/convkp.html

Third Assessment Report of IPCC at http://www.ipcc.ch

UNFCCC Guide on Kyoto Protocol at http://unfccc.int/resource/guideconvenkp-p.pdf

U.S. State Department Report on Climate at http://epa.gov/globalwarming/publications/car/index.html

CHAPTER FOURTEEN

"Let Them Drink Oil"
RESOURCE CONFLICT IN THE NEW CENTURY?

PRÉCIS

The desire, even necessity, to control natural resources and conflict over those resources are as old as human history. Major wars have been fought over access to precious gems, metals, food, and exotic spices, to name a few examples. In the second half of the twentieth century, the most well-publicized resource conflict was over access to the oil reserves of the Persian Gulf region. What types of resources will cause what kinds of conflicts in the first part of the twenty-first century?

This case examines three "mini-cases" of resource conflicts with roots in the last century but that continue into the current era. The first deals with access to water in the Middle East, and it is primarily a conflict between Turkey and downstream riparians within the Tigris-Euphrates river system and, to a lesser degree, between Syria and Israel over the headwaters of the Jordan River. The second mini-case deals with petroleum, but within the context of the large oil reserves of the Caspian Sea area. This case combines the desire to exploit the oil with the geopolitical struggle to determine how the oil will be moved from central Asia to potential consumers. The third case centers on the desire for diamonds and the extraordinarily brutal methods employed to guarantee access to them. The focus is on the recently concluded civil war in Sierra Leone.

Conflict and war over the ability to control, monopolize, or deny access to valued resources is as old as recorded human history. Men have fought and died, armies have swept across countless expanses, and empires and states have risen and fallen in the name of precious resources. Whether it was control of the silk route across Asia or the exotic foodstuffs of the Spice Islands, the diamonds and gold of southern and central Africa, El Dorado in the new world, or the petroleum wealth of the Middle East, the struggle for natural, scarce, and valuable resources has been a recurrent theme of human history and the relations between individuals and groups.

How will this historic theme be enacted in the twenty-first century? Resources clearly remain scarce (meaning there are more claimants to them than can simultaneously be accommodated), and some are becoming scarcer as either natural stores are depleted (petroleum and other forms of fossil fuel, for instance) or increasing numbers of people with increasing demands put additional pressures on existing stores (rare gemstones). At the same time, there is little indication that human greed to control and profit from those resources that others want is on the wane.

At this early juncture, we cannot confidently project very far into the new century in terms of the kinds of conflicts that will occur over scarce resources. Instead, the best we can do is to look at the kinds of resource conflicts that have transcended the end of the twentieth century, and extrapolate from them into at least the near future. Such an examination will provide the context for speculating about resource conflict in the new century.

To explore this subject, we will examine three "mini-case studies" of these conflicts with roots in the 1990s but that remain on the agenda for a new millennium. All three share their location in the developing Afro-Asian world, but they differ significantly in content and in the current severity that they present to their region and to the international system generally. When viewed in combination, they will provide some insight into the future.

The cases are presented in reverse order of their current trauma to the international system. The first, from which the title is drawn, analyzes the problem of water scarcity in the Middle East, and more specifically, the division of water from the Tigris and Euphrates River system between Turkey and the downstream riparian states, notably Syria and Iraq (the quote has been attributed to an unnamed Turkish official reacting to Iraqi demands that Turkey provide more water for their use). The second case moves northward and eastward and involves the oil and natural gas reserves in the Caspian Sea, and more specifically, the continuing difficulty of finding a geopolitically acceptable way to get this alternative source of energy to Persian Gulf oil to market. The third case looks at a very different kind of resource, diamonds, and the tragedy their exploitation has created in central Africa, and especially Sierra Leone.

The cases also vary considerably in the violence or violent potential they threaten in their region and more broadly. While the question of water rights produces a good deal of heated debate in the Middle East that will doubtless increase as time goes by and demands for the basically inelastic supply of potable water further outstrip supplies, Turkey is so much more powerful than the other states with claims to the water that violence seems a remote prospect for the foreseeable future. In Azerbaijan, the possible renewal of war between that country and Armenia lurks behind plans for shipping Caspian Sea oil to market; activation of the Turkish and other pipeline solutions contains within it the lively possibility of Armenian efforts to disrupt the flow (or certainly to threaten to do so), and other "solutions" are mired in the problem of the attempted secession by Chechnya from Russia. The pursuit of diamonds in Sierra Leone has already produced one of the grisliest civil "wars" of the era, and it is a conflict that could return at any time and that currently has engaged the attention of UN peacekeepers.

MIDDLE EASTERN WATER

The adequacy of supplies of potable water to grow food and to provide for basic human needs is a growing global concern for the present and certainly for the future, and many environmental scientists now argue that access to water could be the most important environmental issue of this century. In the arid Middle East, a combination of factors has made the problem a current, rather than a future, area of major concern. In a nutshell, growing populations and increased demands for additional water fueled by both population and economic factors are placing greater and greater demands on a water supply that is finite and, in its present form and usage, inadequate for the future. The problem is simple: the demand for Middle Eastern water exceeds supply, and the problem can only get worse as time goes by. Water could supplant oil as the region's most valuable commodity.

In this circumstance, access to and control of water becomes a major geopolitical matter; as the quote in the title suggests, water could also easily supplant petroleum as the major geopolitical concern of states. The oil-producing states have held sway in the region for years, sometimes with considerable haughtiness, but by and large, they are the most water-poor states in the region. It is by no means fanciful to suggest they may find themselves digging into their oil profits to buy water in much the same way that other states have had to come to them for oil.

Statement of the Problem

The water problem is endemic to the Middle East. Although the region is surrounded by seas and oceans, their waters are saline and unusable. Within the region itself, there are only two major river systems (if one excludes the Nile, which flows through only two regional states, Egypt and Sudan). These are the Tigris-Euphrates River system, which provides most of the water for Turkey, Iraq, and Syria, and the Jordan River Basin, which contributes to the water supply of Syria, Israel, Lebanon, and Jordan. Most of the region is arid or semi-arid.

Of the two systems, the Tigris-Euphrates is the subject of the most immediate physical and geopolitical concern. The Jordan system came into conflict in the 1960s, when the Islamic countries contemplated restricting or cutting off Israeli access to this water source, which was vital to Israel's survival. One of the major purposes for which Israel fought the 1967 Arab-Israeli War was to gain control over the river and its tributaries (including the Sea of Galilee and streams flowing into it). This end was accomplished with the occupation of the Golan Heights, which gave Israel secure control over the headwaters of its water supply. Finding a way to reconcile Syrian demands for a return of occupied territories with Israeli insistence on control of vital water access remains one, and possibly the most important, hurdle confronting a Syrian-Israeli peace accord.

The major regional conflict is over the uses of the Tigris-Euphrates system. As the map indicates, the headwaters of both the Tigris and Euphrates are in eastern Turkey, which is the largest and most powerful country in the region. The Euphrates, which at 1,800 miles in length is the longest river in southwest Asia, flows south from Turkey into Syria, and from Syria into Iraq, where it eventually meets the Tigris at the town of al Qurnah, forming the Shatt al Arab waterway that flows into the Persian Gulf and forms the boundary between Iran and Iraq. The Tigris, on the other hand, begins its 1,180-mile flow in eastern Turkey but flows south directly into Iraq (although it briefly forms a boundary between Turkey and Syria).

Water from the Tigris-Euphrates system is important to all three states, although it is not equally vital to all. Access to the waters is particularly important to Syria, and even more so to Iraq, because the system provides the majority of the water each uses for irrigation as well as drinking water, for which there are no ready substitutes. Expansion of the agricultural sectors for each depends on a reliable supply of water, and growing populations in each country place additional stress on current available supplies. Both Syria

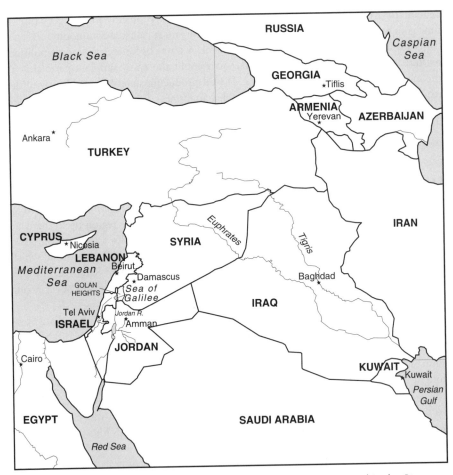

Map 14.1 Map of the Middle East, including the Tigris-Euphrates system and Jordan River.

and Iraq demand that Turkey increase the amount of flow of the river out of Turkey and guarantee the amount available to them.

Turkey is much less dependent on the system, because it enjoys more rainfall than Iraq and Syria and because it has other river systems that run through the country. Although Turkey is classified as having a water surplus, the Turks have claims on and plans for the system that threaten the access of downstream riparian states. For the Turks, the waters of the Tigris and Euphrates system are an integral part of their plans for the economic and political development of eastern Turkey. The mountainous area is the site of the Greater Anatolia Project (GAP), and central to that project is the development of a series of hydroelectric dams and reservoirs on the two rivers. In addition to allowing Turkey to control the flow of the rivers, these dams are designed to allow agricultural development of the eastern part of the country through irrigation and also to promote recreational uses of the resulting lakes and thus tourism in the country's poorest region.

The GAP has geopolitical ramifications and purposes as well. The area in which the development is taking place is known to many of its inhabitants as Kurdistan, and the Turkish Kurds have been engaged in a recently suspended, long-term civil war against the Turkish government, resulting in many deaths and alleged atrocities that have blackened Turkey's eye in international circles (ending the civil war, for instance, is one of the preconditions for consideration of Turkey's admission to the European Union, a primary objective of the regime in Ankara). Part of the Turkish government's strategy for creating a stable relationship with the Kurds is to make their homeland in Turkey prosperous enough that they will perceive a stake in remaining a part of the country and thus will abandon their insurrection.

Other regional countries gain a stake in the resolution of the problem in a kind of ripple effect that arises because Syria has claims against both Euphrates and Jordan River waters. In the absence of a satisfactory guarantee that Turkey will keep the water flowing (and Turkey is capable physically of reducing or interrupting the flow altogether), Syria continues to demand a share of the water from the Jordan Basin, which is a matter of considerable concern for Israel, Jordan, and Lebanon (the other users of Jordan River water). To make matters even more complicated, Israel has a nascent alliance with the Turks that may, among other things, result in the importation of Turkish water directly to Israel, providing for them a further interest in Turkey's water situation. Because Saudi Arabia is also a water-poor, oil-rich state that has some interest in importing Turkish water, even it has at least an indirect stake in the problem.

The situation has been intractable, because geopolitics becomes intertwined with the issue of water equity. The issue is clearly defined: Syria and Iraq want and demand concrete, inviolable guarantees to an increasing portion of the water from the two rivers, a demand that reverberates through the interests of the others. Turkey, on the other hand, is perfectly content with the status quo, because that status quo leaves the Turks in control of the situation regarding the supply and control of the water and maximizes their freedom of action.

The problem thus becomes one of claims and counterclaims and leverage. The downstream states base their claims for additional water on demographics like population increases, which no one denies. The Turks, however, counter that the problem is not how much water the Iraqis and Syrians have from the river system, but how they use it. To cite two Turkish examples, the Turks allege that both the downstream states grow crops that are inappropriate in their use of water for the amount of water available and given their needs (cotton, for instance), and the Turks allege that downstream riparians use primitive irrigation techniques that result in a large amount of water being wasted through evaporation. The Turks thus claim that Iraq and Syria receive enough water to sustain themselves if they only use it properly.

With good arguments on both (or all) sides, resolution incorporating change requires leverage to induce agreement. To this point, all the leverage has resided with the Turks. They control the source of the water, they are the most militarily powerful state in the region (thereby ruling out military action to seize the water), and there is nothing that Syria and Iraq have that Turkey needs badly enough to compel the Turks to concede on the water issue. In this region where water is king, the Turks would seem to hold the upper hand.

Possible Means of Resolution

Although discussions have been held periodically between Turkey and the downstream riparian states about the Tigris-Euphrates system, the discussions have not yet approached the point where anything resembling a solution about equitable distribution has been found. Partly, this is the case because the requirements of the downstream states have not become so critical that Iraq and Syria feel the need to try to force the issue. At the same time, both complainants have other, more immediate concerns: Syria has been in the middle of the succession of the late Hafiz al-Assad to his son Bashar, it has the settlement of hostilities (which incorporate a water dimension, of course) with Israel on its diplomatic plate, and more recently it has faced demands that it end its occupation of Lebanon. The American invasion and occupation of Iraq and the subsequent armed resistance and attempts to reestablish Iraqi sovereignty fills the agenda in Baghdad; any inconveniences caused by water flows from the Tigris and Euphrates pale by comparison. There are no particular outside pressures on Turkey to accommodate either the Syrians or the Iraqis; both are considered international rogues and have few friends who will bring pressure to bear on them.

What, then, are the possible alternatives that might lead to some form of agreement dividing the waters of the Tigris-Euphrates in a manner that would satisfy all parties? One can safely omit the possibility of military action—an attempted seizure of Turkish land to gain control of the waters, for instance. The armed forces of Turkey are much larger and more powerful than those of either Syria or Iraq (whose military was, of course, disbanded in 2003 and is slowly being rebuilt). As a member of NATO, Turkey can boast of forces that are much better equipped than the others. Military threats would be greeted with derision in Ankara.

Although none are very hopeful, there are four other possibilities for bring resolution to the water issue. The first is a *negotiated reallocation* of the current formula for allocating flow from the rivers. Such a negotiation would almost certainly have to be multilateral, probably with outside help provided by some general agency like the United Nations; a regional actor like the Arab League; or a more specialized intergovernmental organization (IGO) like the Water Resources Working Group (WRWG), an organization founded in 1992 to "foster cooperation on water related issues while creating confidence building measures, and cooperative efforts to alleviate water shortages." The problem with this solution, of course, is the asymmetry of incentives to enter into negotiations; the Turks, after all, see no need to change the formula under which water is currently allocated, and the Syrians and Iraqis can offer few incentives to convince the Turks to change their position. In those circumstances, Turkey would likely be especially unwilling to enter into any discussion that might end with some mandatory reallocation that they might oppose. In such circumstances, the Turks might well decide that no negotiations are better than negotiations that might provide an unacceptable outcome.

A second approach, advocated vociferously by Turkey, is *improved usage of existing supplies*. As already mentioned, Turkey has maintained all along that the problem Syria and Iraq face is not how much water they receive from the Tigris and Euphrates, but how efficiently and effectively they use it. As noted, Turkish charges are two-fold. First, they maintain that neither country has taken sufficient steps to modernize its irrigation system. Irrigation water from the rivers instead is allowed to flow through open ditches and evaporate in the Middle Eastern heat. In the Turkish view, the solution to the downstream water problem is agricultural modernization. Further, they maintain that both countries need to concentrate on growing crops that require less water, such as wheat, rather than crops that require extensive irrigation. While these charges are largely valid, it is not clear where either Iraq or Syria would obtain the resources necessary to engage in the modernization it is alleged they need to undertake. Syria has largely isolated itself from global sources of funding, and recovery from the war continues to dominate the badly disrupted Iraqi economy.

A third approach to the problem is *alternate sources of water*. This supply–side approach is one being pursued throughout various parts of the Middle East, because very few states in the region (Turkey, ironically, is one of the few exceptions) have adequate water within their boundaries. Desalinization of seawater has been a popular proposed enterprise (especially in Israel), but it has been dogged by problems of expense; if Israel has trouble paying for desalinated water, how could much poorer Syria and Iraq afford the effort? The fact that Syria is landlocked further complicates its problem—unless it controls Lebanon—and Iraq has a very short coastline as well on the Persian Gulf. Bringing water from countries where it is in excess to the Middle East has attracted attention in countries like Saudi Arabia, and Israel and Turkey have been pursuing the possibility of transporting Turkish water to Israel. The problem with both these "solutions" is that they are expensive and thus are available possibilities only for the richer countries of the region; Iraq, and especially Syria, clearly do not fall into that category.

Finally, some have suggested *regional cooperation* as a potential solution. The idea here is that if all the states of the region (probably excluding Israel) could come together and view their mutual water problem as an integral, regional problem, then possibly they could fashion regional solutions from which all would benefit. The problem is that the incentives to cooperate are, once again, differential. Certainly, mutual cooperation among those who are water deficient might yield benefit. In this particular situation, however, Turkey is *not* water deficient, and it is hard to see what benefit it would derive from mutual action and thus what the incentive would be to become involved in the enterprise.

The Prospects

The ongoing barrier to solving the problem of water from the Tigris-Euphrates system is creating incentives for Turkey to agree to change. At the moment, there is little incentive other than humanitarian concern for its neighbors, and that is normally insufficient to bring about change, especially when the deprivation being endured by the others is not yet critical.

There is some irony and bitterness in the phrase, "let them drink oil." While Turkey has adequate water supplies, it is not one of the petroleum-rich countries of the region and has not benefited from the prosperity heaped upon the oil producers. Now the shoe is on the other foot, and the Turks have to be enjoying the discomfort of their fellow Muslims.

To make progress, Turkey will require some geopolitical incentive to accommodate downstream riparian states. The hinge may be Turkey's desire to become a prosperous, developed state that can, as Turkey has sought to do for a decade, become eligible for admission to the European Union. One requisite for economic development is reliable access to sufficient energy resources to fuel a modern state. In the form of petroleum, that is something the water-poor states (other than Syria) have. A water-for-oil deal may be the best incentive the downstream states can offer. Whether that is attractive enough to whet Turkey's interest depends on whether there are alternative sources for Turkey. One of the most obvious alternatives is the petroleum wealth of the Caspian Sea area, to which the discussion turns as the subject of the second mini-case in this chapter.

CASPIAN SEA OIL

Petroleum was the most geopolitically potent natural resource of the twentieth century, and especially the latter half of that century, when the concentration of production shifted to the Persian Gulf littoral and the oil-rich states of that region gained control of the wealth under their soil from the major Western oil companies (known in the area as the Seven Sisters). Previously poor and underdeveloped countries became strategic prizes in the East-West competition, favor was curried, wars were fought, and American President Jimmy Carter declared the security of the Persian Gulf vital to United States interests. As if to prove the gravity of his assertion in what became known as the Carter Doctrine, the United States led a coalition of more than twenty-five states to expel the invading Iraqis from Kuwaiti soil in 1990–91.

Western dependence for energy on the Persian Gulf, which possesses nearly two-thirds of the world's known petroleum reserves, has never been entirely comfortable for the oil consumers. This dependence ties the developed countries to the often volatile politics of the region, leaves them subject to periodic extortion when oil supplies are withheld and leads to increased prices at the pump, and necessitates the devotion of military and other resources to a region of the world that would not otherwise warrant the expenditure. The problem and the solution, of course, is how to reduce that dependency.

The basic problem is not, as is sometimes advertised, a shortage of alternate sources of energy. There is, for instance, a large amount of unrecovered oil in the United States, but the cost of extracting it is either too high to make it economical (there is plenty of oil under Texas, but no one wants to pay the $60 a barrel or so to recover it), or the effort runs afoul of environmental or other concerns (the current controversy over exploiting the Alaska wilderness, for instance). There are also large reserves in or adjacent to the west coast of Africa, Venezuela, Indonesia, and a number of other places where the politics are nearly as complicated as in the Persian Gulf. It also might be possible, of course, to reduce dependency by lowering levels of usage and hence demand, a source many governments (especially the United States) have been politically unwilling to embrace and champion seriously. Even the question of global warming from burning fossil fuels enters the equation.

In these circumstances, the desire to break dependence on Persian Gulf oil has led the world's oil consumers to the small Soviet successor state of Azerbaijan. Its capital, Baku, sits on the banks of the Caspian Sea (which is actually a salt lake and the world's largest inland body of water), under which some of the richest deposits of petroleum and natural gas left in the world lie. The largest of these deposits are about sixty miles offshore from Baku, making it the focus of concerted exploration and exploitation.

The existence of Caspian Sea petroleum is nothing new. In fact, oil was discovered in the area in the second half of the nineteenth century, and by the beginning of the twentieth century, the region supplied most of Russia's oil needs (Imperial Russia completed its annexation of Azerbaijan in 1828). Although Azerbaijan declared its independence in 1918, it was absorbed into the Soviet Union in 1920. During the period when it was a republic of the Soviet Union, Azerbaijan was clearly not an alternative source of petroleum for an increasingly addicted West, however, because of the nature of the Cold War competition and Western unwillingness to become dependent on Soviet-controlled petroleum reserves.

The demise of the Soviet Union opened the floodgates for Western entrepreneurs to be drawn to Baku and elsewhere along the shores of the Caspian Sea. When Azerbaijan declared its independence from the Soviet Union on August 30, 1991, the oil companies were not far behind, engaging in a flood of speculation and exploration that many veteran oil industry experts say had not been seen since the opening of the Texas oil fields in the early 1900s. By the middle 1990s, the Caspian Sea fields were widely being extolled as the means by which the developed world would break the stranglehold imposed by the Persian Gulf oil-producing states. Yet today, hardly a drop of Caspian Sea oil finds its way to the West, and the prospects for that situation changing in the short term are unpromising.

Why is this the case? There is certainly no lack of interest among Western governments and the private oil companies in exploiting and bringing to market the petroleum riches lying beneath the Caspian Sea, and there are no major technical or engineering barriers present. But there are geopolitical problems; one is the political instability of the region; another is the geopolitics of piping the riches to market because of competing routes with different advantages and barriers.

Regional Instabilities

Five states (Azerbaijan, Russia, Kazakhstan, Uzbekistan, and Turmenistan) have claims to parts either of the oil or of the natural gas under or surrounding the Caspian basin. The three northern states (Azerbaijan, Kazakhstan, and Russia) have agree to a division of the resource contiguous to their shores, but the oil still does not flow. The reason it does not are most clearly exemplified by the situation in Azerbaijan.

The major geopolitical liability for Azerbaijan centers on two enclave areas that are points of major contention between Muslim Azerbaijan and neighboring Christian Armenia: Nagorno-Karabakh and Naxcivan (sometimes known as Nakichevan). Of these two disputes, the ongoing conflict over Nagorno-Karabakh has been the more serious and has created the most difficulties for Azerbaijan generally and for exploiting the oil in particular.

Nagorno-Karabakh was an enclave with a majority Armenian population that is located physically in Azerbaijan. There has been a long history of accusations by residents of the enclave that they have been mistreated by their Muslim rulers, and this has accompanied an unease with being physically separated from their Armenian brethren, as the accompanying map shows.

Map 14.2 Map of Azerbaijan and surrounding areas (Armenia, Chechnya, and Turkey).

The contest over the status of Nagorno-Karabakh, which was treated as an autonomous region within Azerbaijan by the Soviets, goes back to the latter days of the Soviet Union. In 1988, the Armenians petitioned Moscow to cede Nagorno-Karabakh to Armenia and were rebuffed by the Soviets. When Azerbaijan declared its independence, it announced that the region would lose its autonomous status and become an integral part of Azerbaijan, an action that sent residents into opposition. War broke out between secessionists from Nagorno-Karabakh and Azerbaijan, and Armenian troops entered the fray in support of the ethnic Armenians. By August 1993, Armenian forces had occupied the area and had also taken control of the corridor linking Nagorno-Karabakh to Armenia. A cease-fire was arranged in 1994, but the issue has never been permanently settled. In the meantime, Armenia remains in control of one-sixth of Azerbaijani territory that constitutes Nagorno-Karabakh and the corridor, and the possibility that fighting will resume remains an ever-present likelihood in this undeclared war.

The fighting over Nagorno-Karabakh has left two legacies with which Azerbaijan must struggle. Of the most immediate concern are Azerbaijani refugees from the war zone. It is estimated that the refugees number more than a million, which is the largest percentage of refugees (as a part of the population) in any country in the world, and most of them live in the most wretched of conditions within Azerbaijan. Getting the oil to market and hence gaining the revenues that oil will put into government coffers has the potential greatly to ease this problem.

The other legacy is the danger of renewed violence, which affects thinking about where pipelines can be constructed to get the petroleum to the west. The Armenians have made no secret that they are in a physical position to disrupt any lines going near Armenian territory and that they would not be reluctant to engage in disruption if they felt they needed to.

The other political problem in Azerbaijan surrounds the government of the country itself. The head of government is Heydar Aliyev, a former first secretary of the Azerbaijan Communist Party who was removed from office by Mikhail Gorbachev in 1987 on charges of rampant corruption. Aliyev returned to the political arena in 1995 as the leader of something called the New Azerbaijan Party (NAP) and was elected president of the country. According to the *CIA Factbook 2004*, corruption in the country is "ubiquitous." The 1999 Corruption Perceptions Index, produced by Berlin-based Transparency Inc., rates the Azerbaijan government as the third most corrupt regime in the world after Cameroon and Nigeria and right before Indonesia (see Chapter 9, "Debating Globalization"). In addition, there have been charges of nepotism and cronyism against the Aliyev family. Dealing with the regime is a major source of frustration for the oil industry and casts doubts, among other things, about how much of the projected oil revenue would be applied to problems like the refugees as opposed to lining the Aliyev family's pockets.

The Pipeline Problem

The problem of exploiting the Caspian Sea oil and gas fields is not technical in nature; rather, it is almost entirely political, or, more specifically, geopolitical. In the decade or so since the demise of the Soviet Union, the major global oil companies have descended on the Caspian region, generously laden with Western expertise and funds, and have transformed the rickety petroleum industry run by the communists into a modern Western-style operation. Although it is true that the Abseron Peninsula on which much of the Baku refining capacity resides has been proclaimed one of the most polluted places on earth, the oil companies are ready and eager to make the oil flow.

The problem is finding a way to get it safely and securely to market to help relieve the world's dependence on the Middle East. To this point, there have been three proposals for an Azerbaijani pipeline to the west; none of them meet the dual criteria of security and avoidance of the Persian Gulf. The three routes under consideration go through Russia, Turkey, and Iran. Each is flawed in some political manner.

The Russian pipeline would run across Azerbaijan's northern boundary with Russia and would make its way to either the Black Sea or the Baltic Sea, from which it could then be shipped to Western markets. As might be imagined, the Russians are very strong advocates of this route, because they would be able to charge a duty on the petroleum as it is transshipped across Russian territory, thereby providing needed money to aid the transformation and development of the Russian state.

Aiding and stabilizing the Russian state has considerable support in the West, and especially the United States, but the Russian "solution" raises two objections. The first is that the Russian government has proven so inept that it would likely squander the revenues or have them skimmed off by corrupt officials or other criminal elements in the country, a situation that Russian President Vladimir Putin vows to remedy but has not yet done. More fundamentally, however, the pipeline route traverses the rebellious province of Chechnya. The Russians realize that no one is going to endorse a pipeline scheme that could be held hostage by rebellious Chechens, and the recent spate of Chechen terrorism cools a good deal of the enthusiasm for this solution for getting Azerbaijani oil to market.

The Turkish solution has the same kind of problem. The idea here is to build a pipeline across Turkey that would connect to the country's existing oil refineries in the northwest part of the country (which, unfortunately, have been the site of major earthquakes in the past few years). The oil would then be shipped through the Black Sea into the Mediterranean and to market.

The geopolitical problem in this case is that the Turkish pipeline would have to be built across or adjacent to Armenian territory, thereby enmeshing it in the volatile relations between those two successor states. Azerbaijan has no direct border with Turkey. The shortest route to Turkish soil from Azerbaijan is through Armenia (and possibly Nagorno Karabakh, depending on how a route might be fashioned), which is clearly untenable as long as the conflict between the two states exists. The alternatives would be to go around Armenia to the south through Iran, which hardly solves the problem of dependence on the Persian Gulf, or through Georgia. Georgia itself has been unstable, with Abkhazian secessionists periodically causing problems, leading to a Russian army occupation of parts of the country, and it is doubtful the Armenians would hesitate to violate Georgian soil to damage the pipeline if they felt the need to do so. An Iranian pipeline would go to the Persian Gulf.

The Prospects

Because the dual criteria of pipeline security and lessening dependence on Persian Gulf oil have not been met, the Caspian Sea fields remain largely dormant, certainly not pumping the quantities of oil that could make a difference in worldwide supply and thus price. Other issues remain that contribute to the standstill. There is currently only partial agreement on boundaries in the Caspian Sea among the five littoral states, although the Azerbaijanis, Russians, and Kazakhs have announced an agreement between them on division of rights. Disagreements such as this are not, however, fundamental. What is needed is an agreement on a pipeline route and a guarantee that the route will be secured so that interruptions in supply do not occur.

It is not clear that the principals can make that guarantee at this time. The proximity of Azerbaijan to Chechnya and the Russians' continuing problems there suggest they would have great difficulty providing adequate assurances that Chechen separatists would not act to interrupt the flow. Georgia does not have the might to block the Armenians. Those proposing alternative routes simply lack the leverage to make the necessary assurances to get the pipeline going.

What will have to happen to break the impasse? The probable answer involves extra-regional action. Regional powers cannot or will not act effectively. Russia is too weak to squelch the Chechens, and Turkey is certainly in no political position to suppress Armenian interruptions, given the genocide of the Ottoman Turks against Armenia early in the twentieth century (although Turkey and Armenia were meeting in early 2001 to explore ways to resolve their historical and ongoing differences). That means the impasse will remain until those who have the most vested interest in access to Caspian Sea reserves decide to act themselves. Direct Western involvement opens up so many unpleasant prospects that, for now, it is far easier to dream of the prospects of Caspian Sea oil than to bring it home.

DIAMOND WARS

The third mini-case moves out of the Middle East into Africa, and more specifically the small West African country of Sierra Leone. It is a country that normally would not draw much international attention; one of its major claims to historic fame is the fact that natives of Sierra Leone carried out the mutiny on the slave ship *Amistad*. But a bloody civil war raged off and on from 1991 to 2002, and it has produced some of the most gruesome carnage in the decade of the 1990s in the forms of mass amputations of innocent civilians by so-called "rebel troops" and the displacement of nearly one-third of the population. In turn, the violence in Sierra Leone has triggered both African and broader, extra-regional international efforts to end what has gone on, including the fielding of the largest peacekeeping mission in United Nations history in this country, which is roughly the size of South Carolina.

What has caused the atrocities of Sierra Leone? At the most general level, the civil violence of Sierra Leone is simply part of the tapestry of political instability in its part of Africa. When fighting broke out in 1991, many observers considered it an extension of the chaotic bloodshed in contiguous Liberia, and the Liberian government of Charles Taylor (itself the result of a bloody civil conflict that featured the so-called "child soldiers," 10- to 12-year-olds enlisted into the violence) was one of the few but consistent supporters of the Revolutionary United Front (RUF), the largest of the organizations that waged the war.

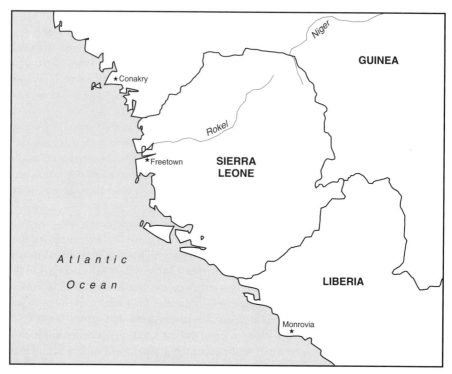

Map 14.3 Map of Sierra Leone.

But the war in Sierra Leone is about more than simply a power struggle among competing tribes in a poor and backward African state. Sierra Leone has a rich supply of a highly scarce and valuable resource—diamonds. The power struggle in that country cannot fully be comprehended other than in the context of controlling the diamond-producing regions that form the country's primary economic resource and thus source of foreign exchange. Sierra Leone would probably be unstable to some extent were there no diamonds in its soil because of its location; destabilizing the government as a means to exert de facto control over the gems of Sierra Leone provided the incentive to conduct a bloody conflict that could not be justified otherwise.

The Background

A former British colony, Sierra Leone gained its independence in 1961, as one of the earlier African states to complete that process. Its early history was marred by instability and violence, and some semblance of order did not appear until 1978, when it was reorganized as a one-party state. Between 1978 and 1991, the country experienced periods of civilian and military rule, and in 1991, a new constitution was ratified with the purpose of returning the country to civilian rule. A coup overthrew the government that same year, and the RUF emerged in the countryside from near the border with Liberia in opposition to the military government.

Fighting continued between the RUF and the military government of Sierra Leone (bolstered by observers from the Economic Community of West African States or ECOWAS and later troops under the ECOWAS authority). In 1995, UN Secretary General Boutros Boutros-Ghali appointed a special envoy to Sierra Leone, Berhanu Dinka, to negotiate a cease-fire and to return Sierra Leone to civilian rule. To that end, presidential and parliamentary elections were held in February 1996, and Dr. Ahmed Tejan Kabbah took power. The RUF boycotted the election and remained in opposition until November 1996, when the government and RUF signed a peace agreement known as the Abidjan Accord.

The accord did not last long. Unhappy with the accommodation that had been reached, the Sierra Leonean armed forces once again staged a coup d'état in May 1997. The army actually formed a ruling junta with the RUF, and the Kabbah government fled into exile in Guinea. On October 8, 1997, the UN Security Council imposed an oil and arms embargo and authorized ECOWAS to employ observer group (ECOMOG) troops to enforce it. The junta refused to accept the sanctions or an October 23 cease-fire among the parties.

In February 1998, ECOMOG came into combat with the Sierra Leonean forces, defeating them and their RUF allies. The junta collapsed and on March 10, President Kabbah and his government returned to the country. In order to support the government, the UN established the UN Observer Mission in Sierra Leone (UNOMSIL) in June 1998. The rebels, forced into the countryside, began their campaign of terror, including amputating the hands and feet of numerous citizens in a more or less random manner. These actions were witnessed by UNOMSIL members (who were protected by ECOMOG forces). In order to deal with the chaotic situation, the Security Council authorized the establishment of the United Nations Mission in Sierra Leone (UNAMSIL) on October 22, 1999, with an initial force maximum of 6,000 personnel, which was increased in May 2000 to 13,000 military personnel and 260 military observers, the largest such mission in UN history. In September 2000, there were discussions of raising the authorized limit to 20,500 troops, but it was largely being disbanded in 2004.

Two major points come from this extraordinary chronology. The first is the almost pathetic level of instability in this small country. The term "failed state," originally coined in the early 1990s to describe Somalia and other states chronically unable to govern themselves, clearly applies to Sierra Leone. The country has endured an unbroken string of political woes: elections overturned, coups and countercoups, insurrection, and the alliance between the military and the terrorists-rebels. The second is that the only apparent source of stability in the country has been imposed by outsiders. ECOWAS (and forces under the banner of ECOWOG) were crucial in restoring order at the end of the decade, and now the UNAMSIL is in place. It is not clear what will happen when they leave; one possibility is a return to the chaos of the 1990s.

It's the Diamonds, Stupid!

The conditions in Sierra Leone are objectively horrible enough to raise our sympathies: Christopher Wren in the *New York Times* recently reported that more than 300,000 people have been "internally displaced" in the country, and many more have fled across the border into neighboring Guinea and Liberia. In addition, the terrorist campaign of the RUF has left literally thousands of Sierra Leoneans with neither hands nor feet (or both), creating a prosthetic emergency of the most major proportions.

Given the meager status of Sierra Leone, one initially wonders why it has received the attention it has. Why, for instance, has the RUF and its currently imprisoned leader, Foday Sankoh, engaged in the spectacular, gruesome campaign that has plagued the country for years and is Sierra Leone's principal, overwhelmingly negative, distinction in the new millennium?

The answer, of course, is diamonds. Before the civil war began, Sierra Leone was one of the world's leading producers of commercial and gemstone diamonds, ranking fourth or fifth in total production at different times during the 1970s. The wealth produced by the diamond trade (much of which has traditionally been smuggled illegally out of the country) provided the incentive for fighting and enhanced the ability of the RUF to buy weapons and hence carry out their campaign. Recognizing that diamond wealth was being used to underwrite the atrocities, a suspension of the diamond trade emanating from Sierra Leone was part of sanctions imposed on the country during the 1990s, and the sanctions have just recently been lifted in an attempt to revive a Sierra Leonean economy that has been devastated by the civil war. Without the lures of diamond wealth, one wonders if the principals would have gone to the ends they have in the war.

The Prospects

The outside world has taken an active interest in Sierra Leone's travail, which may be its major hope for the future. As already noted, the UN has become actively involved through the augmenting of ECOMOG forces into UNAMSIL. In October 2000, for example, the UNAMSIL force included personnel from thirty-two member countries as diverse as the People's Republic of China and the Russian Federation to Croatia and Uruguay. Eight of the thirty-two participating countries were African. In addition, twelve countries have contributed personnel to the civilian police force (six of which are African). The hopes of restoring and maintaining order rest largely with these forces.

On October 5, 2000, the UN Security Council was presented with a plan for a war crimes tribunal for Sierra Leone. Aimed specifically at the atrocities committed largely by the RUF, its jurisdiction will include the crimes of murder, torture, terrorism, rape, sexual slavery, mutilation, hostage-taking, pillage, and attacks on civilians. The most obvious objective is to bring to justice those guilty of the enormous number of amputations. Ironically, many of the perpetrators of these crimes recorded their grotesque deed on videotape or still photographs to impress their superiors, but when this documentary evidence was captured by the UN, it came to serve as stark evidence of atrocity. The tribunal, which is the fourth war crimes body formed since the end of the Cold War (see Chapter 4, the case study on war crimes), will be jointly conducted and administered by the UN and the government of Sierra Leone. Major questions to be decided include the minimum age of individuals to be tried (because many of the "soldiers" of the RUF were young teenagers) and what to do with Sankoh and the rest of the RUF leadership.

Finally, it is almost certain that a major humanitarian effort will be mounted to deal with the tragedy of the Sierra Leonean amputee problem. In all likelihood, the bulk of the effort will come from nongovernmental organizations (NGOs) who are willing to provide services and manufacturers of prosthetic devices to alleviate the suffering of those victims of the war. The French-based *Medecins sans Frontieres* (see Chapter 2) has announced a major initiative in this regard.

CONCLUSION

In this case study, we have looked at the very different impact that conflicts over scarce resources can have on international or domestic politics. In each case, a resource that more parties want than can have simultaneously (the definition of scarcity) has resulted in conflict. In Sierra Leone, that conflict has been bloody, vicious, and atrocious, tearing apart the internal politics of an otherwise unexceptional West African state. In the Caucasus, the effects of international conflict (Nagorno Karabakh) and internal strife (Chechnya) complicate and, to this point, make impossible the exploitation of a scarce resource to an outside world anxious for its use. In the region serviced by the Tigris-Euphrates River system, the conflict remains dormant and the geopolitics seem to militate against violence, but tension remains.

The point of the discussion is to highlight the diversity of potential situations in which scarce natural resources have affected worldwide situations in the near past and present, as some indication of the kind of role resource scarcity may play in the future. As the world's population continues to grow, there will be an increasing demand for potable water in an environment of limited elasticity: the supply can be increased by bringing water from water-rich to water-poor areas or by increasing the supply through desalinization, but both solutions are economically prohibitive. As the global economy grows to encompass more states, that participation will place added demands for the energy that undergirds much economic activity. Greater industrialization will create the need for more commercial diamonds. And while it is difficult to detail all the possible areas where resource scarcity will result in political conflict in the future, there is no doubt at all that such conflicts will arise and be troublesome.

STUDY/DISCUSSION QUESTIONS

1. Resource scarcity and its geopolitical implications has not been a prominent topic in international relations to this point. What is the actual and potential problem that scarce resources can have? How might this be a bigger problem in the future?

2. Describe the problem created by excess demands made on the waters of the Tigris-Euphrates water system (including how it spills over into the Syrian-Israeli debate over the Golan Heights). What is the status of the dispute, how can it be resolved, and why is violence unlikely to be the means of resolution?

3. Why is access to Caspian Sea oil and natural gas such a large international priority? What political factors are interfering with the ability to bring this resource to market? What can be done to break the impasse?

4. Given the number of civil conflicts in Africa, what is distinctive about the chaotic conflict in Sierra Leone? Would the war have been the same without access to diamonds? How can the situation be resolved?

5. Can you discern any patterns from the three mini-case studies included in this chapter? Can you think of other examples of resource conflicts that carry out the same or different themes from those presented here?

READING/RESEARCH MATERIAL

"Azerbaijan." *Microsoft Encarta Online Encyclopedia 2000.* Microsoft Corporation, 2000.
"Azerbaijan." *CIA World Factbook 2000.* Washington, DC: Central Intelligence Agency, 2000. http://www.odci.gov/cia/publications/factbook/geos/aj.html
BBC News. "Q&A: Why Does Nagorno Karabakh Matter?" BBC News, March 31, 1998.
Commission on Global Governance. *Our Global Neighborhood.* New York: Oxford University Press, 1995.
Daniel, D., and R. Matthews. "Environment and Security: Muddled Thinking." *Bulletin of the Atomic Scientists,* April 1991, 8–23.
Elhance, A. *Hydropolitics in the Third World: Conflict and Cooperation in International River Basins.* Washington, DC: United States Institute of Peace Press, 1999.
Homer-Dixon, T. "Environmental Scarcities and Violent Conflict: Evidence from Cases." In *Global Dangers: Changing Dimensions of International Security,* edited by Sean Lynn-Jones and Steven Miller, pp. 144–179. Cambridge, MA: MIT Press, 1995.
Lowi, M. "Bridging the Divide: Transboundary Resource Disputes and the Case of West-Bank Water." *International Security* 18, 1 (1993), 113–138.
"Sierra Leone News." October 3, 2000. http://www.sierra-leone.org/slnews.html
"UNAMSIL." New York: United Nations, October 13, 2000. http://www.un.org/Depts/dpko/unamsil/UNAMSIL.htm

WEB SITES

Overview of the Tigris and Euphrates damming project from Turkish view
The G.A.P. Project at http://www.mfa.gov.tr/grup;d/dc/dcd/gap.htm
Information on water resources as well as data on global freshwater issues
The World's Water at http://www.worldwater.org
Focus on water in the Israeli-Palestinian conflict and Jordan River basin
Water and Conflict at http://aternet.rug.ac.be
Analysis of Caspian Sea mineral wealth dispute
EIA: Caspian Sea Region at http://www.eia.doe.gov/emeu/cabs/Caspian.html
Political, cultural, and humanitarian information on Sierra Leone
Sierra Leone Web at http://www.sierra-leone.org

CHAPTER FIFTEEN

Worse Than the Bubonic Plague

AIDS IN AFRICA AS A TRANSSTATE ISSUE

PRÉCIS

By now, the dimensions of the human tragedy being inflicted on most of the countries of sub-Saharan Africa by the HIV-AIDS pandemic are known to most, at least in general terms. The list of lives lost, and the demographic consequences of those losses for the generations yet to come, have received widespread publicity. The pandemic is real, it is serious, and it is getting worse.

This case study attempts to examine the AIDS crisis from the vantage point of a transstate issue that can only be approached and solved through an international effort. The case reviews the dimensions of the problem and its suggested solutions, a matter made more public by then U.S. Secretary of State Colin Powell's adoption of the problem in 2001 and echoed by President Bush in 2003. It then raises the question of whether there is sufficient international will and interest to tackle the problem and whether thinking about this health disaster and its solution is a precedent for dealing with future health disasters (an outbreak of the Ebola virus is used as an example) might produce an international reaction.

It has been described as the world's most severe health crisis since the bubonic plague ravaged Europe during the Middle Ages, with current projections that more people will die from it than succumbed to the black death. Those who observe its deadly progress no longer refer to it as an epidemic; instead, it is now universally called a "pandemic" because its effects encompass a whole continent and threaten to become a worldwide disaster. Former U.S. Secretary of State Colin S. Powell adopted its solution as a personal cause, as has President George W. Bush.

Its effects, which have been widely publicized in recent years, are staggering in their human toll. Left unchecked, several countries that are most affected could see life expectancy, which has been declining for a decade, dip below 30 years within the next decade, according to some projections. A whole generation of children has been orphaned as their parents have died from the disease, and their countries will soon face a ghastly situation where the leadership the parents of those orphans were supposed to provide will instead be a void, producing a generation lost. We could even see the absolute decline in population on those parts of the continent most adversely affected.

The problem, of course, is AIDS, and the pandemic is at work on the continent of Africa. It is a human disaster with which we all have by now at least a passing acquaintance, due to the tireless efforts of those with an interest and desire to treat and cure the grisly results. Yet despite a generalized awareness that there is a global problem, AIDS in Africa hardly dents the international agenda. Among the dedicated medical caregivers who seek to lessen the suffering, there is great, even heroic effort both to publicize and to treat the disaster. The international community, including those with the ability to address and ameliorate the problem, basically averts its eyes when asked for help, and, if it cannot completely ignore the cries for assistance, it does less than the advocates say it should. The United States has pledged $15 billion to help cope; even if the money all is eventually spent, it will be a small drop in a very large bucket.

Why is this the case? One part of the answer almost surely comes from the fact that the disaster is occurring far away, in central and southern Africa, in the most distant and obscure part of the world physically and in terms of consciousness for most people who do not live on or study the continent. The AIDS epidemic in the United States, which the African pandemic absolutely dwarfs as a physical problem, has received massive publicity and the most concerted medical research and pharmaceutical efforts. Africans, suffering monumentally more, have benefited relatively little from these efforts.

Part of the reason for this inattention is economic. AIDS "cocktails" widely available to Western sufferers from HIV and AIDS typically cost between $10,000 and $15,000 a year, a sum far in excess of the per capita income in most African states, which measure annual per capita income in the *hundreds* of dollars. Even treatments for the side effects of AIDS-caused immunity deficiencies like pneumonia and tuberculosis that cost far less are unavailable in most African countries. In the United States, a person diagnosed with HIV or AIDS has the medical doors opened wide and the treatment options spelled out. In many African countries, all a doctor who diagnoses a patient with the disease can do is to tell the victim's loved ones to take the patient home to die.

One result has been a virtual scandal between the pharmaceutical firms most heavily involved in HIV-AIDS and third world drug firms intent on manufacturing cheaper versions of medication, pitting international patent regimes against humanitarian concerns. The drug companies, buffeted by worldwide accusations of profiteering at the expense of massive human suffering, recanted in 2001 and agreed to sell HIV-AIDS drugs at a greatly reduced price (although still well above the means of many in Africa).

International inattention to this horrible plague is difficult to understand, and it is the purpose of this case study to try to shed some light on both the pandemic and how it is a broader concern than for only its direct victims. The AIDS pandemic is a classic, although hideous, transstate issue, but it remains in the international shadow of more popular international problems like the environment or human rights. We will try to see why. In order to do so, we will proceed in three steps. First, we will examine the AIDS problem in Africa through the lens of the structure of other transstate issues, in the process trying to establish if African AIDS has the same characteristics as more familiar, orthodox issues spanning the globe and spilling across international boundaries. Second, we will look at some of the characteristics of this particular transstate problem, both as primer (or refresher) for the reader and as a way to see how this issue differs from or is similar to other transstate issues. Third, we will examine how other transstate issues have been addressed internationally to see if similar efforts either have been attempted in the AIDS case or might prove helpful in attacking the tragedy of AIDS in Africa. We will conclude by suggesting that what is learned from treating HIV-AIDS as a transstate issue may provide a relevant model for similar international outbreaks of diseases in the future, such as the Ebola virus that currently affects Africa and could spread elsewhere.

THE PANDEMIC AS A TRANSSTATE ISSUE

A word about terminology is necessary at this point. Although there is not complete consensus on a definition of a transstate issue, this one derived from Snow, *United States Foreign Policy*, will suffice: a transstate issue is a "problem caused by the actions of states or other actors that cannot be solved by the actions of individual states or other actors within individual states alone." The heart of this definition is its assertion of two common, interrelated characteristics of a classic transstate issue: both its causation and its solution go beyond the ability of individual sovereign jurisdictions.

Not all the problems normally identified as transstate issues meet the criteria of this definition. Some of the environmental problems such as ozone depletion and the greenhouse effect do, but others like human rights do not. In the case of human rights, for instance, it is not physically impossible for individual states to enforce a uniform set of human rights standards; the problem is that some states choose not to do so, and the international community has to this point not been able to agree completely on appropriate standards and the means to enforce them. Problems that could be solved by individual states but are not we can refer to as *semi-transstate issues.*

There are also global problems that may rise to the severity of transstate issues but that have not achieved that level of severity or notoriety in people's minds, depending on one's individual vantage point. Global overpopulation is recognized by many demographers and futurists as a grave future threat to the world, and it has engaged the efforts of many population planners and the like. Despite demographic projections of future doom, however, the results have not been so devastating to this point that they activate universal concern or action. Transstate issues in this category can be thought of as *potential transstate issues.*

Clearly, these distinctions form a hierarchy of international concerns. Potential transstate issues are at the bottom of the hierarchy (although by no means necessarily at the bottom of the list of international problems that the international system must consider), because they are less immediate in their effects than full-scale transstate issues.

Likewise, semi-transstate issues are less worrisome than full-blown transstate issues because the problems are solvable if the international actors show the willingness to engage in the actions that would solve them.

Transstate issues, on the other hand, are the most intractable and difficult. Partly this is the case because, by definition, they require cooperative actions across sovereign state boundaries, which often generates friction and suspicion of intrusion on state prerogatives. At the same time, the solutions, where they are known, are often controversial. To cite an example from Chapter 13, how much reduction in greenhouse gas emissions is necessary to eliminate how much surface warming, and who will have to reduce how much? Where solutions to these issues are known, they are often quite expensive and must compete for scarce resources with other domestic and international priorities for attention and funding. Where the effects of the problem are distant—either in time or in who is affected—attention to the solutions may be disadvantaged in the competition for resources, and especially funds. Finally, when the transstate issue has a North-South, developed world–developing world overlay, as they often do, the heart of the debate often gets swept up in the ongoing differences regarding the "obligations" of the developed world more aggressively to address the developmental needs of the less-developed countries.

How does the African AIDS pandemic rate in this scheme of concerns? Clearly, it is not a potential problem, because, as noted in the introduction, millions of people have already died from the disease, millions are infected with HIV or AIDS and likely will die, and the fact and trend of infection will not abate without intervention. One can make a partial case, at least early on in the progression of the pandemic, that African AIDS has some of the characteristics of a semi-transstate issue, in that the efforts of states have either been inadequate to stem the problem before it reached such enormous proportions or, in some cases, in the physical denial that the problem existed (or even that it does exist). That may have been true earlier, but it is no longer the case. One of the major newer sources of HIV infection has been from African soldiers. Some soldiers sent into other African countries as peacekeepers have acquired the virus through sexual contact with infected natives and then taken it home and transmitted it to their fellow countrymen. At the same time, already infected peacekeepers may spread the disease in countries where they serve through sexual contact with natives. Other than somehow enforcing abstinence or safe sex, it is not clear how the actions of individual states acting alone could stop that problem.

The pandemic thus has risen to the status of a full-scale transstate issue, with all the characteristics and problems associated with such an issue. Clearly, the divisions between states exacerbate the problem by making cross-boundary cooperative treatment programs impossible or ineffective. The motto of the World Health Organization (WHO), that "disease knows no frontiers," clearly applies to the pandemic; the response that solutions should be coterminus with the problem has not yet become the norm.

The other common characteristics apply as well. There is basic disagreement not only about causes of the pandemic but also about the solutions. Within the scientific community, there is a small fringe that denies the relationship between HIV and AIDS and denies the disease kills anyone, a position endorsed by the president of one African country (South Africa) and vociferously denounced by virtually all of the global medical community. Solutions tend to center on the provision of cheap drugs to treat the disease or its symptoms, putting advocates into conflict with the pharmaceutical firms who produce HIV-AIDS drugs and activating debates over whether prevention or treatment is the best approach. The matter of treatment raises the question of cost, which most of the African states simply cannot come close to bearing and which can only be approached with either massive subsidizing of current drugs by the most developed states or the discovery of much cheaper alternatives. Major drug companies have offered substantial subsidization, but it is not clear this is adequate given the paucity of African health budgets. Finally, the issue also is tinged by the matter of developmental obligations, because AIDS is arguably the single greatest barrier to African development today and because, it is alleged, ultimately the most effective way to stem the behavior that creates the problem is through the economic development of the societies in which it is occurring.

DIMENSIONS OF THE PROBLEM

For most of the world, the severity of the problems facing African countries is almost inconceivable, and as long as the rampant spread of the disease is essentially isolated to the most marginalized continent of the globe, confronting and coming to terms with its effects will be difficult for most people. Yet, there is reason to do so on two counts that go beyond but by no means ignore the immediate horror.

One of these reasons is that the pandemic will almost certainly spread to other continents. There is, for instance, some evidence that AIDS is increasing in parts of Asia, where there are much larger populations that could be subject to infection but where the resources to deal with the problem are not much greater than they are in Africa. An AIDS pandemic in a country like China—where as many as a million cases have already been reported—could be catastrophic. The same is true of India. The other reason is that the way the AIDS pandemic is dealt with may provide a model, for good or bad, of how the world might deal with similar problems in the future.

Directly connected to the immune deficiencies associated with AIDS has been the recurrence of some diseases (smallpox, for instance) that had virtually disappeared from the world but are returning. At the same time, there are other virulent diseases now isolated geographically that could also spread and become transstate problems. Prominent among these currently incurable diseases is Ebola, a highly contagious virus so far isolated to Africa that kills up to 90 percent of those who are infected by it. The West got a chilling portent of this possibility when a Congolese woman, who entered Canada by air in January 2001, was suspected of carrying Ebola (she was not in fact infected). As we shall suggest in the conclusion, the ways in which the AIDS pandemic is treated may have value as a precedent for dealing with other potentially international pestilences such as Ebola and other diseases that may emerge in the future. How the African AIDS transstate issue is handled, in other words, has both substantive and procedural importance for the future.

Origins and Parameters of the Pandemic

The AIDS virus was first identified in an African country, the then Belgian Congo, in 1959. Although public awareness of the disease in the developed world is generally associated with its outbreak in the United States in the 1980s and 1990s, the fact that the origins of the disease are African has helped mold the way Africans and the world view the disease. The currently most widely held explanation suggests that the disease first occurred in chimpanzees and was somehow transferred to humans, a point of some sensitivity among many Africans because of racist implications concerning the interactions between Africans and the primates. In Africa, there is greater ignorance and denial of AIDS, and at least part of the reason for this denial is the imputation that AIDS is an "African disease."

Certainly the continent has suffered the bulk of the ravages of the pandemic, and there is no predictable end in sight. The raw statistics are staggering. According to UNAIDS—an umbrella group of UN agencies, the World Bank, and the WHO—42 million people worldwide had AIDS in 2003, and 30 million of them are African (about 70 percent of the total). Already, nearly 19 million people have died from AIDS, of whom 3.8 million were children younger than 15 years. In 1999, 4 million out of an estimated 5.4 million infected were African (about 74 percent), and 85 percent of the 2.8 million killed in 1999 by the disease were African. Approximately 13.2 million children have been orphaned by the disease; 12 million of them live in Africa (more than 90 percent). Possibly most chillingly according to a CNN report, "The U.S. Census Board projects that AIDS deaths and the loss of future population from the deaths of women of child-bearing age means that by 2010, sub-Saharan Africa will have 71 million fewer people than it would have otherwise." According to 2004 UNAIDS figures, in seven sub-Saharan African countries—Zambia, Zimbabwe, Swaziland, the Central African Republic, Lesotho, Mozambique, and Malawi—life expectancy for a newborn child is less than 40 years. The overall AIDS infection rate on the continent is 8.6 percent (the worldwide average is 1.1 percent), with the highest rates in Swaziland (38.3 percent), Botswana (37.3 percent), and South Africa (25 percent). By contrast, 30 million people were estimated to have died in medieval Europe during the bubonic plague, thereby explaining the title of this case study. Because the population of Europe at the time was much smaller than the African population today, a higher proportion of Europeans died of the plague, so the analogy between the two events is not perfect.

Why did this situation happen and why does it continue to happen? Some understanding of why the problem has reached the proportions that it has and of why it continues largely unchecked is necessary to understand the problem itself, its transstate nature, and how and whether there is an analogy between this tragedy and other similar transstate problems in the future.

There is not general consensus on the reasons why the pandemic has reached the levels it has achieved, and thus any list will be subject to challenge and disagreement. Having said that, we can identify at least six factors that have contributed to the current state of affairs. The reader is encouraged to think of others.

Ignorance and Denial. Part of the problem is ignorance of the disease and its consequences among many African citizens, and especially those who are undereducated and reside in the rural areas of the continent. In most countries (Uganda is a notable exception), governments have not mounted aggressive campaigns of citizen education about the dangers and consequences of HIV-AIDS and how personally to lessen those dangers. Originally, this absence itself was a form of denial of the severity of the problem, and it is currently made worse by limitations on government health budgets and the absence of treatments to give hope to those identified as infected.

Some of the results of ignorance and denial are macabre. In some parts of the continent, for instance, there is the belief that having sexual intercourse with a virgin will cure the disease in a male, thereby assuring a maximally high level of infection among young teenaged girls.

The most insidious form of denial comes from a small segment of the scientific community, which denies that the disease exists. The leading spokesman of this position is University of California at Berkeley molecular biologist Peter Duesberg, whose book *Inventing the AIDS Myth* argues there is no link between HIV and AIDS, and that the only reason the connection is maintained is because of the amount of research funding available to the scientific community to study the relationship. A variation of this theme is propounded by Ghanaian magazine publisher Baffour Ankomah, who maintains there is no such thing as AIDS and that the anti-AIDS campaign is nothing but a foreign plot to "destroy" Africa. In his magazine, *New African,* he has gone so far as to suggest, "What we call AIDS is actually U.S. biological warfare gone wrong." Among highly visible public figures, the most prominent skeptic of the existence and effects of the disease is South African President Thabo Mbeki.

Taboos on Discussion of the Pandemic. In a number of African countries, there is a strong reluctance to engage in open discussions of AIDS. Part of the reason for this reluctance can be found in social taboos about discussing sexuality and death. One result is that obituaries rarely refer to AIDS as the cause of death, preferring vague references to succumbing from a "long illness" or the like. This aversion to discussing sexual matters has also made things like "safe sex" programs promoting abstinence or contraception less effective than they might otherwise have been.

In some cases, the reluctance to discuss the disease has more practical grounds. In a number of countries, public reportage of the pandemic is opposed on the grounds that publicizing it would discourage tourism, a principal source of foreign exchange for some states. Because they generally lack the resources to do anything about the pandemic anyway, many politicians are reluctant to discuss it, because their inability to treat sufferers makes them appear less effective as public servants. As evidence that ignoring the problem may appear a viable strategy to African leaders, the 11th International Conference of AIDS and STDs (Sexually Transmitted Diseases) in Africa, held in Lusaka, Zambia, in 1998, was not attended by a single African head of state.

Civil Wars. Particularly during the past decade, a number of African countries have been the victims of internal violence. In most cases (Liberia, Sierra Leone, parts of the Democratic Republic of Congo) these conflicts rarely rise to the level of organized conflict that a professional soldier would call war. Rather, they tend to involve attacks against the civilian population by more or less organized armed groups whose members are likely to be referred to as "fighters" rather than "soldiers." Often, the purpose of these activities is criminal. For instance, a basic motivation of the Revolutionary United Front (RUF) of Sierra Leone is to destabilize governance and thereby to facilitate their plundering of that country's diamond mines (see the discussion in Chapter 14).

In these circumstances, a major purpose of the "revolutionaries" is terrorizing and humiliating the target population (or portion of the general population), and an important tactic of that terror is often the systematic rape of females in the combat zones. Because many of the fighters are young teenagers, the result is increased infection rates among the young, a contributory factor in lowering life expectancy. There is also a chain effect, as young women are infected by HIV-positive fighters and then pass the disease along to other sexual partners. As noted earlier in discussing the transstate nature of the problem, when international peacekeepers are imported to quell the violence, they also sometimes contract the disease and take it back to their countries, or begin the cycle by infecting the natives they are charged with protecting. Finally, an important effect of these civil conflicts is to disrupt the provision of public services, including the primitive health-care systems found in most African states, and to force the diversion of resources that might have otherwise been devoted to the pandemic to treating the more immediate and direct effects of the war effort.

Debt and Poverty. Even in countries not prone to violence, the existence of enormous poverty, often exacerbated by the widespread foreign debt under which many African countries labor, makes matters worse. Poverty means the resources to try to treat the disease are unavailable, and this in turn has a multiplying effect. As Lawrence Altman explained in the *New York Times* in July 2000, "while a virus causes AIDS, social conditions feed the epidemic. Patterns of behavior—fed by poverty, ignorance, and despair—have resulted in a disease so widespread that it has left millions of orphans and threatens to destroy much of Africa's economy and to wipe out a generation of young people."

A contributing factor to this dismal condition is the crushing level of external debt that permeates many countries on the continent. As a result, scarce resources that might otherwise be devoted to education about HIV-AIDS, preventive programs such as the distribution of condoms, or treatment of victims are instead funneled into debt service (usually only paying off the *interest* on the accumulated debt, not reducing the principal). There are currently a number of African states that spend as much as four times the amount of money on debt service that they spend on their health systems as a whole, much less on the specific problem of HIV-AIDS.

Expense of Treatment. The extremely high death rate associated with the African AIDS pandemic is the result of the virtual absence of treatment options that are widely available in the West to prolong life and even to arrest the progress of HIV. The culprit, of course, is the cost of the treatments.

Slowing or arresting AIDS in patients in places like the United States, of course, is made possible through the administration of a combination of drugs known collectively as a "cocktail." The medicines in the cocktail are, however, quite expensive, with annual costs running at $10,000 or more per patient, as noted earlier. Using this lower figure, the Washington Office on Africa, an advocacy group for the continent, estimates that the cost of providing this kind of treatment for African AIDS patients would be roughly *$220 billion per year.* Given that the majority of African countries caught up in the pandemic are among the one-half the world's population that subsists on an average income of $2 per capita per day (South Africa being the notable exception), the resources are simply not available even to begin reasonably modest programs of treatment. Instead, as already noted, about all the medical system can do is in effect perform triage on sufferers, sending them home to die rather than having them burden an already overly stressed health-care system. Although newer and cheaper drug treatments are under development, pharmaceutical firms (as we shall see in a subsequent section) have shown some reluctance to bring these rapidly and widely to market in places like Africa while they are recovering the research costs by marketing other, more expensive AIDS medications through the high-priced cocktails, a situation that came to a head in 2001 and that caused embarrassed firms to lower prices.

Relative Powerlessness of Women. One of the more notable aspects of the pandemic is that more women in Africa are infected with HIV-AIDS than men. The United Nations reported in late 1999 that, for the first time, the infection rate for females exceeded that for males. As reported in the *New York Times*, 55 percent of infections occurred in women in that year. More dramatically, the UN report also stated that several studies completed in Africa indicate that African girls aged 15–19 years are as much as five or six times as likely to be infected than their male counterparts.

The main reason for this phenomenon is the relatively dependent status of women in many traditional African societies. In many places, women have little control over reproductive decisions, and if a woman suggests the use of a condom, for instance, the result may be physical retribution. Despite international emphases on human and women's rights in recent years, translating that movement into sexual empowerment remains an uphill fight in numerous places where HIV-AIDS is rampant.

The list of factors contributing to the severity of the AIDS pandemic is not, as suggested earlier, intended to be exhaustive, and certain factors differ in emphasis from country to country and region to region. In a few countries like Uganda, the pandemic is actually abating, as a large government effort in sex education (centering on the use of condoms) has had the effect of lowering infection rates in important target groups in the population such as teenagers. Nonetheless, the problem remains monumental on the continent. Before looking at what is or might be done to staunch the pandemic, some discussion of its dimensions is in order.

Effects of the Pandemic

When the bubonic plague swept through Europe (and parts of Asia) during the middle 1300s, the "black death" (as it was known) claimed roughly one-quarter of the population as its victim. The epidemic finally ran its course, but because modern medicine had yet to come into existence, there was essentially nothing that could be done either to prevent infection or to treat the disease when it occurred. Today, there are vaccines against the black death and antibiotics to treat anyone who might contract it. At the time, there was nothing but suffering and death.

The AIDS pandemic bears similarities to and differences from the great plague. Certainly the levels of human suffering are parallel; the social and economic fabric of affected African countries are being torn apart as surely as those medieval societies were destroyed. Now, as then, countless lives will be lost or cut tragically short.

There is also a significant difference. Through an aggressive program of biomedical research, there now exist treatments to deal with this disease that simply had no parallel during the Middle Ages. Very expensive treatments have been available to those who could afford them for a decade or so, and more affordable drugs are on the way. Although it is impossible to predict precisely when it will occur, research scientists believe a vaccination will soon be available with which to inoculate the uninfected. It is hoped that both of these latter developments will bring the pandemic to an end. In the meantime, the suffering continues on a scale rivaling the great plague.

This is not the place to describe the structure of human suffering in any detail, because our focus on the AIDS pandemic is as a case in international action. However, we can mention illustrative effects that could recur in the future and that may have accompanied the bubonic plague during its course.

A notable attribute of AIDS is that it is, for many purposes, a young people's disease. Due to the nature of its transmission, it strikes particularly at people in their most sexually active stage of life, from early teenage years into their twenties and thirties. When there are no treatment options and the infected are just allowed to die, the result is a severe societal and demographic problem and imbalance that it will take years, even generations, to correct.

A major consequence of the pandemic is that it is robbing the countries most affected of a future generation of leaders and productive workers. Attention has quite appropriately focused on indicators of the tragedy such as dramatic reductions in life expectancy that are the result of the fact that "people are dying in their young adult years, not after leading full lives and then dying," as Karen Stanecki of the U.S. Census Bureau puts it. In 1999, the American Foundation for AIDS Research noted that 80 percent of those succumbing to the disease worldwide are between ages 20 and 50 years, workers in their prime.

What will happen with so many members of the generation dying in their twenties—who will assume leadership in their countries? Who will provide the working class that can contribute to the economic development of countries desperately in need of economic modernization? Where will the soldiers for the army come from? For that matter, who will parent the generation after that, when AIDS is, we hope, a matter of history but its demographic consequences are not? And then there are the 12 million orphaned children. What will their psychological and developmental fate be? In the desperate rush to staunch the rampaging disease, many of these questions have only been asked, with the answers unknown or undiscovered.

We have no close parallels from which to devise answers. The black death killed a higher percentage of people than current estimates presumed will die from AIDS, but the plague was presumably not demographically selective in the same way; the next generation of Europeans was diminished in numbers but presumably each age group was affected more or less equally. The enormous disruptions caused by forced displacement as the result of Africa's civil wars has affected large numbers, for instance, but the generational gap associated with the AIDS pandemic is producing is not so obvious.

There is also the question of the broader health implications of the pandemic. As already noted, a major part of the classification of the pandemic as a transstate issue arises from its progression across national borders in ways that have to this point evaded control.

At the same time, the immune deficiencies that AIDS creates also leave the human body vulnerable to other diseases that are now occurring or recurring as public health problems—things like measles and smallpox, for instance. At a time when some diseases are developing resistance to treatment by antibiotics, the revival of old diseases or the emergence of new diseases (drug-resistant tuberculosis, strains of Ebola, for instance) present some chilling prospects for the future.

The AIDS pandemic in Africa has, by and large, been treated as an African problem, but the time may be running out on our ability to sustain that luxury. The disease is spreading geographically to parts of Asia, the continent on which more than one-half of mankind resides. At the same time, the pandemic threatens to affect the rest of the world as well. Speaking in January 2000, Richard Holbrooke, then U.S. ambassador to the United Nations, warned, "If we don't work with the Africans themselves to address these problems, we will have to deal with them later when they get more dangerous and more expensive." Looking directly at the economic consequences, retired World Bank President James Wolfensohn adds, "Many of us used to think of AIDS as a health issue. We were wrong. AIDS can no longer be confined to the health or social sector portfolios. AIDS is turning back the clock on development."

TRANSSTATE SOLUTIONS

As the discussion immediately above indicates, there is a growing recognition in the international community of both the AIDS pandemic in Africa and the fact that it is more than an African health problem. The result has been a modest international effort to try to come to grips with the problem. Although there is little evidence that the precedent being set in that effort may be important in how we will deal with future crises, that should be a matter of concern for us as well.

The 13th International AIDS Conference was held in July 2000 in Durban, South Africa (the 15th conference was held in Bangkok in 2004), to report on the state of the worldwide problem and efforts to control the disease. The location of the conference was of major symbolic importance on two counts. It was the first time that the meeting had been held in Africa, and it was held in South Africa, whose president, as noted earlier, has been one of the major politicians who are skeptics about the link between HIV and AIDS.

Beyond the recitation of the many horrors associated with the pandemic—including projections of population consequences in Africa—the conference focused on the progress that has been made in developing cheaper medicines to treat the disease. The conference noted that the progression of the AIDS pandemic was far enough along that the population will actually begin to drop in absolute terms in countries such as Botswana, South Africa, and Zimbabwe by 2003. At the same time, the 10,000 conferees were also presented with evidence that more affordable drug treatments that may reduce the rate of progression from HIV to full-blown AIDS are becoming available. The U.S. Centers for Disease Control (CDC), for instance, reported that an antibiotic marketed by Bristol Myers Squibb and Glaxo-Wellcome has been effective in treating a form of pneumonia that "indicates an HIV-infected person has developed AIDS" and can be administered to patients for about $60 a year. While even that reduction is beyond the public health budgets of most African countries, it is nonetheless an indication of progress. Likewise, drugs cheaper than AZT have been developed that prevent the transmission of HIV from infected mothers to their unborn children.

The efforts reported at Durban are hopeful, but they are not the solution to what Dr. Roy M. Anderson of Oxford University described at the conference as "undoubtedly the most serious infectious threat in recorded human history." That is a very broad, serious statement, and one that you would think would produce a worldwide crash effort to contain. While the research efforts to treat and eradicate AIDS are not inconsequential, neither are they of the monumental dimensions the disease would seem to merit. Why not?

The general experience with transstate issues suggests at least some partial answers to this question. Undoubtedly, they are inadequate to explain the phenomenon fully, and they are offered more to stimulate discussion than to foreclose investigating other solutions to the problem. To this end, three observations that have emerged from viewing transstate issues like the environment may be relevant to understanding international reaction to the AIDS pandemic.

The first is the *seriousness and immediacy of the problem.* In problems as diverse as dealing with carbon dioxide emissions and chlorofluorocarbons (CFCs), a major barrier to action is that the problem does not have an immediate injurious effect on those causing the problem and whose behavior will have to be amended to solve it. People who drive large sport-utility vehicles (SUVs), for instance, might be chastened to change to more fuel-efficient and environmentally friendly forms of transportation if it somehow physically hurt when you drove the SUVs and if you felt physical pleasure when you drove 70-mile per gallon vehicles. Obviously, this does not happen, and advocates must rely on more abstract, less immediate arguments such as the effects of global warming on future generations.

The AIDS pandemic is the same way for most people outside Africa. One can read the kind of horrible tales and demographic consequences that have been detailed here, but they have no serious personal effects on the reader. Just as the producers of carbon dioxide (the developed countries) tend to blame the countries of the equatorial green belt for cutting down rain forests that are natural "traps" for carbon dioxide rather than blaming their own driving habits, there is a tendency to treat the AIDS pandemic as someone else's problem. When the Clinton administration publicly elevated the pandemic to the status of a threat to U.S. national security in 2000 (on the grounds that the demographic effects could destabilize African states and thus threaten U.S. interests in those states), hardly anyone outside the AIDS community took notice.

This leads to the second and related problem, the *lack of personalization* of the effects of the problem on most people. The worldwide drug epidemic, which is arguably a form of transstate issue, offers an example. Drug enforcement officials maintain that their problem would be much easier if the immediate personal effect of drug use was negative; if, for instance, smoking marijuana caused respiratory congestion or ingesting cocaine caused sharp pain. Neither is the case, and so entreaties to avoid use fall on at least some deaf ears.

The problem with AIDS in Africa is in some ways similar. The impact of the pandemic is certainly affecting people on that continent, but the effects remain essentially isolated and concern is not personalized outside the continent. What this may suggest is that the only, or at least most effective, way to gain and focus global attention is for there to be concrete negative consequences of not solving the problem. The journalist Robert D. Kaplan (in *The Coming Anarchy*), for instance, argues that a good reason for the rest of the world to deal with the general deterioration of the quality of life in much of Africa is that eventually it will spill over into the rest of the world in the form of migration from that continent to the developed world. Similarly, as the immune deficiencies central to AIDS spawn the birth or rebirth of other diseases that could spread to other areas, the problems of the lack of seriousness and personalization may be overcome as well in developed societies suddenly vulnerable to those diseases.

The third problem is the *low prioritization of the problem, especially in the area of international funding*. As noted, Africa cannot afford to provide adequate funds even to attempt to control AIDS or its treatment, and thus help must come from elsewhere. In his 2003 State of the Union address, President George W. Bush appeared to adopt African AIDS as a personal cause, pledging $15 billion for AIDS treatment, but the pledge has languished among other priorities. The president asked for only $200 million for the Global Fund to administer the program for 2004 (Congress appropriated $550 million), and the funds come with ideological strings: one-third of the funds must be given to faith-based groups "which preach abstinence," according to a July 2004 BBC Online report. Moreover, the administration has resisted committing funds to purchasing WHO-approved generic AIDS drugs, insisting it will only pay for drugs currently under patent to pharmaceutical companies and thus much more expensive than the generics.

The professional AIDS community knows what steps must be taken to gain control of the AIDS pandemic in Africa. The infection rate must be reduced through education about how AIDS is transmitted. Some countries, such as Uganda, have made major progress in "safe sex" education programs that have reduced infection rates, as already noted. Other countries, unfortunately, have not. In order to lessen the impact of AIDS infection, cheaper, more universally available treatments need to be made available, both to reduce suffering and to prolong useful life. Such treatments are available at great expense in the West; they are currently unavailable to almost all Africans. Ultimately, the pandemic can only be halted and the disease eradicated through the development of a preventive vaccine. AIDS research is reportedly not far from developing such a vaccine. Whether such a vaccine will be affordable and available where it is most needed is not yet certain.

It is easy to recite the steps necessary to cope with this catastrophic health problem, and what is frustrating is that it is a tragedy the effects of which can be ameliorated, if they cannot be eliminated. In that sense, the parallel between the AIDS pandemic and the black death of the Middle Ages does not hold. There simply was no possible way that the knowledge base of the thirteenth century could begin to cope with the plague, treat its victims, or find ways to eradicate the problem. AIDS can be, and eventually will be, eradicated. The question that will be asked in retrospect is why more resources were not made available more rapidly and massively to confront the problem. Why did it take so long?

CONCLUSION

The African AIDS case is fascinating for a number of reasons that include the dynamics of why it came about, what is being done about it, and how it can be viewed as a form of transstate issue. But the pandemic is more than a case in medical or international dynamics. In addition, there is the possibility that we may learn from the handling of the AIDS crisis how we should and should not deal with future health crises with international repercussions.

One health threat that currently holds great potential horror is the Ebola virus. Like AIDS, it is a disease that is recent in origin (it was first observed in 1976), and its origin is African (its first outbreak occurred in Zaire in the area adjoining the Ebola River, from which it takes its popular name). Ebola has not yet spread beyond Africa nor has it taken lives in the staggering numbers that AIDS has. It is, however, an enormously infectious disease that is easily transmissible, its existence is very difficult to detect until its symptoms appear in an infected person, and it has a very short and painful effect on its victims, most of whom die (in recent outbreaks, upwards of 90 percent of those infected have died). There is no known cure for the disease.

Because there is an incubation period of several weeks between contraction of Ebola and the appearance of its symptoms, it is entirely possible for a person to have the disease and not know it, thereby raising the possibility of "innocent" infection of others by an unaware carrier of the virus. At the same time, medical personnel treating a victim who do not know that Ebola is present are particularly vulnerable to infection themselves (it is passed from person to person through the body fluids of the infected, including their corpses).

For these reasons, it is only a matter of time until Ebola escapes Africa unless a cure or preventive vaccine is found. Because this has not yet occurred, the prospect of an Ebola epidemic breaking out at any of a number of places around the world remains a potential transstate issue. The Canadian case, where the woman suspected of having the virus had arrived only weeks earlier on a commercial airliner (an ideal closed environment for spreading the virus from unaware carrier to unsuspecting victims), may be a harbinger of things that might occur in the future.

Ebola has currently not risen to the status of a full-scale international issue for several reasons. One is its relatively recent discovery and the isolation and comparative infrequency of outbreaks of the disease. There have been outbreaks in Zimbabwe, South Africa, and Kenya, and as of late 2000, there was an epidemic in Uganda as well. The disease tends to appear in rural areas where sanitation facilities and practices are reasonably primitive. The practical result is that outbreaks do not receive the publicity and public outcry they would if they happened in urban settings or more geopolitically prominent locations. Also, the nature of the disease and where it has occurred have resulted in comparatively small numbers of deaths, generally in the hundreds in each individual outbreak. Partly, this is the result of outbreaks in rural areas where the population is not concentrated and there are consequently fewer potential victims. In addition, however, the disease kills so quickly that epidemics tend to run their course in short periods. As one newsletter devoted to the study of the virus puts it, "Ebola's virulence may also serve to limit its spread: its victims die so quickly that they don't have a chance to spread infection very far."

The Ebola problem thus clearly does not yet rise to the level of transstate concern that AIDS has, and quite possibly it never will. The AIDS pandemic is of a vast order of suffering and consequence, whereas Ebola strikes quickly but also passes quickly.

Nonetheless, it is probably just a matter of time until there is an outbreak somewhere else in the world. If the disease is misdiagnosed in new places (what hospitals in the United States, for instance, are currently geared to look for it or related hemorrhagic diseases among patients?), the result could be an outbreak in which hundreds or thousands would die an excruciating death. At that point, would there be an international cry for a concerted effort to find a cure? There has been some promising research in the United States using steroids that seem effective in treating Ebola. Would it be greatly accelerated in those kinds of circumstances?

There is the broader precedent that might be set. Will the AIDS pandemic provide the international community with a "wake up call" regarding the consequences of not engaging the problem with all available resources earlier than it has? Will our retrospective on the devastation of Africa reveal that it might have been mitigated had we acted sooner and placed greater resources into finding vaccines and cures? Will our analysis provide some useful guidelines for dealing with present problems like Ebola before they emerge as larger, more hideous disasters? Or, will we require a major Ebola outbreak in a European or North American location before we mount a major effort aimed at eradicating the problem?

And then there is the future. AIDS and Ebola are unlikely to be the last major health problems with some or all the characteristics of a transstate issue. Will the experience to date inform the approaches the international community takes to the problem? It will be interesting to see.

Finally, there is a question that has only been addressed by indirection. Is the reason for the relative slowness and inattention to AIDS, and by extension Ebola, the result of where the outbreaks have taken place? When AIDS was detected in the United States, action was initially less rapid than it might have been because it was equated, rightly or wrongly, with the gay community. When the disease reached significant numbers in the heterosexual, "straight," community, then efforts appeared to redouble. Is that the problem, in a geographic sense, with AIDS in Africa? It is a terrible moral indictment to suggest the treatment of great suffering depends on where one is from, but that may have been the case with this disaster.

STUDY/DISCUSSION QUESTIONS

1. What is a transstate issue? What are its characteristics? How well does the AIDS pandemic in Africa meet the criteria?

2. How did the AIDS pandemic come about? How has it progressed? What are its demographic consequences?

3. Part of the problem of AIDS in Africa arises from impediments for dealing with it on that continent. What are these impediments? Are they similar or different from other transstate issue impediments? Can you think of other barriers to confronting the problem?

4. Think about the long-term effects of the pandemic on Africa. What will it take for Africa to recover from the effects (if it can)?

5. What international efforts have been undertaken to deal with the pandemic? Based on the experience of dealing with other transstate issues, what can one expect in the future? Have, for instance, the major pharmaceutical firms done a responsible job of responding to the pandemic?

6. Apply the experience of AIDS in Africa as a transstate issue to other current and potential health disasters like Ebola. What can we learn from one experience to help with others?

READING/RESEARCH MATERIAL

"AIDS Orphans in Africa." *The Washington Office on Africa*, 2000. http://www.woaafrica.org/Aorphans.htm

"AIDS Pharmaceuticals and AIDS in Africa." *The Washington Office on Africa,* 2000. http://www.woaafrica.ord/Atrade.htm

Christensen, John. "AIDS in Africa: Dying by the Numbers." *CNN.com,* November 8, 2000.

———. "Scarce Money, Few Drugs, Little Hope." *CNN.com,* November 8, 2000.

"Ebola." http://www.nyu.edu/eduation/mindsinmotion/ebola/htm

"International AIDS Conference Offers Good News about Cheap Drug Treatments." *CNN.com,* July 11, 2000.

Kaplan, Robert D. *The Coming Anarchy: Shattering the Dreams of the Post Cold War.* New York: Random House, 2000.

Murphy, Claire. "Bush's Affair with Abstinence." *BBC Online*, July 12, 2004.

"Report: AIDS Pandemic Declared Threat to U.S. National Security." *CNN.com*, April 30, 2000.

Snow, Donald M. *United States Foreign Policy: Politics Beyond the Water's Edge*, 3rd edition. Belmont, CA: Thomson Wadsworth, 2005.

Wehrwein, Peter. "AIDS Leaves Africa's Economic Future in Doubt." *CNN.com*, November 8, 2000.

Wooten, James. "Africa's AIDS Tragedy: Monumental Health Crisis May Become Moral Catastrophe." *CNN.com,* November 8, 2000.

WEB SITES

Official Web Site for United Nations Programme on HIV-AIDS

UNAIDS at http://www.unaids.org

Lists of reports, fact sheets, U.S. government agencies and other online resources

Global Issues: HIV/AIDS at http://usinfo.state.gov/topical/global/hiv

Regional AIDS updates and World Bank HIV-AIDS programs

World AIDS Day at http://worldbank.org/worldaidsday

Official U.S. government programs, activities, and publications

Office of National AIDS policy at http://www.whitehouse.gov/onap/aids.html

CHAPTER SIXTEEN

Understanding and Organizing a Post–September 11, 2001, World

THE CONTINUING CAMPAIGN AGAINST EVOLVING TERRORISM

PRÉCIS

The terrorist attacks of September 11, 2001, were a major trauma for the United States and the world at large, thrusting international religious terrorism onto center stage. It was a force that had been building for the better part of two decades but had previously not achieved the level of notoriety that the attacks evinced. Efforts to respond to the actions of Al Qaeda (the principal international terrorist group) have, in turn, caused the nature of the threat itself to change, a process of terrorism suppression and terrorist group adaptation that is likely to continue.

The purpose of this case is to investigate the nature of the terrorist problem, how it is changing, and what can be done about it. We begin by examining the dynamics of terrorism: what is it, what do terrorists seek to do, who are they, and what causes people to become terrorists? We then move to how terrorism has evolved as a problem since September 11 and what kinds of efforts we can mount against terrorism. Based on this information and perspectives raised throughout the case, we conclude by suggesting some elements of a comprehensive terrorism suppression strategy.

The tragic terrorist attack by the Islamic terrorist group Al Qaeda against the World Trade Center towers and the Pentagon on September 11, 2001, was a seminal international and national event. Internationally, it signaled a new and frightening escalation of a problem that had troubled Europe and other parts of the world for a long time, and it produced an enormous outpouring of sympathy and support for the United States as the victim (which has largely dissipated). Nationally, the attacks traumatized an American population suddenly aware of its vulnerability, even mortality, and spawned a major national priority to deal with this problem under the official sobriquet of the "global war on terrorism," or more compactly, GWOT.

The GWOT is now roughly four years old. It has had some successes, notably in capturing or otherwise suppressing elements of the old Al Qaeda network, but the problem of terrorism has by no means diminished, much less abated. The apparently monolithic threat posed by Al Qaeda is smaller than it was in 2001, but not the problem of terrorism itself: new permutations have arisen that are, if anything, more provocative and dangerous. Most groups share radical Islam as a foundation, but from Chechnya to Indonesia, new and different organizations have emerged as new challenges: international terrorism has become a hydra-headed beast.

The purpose of this case is to examine how the problem of international terrorism has evolved and is evolving and how to deal with it. In the process, we will describe in some detail aspects of the problem including defining terrorism and describing how it works, looking at different ways to think about terrorism, considering how it has evolved since September 11, and discussing how we deal with terrorism. This discussion is preface to the central purpose and task of the case, which is thinking about how to devise a comprehensive strategy to combat the terrorist threat. This exercise, toward which the rest of the case is aimed, will occur in the concluding section of the study.

Before turning to the examination of the phenomena, three related observations are necessary to condition the comments that follow. First, although we speak of a GWOT, the use of the term "war" is unfortunate, deceiving, and distorting. As the term is usually used, war refers to armed combat between combatants organized as states or states versus organized oppositions within states. War, in other words, is an action that pits people against other people, where the groups attack one another to impose their will on those other people. Terrorism, on the other hand, is a more intangible idea, a method by which people seek to accomplish goals. One cannot attack and subdue an idea. What one can do is to oppose and subdue people who act from ideas—we can make war on terrorist organizations like Al Qaeda (although their lack of a territorial base makes subduing them difficult); the best we can do with an idea is to discredit it.

The second observation flows from the first. The war analogy is further flawed because it implies that the opposition can be defeated: that the purpose of the war is to suppress and eliminate the opposition. Terrorism is an ancient practice that transcends efforts to suppress and defeat individual manifestations—defeating Al Qaeda or any other terrorist organization will not eliminate the phenomenon, just particular practitioners. There will always be terrorists somewhere, and the purpose of those opposed to terrorism is to *contain* the problem, not eliminate it.

Because terrorism cannot ever be eliminated altogether, then efforts in opposition to it are exercises in *risk reduction*, not risk elimination. Risk, for our purposes, is the difference between threats to our interests and our capabilities (or resources) to counter, contain, or eliminate those threats. Although the level of terrorist threat ebbs and flows across time, it is essentially always potentially greater than the resources available to effectively thwart all manifestations of the threat. Terrorism, to paraphrase former German Chancellor Helmut Schmidt, is a problem to be worked, not solved for once and for all.

Any strategy or policy that is aimed at "smashing" or "defeating" terrorism is bound to come up short.

In order to facilitate our discussion, we will largely use three different organizations or movements that have been deemed terrorist as the examples for the discussion. For obvious reasons, a good deal will focus on Islamist (more properly *jihadist*) Middle Eastern groups featuring Al Qaeda and its successors. Because they burst on the international public stage with such fury in 2004, the Chechen separatist movement will also be mentioned. To a lesser degree, the Indonesian terrorist movement Jemaah Islamiyah (first mentioned in Chapter 9) will also be included.

WHAT IS TERRORISM?

The first step in coming to grips with terrorism is defining the term. It is an important consideration, because so many phenomena in the contemporary international arena are labeled terrorist. This makes a definition particularly important as a means to measure whether a particular movement or act is terrorist or not. Without a set of criteria to tell us what does and does not constitute terrorism, we are left disabled in trying to make a determination.

This is not a merely semantic exercise. Take, for instance, the current emphasis on Chechen separatists and their campaign that the Russian government has called terrorist. Certainly, actions such as enlisting suicide terrorists to blow up two Russian airliners and the brutal siege of the school in Beslan in the Caucasus were hideous, brutal acts that comport with an understanding of terrorism, but is it correct to label the movement that commissioned and carried out the acts terrorist as a result? In context, when the Russian government of then President Boris Yeltsin used the Russian army to attack Chechnya in 1995 to wipe out the secessionist movement there (among other things, leveling the capital of Grozny) and current President Vladimir Putin renewed the campaign in 1999, there were widespread international accusations that the Russian government was terrorizing the Chechens and engaging in crimes against humanity (acts of state terrorism). So who is the terrorist here?

Having an agreed definition of terrorism would help answer this and similar questions about other potentially terrorist activities, but unfortunately, such an agreement does not exist. Rather, there are virtually as many different definitions as there are people and organizations making the distinctions. There are also some commonalities that recur across definers and will allow us to adopt a definition for present purposes. A few arguably representative examples will aid in drawing distinctions.

The United States Department of State offers the official governmental definition, which is applied in its annual survey of international terrorism. Its definition of terrorism is "premeditated, politically motivated violence perpetrated against noncombatant targets by subnational groups or clandestine agents, usually intended to influence an audience" (quoted in Krueger and Laitin). In *Attacking Terrorism,* coauthor Audrey Kurth Cronin says terrorism is distinguished by its political nature, its nonstate base, its targeting of innocent noncombatants, and the illegality of its acts. Jessica Stern, in *Terrorism in the Name of God,* defines terrorism as "an act or threat of violence against noncombatants with the objective of exacting revenge, intimidating, or otherwise influencing an audience." Alan Dershowitz (in *Why Terrorism Works*) offers no definition himself, but notes that definitions typically include reference to terrorist targets, perpetrators, and terrorist acts.

These definitions, and similar ones from others in the field, differ at the margins but have common cores. All share three common points of reference: terrorist acts (illegal, often hideous and atrocious), terrorist targets (usually innocent noncombatants), and terrorist purposes (political persuasion or influence). The only difference among them is whether they specify the nature of terrorists and their political base: the State Department, Cronin, and Dershowitz all identify terrorist organizations as non–state based actors. Cronin in particular emphasizes that "although states can terrorize, by definition they cannot be terrorists."

This brief discussion allows me to adopt my own definition, which incorporates the three components of terrorist acts, targets, and purposes, but not the criterion of terrorist organizations as non–state actors. Historically, states have been leading terrorists, either through the actions of government organizations like the secret police or in creating, commissioning, or controlling the activities of terrorists. In the contemporary setting, almost all terrorist organizations are non–state based, and this fact is at the heart of our difficulty in dealing with them. Defining terrorism as a non–state based activity, however, removes an important category of past (and conceivably future) activity from the definitional reach of terrorism. The non–state basis is a characteristic of modern terrorism, not a defining element.

For the rest of this case study, terrorism will be defined as "the commission of atrocious acts against a target population normally to gain compliance with some demands the terrorists insist upon." Terrorism thus consists of three related phenomena, each of which must be present in some manner for something to be considered an act of terrorism. The fourth element in other definitions, perpetrators of terrorism, is implicit in the three criteria. Discussing each helps enliven an understanding of what constitutes terrorism.

Terrorist Acts

The first part of the definition refers to *terrorist acts*, which are the visible manifestation of terrorism and the part of the dynamic of the phenomena with which most people are most familiar. Several comments can be made about terrorist acts.

One comment is that terrorist acts are distinguished from other political expressions in that they are uniformly illegal. Terrorist acts are intended to upset the normalcy of life through destructive acts aimed at either injuring or killing people or destroying things. Regardless of the professed underlying motives of terrorists (normally couched in lofty political terms), the actions they commit—and especially their focus on noncombatants whose only "guilt" is being part of the targeted group—break laws and are subject to criminal prosecution. By raising the rhetoric of terrorist actions to acts of war (currently holy war or *jihad*), terrorists may seek to elevate what they do to a higher plane ("one man's terrorist is another man's freedom fighter"), but the simple fact remains that terrorist acts are criminal in nature.

The general purpose of terrorist acts is to frighten the target audience; indeed, the word terrorism is derived from the Latin root *terrere*, which means to frighten. The method of inducing fright is through the commission of random, unpredictable acts of violence that seek to induce such fear that those who witness the acts (or learn of them) will conclude that compliance with terrorist demands is preferable to living with the fear of being future victims. Acts of terrorism are not particularly aimed at the actual victims themselves (who are normally randomly selected and whose fate does not "matter" to the terrorist) but at the audience who views the actions. As Brian Jenkins puts it, "*Terrorists want a lot of people watching and a lot of people listening, and not a lot of people dead.*" [emphasis in original] The dynamic of inducing this fright is the disruption of the predictability and safety of life within society, one of whose principal functions is to make existence predictable and safe. Ultimately, a major purpose of terrorism may be to undermine this vital fiber of society.

Beyond frightening the target audience, individual terrorist acts are committed for a variety of reasons, not limited to the normally expressed political goals of particular terrorist organizations. Al Qaeda, for instance, says its most fundamental goal is the expulsion of the West (especially the United States) from the holy lands of Islam, and that its acts (especially those serving bin Laden's *fatwa* calling for killing Americans everywhere) are intended to further that goal. But that is not the only motivation for particular actions.

Terrorists may also act for a variety of other reasons. Jenkins provides a list of six other, generally less lofty, purposes for terrorist actions. First, terrorist actions may be aimed at exacting special concessions, such as ransom or the release of prisoners (generally members of the terrorist group), or at publicizing a message. The capture and threatened (or actual) beheading of foreigners by Iraqi resistance groups to force countries to withdraw their nationals from Iraq is a case in point in the use of terrorist actions for gaining concessions. In that case, the capture of foreign nationals was at the base of demands for prisoner release and to force foreign countries to withdraw from the international relief effort in that country. Jemaah Islamiyah carried out its 2004 attack on the Australian embassy and promptly announced that it would perpetrate similar attacks if its leader, Abu Bakar Bashir, was not released from prison.

Second, terrorists may act to gain publicity for their causes. Before Palestinian terrorists kidnapped a series of airliners and then launched an attack on the Israeli compound at the Munich Olympics in 1972, hardly anyone outside the region had ever heard of the Palestinian cause; the terrorist actions got them that global awareness. The publicity may be intended to remind a world that has shifted its attention away from a particular group and its activities that it is still active and that it is still pursuing its goals. One of the apparent reasons for the spate of Chechen violence in 2004 for which Chechen leader Shamil Basayev claims credit was to remind the world that the Chechen movement to gain independence from Russia is still alive.

A third, and more fundamental, purpose of terrorist acts is to cause widespread disorder that demoralizes society and breaks down the social order in a country. This, of course, is an ambitious purpose, and one that presumably can only be undertaken through a widespread campaign that includes a large number of terrorist acts, and it is the kind of objective most likely to be carried out by governments or semigovernmental actors. The suicide terror campaign by Hamas against Israeli civilians (and the Israeli counterattacks against Palestinians) could be an example of terrorism for this purpose.

A fourth, more tactical use of terrorism is to provoke overreaction by a government in the form of repressive action, reprisals, and overly brutal counterterrorism that may lead to the overthrow of the reactive government. This was a favorite tactic of the Viet Cong in the Vietnam War, and it evoked the ironic analogy of building schools during the day (as a way to pacify the population) and then bombing those schools at night (because they became the source of Viet Cong actions after nightfall). It is not clear that some of the acts committed against American forces in Iraq by the resistance have not been to try to elicit American overreactions and thus fuel anti-Americanism among Iraqi citizens.

A fifth purpose of terror may be to enforce obedience and cooperation within a target population. Campaigns of terror directed by the governments of states against their own citizens can have this purpose, which is often assigned to a secret police or similar paramilitary organizations. The actions of the KGB in the Soviet Union, the Gestapo and other similar organizations in Nazi Germany, and the infamous death squads in Argentina during the 1960s and 1970s are all examples of the use of government terror to intimidate and frighten their own population into submission. At a less formal governmental level, many of the actions of the Ku Klux Klan during the latter nineteenth and early twentieth centuries against African Americans would qualify as well.

Jenkins's sixth purpose of terrorist action is punishment. Terrorists often argue that an action they take is aimed at a particular person or place because that person or institution is somehow guilty of a particular transgression and is thus being meted out appropriate punishment for what the terrorists consider a crime. Although the Israeli government would be appalled at the prospects of calling its recently rescinded counterterrorist campaign to bulldoze the homes of the families of suicide terrorists (or bombing the homes of dissident leaders) as acts of terror, from the vantage point of the Palestinian targets of the attacks, they certainly must seem so.

Stern adds a seventh motivation that is internal to the terrorist organization: morale. Like any other organization, and especially terrorist groups in which the "operatives" are generally young and not terribly mature, it may be necessary from time to time to carry out a terrorist attack simply to demonstrate to the membership the continuing potency of the group as a way to keep the membership focused and morale high. As Stern puts it, "Attacks sometimes have more to do with rousing the troops than terrorizing the victims." Improving or maintaining morale may also have useful spin-off effects, such as helping in recruiting new members to the group or in raising funds to support the organization's activities.

A final comment about terrorist acts is whether, or to what degree, they are successful. The answer is rather clearly a mixed one that has to do with the scale of the actions and their intended results. In some cases, terrorism has been highly successful, but usually in relatively small ways where the terrorists' purposes were bounded and compliance with their demands was not overly odious. To cite one example, terrorist demands to release what they view as political prisoners (usually jailed members of their group) have, on occasion, been complied with, although some countries are more prone to comply than others. Likewise, the Iraqi resistance's campaign of kidnapping and threatening to execute foreign nationals if the countries did not leave the country has been somewhat successful and will almost certainly be duplicated in the future.

It is when terrorists make large demands and follow them up with sizable actions that they tend to be less successful. When terrorists come to pose a basic perceived threat (often because of the audacity of what they have done) to the target country, the reaction by the target may be, and usually is, increased resolve rather than compliance. The September 11, 2001, attacks, after all, did not result in a groundswell of sentiment for the United States to quit the Middle East (especially Saudi Arabia) as bin Laden and Al Qaeda demanded; rather, the attacks stiffened the will of the country to resist. This poses something of a quandary to the terrorist: the more ambitious he becomes, the more likely he is to increase opposition to achievement of his goals. On the other hand, sizing terrorist acts downward to levels that will not increase resolve may result in positive, but less than satisfying, outcomes.

What this discussion of terrorist acts seeks to demonstrate is that, like virtually everything else about the subject, the acts that terrorists commit occur for a variety of reasons. Some of these are more purposive and "noble" than others, but it is not clear what may motivate a particular action. Moreover, different reasons may motivate different groups at different times and under different circumstances. Knowing that a terrorist attack has occurred, in other words, does not necessarily tell you why it has been committed.

Terrorist Targets

Akin to the military objectives in more conventional war, the targets of terrorists can be divided into two related categories. The first is people, and the objective is to kill, maim, or otherwise cause some members of the target population to suffer as an example for the rest of the population. The second category involves physical targets, attacks against which are designed to disrupt and destroy societal capabilities and to demonstrate the vulnerability of the target society. The two categories are obviously related in that most of the physical targets worth attacking contain people who will be killed or injured in the process. As well, attacking either category demonstrates the inability of the target population to provide protection for its members and valued artifices, thus questioning the efficacy of resisting terrorist demands.

There are subtle differences and problems associated with concentrating on one category or another of target. Clearly, attacks directly intended to kill or injure people are the most personal and evoke the greatest emotion in the target population, including the will to resist and to seek vengeance. From the vantage point of the terrorist, the reason to attack people (beyond some simple blood lust) is to attack their will to resist the demands that terrorists make. In Snow and Drew, we refer to this as *cost-tolerance,* the level of suffering one is willing to endure in the face of some undesirable situation. In the case of terrorist targeting, the terrorist seeks to exceed the target's cost-tolerance by making the target conclude that it is less painful (physically or mentally) to accede to the terrorist's demands than it is to continue to resist those demands. The terrorist seeks to exceed cost-tolerance by maximizing the level of fear and anxiety that the target experiences because of the effects (often hideous) of attacks on other members of the target group. The terrorist wants the target group to become so afraid of being the next victim that they cave in and accept the terrorist demands. If cost-tolerance is exceeded, the terrorist wins; if the target remains resolute, the terrorist does not succeed (which may not be the same thing as saying the terrorist loses).

Overcoming cost-tolerance is not an easy task, and it often fails. For one thing, terrorist organizations are generally small with limited resources, meaning that they usually lack the wherewithal to attack and kill a large enough portion of the target population to make members of that population become individually fearful enough to tip the scales (blowing up people on airplanes may be a partial exception). One of the great fears associated with terrorist groups obtaining and using weapons of mass destruction is that such a turn of events would change that calculus. For another thing, attacking and killing innocent members of a target group (at least innocent from the vantage point of the group) may (and usually does) infuriate its members and increase, rather than decrease, the will to resist. That was certainly the case during World War II in Germany, where constant aerial bombardment failed to destroy the German people's will to survive.

Standing up to terrorist attacks on human targets is not always easy, as the example of hostage-taking in Iraq shows. In that instance, officials are placed in an obvious quandary. On one hand, when hostages are taken and their execution threatened if some demands are unmet, there is an obvious and understandable instinct to try to save the hostage(s), and in the absence of an ability to rescue them physically (which, in the Iraqi cases, was apparently impossible), the only means available is to accede to their demands (have cost-tolerance exceeded). On the other hand, doing so means the terrorists succeed and are likely to be emboldened to do the same thing again, as was the case in Iraq when several countries pulled their workers out after some of their nationals were kidnapped and threatened with execution. The Americans and British refused to accede in these demands and had a number of their citizens executed. In those cases, the terrorists did not prevail, but they also did not visibly lose, because (at this writing) none of them had been captured and brought to justice for their deeds.

When the targets are physical things rather than people per se, the problems and calculations change. When the target of terrorists is a whole society, the range of potential targets is virtually boundless. In attacking places, the terrorist seeks to deprive the target population of whatever pleasure or life-sustaining or life-enhancing value the particular target may provide. The list of what we used to call *countervalue* targets when speaking of nuclear targeting (things people value, such as their lives and what makes those lives commodious) covers a very broad range of objects, from hydroelectric plants to athletic stadiums, from nuclear power generators to military facilities, from highways to research facilities, and so on. Compiling a list for any large community is a very sobering experience.

It is unreasonable to assume that the physical potential target list for any country can be made uniformly invulnerable. There are simply too many targets, and the means of protecting them are sufficiently discrete that there is little overlap in function (protecting a football stadium from bombers may or may not have much carryover in terms of protecting nuclear power plants from seizure). As a result, there will always be a gap between the potential threats and the ability to negate all those threats, and the consequence is a certain level of risk for which there are simply inadequate resources to cancel.

Terrorist Objectives

The final element in the definition of terrorism is the objectives, or reasons, for which terrorists do what they do. These objectives, of course, are directed against the target population and involve the commission of terrorist acts, so that the discussion of objectives cannot be entirely divorced from the other two elements of what constitutes terrorism.

For present purposes, our discussion of terrorist objectives will refer to the broader outcomes that terrorists seek (or say they seek) to accomplish. Objectives are the long-range reasons that terrorists wage campaigns of terrorism. In the short run, terrorists may engage in particular actions for a variety of reasons, as already noted (group morale or recruitment, for instance). What they seek ultimately to accomplish is the province of terrorist objectives.

It will be useful to make a distinction here among types of goals terrorists pursue. The major objectives of terrorists, their ultimate or strategic goals, refer to the long-term political objectives to which they aspire. For Al Qaeda, for instance, the removal of Americans from the Arabian Peninsula is a strategic goal; for Chechen separatists, independence from Russia is the ultimate objective. At the same time, terrorists also pursue interim, or tactical, goals, which generally involve the successful commission of terrorist acts against the target population. The purpose, in the case of tactical objectives, is to demonstrate continuing viability and potency, to remind the target of their presence and menace, and to erode resistance to their strategic goals.

Because most terrorist groups are ultimately political in their purposes, terrorist objectives are political as well. To paraphrase the Clausewitzian dictum that war is politics by other means, so too is terrorism politics by other, extreme, means. Likewise, the objectives that terrorists pursue are extreme, at least to the target population if not to the terrorists themselves. Sometimes, terrorist objectives are widely known and clearly articulated, and at other times they are not. Ultimately, however, campaigns of terror gain their meaning in the pursuit of some goal or goals, and their success or failure is measured to the extent that those goals are achieved.

Terrorism is, of course, the method of the militarily weak and conceptually unacceptable. The extremely asymmetrical nature of terrorist actions arises from the fact that terrorists cannot compete with their targets by the accepted methods of the target society. Terrorists lack the military resources to engage in open warfare, at which they would be easily defeated, or in the forum of public discourse and decision, because their objectives are unacceptable, distasteful, or even bizarre to the target population. Thus, the terrorist can neither impose his purposes on the target nor persuade the target to adopt whatever objectives he wants. These facts narrow his options.

The fact that terrorist objectives are politically objectionable to the target sets up the confrontation between the terrorists and the target. Normally, terrorist goals are stated in terms of changing policies (Palestinian statehood or the right to repatriation within Israel, for example) or laws (releasing classes of detained people)—changes that the majority in the target state finds unacceptable. Because the terrorists are in a minority, they cannot bring about the changes they demand by normal electoral or legislative means, and they are likely to be viewed as so basically lunatic and unrealistic by the target audience that it will not accord seriousness to the demands or those who make them. To the terrorists, of course, the demands make perfect sense, and they are frustrated and angered by the treatment their demands are given. The stage is thus set for confrontation.

Terrorists achieve their objectives by overcoming the will of the target population to resist, or what we have already called cost-tolerance. The campaign of terrorist threats and acts is intended to convince the target population that acceding to the terrorist demands is preferable to the continuing anxiety and fear of future terrorism. If the target population concludes that giving in to the terrorist demands is better than continuing to resist, cost-tolerance has been exceeded, and the terrorist wins. If continuing resistance (even increased defiance) is the outcome, then cost-tolerance is not exceeded and the terrorists do not succeed.

The failure to achieve strategic objectives is not the same thing as total failure, however. The successful terrorism of a large society by a small group of terrorists is a tall order, and one for which the terrorists (almost by definition) do not have the resources to achieve. At its zenith, after all, Al Qaeda consisted of probably less than 10,000 active members, who could hardly bring the United States to its knees. Terrorism is, after all, the "tactic of the weak," and there are real limitations on the extent of the danger such groups can physically pose.

Determining whether terrorists achieve their goals or fail is complicated by the contrast between the tactical and strategic levels of objectives, making the compilation of a "score card" difficult. Modern terrorists have rarely been successful at the strategic level of attaining long-range objectives. Al Qaeda has not forced the United States from the Arabian Peninsula (although American presence is declining), Russia has not granted Chechnya independence, and Jemaah Islamiyah has yet to achieve a sectarian Islamic state in Indonesia. At the same time, the terrorist record at achieving tactical objectives (carrying out terrorist attacks) is, if not perfect, not a total failure either. As long as terrorists continue to exist and to achieve some of their goals, they remain a force against their targets. Thus, the competition between terrorists and their targets over the accomplishment of terrorist objectives continues to exist within a kind of netherworld where neither wins or loses decisively and thus both can claim some success: "We do not give in to terrorism" defined as resisting terrorist strategic objectives, versus "We succeed against the infidels" defined as the successful commission of acts of terrorism.

THINKING ABOUT TERRORISM: PERSPECTIVES AND CAUSES

For most of us, terrorism is such an alien phenomenon that we have difficulty conceptualizing exactly what it is and why people would engage in acts of terrorism, up to and including committing terrorist acts that include their own planned deaths (suicide). And yet, the historic and contemporary public records are strewn with enough instances of terrorism to make confronting the conceptual "beast" necessary for understanding and coping with the reality around us.

Terrorism is too complex a phenomenon to capture entirely in this brief case study, but one can gain some insights into it by viewing it through two lenses. The first will be by examining three perspectives that try to capture terrorism and its place in international politics. The second is to look at three of the explanations that are commonly put forward to answer the question, "why is there terrorism?"

Three Perspectives

Where does terrorism fit into domestic and international politics? Is terrorism ever a legitimate enterprise, or is it always something outside the realm of legitimacy? Answers to these questions depend on one's perspective, as captured in a typecasting of terrorism as legitimate or illegitimate behavior. There are two polar opposite perspectives that are typically the basis for such a discussion: terrorism as crime and terrorism as war. To these two distinctions, we will add a third, which is terrorism as a specific kind of warfare, asymmetrical war.

The basic distinction serves two purposes. On the one hand, it speaks to the legitimacy of terrorism: a depiction of terrorism as crime clearly stamps it as illegal and thus illegitimate, whereas depicting it as war (of one sort or another) raises its status among actions of states and groups. The distinction also suggests the appropriate approach to dealing with terrorism either as a legal system issue or military problem.

The *terrorism as crime* perspective focuses on terrorist acts and their acceptability, with an emphasis on their illegality. All terrorist acts against people and things violate legal norms in all organized societies: it is against the law to murder people or to blow up things, after all, regardless of why one does so. If acts of terrorism are, at their core, criminal acts, then terrorists are little more than common criminals and should be treated as such. Terrorism thus becomes at heart a criminal problem, and terrorists are part of the criminal justice system subject to arrest, incarceration, trial, and, where appropriate, imprisonment or execution.

Terrorists simultaneously reject and accept this depiction. They reject the notion that what they do is criminal, because their acts—while technically illegal—are committed for higher political purposes, as discussed earlier. Terrorists kill people, but—in their minds—they do not murder them. Terrorists are not criminals; rather, they are warriors (in contemporary times, "holy" warriors). Thinking in this manner elevates the status of the terrorist from criminal to soldier, a far more exalted and acceptable position. At the same time, terrorists prefer for target societies to think of them as criminals in those situations where they are captured and brought to justice (assuming the capturing society adheres to its own criminal procedures, which is not always the case). The reason is simple: at least in the West, criminal measures are considerably more stringent in procedural and evidentiary senses than military law, affording the terrorists greater protections under the law and making their successful prosecution more difficult. Attempts in the United States to relax criminal safeguards regarding terrorists seek to change that status but have created controversy in civil rights and liberties terms.

Terrorists prefer the second perspective, *terrorism as war*. This viewpoint emphasizes the political nature of terrorism and terrorist acts, adopting the Clausewitzian paraphrase that "terrorism is politics by other means." If one accepts the basic premise of this perspective, then terrorist acts are not crimes but acts of war, and as such are judged by the rules and laws of war rather than by criminal standards. The interactions between terrorist organizations and their targets are thus warlike, military affairs. Whereas outside situations of war killing is always illegal, within war it is permissible, at least within certain bounds regarding who and in what conditions killing is deemed permissible.

The current global war on terrorism implicitly accepts this perspective, if not its implications. Within the GWOT, the term "war" is used rather loosely and almost allegorically rather than literally, and almost all apostles of the designation do not view terrorists as warriors but rather as wanton criminals to be brought to justice or to their demise. Within the antiterrorism campaign in Afghanistan, for instance, members (or alleged members) of Al Qaeda were not treated as prisoners of war, which would have afforded them certain legal rights under the Geneva Conventions on War, but instead treated under the legally vague designation of "detainees," who apparently do not possess Geneva Convention protections.

The problem of treating terrorism as crime or as war is that, in most cases, it is both. Terrorists do engage in criminal acts but they do so for reasons more normally associated with war. This fact suggests that there should be a third way of depicting terrorism, which we will call *terrorism as asymmetrical war*. As Chapter 10 suggested, asymmetrical warfare is different from the conventional forms of warfare that are covered by the traditional laws of war; indeed, a major characteristic of asymmetrical warfare is the rejection of traditional norms and rules as part of the attempt to level the playing field of conflict. As noted earlier, for instance, the asymmetrical warrior does not distinguish between combatants and noncombatants, just as the terrorist considers all members of the target group as equally culpable and thus eligible for attack. Terrorism was depicted as one form of asymmetrical warfare in Chapter 10 because it is a tactic of a movement that cannot possibly compete under the acceptable rules of engagement.

Terrorism as asymmetrical war is a hybrid of the other two perspectives. The terrorists' rejection of accepted rules means they can treat their actions as acts of war while the target society rejects this contention and can continue to consider their actions as crimes against mankind. The status of asymmetrical warriors as warriors may be ambiguous within the rules of war, but leaving their actions within criminal jurisdiction satisfies the target society's depiction while affording captured terrorists the legal protections they seek. This perspective also allows terrorism to be depicted as both a criminal *and* a military problem, which it is, and thus to allow both law enforcement and military responses to terrorists. The only difficulty is in determining the appropriate mix of criminal justice and military responses generally and in specific situations.

Three Causes

What motivates individuals and groups to become terrorists and to engage in the often gruesome and dangerous acts that typify terrorism is also the source of considerable speculation and disagreement among experts and lay observers. Much of the difficulty in making such assessments derives from the absolute inability most of us have in imagining why anyone would become a terrorist and kill what, from our perspective, are innocent people. Whatever leads people to become terrorists is so alien to us that we cannot draw analogies from our own experiences or those arising in our society as we know it (which has, of course, produced its fair share of terrorists).

Three vantage points on what causes people and groups to adopt terrorism are often put forward, reflecting in some ways the disciplinary vantage points that various students of the phenomenon represent. Most of these explanations surfaced during the 1960s and 1970s, during the third or "New Left" wave of modern terrorism, according to David C. Rapoport (the first two were anarchism and anticolonialism, the fourth and present wave is religious). This is worth noting because the 1960s and 1970s tended to be more tolerant, even sympathetic, with politically aberrant movements than is true today. At any rate, terrorism is typified as primarily a societal, a psychological, or a political problem. The three explanations are neither mutually exclusive nor agreed upon.

The *societal* argument is that social conditions provide the breeding grounds for terrorism. Societies that consistently underachieve, fail to provide adequate material or spiritual advances or hope, and in which the citizens live in an unending and hopeless condition of deprivation provide a kind of intellectual and physical "swamp" in which terrorism "breeds" a ready supply of potential followers who are willing recruits for terrorism causes that promise to bring meaning and direction to their lives. These "failed societies" may oppress specific groups that are even more prone to the appeals of terrorism recruiters. A variant of this argument also suggests that some societies' values may be better suited for producing terrorists than others. In the contemporary setting, for instance, some observers note that Islam has a more prominent, positive role for religious martyrdom than other religions, making the terrorist path and especially suicide terrorism more acceptable than it would be in other places.

If this argument is substantially correct, it leads to a potential solution to the terrorism problem: if the wretched conditions are removed and the society ceases to be a failed one, then the conditions that breed the terrorists may also be removed. This is the heart of the argument for "draining the swamp" as a way to combat terrorism. The tool for doing so is the infusion of (probably massive) amounts of developmental assistance to create the physical basis for greater prosperity and a sense of meaningful futures: people do not volunteer for potential self-immolation (such as suicide terrorist missions) if they have hope for the future. In the current debate, feeding resources into the Pakistani education system to create a peaceful alternative to the religious *madrassa* schools that teach anti-Americanism is a prime example of the application of the societal argument.

Critics point to a hole in this explanation of what creates terrorism. That argument is that many modern terrorists are not the product of societal deprivation. Sixteen of the nineteenth September 11 terrorists, after all, were Saudi citizens, who could hardly be accused of coming from deprived backgrounds. Such an observation is obviously true but it does not completely negate the argument that inferior societal conditions produce terrorists. Rather, the observation conditions the argument by saying that *not all* terrorists come from societally deprived backgrounds. Most terrorist leaders, it appears, and some of their followers come from middle, even upper-class backgrounds (bin Laden, for instance), but a lot of their followers indeed emerge from the "swamp."

The second explanation moves from the group to the individual. Rather than focusing on failed societies, the *psychological* argument shifts the emphasis from the failed society to failed peoples. The psychological argument is not entirely divorced from the societal argument, in that it basically contends that there are certain traits in people, certain psychological states, that make them more susceptible to the terrorist appeal and thus more willing to commit terrorist acts than is true of other individuals. Because not everyone who possesses these traits becomes a terrorist (lots of people are frustrated but do not react by becoming suicide terrorists, for instance), then there must be triggering societal conditions that activate these tendencies.

Terrorist profiling is a clear example of the psychological explanation of terrorism. In many contemporary arguments, for instance, it has been observed that many of the individuals who perpetrate religious-based terrorism from Middle Eastern settings share several characteristics. Most of the terrorist followers (as opposed to the leaders who recruit, train, and direct them) tend to be teenaged boys with high school educations who do not have jobs at all or if they do, jobs that pay them insufficiently poorly that they have few prospects. They tend to be unmarried with few prospects of finding a wife (often because they cannot support one). They also tend to have low self-esteem intermixed with a high sense of helplessness and hopelessness about their futures. These perceptions lead to a high sense of humiliation, embarrassment, and impotence toward the future. Individuals with this kind of profile are believed to be especially vulnerable to recruitment by terrorist leaders who promise to restore meaning and purpose and thus a sense of self-esteem. A particularly troubling recent trend has been the emergence of females with similar profiles in terrorist roles.

This profile is particularly disturbing, because the Middle East has a population "bulge" that includes a large number of young males who meet the basic enabling characteristics described in the profile. Moreover, the societal conditions in most Middle Eastern states offer few prospects for reducing the conditions, notably of employment, to turn the situation around. As long as life does not contain meaningful prospects that can prevent the triggering of psychological processes leading to terrorism, there will be fertile breeding grounds for new generations of terrorists. It might be added that there are far fewer studies that suggest similar profiles for terrorist leaders, except that they come from higher socioeconomic situations.

The third explanation is *political*, that it is failed governments that produce the societal and psychological conditions in which terrorism emerges or that produce conditions in which terrorists emerge or are nurtured. Although it hardly exhausts the possibilities, state action can lead to terrorism in two ways. First, state oppression (indeed, including the use of terrorism *by* the government) may lead to political opposition that must be clandestine and resort to terrorism as their only means of survival (terrorism as the tool of the asymmetrical warrior). The Chechen resistance would certainly view itself in this manner. In other cases, the government may be so inept or ineffective that it provides a haven for terrorists to exist without being able to do anything about it. The ineffectiveness of the Pakistani government in suppressing remnants of Al Qaeda and other sympathetic groups in the mountainous areas bordering on Afghanistan is an example. In yet other cases, sympathetic governments may even provide refuge and sanctuary for terrorist organizations. The relationship between Afghanistan's Taliban regime and Al Qaeda is a frequently cited example.

As with the other explanations, the political model also suggests remedies. If it is bad governments that create, put up with, or consort with terrorists, then there are two ways to deal with the problem. One is to convince the government to abandon the terrorists, quit creating them, or capture/apprehend them, using either positive inducements (military or economic assistance) or threats of some form of sanctions to induce compliance. This has been the basic American strategy with Pakistan. If those efforts fail, a second option may be to replace those governments with more compliant regimes. That, of course, is at least part of the rationale for the American invasion of Iraq.

As noted, these explanations are not mutually exclusive. Failed governments have failed societal conditions as one of their causes and consequences, and it is failure at these levels that creates the triggering conditions for psychological forces that activate terrorists. It may be, as well, that these explanations are not comprehensive, but may be characteristic of the 1960s and 1970s variants of terrorism, which were, among other things, noticeably secular rather than religious. Strategies for dealing with the terrorism problem include sorting out the influences of various explanations and deciding how well they apply to the current and evolving forms of terrorism.

EVOLVING TERRORISM SINCE SEPTEMBER 11

The events of September 11 understandably focused national attention on a specific terrorist threat posed by Al Qaeda. The focus was natural given the audacity and shock value of the actual attacks and by the novelty of an organization such as Al Qaeda. To the extent that Americans had much of any understanding of terrorism, it was associated with more "classical" forms, such as highly politicized anticolonialist movements like the Irish Republican Army (IRA), state terrorism in the form of suppression by totalitarian regimes like Hitler's Germany or Stalin's Soviet Union, or isolated anarchist assassinations or individual acts like the bombing of the Murrah Federal Building in Oklahoma City.

Understanding the nature of the threat has been difficult for at least two reasons. First, the contemporary form of terrorism is different from anything we have encountered before. It is non–state based terrorism that does not arise from specific political communities or jurisdictions but instead flows across national boundaries like oil slipping under doors. This makes it conceptually difficult to make it concrete and to counter it. It is also religious, showing signs of fanaticism that are present in all religious communities (including our own historically) but are alien to our ability to conceptualize. Slaughter in the name of God goes beyond most of our intellectual frameworks. It is also fanatically anti-American and thus in sharp contrast to the general pro-Americanism that we at least believed dominated the end of the twentieth century. It also employs methods such as suicide terrorism that, if not historically unique, are deviant enough to go beyond most of our abilities to conjure.

Second, our understanding is made more difficult by the changing nature of contemporary terrorist opponents. The Al Qaeda of 2001 was hard enough for us to understand, but it has evolved greatly since then. Partly this is because international efforts since 2001 have been quite effective in dismantling the old Al Qaeda structure by capturing and killing many of its members. This success, however, has caused the threat to disperse and transform itself into forms that we find even less recognizable and thus more difficult to identify and attack. Thus, a discussion of organizational evolution is necessary to clarify the nature of the current terrorist threat.

Jessica Stern, in *Terrorism in the Name of God*, lays out the requirements for a successful terrorist organization. The effectiveness of a terrorist organization is dependent on two qualities: resiliency (the ability to withstand the loss of parts of its membership or workforce) and capacity (the ability to optimize the scale and impact of terrorist attacks). The larger the scale of operations that the terrorist organization can carry out without large losses to its members through capture or death, the more effective the organization is. Conversely, if an organization can only carry out small, relatively insignificant acts while having large portions of its membership captured or killed, the less effective it is.

Resiliency and capacity are clearly related. For a terrorist organization to carry out large operations such as the coordinated attacks on Spanish commuter trains in 2004, it must devise a sophisticated, coordinated plan involving a number of people or cells who must communicate with one another both to plan and to execute the attack. The Achilles' heel in terrorist activity is penetration of the organization by outsiders, and the key element is the interruption of communication that allows penetration into the organization and movement through the hierarchy to interfere with and destroy the organization and its ability to carry out attacks (in other words, to reduce its resiliency). The most effective way for the terrorist organization to avoid penetration is to minimize communications that can be intercepted, but doing this comes at the expense of the sophistication and extent of its actions (reduction in capacity).

The result is a dilemma that is changing the face of contemporary terrorist organizations. Historically, according to Stern and others, most terrorist organizations have followed an organizational form known as the *commander-cadre* (or *hierarchical*) model. This form of organization is not dissimilar to the way complex organizations are structured everywhere: executives (commanders) organize and plan activities (terrorist attacks) and pass instructions downward through the organization for implementation by employees (cadres). In order to try to maintain levels of secrecy that improve resiliency, terrorist organizations structure themselves so that any one level of the organization (cell) knows only of the cell directly above and below it.

Commander-cadre arrangements have the advantages of other large, complex organizations. They are able to coordinate activities maximizing capacity (the African embassy bombings, for instance); can organize recruitment and absorb, indoctrinate, and train recruits; and can carry out ancillary activities such as fundraising, dealing with cooperative governments, and engaging in commerce and other forms of activity. The disadvantage of these organizations is that they may become more permeable by outside agencies because of their need to communicate among units. Modern electronics become a double-edged sword for the terrorist: things like cell phones facilitate communications in executing attacks, but those communications can be intercepted, leading to resiliency-threatening penetration. In fact, electronic surveillance of terrorist communication has been extremely helpful in the pursuit of Al Qaeda to the point that the old organization of the 1990s, which basically followed the commander-cadre model, has been reduced in size "from about 4,000 members to a few hundred," according to Gunaratna in the Summer 2004 *Washington Quarterly.*

The result of the campaign against Al Qaeda has been to cause it to adapt, to become what Stern refers to as the "protean enemy" that has "shown a surprising willingness to adapt its mission" and to alter its organizational form to make it more resilient. Al Qaeda is no longer a hierarchically organized entity that plans and carries out terrorist missions. Instead, it has adopted elements of the alternate form of terrorist organization, the *virtual network* or *leaderless resistance* model and has dispersed itself into a series of smaller, loosely affiliated terrorist organizations (Jemaah Islamiyah is a prime example) that draw inspiration from Al Qaeda. The announcement by Iraqi resistance leader Abu Musab al-Zarqawi of allegiance to bin Laden's goals in October 2004 (Zarqawi is sometimes mentioned as a possible successor to bin Laden) may be another case in point of this evolution. If it ever was a monolithic dragon, Al Qaeda has instead become a hydra-headed monster.

The virtual network organizational model was apparently developed in the United States by the Aryan Nation hate group. Its problem was that its membership was constantly being penetrated and disrupted by law enforcement organizations like the FBI, which used extensive electronic surveillance (wire tapping) to uncover and suppress illegal Aryan Nation activity and to prosecute both the planners and the executioners of its actions. The solution for Aryan Nation, recently adapted and adopted by international terrorist organizations like Al Qaeda, is the virtual network/leaderless resistance.

The core of this model is the reduction of direct communications between the leadership and its members. Rather than planning operations and instructing operatives to carry out plans, leaders instead exhort their followers to act through public pronouncements (for instance, through the use of Web Sites). Leaders may issue general calls to action, but they have no direct communications with followers that can be intercepted or used as the basis for suppression or conspiracy indictments. The leader has no direct knowledge or control of individual terrorist acts, which he or she may inspire but not direct.

The "Army of God" movement in the United States is an example; its leaders condemn abortion doctors and suggest to followers that they should be suppressed, including the use of physical violence. The hope is that a devoted follower like Eric Rudolph (indicted for killing an off-duty policeman in an attack against a Birmingham, Alabama, abortion clinic in 2000) will be inspired to carry out the mission. The advantage of this model is that it maximizes the resiliency of the organization and protects its leadership from capture or prosecution; its principal drawback is reduced capacity to order specific "desirable" actions (this is also a problem for law enforcement, because nobody but the individual inspired terrorist knows in advance what he or she plans to do).

With the success of terrorist suppression after September 11, Al Qaeda and its affiliates have apparently adopted some of the characteristics of a virtual network. Leaders like bin Laden continue to organize some operations in the traditional commander-cadre manner, but increasingly, bin Laden is seen as a virtual leader whose principal role is to make pronouncements that inspire the membership and that of affiliated organizations to continue the *jihad* that bin Laden has declared and continues to champion.

Part of this shift has taken the form of a dispersion of terrorist organizations. During the 1980s and 1990s, bin Laden and his associates trained literally thousands of religious terrorists, who have now formed movements of their own in their home countries. Levels of affiliation and control of these "franchises"—as they are sometimes known— vary considerably, but they do change the nature of the terrorism problem. Cutting off one "head" (capturing or killing bin Laden, for instance) would not decapitate the movement he leads, because other heads exist and doubtless yet other leaders would arise to replace and play the role of the fallen leader.

The nature of the terrorist threat is thus changing. It is becoming more diffuse as terrorist organizations become more adaptable organizationally and otherwise (become more "protean" in Stern's term). This means that the nature of trying to control or dismantle the problem of terrorism is becoming more complex as well.

DEALING WITH TERRORISM: THE GWOT

There is great rhetorical agreement in the United States and elsewhere that the threat posed by international terrorism—which primarily means the threat posed by militant

Islamic terrorist groups and most popularly associated with Al Qaeda—must and will be defeated: we are committed to "winning the global war on terrorism."

But what does that robust rhetoric mean? Is the GWOT really a war at all, or something else (in the immediate wake of September 11, French President Jacques Chirac suggested calling it a "campaign" to remove some of the military emphasis)? Is it really possible to make war, as we generally think of the term, against a method or idea, as opposed to some identifiable group of people? For that matter, how does one attack and defeat a non–state based enemy organization that has no territory or identified population base that can be subjected to military actions?

All of these are valid questions for which definitive, consensually agreed answers do not exist. Begin with the war analogy. It is frequently argued that it makes no sense to talk about war against an abstraction, and the idea of terrorism is the application of an idea. Can you "kill" an idea in some concrete or abstract manner? If so, how do you know you have accomplished the task? Where, quite literally, are the bodies or the surrendering enemies? Wars, at any level, are contests between members of different groups to assert control. But people and their ideas are not the same thing.

The war analogy suffers even if one switches emphasis and says the GWOT is a war on global terrorists. Switching the emphasis at least has the virtue of making a war of people against other people (a conceptual improvement), but it still retains two problems in the current context.

First, warfare against terrorists is war against asymmetrical warriors, as noted in Chapter 10. That means the countries seeking to defeat terrorism are militarily superior in conventional terms and that terrorism is the means by which terrorists seek to create a situation where they have a chance to succeed. The problem here lies in the criteria for success for those seeking to snuff out terrorists and the terrorists themselves. For the United States (or any other country engaged in terrorism suppression), the criterion is very exacting: the war cannot be won until terrorists everywhere specified by the war (the globe as currently defined) have been defeated. Those seeking to suppress terrorists must crush their opponents; in a phrase, they can only "win by winning."

The situation is different for the terrorists. Terrorists know that they cannot win in the traditional sense of crushing their enemies (win by winning), but equally, they know their enemies cannot validly claim victory as long as the terrorists can continue to operate. Thus, terrorists (much like guerrillas) realize that their criterion for success is to avoid being defeated, and that the longer they remain a viable force, the more likely they are to becoming a sufficient irritant that their opponents conclude acquiescence to their demands is preferable to continuing the frustrating struggle against them. The terrorists, in other words, can "win by not losing," or, at a minimum, prevent their opponent from declaring victory by avoiding losing.

The problem of defeating terrorists is made more difficult by a second problem associated with modern asymmetrical warfare: contemporary international terrorist organizations are non–state actors. We know that most of the contemporary religious terrorists are Muslims who come from or have connections to parts of the Islamic Middle East. We also know that not all Muslims in the Middle East support the terrorists or what they do (although enough do to provide safe haven in which terrorists can hide), and that no state government has claimed association with major terrorist organizations since the overthrow of the Taliban in Afghanistan. To make matters worse, these non–state actors generally imbed themselves within physical areas and among people sympathetic to them; they move around, including across international borders; and they rarely establish public physical symbols that can be identified with them (some Islamic charities that serve as fronts for terrorist activities such as recruitment and fundraising are partial exceptions).

The problem this creates for a "war" on terrorists is finding and specifying targets that can be attacked and defeated. When Al Qaeda was openly running training camps in Afghanistan, this was not so much of a problem, and occasionally a military attack would be made on one of these facilities (for instance, cruise missile attacks on Al Qaeda training camps in 1998 in retaliation for the bombings of American embassies in Africa). Since the fall of the Taliban and the dispersal of Al Qaeda into greater non-state anonymity, military actions directly against Al Qaeda or its associates have essentially ceased. The problem, quite literally, is that we do not know what to attack, and especially what we could attack that would move us measurably toward "victory." The most important military limitation is the inability to find and target the most vital parts of the terrorist existence—the so-called "centers of gravity" on which the terrorists rely for continued viability. The result, according to Audrey Kurth Cronin, is "that it is virtually impossible to target the most vulnerable point in the organization." Until (or unless) these problems are surmounted, military efforts are likely to remain frustrating.

Then there is the more specific problem of the ultimate non–state based opponent, Al Qaeda. In one sense, Al Qaeda remains the major focus because it remains the center of the (increasingly virtual network) movement, but as it has morphed into many smaller groups with varying degrees of affiliation, the problem of rounding up and punishing the entirety becomes even more difficult, especially in a military sense. Al Qaeda is now as much an inspiration for others as it is a concrete opponent. Having said that, it has probably increased its resiliency at the expense of capacity to carry out devastating attacks. Ultimately, however, resiliency is more important to Al Qaeda than capacity, since resiliency is another way of saying survival and guaranteeing that Al Qaeda does not lose the war.

In some sense, the GWOT requires a continuing Al Qaeda presence. As CIA official Paul R. Pillar explains, "the existence of a specific, recognized, hated terrorist enemy has helped the United States retain its focus. As long as Al Qaeda exists, even in its current, severely weakened form, it will serve that function." Were we to capture or kill bin Laden and his cohorts, we would destroy a terrorist focus, but we would not destroy terrorism; someone else would pick up the gauntlet. Al Qaeda and bin Laden help us keep our attention focused.

The continuing role of Al Qaeda is illustrated by a terrorist incident that occurred in October 7, 2004, at seaside resorts on Egyptian soil in the Sinai Peninsula. Bombs tore apart a series of resort hotels where many of the occupants were Israelis celebrating the end of the Yom Kippur holiday. The immediate question was who was responsible, and within a day's time, Al Qaeda had been identified as the likely culprit. While bin Laden has publicly condemned Israel for its suppression of the Palestinians, there are not publicly known instances of Al Qaeda attacks against Egyptian targets. So, was Al Qaeda really to blame directly (did, for instance, bin Laden order the attacks)? Or could the attacks have been carried out by an affiliate or franchise of Al Qaeda acting independently or simply deriving the inspiration to do so from bin Laden's general exhortations? For purposes of the GWOT, simply blaming Al Qaeda removed the need for such nuanced public judgments.

This introduction to dealing with terrorists is intended to convey that the problem is both physically and intellectually very difficult, and that any simple, sweeping anti-dotes to solving the problem of terrorism are likely to be inadequate and to result in fail-ure. That does not mean the task is hopeless or that things cannot be done to manage or mitigate the problem. In the paragraphs that follow, we will explore dealing with terror-ism through three lenses: conventional methods of suppressing terrorism (what we can do), levels of effort (who can do it), and a focus on undercutting terrorist appeal (how can we make terrorism less attractive).

Suppressing Terrorists: Antiterrorism and Counterterrorism

In conventional terrorism-suppression circles, two methods for dealing with the terror-ist problem are most often invoked: antiterrorism and counterterrorism. The two terms are sometimes used interchangeably, although each term refers to a distinct form of action with a specific purpose. Any program of terrorist suppression will necessarily contain ele-ments of each of them, but failing to specify which is which generally or in specific appli-cations only confuses the issue.

Antiterrorism refers to defensive efforts to reduce the vulnerability of targets to ter-rorist attacks and to lessen the effects of terrorist attacks that do occur. Antiterrorism efforts thus begin from the premise that some terrorist attacks will indeed occur, and that two forms of effort are necessary. First, antiterrorists seek to make it more difficult to mount terrorist attacks. Airport security to prevent potential terrorists from boarding air-liners or the interception and detention of possible terrorists by border guards are exam-ples. Second, antiterrorists try to mitigate the effects of terrorist attacks that do occur. An example might be blocking off streets in front of public buildings so that terrorists can-not get close enough to destroy them.

There are at least three related difficulties with conducting an effective antiterrorist campaign. One is that antiterrorism is necessarily reactive; terrorists choose where attacks will occur and against what kinds of targets, and antiterrorists must respond to the ter-rorist initiative. A second problem is the sheer variety and number of targets to be pro-tected. As suggested earlier, the potential list of targets is almost infinite, and one of the purposes of attacks is randomness so that potential victims are always off guard and antiterrorists will have trouble anticipating where attacks may occur. The third problem is target substitution: if antiterrorist efforts are sufficiently successful that terrorists deter-mine their likelihood of success against any particular target (or class of targets) is sig-nificantly diminished, they will simply go on to other, less well-defended targets. Given the variety of targets available, finding places and things that have not been protected is not impossible.

The other form of terrorist suppression is *counterterrorism*, offensive and military measures against terrorists or sponsoring agencies to prevent, deter, or respond to terror-ist acts. As the definition suggests, counterterrorism consists of both preventive and retal-iatory actions against terrorists. Preventive acts can include such things as penetration of terrorist cells and taking action—including apprehension and physical violence against terrorists—before they carry out their acts. Retaliation is more often military and paramilitary and includes attacks on terrorist camps or other facilities in response to terrorist attacks. The purposes of retaliation include punishment, reduction of terrorist capacity for future acts, and deterrence of future actions by instilling fear of the consequences.

Counterterrorism is inherently and intuitively attractive (which may be why there is a tendency to lump antiterrorist and other activities under the banner of counterterrorism). Preventive actions are proactive, taking the battle to the terrorists and punishing them in advance of creating harm. In its purest form, preventive counterterrorist actions reverse the tables in the relationship, effectively "terrorizing the terrorists." Pounding a terrorist facility as punishment from enduring a terrorist attack at least entails the satisfaction of knowing the enemy has suffered along with the victim.

The problem with counterterrorism, like antiterrorism, is that it is insufficient on its own as a way to quell terrorism. Preventing terrorist actions requires a level of intelligence about the structures of terrorist organizations that is quite difficult to obtain, and it has been a central purpose of terrorist reorganization discussed above to increase that difficulty. If one does not know the terrorist organization in detail it is, for instance, difficult to penetrate, learn of its nefarious intentions, and interrupt those activities. The absence of a state base that can be attacked means it is more difficult to identify terrorist targets whose retaliatory destruction will cripple the organization, punish its members, or frighten it into ceasing future actions.

Ideally, antiterrorism and counterterrorism efforts act in tandem. Counterterrorists reduce the number and quality of possible attacks through preventive actions, making the task of antiterrorist efforts to ameliorate the effects of attacks that do succeed less frequent and thus more manageable. Counterterrorist retaliation then, it is hoped, can reduce the terrorists' capacity for future mayhem. In practice, however, these efforts sometimes come into operational conflict. The antiterrorist emphasis on lessening the effects of attacks may lead to publicizing the possibility of particular attacks as a way to alert citizens (the color-coded warning system, for instance), whereas counterterrorists prefer to keep operations as secret as possible to facilitate clandestine penetration and interruption. We will return to this problem in the conclusion.

International versus National Efforts

There has been considerable discussion since September 11 about the appropriate level at which to conduct operations aimed at suppressing this current wave of international terrorist activity. In the immediate aftermath of the attacks, there was an enormous international outpouring of sympathy for the United States and willingness to join a vigorous international effort to deal with terrorists around the globe. That resolve resulted in a good deal of international cooperation among law enforcement and intelligence agencies in various countries, much of which continues quietly to this day. The more visible manifestations of that internationalization have faded as the United States has "militarized" the terrorist suppression effort (the GWOT as primarily "war") and moved toward actions opposed by the major allies in the law enforcement and intelligence efforts through unilateral actions in places like Iraq.

As already reported, the post–September 11 international effort has experienced apparent successes in reducing the size and potency of Al Qaeda as it existed at the time. The nature and extent of that reduction has been a matter of disagreement, as evidenced in disagreements in the 2004 American presidential debates (what percentage of leaders as opposed to followers have been killed, how many new members have replaced them in new organizations, etc.). The international problem has, however, clearly changed, and the question is how this change is and should be reflected in the degree to which ongoing terrorism should be treated as a national or international effort.

Within the United States, most of the visible activity on reforming the effort has been national. *The 9/11 Commission Report*, for instance, emphasized reform within the American government (principally in restructuring the intelligence community) as a way to respond to the evolving problem. One section in its recommendations chapter is titled "Unity of Effort Across the Foreign-Domestic Divide," but its primary function is to suggest improvements in the American ability to cooperate with foreign sources. Emphases on problems like border protection—port security, for instance—generally have a primarily national content.

Does the nature of the new threat suggest a greater inward or outward turning of efforts? CIA expert Pillar suggests that the evolving nature of the threat reinforces the need for greater internationalization. As he describes it, "In a more decentralized network, individuals will go unnoticed not because data on analysts' screens are misinterpreted but because they will never appear on those screens in the first place." Much of the added data on the successors to Al Qaeda can only be collected in the countries where they operate, but Pillar sees two barriers to sustained international cooperation. First, "an underlying limitation on foreign willingness to cooperate with the United States is the skepticism among foreign publics and even elites that the most powerful nation on the planet needs to be preoccupied with small bands of radicals." This leads to a second misgiving, which is the perceived "ability to sustain the country's own determination to fight" the terrorist threat.

Other Aspects of the Problem

A final problem of the conceptual nature of the GWOT is that it does not capture the entirety of the problem that it has been asked to solve. The GWOT, as suggested, is really an effort aimed at suppressing terrorists, as are the forms of dealing with terrorists discussed immediately above. Somehow capturing or killing all the existing terrorists does not, however, destroy *terrorism*, which is the underlying purpose of the entire enterprise. As long as individuals and groups choose terrorism as the means to realize their ideas, terrorism cannot be wholly eradicated; only its current manifestations can be contained.

This other part of any effort to suppress terrorism is intellectual, a war of ideas that has two basic parts. The first is the intellectual competition between terrorists and their enemies—the underlying reasons terrorists emerge, and the appeal they have among the populations that hide, nurture, sustain, and form the recruitment base for movements that employ terrorism as a method. In the current wave of religious terrorism, virulent anti-Americanism is the activator; the United States and the American way of life are portrayed as the major threat to Islam and the way of life that it promotes. As long as the

United States (and the West generally) does not compete with this basic idea and assert and convince those in the Middle East that our ideas produce a superior existence *for them*, there will be an endless stream of recruits to the banner that no terrorist-suppression efforts can even hope to overcome.

The second part of the intellectual battle is over the use of terrorism as the method of those whose ideas we oppose. Not only must we compete in the forum of ideas that can lead to terrorism, we must also deal with what causes people to become terrorists. Regardless of what the level of causation one begins at (societal, political, or psychological), one must persuade people that volunteering to be terrorists (in the most extreme case, agreeing to commit suicide to advance the terrorist cause) is not acceptable to them if we are to staunch the flow of recruits of terrorists intent on killing us. This problem, "draining the swamp" in which terrorists breed, is clearly a necessary part of any comprehensive strategy.

CONCLUSION: TOWARD A STRATEGY FOR TERRORISM

One thing has not changed since the terrorist attacks of September 11. The United States did not have a comprehensive, encompassing strategy for dealing with the risks associated with international terrorism then, and it does not have such a strategy today. What it does have is a series of catch phrases and partial approaches to the problem, some of which actually contradict one another (Iraq and the war on terrorism, for instance). The same can be said of the world at large, but the problem is most poignant for the United States, because it is the self-appointed world leader in the GWOT and because of the overwhelming preponderance of American power and resources that can and must be applied to reducing the risk of terrorism. Until the United States gets its act together, in other words, neither will the rest of the world.

The problem with the issue of terrorism is two-fold. First, it is a very complicated, complex problem of the kind with which political institutions are loath to deal. Declaring a GWOT is a great deal simpler than dealing with the incredible complexities only broadly suggested in these pages. Individuals *within* governments can deal with these problems comprehensively, but large, cumbersome organizations with diverse purposes and agendas have a harder time. Second, the suppression of terrorism is not a conflict that can easily be won, if it can be "won" at all. Terrorism as an idea has been around for a long time, and it will likely continue to persist for a long time. The goal of terrorism strategy is to contain terrorism, to reduce the risks arising from it—not to exorcise it from national and international existence. That is not as high flown a goal as obliterating terrorism, but it is more realistic.

What then are the goals and elements of a terrorism strategy? What we must do is raise questions, because there are no agreed answers (if there were and they worked, there would not be the problem there is). Thus, the purpose of this concluding section of the case is to help the reader organize and articulate questions about how a comprehensive strategy toward terrorism might be fashioned, not to provide the definitive answers to those questions.

The first and obvious step in devising a strategy is deciding what its goal should be. It is clearly not enough to say the goal is to "win" the struggle; one must specify what winning means. During the latter stages of the 2004 presidential campaign, the principal candidates effectively—if inadvertently—framed this question. Democratic nominee John Kerry, in one of the presidential debates, argued that the only realistic goal was to contain the problem, to reduce it to the status of a nuisance rather than a central, encompassing fixation; he drew the analogy with containing prostitution and gambling. President George W. Bush replied fiercely that Kerry was wrong and that the goal of the GWOT had to be to hunt down and destroy terrorism everywhere it existed; winning means eradicating terrorism.

Which of these goals should we adopt as the bedrock of strategy? Eradication of terrorism is clearly more emotionally attractive, but is it a realistic or attainable goal for policy and strategy? Terrorism has been around as a more-or-less permanent force for at least 2,000 years (many scholars date it back to the first century A.D. to groups like the Sicarii and the Zealots), and although it has ebbed and flowed in its prominence across time, it has never disappeared altogether. Similarly, terrorist movements, such as the current religiously based terrorism, come and go, but they seem always to be replaced by something else. In that case, is a strategy based on destroying terrorism (more properly, terrorists) bound to fail and frustrate those who pursue it? Or, is it more realistic (if less emotionally satisfying) to aim to minimize terrorism?

Then there is the question of how to implement the strategy. Clearly, any terrorism-suppression strategy must begin with elements of both antiterrorism and counterterrorism, but in what balance? In the last section, it was noted that the two thrusts can be and sometimes are at odds with each other. An example shows this tension.

In August 2004, the American government announced it had seized from a suspected terrorist computer diskettes that contained blueprints for schools in New York City, New Jersey, the District of Columbia, and elsewhere. Coming on the heels of the school hostage-taking and murders in Beslan, Russia, earlier that summer, homeland security officials extrapolated that the diskette might be evidence of a similar intent.

How should the situation have been handled? Through a quiet, behind-the-scenes counterterrorism effort where the potential terrorists were not made aware the government had the diskette, but instead where counterterrorists observed, tried to penetrate, and then squelched any plans? Or through an antiterrorist approach that notified the public of the threat and urged them to take action that would make any attack less effective? The problem was that the two approaches contradicted each other. A counterterrorism approach meant the public would be uninformed, and if an attack occurred, would be unprepared to moderate the disaster. An antiterrorist approach meant any secrecy would be blown, making a counterterrorism effort much more difficult or impossible. In the real case, of course, the antiterrorists won, and the potential plot was widely publicized. Was that the right decision?

There is another structural concern in dealing with existing terrorists. How does one improve the effort to detect, penetrate, and frustrate terrorist activities? At the national level, for instance, the 9/11 Commission made some strong suggestions for reform and consolidation of governmental efforts, but all suggestions entail considerable change in how people go about their business. How much of the commission's efforts will or should be implemented? Further, how much of the effort should be internationalized? Should the United States remain largely independent of others in efforts ranging from counterterrorism to cooperation with United Nations or other international efforts? Or should the United States encourage greater cooperation across borders, even if it disagrees with some of those efforts?

There is the further question of what else is to be done. At least two concerns can be raised in this regard. Clearly, one way to eliminate or lessen the problem of terrorism is to discourage or lessen its appeal to potential terrorists: fewer terrorists, by definition, would pose a smaller terrorism problem. Antiterrorism and counterterrorism efforts may influence the actions of current terrorists, but they apparently do little to discourage, and may actually encourage, the recruitment of future terrorists. Israeli destruction of the family homes of Palestinian suicide terrorists has rather clearly not discouraged others from signing up for that grisly mission, and it is at least arguable that the American military effort in Iraq—regardless of the merit of its stated aims—has the ancillary effect of increasing regional anti-Americanism and thus intensifying efforts to recruit terrorists to oppose Americans.

How does one make terrorism less attractive to potential recruits? One approach is to relieve the human conditions in which terrorism seems to prosper—to "drain the swamp" of terrorism-producing societal, psychological, and political conditions and thus make terrorism a less-attractive alternative. Intuitively, such efforts appear to make sense, but they face objections. One is expense: uplifting societies to the point that terrorism is unappealing to the citizens would require very large monetary and other resources (for instance, what would it cost to fund a Pakistani education system that would make the terrorist-producing *madrassa* system obsolete?). Are we willing to pay for such an effort? In addition, the results are uncertain; as many analysts point out, the 9/11 terrorists came from Saudi Arabia, not some wretched backwater "swamp," and all the developmental assistance in the world would not have changed these individuals.

A second possible thrust of strategy might be to make people less of a target of terrorists. Current Middle Eastern religious terrorism is fueled by a virulent anti-Americanism that we find intellectually ludicrous and incorrect. Should the United States be mounting a much more comprehensive campaign to convince people in the region that the Western model is superior to the worldview that fanatical religious spokespersons are propounding? If we think, as we say we do, that the terrorist proponents are trying to drag the people of the region a thousand years back in time to some imagined caliphate that is more nightmare than dream, why do we not say so more loudly and consistently?

Finally, there is the question of exposure. One reason for the underlying anti-Americanism in parts of the Middle East is the level of supposedly corrupting American physical presence in the region (this has been a particular obsession of bin Laden for some time). The obvious reason for that presence is Middle East oil, and without that need, the reason for American presence is reduced greatly or disappears altogether. If that is the case, should national energy policy not be an important element in terrorism strategy? Some of the most vocal proponents of the GWOT in the United States simultaneously oppose higher fuel efficiency standards for vehicles (the so-called Corporate Average Fuel Efficiency—CAFÉ—standards). Because oil revenue has clearly been linked to private support for terrorists in Saudi Arabia and elsewhere, is it not inconsistent to support strong terrorism suppression while one drives a large, gas-guzzling sport-utility vehicle?

This discussion, of course, only examines the tip of the iceberg of what a comprehensive terrorism strategy would include. The problem to date, reflected in the artificial designation of the effort as a "war," has been to isolate terrorism and its suppression from other aspects of national and international concern. Terrorism, however, is a broader phenomenon that is part of a larger set of problem and international malaise. Until we start treating it for what it is, our efforts are bound to languish.

 ## STUDY/DISCUSSION QUESTIONS

1. Define terrorism. What are its common elements? How does the elaboration of the elements help us understand the nature of terrorism?

2. What do terrorist acts seek to accomplish? In what circumstances do they succeed or fail?

3. What kinds of targets do terrorists attack? What is cost-tolerance? How does it factor into resistance to terrorism and terrorist success?

4. Why do terrorists engage in terrorist activities? What do they seek to accomplish? Why do terrorists adopt asymmetrical means to achieve their objectives?

5. Three perspectives and causes of terrorism are discussed in the case. What are they? Do you find any of them more convincing than the others?

6. How has international terrorism changed since 9/11, notably in terms of terrorist organization? What are the implications of these changes for dealing with terrorists?

7. Discuss the propriety of the "war" analogy when dealing with terrorism. Does it help or distort thinking about and countering the problem?

8. What are the three ways of dealing with terrorism discussed in the text? Describe each as an element in lessening or eliminating the problem of terrorism.

9. What are the elements of a comprehensive terrorism strategy discussed in the conclusion? Can you think of others?

10. The distinction between dealing with terrorism and dealing with terrorists is a recurring dichotomy in the text. What is this distinction? What are the implications for dealing with the problem from one perspective or the other?

READING/RESEARCH MATERIAL

Allison, Graham. *Nuclear Terrorism: The Ultimate Preventable Catastrophe.* New York: Times Books (Henry Holt and Company), 2004.

Atran, Scott. "Mishandling Suicide Terrorism." *Washington Quarterly* 27, 3 (Summer 2004), 67–90.

Burke, Jason. "Think Again, Al Qaeda." *Foreign Policy,* May/June 2004, 18–26.

Cronin, Audrey Kurth. "Sources of Contemporary Terrorism." In *Modern Terrorism: Elements of a Grand Strategy,* edited by Audrey Kurth Cronin and James M. Ludes. Washington, DC: Georgetown University Press, 2004.

Dershowitz, Alan M. *Why Terrorism Works: Understanding the Threat, Responding to the Challenge.* New Haven, CT: Yale University Press, 2002.

Gunaratna, Rohan. "The Post-Madrid Face of Al Qaeda." *Washington Quarterly* 27, 3 (Summer 2004), 91–100.

Jenkins, Brian. "International Terrorism." In *The Use of Force: Military Power and International Politics* (6th ed.), edited by Robert J. Art and Kenneth N. Waltz, 77–84. New York: Rowman and Littlefield, 2004.

Krueger, Alan B., and David D. Laitin. "'Misunderestimating' Terrorism: The State Department's Big Mistake." *Foreign Affairs* 83, 5 (September/October 2004), 8–13.

Laqueur, Walter. "The Changing Face of Terror." In *The Use of Force*, edited by Art and Waltz, 451–464.

Pillar, Paul D. "Counterterrorism after Al Qaeda." *Washington Quarterly* 27, 3 (Summer 2004), 101–113.

———. "Dealing with Terrorism." In *The Use of Force,* edited by Art and Waltz, 469–476.

Rapaport, David C. "The Four Waves of Terrorism." In *Modern Terrorism*, edited by Cronin and Ludes, 46–73.

The 9/11 Commission Report: Final Report of the National Commission on Terrorist Attacks Upon the United States, authorized edition. New York: W.W. Norton, 2004.

Sloan, Stephen. *Beating International Terrorism: An Action Strategy for Preemption and Punishment.* Montgomery, AL: Air University Press, 2000.

Snow, Donald M. *September 11, 2001: The New Face of War?* New York: Longman, 2002.

Snow, Donald M., and Dennis M. Drew. *From Lexington to Desert Storm and Beyond: War and Politics in the American Experience.* Armonk, NY: M. E. Sharpe, 2000.

Stern, Jessica. *Terrorism in the Name of God: Why Religious Militants Kill.* New York: ECCO, 2003.

———. "The Protean Enemy." *Foreign Affairs* 82, 4 (July/August 2003), 27–40.

WEB SITES

Official U.S. government Web Sites dealing with terrorism

The Department of Homeland Security at http://www.Whitehouse.gov/homeland

The State Department at http://www.state.gov

Text of "bin Laden Epistles" at http://msanews.net/MSANEWS199610/19961012.3.html

Reports on future trends from Federal Research Division

http://www.loc.gov/rr/frd/terrorism.html

UN Action against terrorism at http://www.un/org/Docs/sc/committees/1373/

RAND Corporation on Terrorism, Homeland Security at http://www.rand.org/research_areas/terrorism/

Terrorism Research Center at http://www.terrorism.com/

Index

Abbas, Mahmoud, 89, 101
Abdulla, King of Jordan, 99
Abidjan Accord, 253
Absolute sovereignty, 77–78. *See also*
   Sovereignty
Abu Ghraib prisoner abuse, 54, 58,
   68
Aceh, 152–153, 158
Action-reaction phenomenon (ARP),
   185
Afghanistan, 19, 21, 30–31, 39,
   83–86, 178, 286, 291
African AIDS, 257–271. *See also*
   AIDS
Agreement on Trade-related Aspects
   of Intellectual Property Rights
   (TRIPS) (World Trade
   Organization), 136–137
AIDS, 48, 137, 222, 257–271
Al Qaeda, 83, 84, 98, 153, 178, 179,
   273–275, 277, 279, 281–284,
   286–292, 294
Albright, Madeleine, 69
Aliyev, Heydar, 249
Altman, Lawrence, 264
American Civil War. *See* Civil War
American Foundation for AIDS
   Research, 266
American model of economic
   development, 109, 110, 119–121
American Revolution, 76, 77, 128
Anderson, Roy M., 268
Ankomah, Baffour, 263
Anti-Americanism, 39, 297
Anti-Ballistic Missile (ABM) Treaty of
   1972, 187, 190, 195, 196
Antiterrorism, 292, 297
Arab-Israeli War. *See* Six-Day War
   (1967)
Arab League, 244
Arafat, Yasir, 89, 90, 94, 98, 99, 102
Argentina, 278
Aristide, Jean-Bertrand, 43–44
Armenia, 239, 240, 249, 251
Armenians, 74, 248, 249
Army of God movement, 289
Aryan Nation, 288–289
Asia-Pacific Center for Strategic
   Studies, 186
Asia-Pacific Economic Cooperation
   (APEC), 115, 145, 156, 158
Asian model of economic
   development, 109, 111, 116, 155
Assad, Hafez al-, 99
Assad, Mustafa, 99
Association of Southeast Asian
   Nations (ASEAN), 145, 156, 158

Asymmetrical warfare, 162, 165,
   173–179, 284. *See also* Warfare
Australia, 83, 229
Austro-Hungarian Empire, 36
AWACS (airborne warning and
   control system) aircraft, 12
Azad Kashmir, 209, 210
Azerbaijan, 148, 240, 247–250

Bajpai, Shankar, 211, 214
Bangladesh, 233
Barak, Ehud, 94–96, 99
Basayev, Shamil, 277
Bashir, Abu Bakar, 153, 277
Begin, Menachem, 92, 94
Belarus, 38–39
Belgian Congo, 80, 181, 261
Belo, Carlos Filipe Ximenes, 152
Biafra, 22
Biddle, Stephen, 178
Billiard ball theory, 76
bin Laden, Osama, 179, 279, 288,
   289, 292
Blitzkrieg, 170
Bodin, Jean, 75
Borneo, 147, 158
Bosnia, 21, 51, 53–55, 61–65, 67, 84,
   180
Botswana, 262, 267
Boutros-Ghali, Boutros, 61, 253
Brauman, Rony, 24
Bretton Woods, 131–132
Brezhnev, Leonid, 192
Bristol Myers Squipp, 267
Browne, John, 231
Brunei, 9
Bubonic plague, 257, 265, 266
Burma, 158
Bush, George W., 15, 66, 72–73, 85,
   89, 187, 190–192, 195, 258,
   269, 296

Cambodia, 9, 12, 21, 60, 61, 74, 79,
   83
Cameroon, 148, 249
Camp David Accords, 52, 89–105
Canada, 229, 261, 270
Capitalism, 113–114, 156. *See also*
   Crony capitalism
CARE, 28
Carothers, Thomas, 39, 40
Carter, Jimmy, 89, 90, 92, 93, 97, 98,
   246
Caspian Sea oil, 239, 240, 246–251
Centers for Disease Control (CDC),
   267
Central African Republic, 262

Central Intelligence Agency (CIA),
   179
Chechnya, 45, 73, 86, 241, 250, 251,
   255, 275, 277, 281, 282, 286
Chellaney, Brahma, 198
Cheney, Richard, 15
Chiang Kai-shek, 5
China, 1, 3–17, 21, 40, 44, 47, 48,
   60, 112, 121, 124, 136, 137,
   147, 184–187, 189, 190, 193,
   194, 196–198, 216, 230, 261
Chirac, Jacques, 290
Civil War, 56, 128, 167, 175
Clausewitz, Carl von, 109–110
Climate change. *See* Global warming
Clinton, Bill, 47, 48, 60, 66, 89, 90,
   94–96, 98, 115, 192, 204, 211,
   230
CNN, 9
Cold War, 21, 36, 37, 51, 53, 55,
   59–61, 73, 79, 82, 90, 91,
   96–97, 133, 148, 161–162, 164,
   172, 181, 184, 185, 188, 199,
   205, 218. *See also* Post-Cold War
Colombia, 179
Commander-cadre model, 288
Communism, 3, 37, 79
Conference of the Parties (COP), 227
Connally Amendment, 67
Conroalles, Anthony M., 175
Corruption Perceptions Index
   (Transparency International),
   148, 249
Cost-tolerance, 279–280
Counterterrorism, 292–293, 297
Croatia, 61, 63
Cronin, Audrey Kurth, 275, 276
Crony capitalism, 116, 148–149
Cuba, 36
Cyprus, 181

Defense. *See* Military
Democratic Republic of Congo, 80,
   180, 263
Democratization, 2, 35–49
Deng Xiaoping, 6–7
Deregulation, 114, 119–120
Dershowitz, Alan, 276
Deterrence, 186–187, 199
Diamonds, 239, 241, 251–254
Dinka, Berhanu, 253
Diplomacy
   China and, 13–14
Dispute Settlement Body (DSB),
   139
Dispute Settlement Understanding
   (DSU), 138–139

301